INTERACTIVE GROUP THERAPY

INTERACTIVE GROUP THERAPY

Integrating Interpersonal, Action-Oriented, and Psychodynamic Approaches

Jay Earley, Ph.D.

BRUNNER/MAZEL
Taylor & Francis Group

USA	Publishing Office:	BRUNNER/MAZEL *A member of the Taylor & Francis Group* 325 Chestnut Street Philadelphia, PA 19106 Tel: (215) 625-8900 Fax: (215) 625-2940
	Distribution Center:	BRUNNER/MAZEL *A member of the Taylor & Francis Group* 47 Runway Road, Suite G Levittown, PA 19057 Tel: (215) 269-0400 Fax: (215) 269-0363
UK		BRUNNER/MAZEL *A member of the Taylor & Francis Group* 11 New Fetter Lane London EC4P EE UK Tel: +44 171 583 9855 Fax: +44 171 842 2298

INTERACTIVE GROUP THERAPY: Integrating Interpersonal, Action-Oriented, and Psychodynamic Approaches

1 2 3 4 5 6 7 8 9 0

Printed by Edwards Brothers, Ann Arbor, MI, 1999.

A CIP catalog record for this book is available from the British Library.

⊗ The paper in this publication meets the requirements of the ANSI Standard Z39.48-1984 (Permanence of Paper).

Library of Congress Cataloging-in-Publication Data
Earley, Jay, 1944–

    Interactive group therapy : integrating interpersonal, action-oriented, and psychodynamic approaches / Jay Earley.
      p.   cm.
    Includes bibliographical references and index.
    ISBN 0-87630-984-8 (case : alk. paper)
    1. Group psychotherapy.   2. Group psychotherapy Case studies.
I. Title.
RC488.E224   1999
616.89'152—dc21   99-44316
                                                  CIP

ISBN: 0-87630-984-8

CONTENTS

III. FACILITATING THE PROCESS

IV. GROUP-RELATED ISSUES

V. SPECIAL ISSUES

PREFACE

In a recent survey (Dies, 1992), the American Group Psychotherapy Association divided group therapists into three categories: psychodynamic, interpersonal, and action-oriented. The psychodynamic approaches (Rutan & Stone, 1993) are those derived from psychoanalysis where the primary emphasis is on uncovering symbolic material related to the childhood origins of defenses and symptoms. Interpersonal approaches, as exemplified by Yalom's (1995) classic text, focus primarily on the personal interactions and relationships among the group members. Action-oriented approaches include cognitive/behavioral, Gestalt, Transactional Analysis (TA), and psychodrama—the common element being a commitment to action in addition to self-exploration. This not only includes action on the part of group members (e.g., behavioral experimentation or role playing) but also an active leadership stance from the group therapist that may include suggestions, questions, and structured activities in addition to interpretations.

This book presents a new approach that draws from all three of these orientations to form a creative whole of its own, which I believe represents an advance in the field. Like interpersonal approaches, it sees the interactions between group members as the primary means for therapeutic change, focusing on contact and intimacy between group members as an important aspect of therapeutic healing. Like psychodynamic groups, my approach emphasizes insight about unconscious processes and childhood origins of current problems. Finally, like Gestalt therapy (Perls, Hefferline, & Goodman, 1951), it uses an active leadership style that focuses on responsibility, spontaneity, and vitality, and helps members heighten awareness of their moment-to-moment experience.

Action-oriented groups tend to be leader-centered groups, where the group members interact primarily with the leader rather than with each other, and less attention is paid to the relationships among group members and the unfolding of the group process. As a result, this valuable aspect of group work is usually not fully utilized in action-oriented groups. The approach described in this book changes that because it is both action-oriented and group-centered. It encourages experimenting with new behavior and an active leadership stance, while focusing primarily on group process and interpersonal interactions between group members. In addition, my action-orientation prompts me to have a different viewpoint on some crucial group issues such as healing responses from group members, the role of touch, and contact between members outside of group.

Therefore, this book will be of special interest to action-oriented group leaders who want to move beyond leader-centered or structured groups toward a greater emphasis on interpersonal and group process. Because of my background in Gestalt therapy, many Gestaltists and other action-oriented therapists have attended my training program to learn how to lead interactive, group-centered groups.

This book begins with a discussion of the therapeutic change process in group therapy, which then forms the background for the presentation of method and technique. The bulk of the book is devoted to providing practical guidelines for leading groups. I offer detailed suggestions for structuring groups, making interventions, understanding difficult clients, adopting the best leadership attitude, following group process, and a host of other clinical issues. In addition to rich clinical examples and case histories, the book also contains transcripts of group sessions, annotated to illustrate both theory and technique.

☐ Unique Features of This Approach

Therapeutic Change Process.   This book contains a new perspective on the therapeutic change process that emphasizes those interpersonal aspects of change that are particularly important in therapy groups. In addition to helping clients achieve greater insight and access to their feelings, it demonstrates the value of experimenting with new, healthy behavior and receiving healing responses from other group members and the leader.

Active Leadership Stance.   Though the style of leadership advocated here is active, it is empowering for group members. As a leader, you ask questions to elicit clients' awareness of their experience in the moment and the deeper issues that underlie their reactions. You also sometimes make suggestions about new behavior or attitudes that clients can try experimentally. When necessary, you actively intervene to make sure that the group is safe enough for members and is moving in a therapeutic direction. However, group members themselves are responsible for their own therapeutic direction and initiate the details of the work. When an interaction or exploration is proceeding appropriately, you may be silent for long stretches of time. In summary, the leader is active in ensuring that the work is advancing in a therapeutic manner, but this activity is often oriented toward encouraging client responsibility. This book contains a discussion of the internal shift that action-oriented leaders often must make in moving from a leader-centered to a group-centered mode.

The Interactive Norm.   This method actively promotes the norm that the primary focus of the group is the interpersonal interactions between group members. They are expected to initiate work on their relationships with each other and to explore their feelings about being in the group. Rather than waiting for this work to emerge gradually, the leader actively encourages it.

Presence and Contact.   In this approach, we are not only interested in behavior and its unconscious meaning, but also the quality of presence and contact as group members explore themselves and interact with each other. When is a client being purely intellectual? When is she distracted? When is a group member inhabiting her body and feeling her emotions? Is a client taking in the support and caring she is receiving? Is she allowing herself to be touched by others?

Intimacy and Relational Healing.   This method pays special attention to the relationships that develop between group members. These not only activate transferential material, but also have the potential for helping clients heal. When two people work through the transferential difficulties between them and develop a deep connection with each other over time, they can both experience enormous growth.

☐ My Experience

I have been leading therapy groups for two decades and training group therapists for nearly one. Groups have become the major focus of my professional life, igniting my passion and providing fulfillment. As a leader, trainer, and participant, I love therapy groups—the excitement of the here-and-now encounters between people; the intensity of the work; the caring and love that develop among group members over time; the profound therapeutic changes that clients achieve; those special moments of group bonding and the overall sense of community that develops. It is very satisfying to participate in a group that creates the equivalent of a healthy extended family or tribe. I hope that, in addition to educating you about therapy groups, this book will help you appreciate the group therapy experience and perhaps inspire you to include more of this kind of relating in your own life.

☐ Larger Social Issues

My interest in group therapy goes beyond a desire to help group members reduce their suffering and lead happier lives. I am also interested in group work as a way of promoting healthier ways of being and relating to others in our society. The world is in such a serious crisis at this time in human history (Earley, 1997) that we can't afford to focus only on the narrow goals of our profession. We must be interested in changing our culture and society in fundamental ways or the world may be facing serious ecological and social breakdown. This is not just my belief or that of a narrow group. In 1993, a group of 1,600 of the world's leading scientists—including half of all living Nobel laureates in science—published the *World Scientists Warning to Humanity*, which contained the following statement, "We the undersigned, senior members of the world scientific community, hereby warn all humanity of what lies ahead. A great change in our stewardship of the earth and the life on it is required, if vast misery is to be avoided and our global home on this planet is not to be irretrievably mutilated."

Group therapy, of course, can only play a small role in the social transformation that is needed, but that role can be important nonetheless. We have an opportunity to not only alleviate symptoms of mental illness and foster healthy character change, but also to promote empathy, self-reflection, community, appreciation of diversity, healthy ways of dealing with power, and other new ways of being. As a result, group therapy can help us to create a healthier culture and surmount the current planetary crisis.

☐ Organization of the Book

Part I (chapters 2–6) discusses the therapeutic change process in groups along with practical suggestions for facilitating it. Part II (chapters 7–13) describes how to create a therapeutic group culture, including developing healthy group norms and helping clients learn therapy skills. Part III (chapters 14–20) covers a variety of other issues related to facilitating the process of a therapy group. Part IV (chapters 21–25) discusses issues that are specifically related to the whole group process. Part V (chapter 26–29) covers a number of special topics, including groups with special populations, issues, and methods, and the relationship between group therapy and society.

ACKNOWLEDGMENTS

I gratefully acknowledge help in editing this manuscript from Josh Kendall, Sue Friedberg, Steve Schklar, Marla Silverman, Maria Warrack, Bob Harman, Ron DeAngelo, Bonnie Weiss, Elinor Greenberg, Gail Staal, Liza Johnson, Susan Berg, Judith Schaer, Jacques Squillace, Kelly Moreno, Towne Allen, and Iris Fodor.

Introduction

☐ Group Therapy

Let's begin with an overall look at the field of group psychotherapy. Originally a mere offshoot of individual therapy, group therapy was long considered a second-rate form of treatment. Over the years, increasingly sophisticated forms of group therapy have emerged that take advantage of the unique features of the group setting. As a consequence, group therapy has become a powerful treatment modality in its own right. Rather than simply being a more cost-efficient way to provide therapy, group therapy provides many therapeutic advantages over the individual setting.

Group therapy is effective for the entire range of psychological issues and is the treatment of choice for certain problems and clients. It is also useful when combined with individual therapy, either at the same time or in sequence. In addition, groups provide clients with a different kind of growth experience than other modes of therapy, helping them especially to develop interpersonal and group capacities. Of course, individual therapy also has advantages over group therapy. The optimal treatment for a particular client depends on her presenting problem, her personality structure, and her therapeutic goals.

Recent surveys of the research literature on psychotherapy outcome (Dies, 1986; Kaul & Bednar, 1986; Orlinsky & Howard, 1986) indicate widespread endorsement of group therapy as a clearly effective mode of psychotherapy. Moreover, when comparing group and individual psychotherapy, researchers (Orlinsky & Howard, 1986; Toseland & Siporin, 1986) have found that group therapy is generally as effective if not more effective than individual therapy. Given the much greater cost of individual therapy, this conclusion has important implications.

Increasing Importance of Group Therapy. Today group therapy is becoming increasingly prevalent because of managed care's push toward reducing the cost of treatment. Groups are being used more frequently in institutional settings because they are more cost effective. In private practice, clients are often not covered for the full course of therapy they need, and therefore they are turning to groups because they are more affordable.

The Need for Training. As group therapy becomes more widely used, there is a greater need for group therapy education and training. Frequently therapists tell me that they have been given three groups to lead at the clinic, even though they have no training other than a single graduate course in group therapy. It is important for therapists to receive substantial training in group therapy, perhaps even as much as they receive in individual therapy. This should include at least a year program including theory and technique, a personal group experience, and a practicum, along with supervision of a group the trainee is leading. If not provided in graduate school, psychotherapists should seek this at postgraduate training institutes. This book is appropriate for use in such a training program.

General Purpose and Problem-Focused Groups. Therapy groups can be divided into two general categories—general purpose groups and problem-focused groups. Problem-focused groups (McKay & Paley, 1992) tend to be oriented toward specific populations and issues such as bereavement, anxiety, sexual abuse, AIDS, substance abuse, and assertiveness. Usually these groups are structured or use a support-group format. In either case, they aim at helping people through a crisis, improving coping, teaching social skills, or alleviating symptoms. They are often time-limited because they focus on goals such as the above that can reasonably be accomplished in a short time, usually 10 to 30 sessions. Self-help groups are an important and widely used type of problem-focused group, though they can't be considered psychotherapy groups.

General purpose groups accept people with a variety of presenting problems. Instead of focusing on a specific issue, these groups work on all the different behavioral and psychodynamic issues that arise in the course of the group and interpersonal process. In addition to the above-mentioned goals, many general purpose groups aim to help clients make deeper changes in their character structure and therefore they need to operate for a longer time, often 1 to 3 years or more. However, they can also be time-limited, and some therapists have reported success with shorter general purpose groups of 20–30 sessions (MacKenzie, 1990).

The approach presented in this book is oriented toward general purpose outpatient groups for adults. It targets both short-term symptom alleviation and problem resolution, and also long-term characterological transformation. At various points the book discusses how to integrate this approach with other group modalities such as supportive work, psychodrama (Moreno, 1959), structured exercises (Earley, 1990), and individual work in the group setting (R. L. Harman, 1984). Chapter 28 explores how this approach can be modified for problem-focused groups and other populations and settings.

☐ Introduction to This Approach

In keeping with the interpersonal nature of the approach presented in this book, the group work focuses primarily on the relationships among the group members and what is currently happening within the group. The group becomes a microcosm for each member's life (Yalom, 1995), and any interpersonal problems she has will most likely occur sooner or later with someone in the group. Thus, rather than just talking about the problems in their lives, members live them out in the group. This gives them a chance to get feedback on the way they affect others, to become aware of their feelings and motivations, and to experiment with new, healthier behavior.

One common type of interaction involves a dialogue between two members. One person might say, "John, I'd like to talk to you. You know, last week when you confronted Sarah, I felt annoyed at you (or I admired you, or I was intimidated by you)." If John were receptive, he might respond by saying, "Gee, what was it that made you feel that way?" Then the two members would have a dialogue. If there was conflict, they would try to resolve it. If they were confused about what was happening between them, they would attempt to clarify the precise nature of their interaction. If they felt good about each other, they might work on connecting more deeply.

The leader facilitates this process, helping them to be more aware of what they are feeling in the moment, especially in response to what the other person just said, and helping them to improve their communication skills (e.g., assertiveness and sensitivity to others). The leader is particularly interested in helping members to become aware of their interpersonal patterns, such as neediness, avoidance of intimacy, defiance of authority, codependence, etc. For each pattern, the client learns to be aware of when it happens in group, what she[1] is feeling at the time, the underlying motivation, its childhood origin, and the role it plays in her life. Then the client can work on healing the pain that underlies the pattern and experimenting with healthier behavior in the group.

In other common types of group work, one client might explore his feelings about being in the group or the group-as-a-whole might explore an issue that is affecting everyone. The interpersonal work for each client changes over time. When a person first joins a group, he will be working on the way he relates to people whom he is just getting to know. Once someone has been in the group for a year or more, he will have a chance to develop close connections with some other group members, and therefore he will begin to deal with intimacy issues.

Clients develop multiple transferences with the leader, other members, and the group-as-a-whole that provide the raw material for exploring interpersonal defenses and their childhood origins. Ultimately, these relationships also serve as a vehicle for healing these wounds and developing healthy ways of relating.

☐ Basic Concepts

I will now present some basic concepts that are used throughout the book in understanding intrapsychic process and therapeutic change.

---

[1]I have decided to deal with the problem of gender pronouns by alternating between masculine and feminine.

Core Issues

A *core issue* is a structure in the psyche based on past events that influences, often unconsciously, the way people see and feel about themselves, relate to others, and act in the world. Core issues are a way of coding memory so that it can be used in future interactions with people. A core issue is the internal basis for a transference reaction. It usually consists of a self-representation and representation of another. These representations involve more than just beliefs and images; they also include emotion, perception, motivation, body sensation, expression, and action. Core issues are similar to object relations (Kernberg, 1975) and to the concept of schemas used in cognitive therapy (Safran & Segal, 1990). They won't be discussed in more detail in this book because the primary focus here is the practice of group therapy.

Let's look at an example of a core issue. If a girl, Marcy, was consistently rejected by her father, she might develop a core issue with an internal representation of the self as needy and unlovable, and a representation of the other as desirable and rejecting. This core issue would likely influence her self-esteem and the way she relates to men. A core issue may be activated all the time or it may operate only under certain conditions. *For example, Marcy might feel unlovable all the time, or she might feel that way only when relating to a man she is attracted to.* A core issue can be activated by a type of person (e.g., men), a perception about a person (e.g., an attractive man), a situation (e.g., a social situation), an action of the other (e.g., he acts rejecting) or an action of the person (e.g., Marcy reaches out to a man).

Healthy Capacities

Human beings have the potential for a variety of *healthy capacities,*[2] such as assertiveness, intimacy, autonomy, and empathy. These capacities are present to a certain extent in young children, but most capacities develop during childhood (and to a lesser extent also during later life). For optimal development of these capacities, a child requires appropriate parenting and other influences (from siblings, relatives, peers, teachers, and the culture at large).

Each capacity includes both behavioral ability and inner experience. The behavioral aspect has to do with the person's capacity to act in a healthy way in the world. For example, the behavioral aspect of assertiveness is the ability to act assertively—to ask for what one wants, to set limits, to stand up for oneself. The experiential aspect has to do with the person's inner experience or sense of self. In the case of assertiveness, the experiential aspect involves feeling powerful, entitled to take care of oneself, and confident about self-assertion.

When a core issue is activated, it *blocks* a healthy capacity (or capacities). In other words, it interferes with a person's ability to use the capacity. (When talking about children, it can mean interfering with the child's development of the capacity.) Thus, just like a core issue, a healthy capacity may be available only under certain conditions. *For example, Marcy might feel valuable only when she is relating to women.*

---

[2]Healthy capacities are similar to "aspects of essence" in the Diamond approach (Almaas, 1988), a school of transpersonal psychology. The capacities I emphasize in this theory are oriented toward interpersonal issues, rather than those in the Diamond approach, which are oriented toward spiritual development. If one were developing a theory focused on, for example, creativity of social change, then it would emphasize other sets of capacities.

At any given moment, a person's behavior often stems from a combination of healthy capacities core issues.

Basic Needs and Capacities

I have found it helpful to identify four basic interpersonal needs that are central to human motivation: connectedness, safety, autonomy, and value. These needs are crucial to the healthy development of children and also influence adult behavior. If a basic need is not met adequately in a person's early years, there will be a deficiency in the corresponding healthy capacity, resulting in pain and perhaps difficulty in functioning. For example, if a person's need for connectedness—love, caring, nurturing—is not met during childhood, she is likely to feel unlovable, isolated, empty, needy, or fragmented. People react intensely to deprivation of basic needs; they are often driven either to defend against the pain or compensate for the deficiency.

Each basic need has a corresponding healthy capacity, called by the same name, which is simultaneously the capacity to get that need met and to feel confident and deserving in that area. I call these the basic capacities. For example, the capacity for *connectedness* means that a person can reach out to form healthy relationships, and also that she feels connected to others and to herself. Basic needs operate all through a person's life even though they are more critical during childhood. Even if a basic need was met during childhood, the person will still have that need as an adult, but the need will be mild, adult, and appropriate, and the person will have the behavioral ability to get it met in most circumstances. To the extent that the need was not met adequately during childhood, the need will be more intense, infantile, and inappropriate, and the person will have less in the way of behavioral skills to get it met.

A person needs to feel safe from attack, intrusion, control, excessive judgment, or exploitation. A person with a good sense of *safety* trusts that others will respect her boundaries and therefore can allow herself to be vulnerable when this is appropriate, but she is able to protect herself from violation if necessary. She is able to mobilize aggression and stand up to anyone who threatens her safety.

A person who has the capacity for *autonomy* feels free to be himself and to take power and initiative in the world without being unduly influenced by others' desires. Therefore he can freely cooperate with others when appropriate, but he can also assert himself and stand up to others if that is called for.

A person who has an inner sense of *value* feels positively about herself and valuable as a person.[3] To the extent that the need for value was met during childhood by appropriate mirroring and appreciation and a person has developed a sense of value, she has high self-esteem, confidence in herself, resiliency in the face of failure, and the ability for constructive self-criticism (Kohut, 1971, 1977). Even though a child needs appropriate responses from others for value to develop in early years, once value is developed in an adult, it tends to be largely self-sustaining.

---

[3] "Value" is obviously similar to the well-known term *self-esteem*. Following Almaas (1988), I prefer to use the word *value* rather than *self-esteem* for this capacity because value refers to a basic underlying sense of being worthwhile that is ultimately independent of any particular personal qualities or responses from others. It means feeling valuable just for being oneself. Too often, self-esteem has connotations of a more surface level of value based on achievements or personal strengths.

I

THE THERAPEUTIC CHANGE PROCESS

Part I presents an interpersonal perspective on the therapeutic change process in therapy groups. I have decided to start this book with an exploration of therapeutic change because that is the ultimate goal of psychotherapy. Once we understand clearly how change happens, we can discuss how to best structure a group to facilitate the change process. This means, however, that the presentation will not be strictly chronological in terms of group development. This chapter deals with the therapeutic change process, and then, in Part II, we start at the beginning to discuss such topics as how to structure a group and develop appropriate group norms.

In chapters 2 through 5, we present the four aspects of the therapeutic change process—access, healing response, experimenting, and inner healing, including practical suggestions for facilitating each one. Chapter 6 consists of an annotated transcript of part of a group session that illustrates these concepts.

2

CHAPTER

Access

Yalom (1995) has delineated a set of 11 factors that influence therapeutic change in groups, including universality, altruism, interpersonal learning, and group cohesiveness. Over the years, this has spawned an interesting body of research, summarized in chapters 1 and 4 of Yalom, attempting to measure the importance of these and other factors empirically, through clients' or therapists' reports or through correlation of these factors with outcome. Though this is useful research, these factors are related to change in inconsistent ways, as Yalom admits. Some of the factors are preconditions for change, some are peripheral aspects of the change process, some are techniques, whereas one of the factors—interpersonal learning—includes a complex change process in itself. Most importantly, the factors do not constitute a coherent conception of therapeutic change.

This book presents such a framework, which includes not only a variety of factors that influence change but also a detailed description of how these factors relate to each other and the place of each one in the change process. There are four aspects of the change process—access, healing response, experimenting, and inner healing—covered in the next four chapters.

☐ Accessing Core Issues

Access refers to uncovering material buried in the psyche, including feelings, beliefs, impulses, values, and memories. The leader helps the client to explore herself and relax defenses so as to get in touch with both core issues and healthy capacities. Ideally, access is a unitary phenomenon, involving both affect and insight into an issue and its origins. Access is a central aspect of both experiential (R. L. Harman, 1984; Moreno, 1959; Pesso, 1969) and psychodynamic (Rutan & Stone, 1993) group therapies, with experiential groups emphasizing affect and psychodynamic groups emphasizing insight. Access may involve the re-experiencing of early pain, a process called *abreaction*. Working with and letting go of defenses is one of the crucial aspects of access.

Full access is not always possible or practical, so the group leader must often make a decision about how much access to pursue and what kind. Purely intellectual insight can be useful, but by itself, it is not usually sufficient for therapeutic change to occur. Pure feeling without understanding can also be useful but not nearly as much as when it is accompanied by insight, and with some clients it can even be dangerous. The degree of access depends on the depth of affect, the intensity of relational involvement, and the amount of insight. The greater the degree of access, the greater the inner healing that can follow. This view of access as part of the therapeutic change process is consistent with Safran and Greenberg's observation (1991) that "The more fully the schema is accessed, the more amenable it will be to restructuring" (p. 342).

Usually it is a core issue that is accessed. When a client is reacting in a problematic way because of the activation of a core issue, it is important for her to feel the underlying pain and understand her reaction and its childhood origins if possible.

> Suppose that Marcy is confronted by a group member, Ben, and she becomes upset. To access her core issue, Marcy would first need to realize that she feels hurt by Ben because she perceives him as rejecting her. Then she might explore further and understand that she is sensitive to rejection by men in general. She might even explore the origins of this pain and feel the depth of hurt she suffered with her father.

☐ Factors Influencing Degree of Access

Affect.   The degree to which the client feels the emotions associated with the core issue. *For example, the more Marcy can experience the depths of her pain and shame, the greater her access.* In addition, access is enhanced by the degree to which a client is open and vulnerable to her pain. A person may feel her pain in an angry, defended way, but if she is truly open to the pain it provides greater access.

Relational Involvement.   Access is also influenced by the degree to which the client is emotionally involved and invested in her relationship with the group member (or the leader or the group as a whole) who activates the core issue: *in this case, the degree to which Marcy cares about her relationship with Ben, how important he is to her.* The more a client is invested, the greater the access. Access is also deepened by the degree of transference in the relationship: *for example, the degree to which Ben activates Marcy's father core issue with her father.* This is one reason that psychoanalysts encourage patients to develop a transference neurosis; it enhances relational involvement with the analyst and therefore the degree of access possible.

Insight.   The greater the client's insight into her motivations, dynamics, and their childhood origins, the greater the degree of access.

The leader can try to enhance a client's affect and insight during a piece of work. Relational involvement can be encouraged in the long run by fostering group cohesiveness and involvement.

When a person achieves full experiential access, it changes her sense of self dramatically. There is sometimes a wrenching experience of pain, often followed by a sense of relief, vitality, and freedom. By facing this pain, the client is now clear on her problem and open to receive healing responses from others. There is a release of energy and a new sense of self.

☐ Caring

Accessing deep pain often involves processing trauma. Frequently there was trauma associated with the original pain, and experiential access may involve re-experiencing this. In order not to re-traumatize the person, the access must be done in a situation of caring where various actions are taken that calm and care for the person during access. She needs empathy, compassion, and acceptance of her as she is (including her pain and defenses). This can come from the group leader, other group members, or even from the person herself. On some occasions, caring also can take the form of touch—a hand on the arm, holding hands, an arm around the shoulder, or even being held. Touch can convey a sense of soothing that allows the pain to be accessed without further trauma.

Caring is actually a form of healing response (see next chapter) because it involves giving the person something to counteract the original pain. To avoid re-traumatization, the healing response needs to happen simultaneously with the access. Trust is a critical factor in the effectiveness of caring.

In some cases, caring may be present but the client may not be able to take it in. This may prevent her from feeling safe enough to proceed with access, or she may become overwhelmed with the feelings that come up. In these cases, it can help to re mind the client that she isn't alone with her pain this time; now she has the support of the leader and the group. This may help her to experience the accessed feelings in a safe way.

☐ The Value of Access

Accessing core issues influences the degree of inner healing that is possible. Thus if a group member has repeatedly done good work with regard to a certain issue but doesn't seem to be making much progress, she may need deeper access.

> For example, suppose Marcy is dealing with her feelings of insecurity about being interesting and attractive to men. Although she has expressed these feelings and gotten positive responses from some of the men in the group, she still feels insecure. This may be because she hasn't gone deeply enough into the origins of her insecurity or she hasn't fully experienced the hurt and shame behind it. The next time this comes up in a dialogue with a man, before allowing her to get a response from him, you could work with her individually to achieve fuller access. Then when she returns to the dialogue and receives the man's feedback, it may have a more powerful healing impact.

However, even a small amount of access can sometimes be useful in promoting inner healing.

> For example, suppose Richard is afraid to speak in group because he is worried about not being accepted. It will be healing for him to discover that he is indeed accepted by the group, but it would be useful for him to do some exploring before the group gives him this reassurance. Just a little work can help Richard to feel his anxiety and realize that he is afraid of being judged by the group for being stupid. Then you can encourage the group to say how they are responding to him, and this feedback can be specific to his fears. The access may lead Richard to be more open to taking the feedback in and being healed. If appropriate, you could go further with the access by helping him explore his past for experiences in which he was shamed and called stupid, allowing deeper healing to ensue.

Repeated Access.   Clients often proceed to more complete access as they work on a particular issue over time.

> For example, Marcy might at first just feel her insecurity around men. The next time it comes up in group, she might access the pain of feeling uninteresting and rejected. A further step might be to locate the source of this insecurity in her relationship with her father. Then she might let herself feel the pain of her father's rejection. Then she might relive a specific incident in which her father rejected her. Another step might be to realize that he seemed to feel contempt for her when rejecting her, making her feel worthless. Each time she achieves more access, this opens up the possibility for further inner healing.

When a person has repeatedly accessed a certain core issue, she develops a familiarity with it. When the issue is activated, she will often recognize it and access the pain without help from the therapist. She can move directly to experimenting with new behavior or receiving a healing response. This is particularly useful in situations outside of group where facilitation isn't available. It enhances the likelihood of receiving healing responses in everyday life.

Trauma and Loss.   When a traumatic event or loss happens in a person's life, it needs to be fully experienced and integrated into the psyche. When this happens to a child, he often doesn't have the capacity to do this unless there is strong support from his parents and family. Without such support, a full experience of the trauma might overwhelm him and cause emotional damage. Therefore the child may defend against the trauma and hold it in unfinished form, associated with a core issue. By helping clients experience and integrate trauma, the access process can enable them to complete important tasks that couldn't be done in childhood. This is especially valuable for survivors of physical or sexual abuse (Herman, 1992).

In cases where the original pain involves a loss that was not processed sufficiently, the most important aspect of access may be the experiencing and integration of the grief. *For example, suppose a man lost a parent or sibling to death in his late teens, and didn't grieve enough at the time. Accessing this pain and grieving for the loss may be the primary thing that is needed for inner healing.*

☐ Practical Issues

Initiating Access

1. An interaction or event in group triggers a defense against a core issue. As a result of being challenged about this defense, the client lets go of it and accesses the underlying pain. *For example, Richard is withdrawn in group as a defense against his fear of speaking. The group challenges him, and he is able to let go of the withdrawal defense and explore the underlying fear of participating.* Often a great deal of effort over months must go into working through a person's defenses to allow access.

2. A core issue is activated by a person or event in the group, and the client feels the pain that is evoked. The leader then helps him explore and access its meaning. *For example, Richard tells the leader about his fear of speaking up in group, and the leader then helps him to explore this feeling and where it comes from.*

3. The client chooses to experiment with certain behavior that he knows will trigger a core issue to access it. *For example, Richard knows that if he attempts to speak in group, he will be frightened. He nevertheless chooses to do this to access and explore the fear at the moment it is happening.*

Access in Groups.   Access is one of the primary activities of individual therapy, where there is more time to focus on one person's self-exploration. In group therapy, the leader may not be able to spend the amount of time with each person individually that is required for full access. In addition, core issues often get triggered in the middle of interactions, and it sometimes isn't advisable to break up a dialogue with another person to do extended individual work. Too much of this can interfere with the flow of the group and leave other group members feeling excluded and bored. Sometimes experimenting or healing must take priority over access. The leader often faces the choice of whether to let a dialogue between two people continue or to work with one individually to achieve greater access. Such decisions will be discussed in more detail in chapter 17.

Technique.   The techniques for working toward access are similar in many ways to those used in individual therapy, so this book will not discuss them in much detail. Asking questions to elicit clients' awareness of their feelings is an important way of working toward access. Empathic reflection of the client's experience is also valuable. When resistance comes up, work with it rather than trying to get past it, as discussed in chapter 14.

Access Through Dialogue.   Even though access is often achieved by temporarily interrupting a dialogue to work with one person individually, sometimes the reverse is true, and access can be achieved only by continuing the dialogue.

For example, suppose Don is in the process of making contact with Sheldon. They are expressing warm feelings toward each other and a desire to deepen their relationship. Suddenly Don feels afraid and withdraws emotionally. At this point, working with him toward access may produce nothing but intellectual speculation. To achieve access, Don will need to go back into the dialogue, reconnect with Sheldon, and watch for the fear to arise again. Then he has a better chance to access information about what he is afraid of and where the fear comes from.

Access Through Group Exploration.   Sometimes, rather than focusing on one person, it is most useful for a number of group members to share their responses to a particular group event and then explore what it means to each of them (and possibly where their responses come from in childhood). This is discussed in detail in chapter 25.

When Access Isn't Desirable or Possible.   When a group is new or when a client has first joined a group, be careful that emotional access doesn't happen too quickly, before the client or group have developed enough connection to support this. See chapter 21 for further discussion.

Access is not always possible, even when desirable. Sometimes the group member is too defended or out-of-touch to access anything meaningful. In these cases, it may be best to move on directly to healing responses. Though there may be less benefit from the healing responses, sometimes you must proceed in this way until the healing has softened the client's defenses enough so that access is possible.

For example, suppose you try to draw Richard out and explore the feelings and fears motivating his withdrawal, but this leads nowhere. He is not in touch with any feelings and doesn't know why he can't speak. However, if he receives warm, caring interest from the leader and the group, he may gradually develop more trust of the leader and group and also heal some of the pain underlying his withdrawal. This support will make it easier for him to access this pain later.

Affect Versus Insight.   Let's discuss when it is best to focus on affect and when on insight. It is usually best to start with emotion and allow insight to emerge from that, because then it is rooted in the person's experience and has greater meaning for her. If a group member starts with some understanding, then it might be wise to work toward greater emotional involvement. *For example, if Marcy understands the meaning of her reaction to Ben but has shut down emotionally, then it would be best to help her feel her hurt and shame.* In contrast, if the group member starts with feeling, then it's best to work toward greater insight. *For example, if Marcy is upset but has no idea what set her off, your job is to help her understand what Ben's statement meant to her.* Sometimes, however, you need to start with the person's natural strength. If a client has an easier time understanding her psychodynamics cognitively, it may be advisable to let her start there and then move on to feelings. Ultimately, of course, both insight and affect are integral parts of access; they become separated only through defenses.

Problems with Access.   Certain clients have a tendency to become overwhelmed with emotions when exploring themselves. It is best to help them learn to contain their emotions and focus on intellectual insight.

Certain histrionic clients have a tendency to overdramatize their pain during access. Though the pain may be real, they may overdo it because of an unconscious need for caring and approval or because of an investment in being a victim. It may be necessary to challenge them very gently on this issue.

Access in Short-Term Groups.   A short-term group doesn't have time to allow for accessing deep feelings and childhood experiences in a gradual manner. There are two options for dealing with this constraint. The most common one is not to work much on access. The focus of the group is kept to current problems in clients' lives or here-and-now interactions between group members. Clients are not encouraged to regress or to explore deep feelings. Emphasis is placed on feedback and teaching about behavior and experimenting with healthy ways of living, either in the group or in the person's outside life. Because the work in a time-limited group cannot move slowly, this strategy avoids the danger of going too quickly into painful material that may overwhelm fragile clients. Usually the goals of the group are limited so they can be accomplished without deep access. Healing responses are provided by the leader and other group members without being concerned about whether this constitutes gratification.

Another way around this difficulty is to work quickly toward access using role playing and expressive techniques, such as is done in Gestalt therapy and forms of body therapy. This strategy can help clients access deep feelings quickly and can accomplish a great deal in a limited time. Although defenses may not be truly worked through, the access can still be of benefit, especially if it is followed by healing responses. Of course, this strategy can be used only with clients who aren't in danger of opening up material faster than they can integrate it.

☐   Accessing Healthy Capacities

When It Is Important

In addition to accessing core issues, it is sometimes important to access healthy capacities. This work is necessary when a defense is blocking a healthy capacity. Let's look at two possibilities.

1.   Suppose a child is regularly threatened or punished for engaging in certain healthy behavior. In all likelihood, the child will begin to defend against the healthy behavior.

> For example, whenever Jocelyn expressed anger or aggression, her father responded with even more anger. Because this terrified her, she developed defenses against feeling and expressing anger. In another example, whenever Sol expressed joy or good feelings about himself, his parents ridiculed him, so he developed a defense against positive feelings.

In the access phase, in addition to accessing pain, a client may need to access buried capacities, such as aggression or joy. At first the pain and fear will probably surface (*e.g., Jocelyn's fear of her anger or Sol's fear of being joyful*) and the client will need to access this and receive healing responses. After a while, she may be ready to experiment with feeling and expressing the forbidden feelings, but even then these feelings may not emerge spontaneously. Because the feelings are still buried behind defenses, the client may need to do some patient exploring to get in touch with them. In fact, she may not even realize that these healthy feelings are there. You may need to inquire about the absence of a certain healthy feeling, encouraging the client to explore how she might be defending against it.

For example, Jocelyn repeatedly got in touch with various ways that she was neglected by her mother. Her mother both judged and ignored her, telling her in no uncertain terms that there was no room in the family for her thoughts and feelings. Each time Jocelyn would access the core issues involved, she would feel hurt and deep pain. However, after a while I began to wonder about her anger. The pain was genuine, but anger, or even rage, would also have been appropriate. As I questioned her about this over a period of weeks, she gradually began to contact her anger at her mother. As her anger emerged, she became aware of how frightening this was because her father had threatened her whenever she expressed any aggression. She persisted in experimenting with anger and gradually the feeling became clearer and more intense. Eventually, she started feeling stronger and more assertive in the group and in her life. In addition to accessing the core issue, she had also accessed her healthy capacities for aggression and assertiveness.

2. Sometimes a defense closes off another healthy capacity in addition to the one associated with the core issue.

For example, Martin was physically abused by his father, producing a core issue and a deficiency in safety. One of Martin's defenses against this was to close off his loving feelings toward his father, producing a deficiency in connectedness as well. After long work of accessing and healing the abuse issue (including accessing rage), Martin was able to grow further by accessing his buried feelings of love for his father, first in the form of forgiveness.

Accessing Anger

When the healthy capacity that needs to be accessed is aggression, it usually takes the form of anger. However, there are two different kinds of work that can be done with anger, which have very different objectives:

Full expression of anger. When working with a client whose aggression is blocked, it is useful for him to work on expressing his anger (or rage) in a full-bodied way—through yelling, hitting pillows, and other forms of physical expression. This should be done through role playing, where the anger is directed toward a parent or other person who is not present. This is *not* practice in how to express healthy anger in real-life situations, and group members should not express anger directly to each other in this way. Such full expression helps clients break through blocks to their aggression so they can access this healthy capacity. If a person can't be fully angry, he also can't properly stand up for himself in other ways. Once a client has freed his aggression in this way, he can more easily channel it constructively when the need arises.

Constructive expression of anger. This type of work is appropriate for interactive expression of anger in a group. When a client is learning to express healthy anger and aggression toward other group members, he often needs to work on his ability to express himself clearly and forcefully but in a way that facilitates understanding and resolution. This is not a form of access, but rather a form of experimenting. The client needs to learn to stand up for himself and hold his ground if challenged by others. He needs to feel that he has the right to feel his feelings and have them heard. At the same time he should work on learning to express anger in a way that makes it easy for the other person to hear him. One aspect of this is owning his anger rather than using character assassination. *For example, the client might say, "When you act arrogant, I feel put down and resentful" rather than, "You are a snob."* Constructive expression of aggression also leaves room for the other person's feelings and doesn't bully her in an attempt to win a battle. It is also important for the client to show his desire to work through the difficulties with the other person rather than just dumping his anger.

In an interactive group, we work mostly on constructive expression of anger, but it is often useful to make explicit to group members the difference between these two types of anger work. So when someone is working on full expression of anger through role playing, he can express himself freely without imagining that this is a model for healthy communication.

Healing Response

This chapter covers the second of the four aspects of the therapeutic change process. First we discuss caring and disconfirming as healing responses that are useful for almost all clients. Then we discuss the types of healing responses that are needed for three kinds of core issues—deficiency, harm, and punishment issues.

A *healing response* is something the client receives that redresses and heals the effects of the trauma or dysfunctional pattern from childhood that originally caused the core issue. This can be thought of as reparenting, though that term is usually reserved for a situation where the client is regressed or inhabiting her inner child and the other person is taking a parental role. The kinds of healing response discussed in this chapter go far beyond this. A healing response gives the client what she needed as a child or repairs the harmful effects of what she did receive. If the original pain came from deprivation, then healing means receiving what was not given during childhood. If the original pain came from abuse or punishment, healing means other things, which are discussed below. Healing can come from another group member, the leader, the group as a whole, and even from the client herself.

☐ Previous Concepts

Most theories of psychotherapy see access as the primary or only mechanism of therapeutic change. Psychoanalysis traditionally has viewed therapeutic change as "making the unconscious conscious." The concept of "corrective emotional experience," (Alexander & French, 1946) expands this understanding of therapeutic change to include experiences in therapy that correct for negative experiences from the past. However, this concept has until recently been largely dismissed. Now more analytic theorists are recognizing that something like a corrective emotional experience is a central part of therapeutic change (Adler, 1985; Stolorow et al., 1987). However, analysts still tend to assume that clients must learn to recognize and give up archaic needs rather than having them met in a healing way. Gestalt therapy also tends to focus on access only, seeing "awareness" as curative in itself (Beissler, 1970). Other theorists also take the position that access is all that is needed because they believe that healing emerges spontaneously from inside (Almaas, 1988; Grof, 1985).

Although access is important and healing can emerge entirely as an internal process, healing responses from others provide a form of corrective emotional experience that is crucial to therapeutic change. Why then have so many theorists neglected to focus on this key process? One reason is that most theories focus exclusively on the process of individual therapy, and although healing responses are just as important there, they are sometimes less obvious because they come from the therapist. A good therapist naturally responds with acceptance, caring, compassion, and other healing ways of interacting with the client. The therapist/theorist often focuses on the access that the client is engaged in and ignores his or her own healing contribution to the process. Psychoanalysts have historically been averse to gratification while failing to distinguish it from healing responses (see chapter 4), and this has led theorists to ignore the importance of healing.

Some theorists, such as Rogers (1951) and Kohut (1977), recognize the importance of the therapist's empathy and caring, but see these factors only as a prerequisite to other, more important, change mechanisms. Rogers sees change as coming through integrating disowned parts of the self, and Kohut sees it happening during optimal empathic failure through the process of "transmuting internalization." Nevertheless, many self-psychologists now seem to intuitively recognize that therapeutic change derives directly from the therapist's empathic response. I believe that healing responses are a pivotal part of the therapeutic change process, not just a preliminary step.

Recently, concepts similar to healing response have been proposed by various psychotherapy researchers (Dahl, 1991; Safran & Greenberg, 1991; Silbershatz & Sampson, 1991). "Once an interpersonal schema has been accessed, one way of modifying it involves the use of the therapeutic relationship to provide schema-disconfirming experience" (Safran & Greenberg, 1991, p. 342). In control mastery theory (Weiss, 1993), the therapist provides healing responses through passing the client's transference tests.

☐ Forms of Healing Responses

The healing response that is needed varies according to the client's underlying psychodynamic issue and the interpersonal situation. The following is a brief summary of the different forms of healing response.

1. **Caring.** Expressing warmth, understanding, and concern for the client's welfare.

2. **Disconfirming.** If the client's core issue leads him to expect others to treat him in a certain harmful way, you (or group members) don't act that way. You may also go out of your way not to act in a way that can be perceived by the client as a repetition of that harm.

3. **Meeting needs.** You (or the group) meet a basic need of the client that was not met in childhood. This is most effective when it follows access.

4. **Protection.** You (or group members or the client himself) protect the client from harm similar to that which happened as a child.

5. **Reinforcement.** The client experiments with new healthy behavior and receives appreciation or other responses from the leader (or group members) that reinforce this behavior.

6. **Reparation.** When you (or a group member) do something that re-creates an experience similar to that which harmed the client as a child, you acknowledge this (perhaps even apologize) and subsequently change your behavior.

7. **Healing relationship.** The client develops a relationship with you (or group members) in which she learns to act in a healthy manner, and she receives the above forms of healing in a consistent way over a period of time. Such a relationship produces the deepest inner healing.

☐ Generic Healing Responses

I now examine each form of healing response in more detail. Caring and disconfirming are generic healing responses that are valuable for almost any person and situation. I discuss them first before turning to forms of healing that are more specifically tailored.

Caring

The original pain almost always involves a lack of caring, where the parents (or others) didn't have the child's welfare at heart, or their own needs or problems took precedence. Therefore caring is a kind of healing response that is helpful no matter what the underlying core issue. It is valuable not only as a specific response to pain that is accessed, but also as a general support for the vulnerability of the therapy process. It was first studied in connection with healing in the therapist–client relationship by Carl Rogers (1951), who emphasized empathy and unconditional positive regard. Caring can be expressed in the following ways.

1. Empathy: resonating with a person's feelings, experiencing a mild version of what she is experiencing, and communicating that. Empathy enables people to feel safe in being vulnerable.

2. Understanding: comprehending what a person is experiencing, what it means to her, and possibly where it comes from in her past. If done in a caring manner, understanding is reassuring because the person feels seen for who she is.

3. Identification: recognizing that you have (or had) a similar issue or feeling. The person feels safe because you understand her from the inside and therefore aren't likely to judge her. She also realizes that she isn't alone with her pain or difficulty.

Identification usually isn't appropriate for the group leader to share because it often involves more self-disclosure than is safe for the group.

4. Compassion: a feeling of love for someone in pain that supports the person in being vulnerable. Compassion makes it not only tolerable but often rewarding to be with someone in pain. It opens your heart.

5. Acceptance: feeling OK about all aspects of a person, even her defenses and rough edges. Acceptance doesn't mean blanket approval; you might still want the person to change. It does means that you maintain good feelings about her despite any shortcomings you see.

6. Appreciation: seeing and valuing the healthy aspects of a person, her strengths and potential, and especially the ways she has grown. It is particularly helpful to express appreciation to someone for her courage and openness in being vulnerable.

As our society has become increasingly bureaucratic, competitive, and impersonal, caring has diminished as a social norm. However, in the right situation most people are actually eager to care for and love each other, and a good therapy group is just the place to foster this. Once group members have seen through someone's defenses to the pain, vulnerability, and humanity underneath, it is much easier to care for her. Most people really value this opportunity to be healing and supportive to others. In addition, the group setting provides an opportunity to learn to understand and appreciate people who may at first seem strange, different, and threatening. All this is good training for the creation of a more caring society.

Disconfirming

Many core issues cause the client to expect to be treated in a harmful way by others. *For example, a client may expect other people to be controlling or uncaring or manipulative.* The leader or group members can provide a disconfirming healing response by not responding in the way the client expects.

> For example, if the client expects people to be manipulative and the group members are honest and straightforward, this will disconfirm his expectations. If the client expects people to be uncaring, their warm, interested responses will disconfirm this.

Sometimes a client interprets others' behavior as fitting his negative expectations even when it doesn't. As the leader, try to make sure that your behavior can't be construed by the client in this way. *For example, if the client expects others to be controlling, make sure to allow and even encourage him to be autonomous.* This reduces the chances that the client will feel harmed, but it doesn't eliminate the possibility. If a client nevertheless persists in interpreting your behavior or that of others' according to a particular core issue, then he should receive feedback about this. Such feedback often happens naturally during the give and take of an interactive group.

Some clients go even further and act in a way that attempts to elicit or complement the negative behavior they expect from other people. *For example, a client who expects people to be controlling may actually try to comply with their wishes even if they don't want this.* In such cases, the leader may need to challenge the client on this behavior to disconfirm his expectations. *The leader might point out that the client is going out of his way to comply with what he thinks is wanted, and encourage him to decide for himself.* This kind of challenge often comes from group members as well as from the leader.

> For example, if a client expects others to not be interested in her, she might hold back and say little about herself or her feelings. When the other group members question her holding back and express interest in hearing from her, this disconfirms her core image of being uninteresting.

☐ Healing Deficiency Issues

In addition to caring and disconfirming, clients need to receive healing responses that are tailored to their particular psychodynamic issues. For the purpose of the ensuing discussion, I divide these underlying issues into three broad categories: deficiency, harm, and punishment issues.

A *deficiency issue* results from a situation where the child was not given enough of what he needed in terms of nurturing, mirroring, affection, and other varieties of caring. The child's basic need for connectedness or value was not adequately met. The extreme of this is neglect. A deficiency issue leaves the person feeling inadequate or deficient in some way—unlovable, undesirable, uninteresting, incompetent, worthless, etc. This feeling may be kept unconscious under layers of defenses.

Meeting Needs

The healing response for a deficiency issue involves meeting the basic need that wasn't met sufficiently in childhood. *For example, if a person wasn't accepted and appreciated for being himself as a child, then healing means receiving that in the group.* Healing responses can come in many forms. In addition to caring, interest, and nurturing, people may also need respect, encouragement, direction, or love.

The closer the healing situation is to the childhood situation, the more deeply healing it can be. This is why it can be powerful to have a group member receive healing when in a regressed state. *For example, if a client allows himself to contact the pain of deprivation as a young child, then the caring and soothing he receives will be deeply healing.* However, even when the person is not regressed and the healing response is given in a more adult form than originally needed, it can still be quite useful.

Healing and Gratification

It is important to make a distinction between a healing response and gratification. It is well known that it is not advisable to gratify the needs of a client, especially a person with borderline tendencies, because this may encourage him to focus solely on getting his needs met rather than trying to understand himself and grow. However, it *is* thera-peutic to meet a client's needs *after* he accesses a core issue and is particularly open.

> For example, Jim tells the leader that he feels she doesn't care for him like she does for others. Jim perceives the leader as bored and uninterested when he is talking but excited and interested in another group member. Jim's perception is not accurate and seems to be derived from being rejected by his mother, who was more interested in his sister. The leader is, in fact, quite interested in Jim. However, if she reassures him about this right away, it may close off the possibility of Jim's accessing this. If Jim believes her, he will feel OK and have no need to process his feelings any further. I see this as gratification because the leader gave Jim a healing response before he had achieved any access. It may help him to feel better in the moment, but it won't contribute much to therapeutic change. On the other hand, if the leader helps Jim explore his feeling response to her, he may access the under-lying transference and feel the pain of his mother's lack of interest. By delaying the timing of the healing response, the therapist allows Jim to open up emotionally. Then when she does convey her genuine interest in him, he can take it in, allowing some healing to occur.

Healing After Access.   Whenever a client's needs are met after access, this not only contributes to inner healing but also rewards the person for the hard work of access. Thus the person will be more willing to face that kind of pain in the future. It is also important to recognize when a person can meet his needs himself, from his own internal resources, and when he needs healing responses from others. In most cases, a healing response should be provided only when the person can't provide his own.

There is another crucial advantage to meeting a client's needs after access. The leader and the group have the opportunity to know exactly what those needs are, so the healing responses can be targeted specifically. Otherwise, the healing person is likely to meet the need that shows on the surface, whereas the real need is hidden, thereby missing the point.

> For example, suppose a man tends to show off his intellect in group, while admitting that he wants to be admired and have his intelligence and competence validated. If he then explores this further and accesses the deeper need, it may turn out that what he really needs is nurturing, or being valued as a person without performing, or something else other than admiration for his intelligence. The need for admiration is a compensation for his real need, and only meeting the real need can be healing.

I use the term *healing response* to refer to meeting needs after access, and *gratifica-tion* to meeting needs without access or when the person could have met them himself. As mentioned in the previous section, sometimes it is necessary to meet some of a person's needs without requiring access first, especially needs for acceptance, understanding, and compassion. In the early stages of group, this helps to build trust and group cohe-siveness. Certain clients need to have these needs met before they can trust enough to access their pain. With acceptance and compassion, some gratification isn't dangerous. With some other needs (e.g., for caring, touch, or advice), it is usually better to postpone meeting them until after access. If these needs are gratified before access, the client is more likely to avoid self-exploration. The group leader may sometimes have to encour-age group members to hold back on gratifying each other. One person may act out a codependent need of her own to care for others, and another might jump in to assuage someone's pain because it makes him uncomfortable. The leader needs to prevent such nontherapeutic gratification and instead lead the client in self-exploration.

Touch.   Healing responses can even go as far as touching. Many clients have suffered some level of deprivation as children in the area of touch, so after appropriate access it can be healing to have another group member offer supportive touch. Most psychodynamic groups have rules against touch out of a legitimate fear that gratification may prevent a client from accessing her pain. However if a leader excludes touch altogether, in the name of preventing acting out, he is throwing the baby out with the bath water. Under the right circumstances (after access), touch can be very healing. In fact, in some cases touch is absolutely required as a healing response; anything else is a pale substitute. In these cases, it is important that the client not be deprived once again. If a group member accesses a deficiency issue that involves early touch deprivation, it can bring up not only great pain but also powerful needs for physical soothing and comfort. Once accessed in a genuine way, these needs should be met directly.

The disagreement between my position on touch and the psychodynamic position probably derives from theoretical differences. Analysts see therapeutic change as coming from making the unconscious conscious, which is an aspect of access. Therefore they see touch as a distraction from this crucial process and don't recognize its importance as a healing response.

When a client accesses deep pain having to do with deprivation, some group members may feel a natural urge to hold or comfort the client through touch. If they express these desires, you can encourage them to take action, after asking the client's permission. If no one initiates or mentions touch, you may need to bring it up by saying to the client, "It looks to me like you really need to be touched right now." When dealing with touch, make sure that the client receiving the touch is not being violated in any way. Her permission should be asked, and you should check to make sure that her answer is genuine (and not just compliance) before allowing any physical contact to occur.

Relational Healing

Healing happens not only in response to a specific event. More importantly, it happens over time through relationship. Let's look at a detailed example of healing using Marcy and Ben.

> In an early session, as part of some work Ben was doing, I encouraged him to pick someone he wanted to connect with. He chose one woman and indicated a couple of others as alternate choices. Marcy felt hurt that she wasn't even on his list of second choices. In a later group, she initiated some important work by telling Ben about her hurt. Ben explained that he didn't choose her because he felt intimidated by her; she was so sharp and perceptive that she would see right through him. Notice that Ben was put off partly by Marcy's defenses. Marcy had already gotten feedback from the group about her intimidating front and was interested in working on this. Therefore, I encouraged her to move into access by suggesting that she not get caught up in his explanation but instead stay with her feeling of hurt. This allowed her to soften, and her previous front of appearing nonchalant disappeared. Then she experimented with letting Ben know, in an open and appealing way, that she liked him and wanted him to like her too and that she felt hurt.

> Marcy's work had three effects. First, she found that she was strong enough inside to tolerate the hurt feeling and that she didn't judge herself because of it. As she did this kind of

work in group over time, she developed a sense of inner support (see chapter 17) that allowed her to be open and vulnerable without fear. This is a form of access because she allowed herself to fully feel the hurt. It led directly to inner healing in the form of increased self-support for vulnerability. I chose not to encourage her to go further into access because she had already explored the origins of this hurt in individual therapy. Second, she discovered that nothing terrible happened when she showed her vulnerability. She wasn't rejected or ridiculed. This was healing for her because the negative reaction she feared didn't happen. Third, Ben began to appreciate Marcy's openness and softness (along with the earthiness and spontaneity that he had always liked in her). He was increasingly drawn to her. This was a further healing reward for her vulnerability, and as time went on it became increasingly integrated into her personality.

> Marcy: This interaction was a key, a turning point for me. I used to think that I was warm, but other people experienced me as hard. It was with Ben that I began the process of recognizing that I present an imposing or intimidating presence. I remembered people being afraid of me in my life, but I was surprised that was the way people saw me, because that wasn't what I felt inside. Inside I felt warm and open. It was a surprise to learn that my defenses were so hardened that people didn't see me. It was a real surprise that someone like Ben should be intimidated by me.

In a later session, Marcy made a comment about how "the universe moved" when Ben said something to another member. She confessed that she had really meant that the universe had moved when he'd said something special to her. At another point she told him that she had a crush on him (but she wasn't coming on to him). She expressed these vulnerable feelings in an open and contactful way, continuing to experiment with healthy behavior. Ben responded in kind. He was moved by this openness on her part and grew fond of her. As the group continued, Ben and Marcy developed a deep connection. Thus continuing to receive emotional support for her healthy behavior helped her to fully develop her capacity for openness. There was no longer any chance of Ben ignoring Marcy. "I liked Ben very much and once he began to appreciate me more, it had a strong impact. His recognition of me liberated me." This is an example of relational healing. As a result of her relationship with Ben, Marcy developed and solidified her healthy capacities of connectedness and vulnerability. (For a more complete case description of Marcy's work in this group, see Earley [1996].)

With the Group.   Relational healing also happens frequently as a result of the relationship between a group member and the group as a whole. Many people who join therapy groups have never had the experience of belonging to a group where they were seen and cared for. This in itself can be a profound healing experience, especially if the person accesses her pain, distrust, and feelings of exclusion in the process of bonding with the group. Relational healing with the group can also happen around specific issues, such as fear of taking attention, telling secrets, or being powerful.

> For example, remember Richard who was afraid to speak in the group. If he develops a relationship with the group where they clearly enjoy giving him the time and attention to speak, this will have a healing effect.

Relational healing also happens in the relationship between a group member and the leader, which has its own dynamics, difficulties, and advantages because you are an authority figure in the group. I discuss member–leader interactions in detail in chapter 19.

☐   Healing Harm Issues

A *harm issue* originates when a child is actively harmed—by anger, judgment, physical abuse, sexual abuse, excessive control, intrusion, or other means. Healing responses to harm issues can take a number of different forms: (a) avoiding acting in harmful ways or ways that can be perceived as harmful by the client; (b) protecting the client from similar kinds of harm (or the client protecting herself); (c) if the harm undermined a basic need, such as value or autonomy, then healing includes meeting that need; (d) when someone (a group member or the leader) re-creates the original harm with the client, healing means acknowledging this and changing one's behavior; and (e) if the original harm came from someone close to the client, then the healing involves being in a close relationship with the client that is harm-free. Let's look at these last four in more detail.

Avoiding acting in harmful ways was previously discussed under the *Disconfirming* section. Here we look at the last four in more detail.

Protection

If a group member is actually being harmed by another member, then the best healing response is protection from that harm. *For example, Marcy experienced frequent judgment and disgust from her father. Suppose that she experiences a similar disgust coming from Barry, either because of a transference distortion of hers or because Barry really feels that way toward her. Marcy's healing should take the form of protection from the negative impact of his disgust.* This protection could come from a group member or the leader, or it could come from the client herself. In most cases, it is preferable for it to come from the person herself, if she is capable of it. *For instance, Marcy might get angry at Barry and tell him that she doesn't like being shamed. This gives her an experience of her own power and a sense of no longer being a victim of such treatment. It develops her capacity for safety, as well as assertiveness and value.* When the protection comes from the client herself, it constitutes both a healing response and experimenting with healthy behavior (see next chapter).

Protection is appropriate when the other person really is harming the client, *for example, if Barry really is disgusted with Marcy.* However, when a client's reaction is a transference distortion, and the other person isn't really harming her, then the work becomes more difficult to handle because it may not be appropriate for the client to dump her anger on an innocent party. Often the best strategy is to encourage the person to practice protecting herself through role playing standing up to the parent who originally harmed her.

Access Before Protection.   Just as gratification is not very healing for a deficiency issue if there is no access first, anger is often not very healing if there is no prior access. In fact, some clients perpetually express anger at anticipated or perceived harm done to them without getting any healing from this.

> For example, Jody got easily enraged when she perceived that someone was doubting her perception of herself or interpreting her underlying motives in an argument. She also got angry whenever someone gave her feedback that contradicted her view of her behavior.

Whether other people's actions were appropriate or not, Jody would frequently become quite hostile when she felt her experience of herself was being invalidated. This derived from her experience with her father, who constantly told Jody what she was feeling, in complete disregard for Jody's actual experience. For quite a while, Jody was unaware of the transferential source of her anger, and therefore no healing occurred. Eventually she was able to access her experience of violation at her father's hands, feel the rage, and connect this with her reactions in group. Then the leader encouraged her to express her rage directly to her father (through role playing), and this was genuinely healing for her.

With a client who hasn't been able to protect herself in the past, such as a timid or compliant person, anger may be an important part of the change process, even without any access. In this case, expressing anger is constructive because it involves experimenting with healthy behavior. *In the above example with Jody, anger was a familiar part of her repertoire, so there was no experimenting involved. With a timid or compliant person, anger would be a step toward health.*

Protection by Others.   In cases of harm, the client frequently suffers from a deficiency in the basic need for protection. Because protection from harm is a basic need, a child who is not protected (whether it is the parent's fault or not) feels deprived of this fundamental requirement. Therefore, protection that comes from someone other than the client can be a crucial healing response. *In this example, if Barry is really shaming Marcy, someone else in the group might challenge Barry and tell him to stop. If no one speaks up and Marcy can't protect herself, the leader might provide the protection. Marcy will thus feel valued by knowing that Barry's reactions aren't supported and she deserves to feel safe from harm.* If the protection comes from outside, the client doesn't get the chance to develop her ability to protect herself, but she can work on this skill later in her growth process. Protection by others is essential if the client is not yet strong enough to protect herself, but even clients who can protect themselves can sometimes benefit from being protected by others.

One group session was becoming very chaotic because various members were acting belligerent and attacking each other. Before one interaction could be resolved another one would begin. Hostility was increasing and people were feeling frightened and unsafe. The leader called a halt and asked each person in turn to explore the underlying meaning of his or her anger and its origins in childhood. Each time a group member would forget this suggestion and begin blaming the person who had triggered his anger, the leader steered him back on track, exploring the underlying meaning of his anger. This led to much valuable work and an easing of the tension in the group. Afterwards, one member said he felt greatly relieved because his family had been chaotic like the group, and no one had ever intervened to restore order and safety. He felt comforted that the leader had protected him and the group from harm. This is an example of healing protection, where the protection came from another person.

Here we have discussed how a protective kind of healing can come either from inside or outside, from the person herself or from others. This is actually the case for all forms of healing responses as will be discussed later in this section.

Meeting Needs

Support for Autonomy.   If the original harm came in the form of control or exploitation that undermined the person's sense of autonomy, then, in addition to protection, healing responses need to include meeting this basic need—giving the person encouragement and support for autonomous actions such as taking initiative, being assertive, saying no, and thinking for oneself.

> For example, if a woman became passive and compliant as a result of being sexually abused, then she would need support for being assertive and setting limits as part of her healing. People might encourage her to stand up for herself or express her own opinions at appropriate points in group.

Appreciation.   If the original harm caused the person to feel negatively about herself, producing a deficiency in value, then the healing response may include receiving approval and appreciation, especially in the areas where she was shamed. *For example, if Beth was made to feel stupid, then her healing would involve getting feedback that she is intelligent or articulate, or at least competent in these areas.* Of course, as a leader you can't always count on this in the same way as other forms of healing. People must really approve of the person in the specific area (*e.g., they must see Beth as smart*). However, the shame clients feel often bears little relation to their actual ability, so this form of healing is fairly common. Keep in mind, however, that the deepest and most important sense of value is one that doesn't depend on good performance or even on the person having positive personal qualities. It involves feeling valuable for simply being. Therefore, although approval of particular traits or behaviors can provide some healing, it has its limits.

When a client protects herself from harm, she also rejects the negative self-image that resulted from the harm. *In the above example with Marcy and Barry, Marcy's sense of value had been blocked by her father's judgments. By standing up to Barry and protecting herself, she also took a step toward restoring her sense of value.* The healing response of protection often helps to develop both safety and value.

Reparation.   Reparation is a kind of healing response that follows a re-enactment of the original childhood harm in the therapy. It is not uncommon for another person to act in a way that feels similar to what harmed the client as a child. *For example, if a client expects others to not be interested in him because his father wasn't, and a group member does in fact get bored with him, this is a re-enactment of the original harm.* Reparation means that the offending person recognizes what he did to harm the client, acknowledges this, and perhaps even apologizes. He subsequently changes his behavior so that this kind of harm no longer happens to the client. *For example, suppose you as leader are preoccupied with your own problems one day when a client is talking and therefore aren't very interested in her at that moment. The client senses this and she feels hurt. Reparation would mean acknowledging that you were distracted, owning this as your problem, and trying to make sure it doesn't happen again, especially with this client. (This might necessitate working on your countertransference reactions.) Reparation can provide a very powerful healing experience for the client.*

Reparation happens more frequently with other group members. Their own core issues or defenses often cause them to act in ways that can be harmful to others, and they are frequently confronted about this behavior. When this happens, the offending person has an opportunity to own his issue and work on it. When he has made enough progress to change his behavior with the person he has hurt, this can produce a powerful form of reparation for the other person. In addition, two members are often working on their relationship with each other, and both may improve their way of relating to the other.

> In the example with Barry and Marcy, suppose Barry admits that he was shaming Marcy and owns the problem, and then gradually becomes more accepting and supportive of her as he works on this issue. Marcy and Barry develop a relationship[4] in which she is no longer harmed by him. Obviously, this kind of healing can take time, not only for the relationship to develop, but also for Marcy to trust that she won't be shamed by Barry again. However, the results are often profoundly healing.

Relational Healing with Harm Issues

If the original harm came from someone close to the person such as a parent (rather than, say, sexual abuse from a stranger), then another kind of healing response is necessary. The person needs to have the experience of being in a close relationship in which she is not harmed.

> For example, Penny was neglected by both her parents, but her grandfather was nice to her. However, he also abused her sexually. In group, Penny formed a friendship with Harry, an older man with good boundaries who had a great deal of respect and affection for Penny. This relationship gave Penny an experience of having a relationship in which she was cared about without being harmed.

> Let's look more carefully at what I mean by "not being harmed." In the above example with Marcy and Barry, even after they become close, from time to time Marcy may still feel harmed by Barry, sometimes even because he does judge her. Nevertheless, if he doesn't do it often or harshly like her father did and if Marcy can stand up to him, they can work things out to restore their relationship to one of warmth and mutual appreciation. This relationship will have a deep impact on the development of Marcy's capacity for safety and value. Of course, Barry will also be working on and healing his own core issues through the relationship.

I have been describing healing relationships in clinical terms, emphasizing the power they have for therapeutic change. However, the intimate, authentic relationships that develop in a therapy group have a spiritual quality that transcends this function. When people genuinely meet each other in profound moments of pain, joy, and contact, and come to truly love and care for each other over time, these connections have their own intrinsic value. It is an honor to witness the unfolding of these sacred connections.

Relational healing with harm issues also happens in a person's relationship with the group as a whole. Clients who come from dysfunctional or abusive families can

---

[4] This refers to a relationship within the group, not necessarily extending into the person's life outside. I will discuss questions of group members forming outside relationships with each other in chapter 20.

experience profound healing just by being in a group where they feel connected without being harmed. For this healing to happen, they will have to access and work through their fears and defenses so they can actually take in the caring and closeness.

☐ Healing Punishment Issues

As mentioned before, a *punishment issue* derives from a situation where the child was regularly punished or threatened (or experienced negative consequences) when engaging in certain healthy behavior. The healing response that is needed involves appreciating the person for engaging in that behavior. *For example, if Bill was punished as a child for being assertive, then he needs acceptance and appreciation for being assertive in group.*

At first glance, a punishment issue may look similar to a harm issue, but the difference is that a harm issue involves harm that happened to the child in a pervasive way, not only in response to certain behavior. A punishment issue develops when the child was harmed (or otherwise punished) for engaging in specific behavior. Here the problem isn't just the harm, but the fact that the person will now refrain from engaging in that behavior (and defend against associated feelings and impulses) because it has been repeatedly punished. In fact, the punishment may not take the form of direct harm at all; it could be abandonment or withdrawal. *For example, suppose that whenever Bill was assertive, his mother withdrew from him, leaving him feeling bereft.* This is a very effective form of punishment.

Punishment can also take the form of negative consequences of other kinds; it need not be something that the parents intended as punishment. *For example, suppose that whenever Bill became assertive, his mother became frightened and had an anxiety attack. Bill would learn to avoid being assertive even if no punishment was intended by his mother.*

Reinforcement

In all these cases, for healing to happen, the client must first experiment with the healthy behavior that was punished in childhood.

> In Bill's case, he must take the risk to be assertive, at least a little. When he discovers that the punishment is not forthcoming, or he receives reinforcement from the leader or the group, this supports and encourages the healthy behavior.

Some preliminary healing can occur if a client expresses his fear of engaging in the behavior and is reassured by the group that it would be OK with them. However, the most important reinforcement requires that the client actually perform the healthy behavior that he fears will meet with disapproval. Once he does this and becomes afraid of people's reactions, the leader should help him articulate exactly what he is afraid of. *For example, Bill might be afraid that the members would be frightened of his assertiveness.* Then, with his permission, encourage the group members to express their actual reactions, which are usually very different from what the client expects. This helps to disconfirm the client's negative expectation based on his core issue. In fact, group members often appreciate the client's healthy behavior and his willingness to take the risk. This reinforces the client's healthy behavior, increasing the likelihood that he will take the risk again.

In addition, experimenting with healthy behavior frequently gets reinforced because the client actually gets what he wants or feels better inside.

> For example, if Bill takes the risk to be assertive by reaching out to a member, she is likely to respond positively. Or if Bill takes the risk to state his opinion about something, he may feel more of a sense of personal power. These reactions are naturally reinforcing.

☐ Summary

Table 3.1 summarizes the information in this section about the form of healing responses for various core issues.

TABLE 3.1

Healing response	Core issue	Basic needs involved
Caring	Any	Any
Disconfirming the expectation of a negative response	Any	Any
Meeting need not met in childhood	Deficiency	Connectedness, value
Meeting need undermined by harm	Harm	Autonomy, value
Protection against harm	Harm	Safety, autonomy
Reinforcement for experimenting with healthy behavior	Punishment	Any
Reparation	Harm	Safety, autonomy, value
Healing relationship	Any	Any

☐ Forgiveness

In the advanced stages of a client's therapy, it can be healing to forgive her parents for the ways that their parenting wasn't adequate. This should occur naturally, at the client's initiative, after she has worked through underlying pain and anger.

Though the work of forgiveness can, of course, be done in individual therapy, group therapy is especially useful in fostering forgiveness through a healing relationship with another group member. When a client has parental transference with someone, it may not be entirely a distortion. There are often important ways in which the other member really is like the parent, not just superficially but in the way that originally harmed the client. *For example, if the parent was overly controlling, there may be a group member who is also very controlling. If a parent was judgmental or distant, there will be group members who have these traits also.*

When a client discovers a transference reaction to another group member, she will explore it and gain insight, access, and healing from this work. In addition, over time, she will see the other group member working on the very character flaw that caused her so much pain from her parent in childhood. She will see the member exploring the history of how he become so controlling or arrogant or afraid of connection. She will see him accessing the pain that is behind this behavior pattern and why he needed that defense, and she will feel compassion for him. He will gradually be healed and change his behavior in the group. She will likely forgive him and develop a more positive relationship with him partly because of the ways that he has changed and partly because of the ways that she has changed. They may come to care about each other.

All of this will affect how the client feels toward her parent. She will probably come to understand more about how he came to be the way he was. She will know or guess something about his history and how he came to have his character flaws. She will realize at a deep level that it wasn't because of something wrong with her that he treated her the way he did. All this will help her to forgive the parent just as she has forgiven the group member who reminded her of the parent. Her new connection with the group member will help her to open her heart to her parent. Thus group therapy adds an extra dimension to the development of forgiveness.

☐ Healing from Inside or Outside

Self-Healing.   Though healing responses most often come from other people, they sometimes come from the client herself, as discussed above for harm issues. Usually they need to come from others first, from the group or the leader, and then as the person progresses in her therapy, she can more frequently heal herself. In fact, at some point in a person's progress around a specific issue, the healing response *must* come from within. With deficiency issues, for example, the client needs to be able to accept and care for herself, to love and appreciate herself. By internalizing the love and caring she has received from the group and the leader, the person becomes able to heal herself.

> For example, once Marcy has received enough healing from Ben and the group, and has really taken it in, she will develop an image of herself as valuable and lovable. Then when she accesses the pain of her relationship with her father, she will be able to provide an internal healing response of caring and love for herself.

Similarly, with a punishment issue, the client eventually needs to progress to the point where she can engage in the "forbidden" behavior and give herself acceptance and appreciation. *For example, Bill will eventually be able to feel good about being assertive without needing reassurance from the group.*

Sometimes clients continue to ask for reassurance or other kinds of healing responses when they no longer need it from other people, because when they have the internal support to provide the healing for themselves. At this point, the group leader might refrain from providing healing and encourage the group members to also hold back. This forces the client back on her own resources to find the healing within, thus promoting further growth. You need to explain the situation clearly, so the members understand why it is therapeutic for them to restrain their caring impulses.

When Healing Progresses from Internal to External.   Occasionally, this order needs to be reversed. Some clients have learned to give themselves a certain amount of self-healing, in the form of nurturing or caring, as a compensation for their childhood deprivation. However, this may be used as a defense against trusting and connecting with other people. These clients may at first accept healing only from themselves, but they must eventually learn to take in healing from others in order to develop their capacity for connectedness.

> For example, one client had developed the ability to withdraw into isolation and soothe herself when upset. Whenever she felt pain in the group, this would be her first inclination. After much work, she began to feel her need for others and take in caring from group members when she was in pain. This opened her up to deeper connections with people in her life.

☐   Other Aspects of Healing Responses

Healing Response Can Lead to Access.   As discussed previously, a healing response frequently leads directly to inner healing or experimenting with new healthy behavior. However, in some cases, it provides a client with the support that is needed to go more deeply into access.

> For example, suppose that Marcy is able to access some of the pain of her father's rejection of her, and then Ben (or another group member) responds with caring and compassion. This additional support may enable Marcy to soften and feel the pain even more deeply.

Combination Issues.   Frequently a core issue may involve both harm and punishment, or even deficiency as well.

> For example, Harry, who was mentioned in the last chapter, had a mother who was critical of him whenever he wasn't working hard and accomplishing things. She also failed to fully accept him for being himself because he was supposed to be perfect. Thus Harry had a harm issue because the judgment was harmful to his self-esteem and confidence, and a deficiency issue because he didn't get the acceptance he needed. He also had a punishment issue because of being judged for being relaxed and spontaneous. Therefore Harry needed all three kinds of healing in the group. He needed to protect himself from the perceived judgment of the group (harm). He needed to receive people's acceptance of him (deficiency), and he needed to experiment with being relaxed and spontaneous so he could receive the group's appreciation for that healthy behavior (punishment).

The Limits of Healing.   There is a limit to how much healing can happen in psychotherapy, especially with respect to intense early needs for love and nurturing. How much can these needs be met when the person is an adult, and when is this therapeutic? Although healing responses are an important part of therapeutic change, there is a limit to how much can happen in psychotherapy. When a client was severely deprived or abused at an early age, the amount of healing that can occur in a few hours of therapy per week is often not sufficient. If you believe a client can get all her early needs met in the group (or even in individual therapy), you will be disappointed and the client may regress and have a serious negative therapeutic reaction. Besides seeking healing responses from outside, the client must develop her own inner resources and ability to heal herself. She may also have to give up the idea of getting all her early needs met, at least in their original form.

☐ Practical Issues

Many times a healing response happens spontaneously without any intervention from the leader, but sometimes you must ask for feedback from the group at the appropriate time. When necessary, the leader should ask the client's permission to get this feedback. By giving her a chance to explore her fears about what she will hear, you may help her achieve deeper access. In addition, it gives the group members a clearer idea of how to respond.

> For example, Tina is working on accessing and showing her needs for nurturing and support. She has hidden them all her life because her mother responded to her needs with disgust and dismissal. After she has opened herself to her pain about her mother's reaction, you could ask her if it would be OK to get responses from the group. This may intensify her fear of being shamed, leading to deeper access. Then when she is ready for the group's responses, they will know that she is afraid of being shamed and can gear their responses to this issue. If Tina has been open and vulnerable in her access work, most of the group members will feel appreciative and closer to her—just the opposite of what she expects.

The Leader's Healing Response

It is generally a good idea to hold back on expressing your own healing response to a client until most of the group members have given theirs. Because of the power that group members attribute to you, if you come in too soon, you may pre-empt what they have to say. Furthermore, you may unwittingly encourage clients to value you more than each other. Healing responses are often more potent and believable coming from group members. Clients may think that it is your job to give the right responses and therefore distrust what you say.

Once the members have had a chance to give their feedback, you can add yours, especially if you can provide a different perspective. If the group members don't spontaneously offer healing responses, then you should give yours so the client isn't left without any. This may also prime the pump for other people. You should also be aware of situations where a group member needs to hear from you in particular, because of transference issues.

When a Healing Response Is Not Believed

Sometimes the client will be reluctant to hear feedback because she is afraid that people will just be "nice" and not really tell the truth. This, of course, is a real possibility, but it rarely happens as much as expected. Encourage the client to tell the group she wants the truth and to challenge anyone she thinks isn't being honest. While she is getting the feedback, if it seems appropriate, ask her if she believes the person. Usually when people give feedback, they are expressive and detailed enough that the client can tell they mean it.

> For example, Marcy shared with the group that she was involved in a car accident because she was eating while driving. An overeater, she felt deeply ashamed of how her food compulsion had caused the accident. She also imagined that the group members felt somewhat disgusted with her about this. When I suggested she get feedback, she said she wouldn't believe it if people said no. She didn't believe their disgust was intense, but she figured it must be there and she thought people would just be nice and pretend it wasn't. However, she agreed to receive feedback, and the group members shared far more than simply a lack of disgust. They explained in detail what their internal responses had been when Marcy was telling her story. For instance, one person felt compassion for Marcy in her struggle with food. When Marcy heard this level of detail about their feelings, she could believe their statements about not being disgusted with her.

If the client doesn't believe someone's feedback, it is useful for her to say that. The person who gave the feedback can then expand on his response and engage in dialogue with the client. This almost always results in mutual understanding. This issue is less of a problem if the group has a history of honest communication and confrontation. Then when positive feedback comes, it is more easily believed.

The Availability of Healing Responses

What if a client does the work to achieve access and others don't respond in a healing way? In individual therapy, you can arrange to provide a healing response because you are the only other participant in the interaction. In the group situation, where members give a wide variety of responses, there isn't as much surety that the response will be healing. However, this isn't as dangerous as it might seem, because in a well-functioning group, people are attuned to each other in a way that usually produces healing responses. In fact, most people are eager to care for and love each other if the group culture fosters this.

Occasionally the client may be acting in a way that annoys the group or puts them off, so that their responses won't be healing. *For example, if Tina is whining and acting like a victim, the group may not respond positively to her pain and needs.* In some cases, a new group may not respond in a healing way because therapeutic norms haven't been established yet. Use your clinical intuition to decide whether or not it will be healing to encourage the client to get feedback. If in doubt, notice how the group seems to be responding to the person nonverbally. If it looks as if they are put off by the client, don't ask for feedback in a situation where she needs healing. In this case, it may be best to give the healing response yourself.

The client will eventually need feedback about what she is doing that turns people off, but she may not be able to hear it when she is vulnerable and needs healing. *In another group meeting, you might encourage someone to point out Tina's whining to her and tell how it affects him.* If it is necessary to work with the client on her difficult behavior at the time she needs healing, you should probably give the feedback. You are in a position to do this from a neutral, benign place, while if you allow the group members to give her negative feedback, they may do it from an angry or judgmental place. *For example, you might say, "Tina, I notice that you are in a lot of pain, but I sense that there is also a second message you seem to be sending to the group, that you will fall apart if they don't take care of you. Does that fit your experience?"*

Healing Mismatch.

When two people engage in a dialogue and one person accesses pain or experiments with new behavior, the healing response ideally should come from the other person. In the vast majority of cases, that person's natural response *will* be what is needed therapeutically. However, occasionally the other person will be so caught up in his own issues that his response will not be healing. Let's call this a "healing mismatch."

> For example, Tina's needs were ignored when she was a child, so now in group it will be healing if people respond to her needs with acceptance and appreciation, and most of the group does. However, Barry's mother was so needy that she neglected him, so Barry now responds with anger when other people show need. If Tina shows her needs to Barry, this will be a healing mismatch. Barry's response won't be healing; in fact, his anger will reinforce Tina's core issue and re-injure her.

Whenever possible, try to foresee healing mismatches in order to avoid them. In other words, don't encourage a client to experiment with new behavior in an interaction with a person who won't respond well to it. *Don't encourage Tina to bring out her needs with Barry if you know he is likely to respond negatively.* If this can't be avoided, work with each person separately rather than allowing any dialogue between them. *If you work with Barry on his difficulty in accepting Tina's needs, he might access his mother issue, sending a message to Tina that Barry's response is his problem. If necessary, you may also need to work with Tina on her feelings about Barry's response.* Although a healing mismatch is a repeat of a core issue and may stir up intense pain, this can lead to deeper access, followed by healing responses from other group members. A mismatch can even give the client an opportunity to experiment with a self-protective response. *For example, you could encourage Tina to express her disappointment to Barry and stand up for her right to have needs.*

Sometimes a client repeatedly seeks out healing interactions with another group member who reacts with a healing mismatch. This is the famous "repetition compulsion," where the client is drawn to someone who can't provide what she needs. It is often an unconscious attempt to get healing from someone who is similar to the original parent. However, this is doomed to failure unless the other person is able to work through his issues and change his response. In ordinary life this rarely happens, and the person keeps re-creating the harm as it happened in childhood. However, in a therapy group, everyone is working on themselves, so the other person may eventually be able to provide the healing the client longs for. However, if the other person doesn't change, the leader must help the client to see the destructiveness of her attraction and learn not to seek healing from the wrong person.

Experimenting

Experimenting is the third of the four aspects of the therapeutic change process. It means trying out new healthier behavior. The word *experimenting* refers to the fact that the client tries out new behavior with an attitude of experimentation, to see what the results will be, both in his awareness and in the reactions of other group members. Thus experimenting is not just behavioral rehearsal; although it often does lead immediately to behavioral change, it can also lead to increased awareness and interesting feedback. An experimental attitude is one of the hallmarks of Gestalt therapy (Perls, Hefferline, & Goodman, 1951). Although Yalom's text (1995, p. 43) doesn't use the word experimenting, he sees trying new ways of being as a central part of interpersonal learning. Despite the fact that psychoanalytic theory places most of its emphasis on access, most psychodynamic group leaders understand intuitively the value of experimenting with new behavior.

☐ Generating Experiments

Let's look at the various ways that experiments can originate:

1. **Suggestion:** An experiment can be suggested by the leader or the group.

    For example, in the early stages of Richard's work, he discussed his fear of speaking in the group but then kept very quiet. At some point, the leader suggested that Richard experiment with telling the group about a recent difficult episode in his life. Although he had great difficulty doing this, it brought up his fears in a way that promoted awareness and access.

2. **Spontaneously:** An experiment can be undertaken unconsciously and spontaneously by a client because he senses that the group is safe enough to take the risk. He hopes (perhaps unconsciously) that this will lead to a healing response. *For example, when he feels safe enough, Richard might spontaneously speak out more frequently or forcefully in the group.*

3. **Accessed or liberated healthy capacity:** Once a person has accessed a healthy capacity or liberated one through an experience of inner healing, it is natural to experiment with exercising that capacity to solidify and deepen its development. *For example, after Richard accesses and works on his fears and receives healing responses from the group, he may feel a greater sense of value and confidence. This may lead him to speak out more easily and fluidly, consolidating and advancing his inner healing.* Engaging in healthy behavior is intrinsically satisfying and helps to develop the healthy capacity or to extend the conditions under which it is available.

4. **Modeling:** A client will often get an idea for an experiment by watching another group member exercising a certain healthy capacity, or by observing that when he does, he receives positive responses from the group instead of the punishment the client fears. Clients especially model themselves on how other people deal with difficult situations. *For example, if Richard observes how another member handles his fear of taking the group's attention, he can use this as a model for healthier behavior.* Of course, one shouldn't simply try to copy other people. This approach can only be helpful if combined with the client's own access and healing. Other people's behavior can merely suggest options that a client wouldn't have imagined on his own. The impetus for the healthy behavior must come from within, not from an attempt to be like someone else.

5. **Refinement:** Often a client begins with one experiment and then modifies it based on his own feelings about it and feedback from others.

    For example, in the early stages of his work, Richard experimented with giving brief feedback to others. At the time, this was a good first step, but after he had made some progress, this behavior was no longer a therapeutic risk, and the group challenged him to say more. When he tried this, he was able to talk at some length as long as he kept it focused on the other person. Then the next experiment was for him to say more about himself.

☐ The Function of Experimenting

Experimenting serves a variety of functions in the therapeutic change process. Sometimes it occurs near the beginning, leading to increased awareness and access. Sometimes it occurs at the end, leading directly to inner healing and therapeutic change. Sometimes it must happen before certain healing responses are possible.

Leading to Access.   If experimenting with healthy behavior succeeds, it can lead to inner healing. Otherwise the experiment will stir up pain or mobilize defenses, but if handled correctly, this can increase the client's awareness of her process. This often leads to increased access and ultimately a deeper level of change. It is useful to recommend (perhaps in consultations)[5] that people experiment with healthy behavior in order to bring up useful work for them in group.

> For example, if Marcy understands that she has a problem with men, she can attempt to reach out to Ben in order to work on this core issue. She might become frightened after saying she needs to talk to Ben but if she is aware of this, she can explore the fear and learn what it means, what it feels like, and where it comes from.

Leading to Healing Response.   When a client expects to be punished for certain healthy behavior, by experimenting with that behavior, she gives herself a chance to receive healing responses (as discussed in the last chapter). If she performs the behavior that was punished in the past, she will likely receive support and appreciation from the leader and the group, reinforcing it and helping to undo the effects of the punishment. In addition, the healthy behavior is reinforcing and healing in itself because it helps her get her needs met in the present. *For example, by reaching out to Ben, Marcy gives herself the opportunity to receive a welcoming response from him and appreciation from the group instead of the rejection she fears.*

Repeated Experimenting.   Often a group member will repeatedly experiment with a certain type of healthy behavior that she is in the process of developing and stabilizing. She may make an experimenting contract with the group whereby she agrees to try out certain new healthy behavior over time. Alternatively, she may engage in the experimental behavior spontaneously because it is naturally arising in her process of growth. In any case, the client will try out a certain behavior with different people and in different ways. Over time she may uncover more of what it means (access/insight), or feel her feelings more deeply (access/affect), or take a further risk (experimenting), or receive new kinds of healing responses. Each such step takes her further along the path of therapeutic change. Repeated experimenting is especially likely to lead to permanent therapeutic change.

☐ Surface and Depth Work

Frequently in psychotherapy a distinction is made between surface work and depth work, with the implication that depth work is superior because it goes to the root of the problem and provides the chance for more profound character change. Surface work is often seen as providing temporary or symptomatic relief, which leaves the client's deeper character issues unchanged. There is, of course, some truth to this, but the situation is more complex and interesting and can be clarified using the concepts of access and experimenting.

Access corresponds roughly to depth work and experimenting to surface work. As we have seen, access is necessary for profound therapeutic change. How-

---

[5] I think it is important for clients who are not in individual therapy with the group leader to meet with him roughly once a month for a consultation about their work in the group. (See chapter 27.)

ever, experimenting also has its own value, not only in crisis intervention or symptomatic relief, but also in promoting significant behavioral changes. In addition, experimenting can be an integral part of deeper characterological change. Though access and experimenting are often done separately—for example, one in psychoanalysis and the other in cognitive-behavior therapy—they work even better together. In an interactive group, they can enhance each other. Experimenting sometimes leads to deeper access, and access (often following by healing) can pave the way for more advanced experiments.

☐   Mixed Experimenting

Ideally when someone is experimenting, the new behavior will be obviously healthy, so it is easy for the group to fully support the person. However, for a variety of reasons a person may need to experiment with behavior that includes some problematic components. In each case, it is important for the leader to frame clearly what is happening so the group can respond in a healing way.

Healthy Reaction to Misperception.   It often happens that a client perceives another group member incorrectly because of a core issue and reacts in a way that would have been healthy if the perception were accurate.

> For example, Betty was working on her aggression, which had been suppressed all her life because of her fear of her abusive father. She perceived Joseph as being arrogant like her father and responded with considerable anger. The anger was inappropriate because Joseph wasn't actually being arrogant, but her expression of anger would have been appropriate in reaction to someone who *was* being arrogant. In addition, the anger was new for her, so she really was experimenting with healthy behavior; it was just misdirected. In this situation the leader should support the expression of Betty's anger while directing it away from Joseph. The best way to do this is by using role playing (as in Gestalt therapy or psychodrama), where Betty would role play expressing the anger to her father.

Exaggeration.   When a person is experimenting with behavior that was forbidden, he may need to exaggerate it at first. Because he has no experience with the behavior, he hasn't had time to develop a tactful way of doing it. This is especially true with aggression. Sometimes the exaggeration happens because the person must overcome an internal prohibition against the healthy behavior, and so he temporarily suppresses that part of himself.

> For example, a man had been a codependent caretaker all his life, assuming an identity as a "nice" person. In group, he eventually began experimenting with taking care of himself even when other people wanted something different. In doing this, he temporarily closed off his sense of connection with people, and went to the other extreme of not caring much at all. He needed to do this because if he had let himself feel concerned about the other members, he wouldn't have been able to stay in touch with his own needs. After the leader explained this strange behavior to the group, they could put aside their hurt and support his experiment. Eventually he was able to be caring again without losing himself.

Healthy in One Way but Not in Another. Sometimes when someone is experimenting with a new healthy way of being, some aspects of his behavior will still be problematic.

> For example, Darian was extremely needy but hid his needs behind a hard mask of toughness. As his work in group progressed, he was gradually able to feel and show his needs. This was a healthy step in the right direction. However, because his needs were still excessive, he had unreasonable expectations of what he should receive from the group. After the leader framed this clearly, the group could support the expression of Darian's needs even though they were put off by his demands. Darian also realized that although expressing his needs was an important growth step, he couldn't expect them to be fully met. Eventually Darian was able to access the young needy place rather than simply demanding that his needs be gratified. Then the group could respond to him in a caring way without feeling obligated to meet his demands, which was quite healing for him.

Problematic Behavior Excessively Punished. Sometimes a punishment issue originates when a person is excessively punished for engaging in a certain kind of problematic behavior, so that behavior gets deeply repressed. This is close to the Freudian drive-theory view of the origins of neurosis. *For example, suppose Mathew was punished for being mean to his sister, but the punishment was excessive. Let's say he was severely beaten for it. Mathew is likely to not only stop being mean, but also repress healthy behavior associated with being mean, such as anger or any type of assertiveness.* In this case, the client may need to experiment with this problematic behavior and have it accepted by the group as part of his healing. *For example, Mathew may need to experiment with being mean in group.* It is usually best to do this through role playing because it may not be appropriate to encourage real problematic behavior with other group members. However, if it happens spontaneously (e.g., if Mathew is mean to someone), the leader should clarify the reason for the problematic behavior and its potential healing value. This sometimes presents the leader with a dilemma—*for example, how to support Mathew's healthy step while still taking care of the person who receives his hostility.*

☐ Experimenting with Feelings and Beliefs

So far we have looked at examples of experimenting with behavior, the most common kind of experiment. However, clients can also experiment with beliefs or feelings. Because core issues involve beliefs, feelings, motivations, body sensations/tensions, and behavior, we can work with any of these elements.

Experimenting with a Previously Developed Feeling

Even after a client has done significant work on an issue and has developed the related healthy capacity, she may sometimes be caught up in the old issue and problematic feeling.

For example, Rosie became insecure with people she admired and obsessed about whether they liked her. She would experience herself in a one-down position, trying to get reassurance that they approved of her. After much work on this issue, she had accessed its roots, received some healing, and developed a healthier attitude. She began to value herself as a person, feel her strength, and assert herself despite fears of rejection. However, from time to time old insecurities would still crop up.

At these times, the person is often experiencing two things at once—the old painful feeling and the new healthier one. If the old feeling predominates, you may want to remind the client about her new-found capacity and suggest that she get in touch with it as she continues the interaction.

For example, when Rosie was feeling insecure in relating to an admired group member, Gina, the leader reminded Rosie of the feelings of value and confidence she had developed. He suggested she get in touch with them and talk to Gina from that place. This helped her to solidify her previous gains.

When Not to Experiment with Feelings

It usually isn't helpful to suggest that a client experiment with a feeling that hasn't previously been accessed or developed. Though a person can consciously choose to try new *behavior* despite fears or insecurities, it is much more difficult to consciously change a *feeling*. Behavior can be chosen, but feelings can't be controlled consciously—except through defenses, which we don't want to encourage. A person can choose to suppress a feeling, but she can't simply choose to feel a healthier one. In fact, if someone tries to change a problematic feeling without accessing and healing its source, she will end up defending against this feeling and pretending to feel the healthy one.

In the above example with Rosie, if the leader had suggested that she experiment with feeling confident in the early stages of her work before she had legitimately developed this capacity, she could have done it only by suppressing her insecurity and feigning confidence.

Experimenting with Beliefs

Once a person has accessed a core issue enough to understand the irrational belief associated with it it, she can sometimes benefit from experimenting with a new healthier belief. Cognitive therapy often operates on this principle. *For example, suppose Mel uncovers the belief that he can't really get his needs met from other people. As an experiment, you could suggest that he consider the possibility that he might have needs that could be met by the other group members.* In suggesting this kind of experiment, you aren't simply trying to modify a client's dysfunctional belief. You are interested in seeing what happens if he tries out a new belief. *On the one hand, Mel might actually let down some defenses and open himself to connecting with others. On the other hand, his defenses might become stronger and more apparent as a result of contemplating the new belief.* In this case, the leader could help him clarify the defense and the reason for it. No matter how the experiment turns out, something can be learned from it.

Some beliefs lend themselves to this kind of experimenting and others don't. If a client believes that other people can't be trusted, it wouldn't be helpful to experiment with trust. In all likelihood, the client would bury her mistrust under defenses and attempt to fake a sense of trust.

CHAPTER

Inner Healing

Inner healing constitutes the fourth and last aspect of the therapeutic change process. It refers to the internal change whereby the person reorganizes her sense of herself and others. Her self-image and her feelings toward herself change. So do her perceptions of others and her emotional reactions to them.

Notice that the word "healing" has two meanings: (a) An activity that one person does for another. (b) The inner process of becoming healthy. These two meanings correspond to two aspects of the change process, so in order to avoid confusion, this book uses the terms *healing response* and *inner healing.*[6]

The Experience of Inner Healing.   At the moment of inner healing, the client experiences an internal shift, frequently accompanied by a letting go and a feeling of aliveness or presence (see chapter 12). This is the experience of the healthy capacity being liberated or developed. For example, the person may feel open or warm or powerful, depending on the particular capacity. The therapist can aid this process by asking about the person's inner experience when inner healing may be occurring. By focusing the client's attention on her experience at this crucial moment, she is more likely to feel the change. In addition, the therapist gains information about whether the person is blocking inner healing.

☐ The Action of Inner Healing

Inner healing means that a healthy capacity is liberated and developed or becomes available under a wider range of conditions. *Remember that the healthy capacities that were deficient in Marcy were connectedness, value, and the ability to reach out. When Marcy receives*

---

[6] In some cases I will simply use the word *healing* to refer to the combination of the two–receiving a healing response and changing inside.

44

a healing response from Ben (after access), she will feel a greater degree of internal connectedness and value. She will also feel more lovable and better about herself. Perhaps Marcy already felt lovable and worthwhile in her relationships with women, but now the range of these capacities will begin to extend to men as well. She will also develop her ability to reach out to men. Of course, each occurrence of inner healing accomplishes just a small part of the total change that is needed.

Inner healing also means that core issues become less entrenched.

Suppose that Marcy starts out with a father issue that is rigidly ensconced in her psyche. It will tend to be activated by all men, regardless of how they act toward her. It will also tend to evoke intense feelings in her which may be hidden behind powerful defenses. Each healing event will tend to chip away at this core issue, helping to make it more flexible and allowing Marcy's healthy capacities to increasingly come into play in her interactions. The core issue will not be activated as easily, perhaps only when she is actually provoked by a man who is being judgmental toward her. In addition, her reactions will be less severe and her defenses more easily relinquished. She will have more room for healthy feelings, such as warmth, confidence, and groundedness.

Relational Healing.   Deeper healing comes through the development of healthy relationships. Let's look at what happens if Marcy and Ben work through their issues so as to create a relationship of mutual liking and respect. Marcy's healthy capacities will develop in a more profound way than any single healing incident or series of incidents could achieve. The relationship with Ben will have a fuller impact on Marcy's capacities for connectedness, value, and reaching out, especially because Marcy has been involved with Ben emotionally and transferentially. Her relationship with Ben will also change her feelings toward men, helping her trust that men can like her. Relational healing is one of the most satisfying aspects of group therapy. Whereas in individual therapy, only the therapist can provide relational healing, in group therapy, it can come from any of the group members.

☐ Taking in Healing Responses

In order for inner healing to occur, the person must be able to take it in the healing response. For example, by recognizing that he is cared for and allowing the caring to touch him emotionally, he can feel more positively about himself. This is one of the reasons why access is helpful; it opens up the person to take in healing responses.

When a healing response is given, notice whether the client seems to be taking it in. Does he believe a compliment? Does he allow it to affect him emotionally, to touch him? Does the positive response help him to feel better about himself? Does inner healing seem to be taking place? Or does he defend against taking it in? The client may negotiate all the previous phases of the change process but remain stuck because he doesn't take in healing responses. The following are typical defenses against taking in:

(a) changing the subject;

(b) explaining away a compliment ("I just did that because …");

(c) bringing up something negative about himself to balance out the positive;

(d) avoiding contact with the person offering the positive response;

(e) internally dismissing a compliment because he feels he doesn't deserve it;

(f) closing down emotionally; and

(g) focusing on the proper way to respond verbally rather than on the compliment or contact.

A Conflict Between the Core Issue and the Feedback.   Let's examine the situation where a client blocks taking in a healing response. The person has a core issue with a negative self-concept (e.g., needy, weak, or bad) and he is receiving a healing response of caring, acceptance, and appreciation that contradicts this. In fact, this contradiction is what makes the response healing. Even if the client has achieved access and open up his core issue for modification, there will still be a contradiction between the existing self-concept, and the healing feedback. *For example, remember Tina felt that when she showed her needs, people saw her as weak and infantile and were disgusted. As part of the therapeutic change process, she must access the pain of this issue, show her needs, and receive caring and acceptance in response. In their healing responses, in contrast to what she expects, people may see her needs as acceptable or even appealing. They might see her as strong or courageous or open.* Sometimes accessing the pain loosens the core issue enough that the client can directly take in the healing response, allowing inner healing to occur. In other cases, the existing issue blocks the client's receptivity to the healing.

Technique.   Therefore it is often worthwhile to ask the client if she is taking in the healing. At first you may need to explain what you mean, but after a while, clients learn what it means to "take in." Just this understanding by itself can be helpful. Then if the person reports that she isn't fully taking in the healing response, help her to explore how she is blocking it. Maybe she doesn't believe that people are being sincere. She may not think that such positive feelings or images could possibly apply to her. She may not feel she deserves warm, caring responses. She may be afraid of what will be required in return if she takes it in. She may feel afraid that she can't live up to the praise she is getting. She may be closed emotionally—her heart hard or her muscles tense—and this may prevent her from taking in the healing.

The form of the defense may provide useful information about how to work with it further. For example, if the client feels she doesn't deserve positive responses, she can explore possible reasons, or the group members can reassure her that she does. Sometimes you can ask the person who gave the healing response to say it again so that the client can practice letting it in.

Therapeutic Dissonance.   Even when a client does take in a healing response, a kind of diffuse blocking may occur because of the dissonance between the existing core issue and the reality of the healing feedback. Let's call this blocking *therapeutic dissonance*. If the client doesn't pre-empt it, therapeutic dissonance naturally promotes inner healing. You can tell that a client is experiencing therapeutic dissonance if he reports an inner conflict or experiences confusion or dizziness or discomfort. Dissonance is not a state that persists long in a person, as has been shown in studies of cognitive dissonance (Festinger, 1957). In the clash between two realities, one must go. If the leader doesn't allow the client to push away the healing feedback, the core issue will have to change. It will become more flexible and the blocked healthy capacity will become a more available. Therapeutic dissonance is one form of what is known as an "impasse" in Gestalt therapy.

As a leader, you need to encourage the person to take in the healing response enough to trigger the therapeutic dissonance. The client shouldn't try to force himself to take in the healing. He should simply allow himself to experience the therapeutic dissonance. You may need to keep the client from diverting the work in another direction. He may need help in staying with the experience of therapeutic dissonance because it is often uncomfortable. However, if the client allows it, the dissonance itself is healing. Nothing else is necessary.

☐ Therapeutic Change Outside Therapy

Any of the four aspects of the therapeutic change process can occur outside of therapy:

1. *Access* is the step that is most difficult to accomplish outside of group, because it involves the kind of self-exploration that usually takes place only in therapy situations. However, once a person has repeatedly accessed a certain core issue in group, then access can happen naturally outside of group.

   For example, if Marcy has accessed the pain of her father's rejection in group a number of times, then when she feels rejected by a man she is dating, she can remind herself that this derives from her relationship with her father and allow herself to feel the pain from the past. This may allow her to act differently in the present.

   In most cases, access that occurs outside group doesn't go as deep. A client might become aware of when she is engaging in problematic behavior and the feelings and motivations behind it, without going into it very deeply. *For example, Marcy might notice whenever she is acting aloof toward a man and check to see if she feels or expects to be rejected by him.* However, this lighter kind of access can still be quite valuable, especially because the client is taking the therapeutic work into her ordinary life.

2. If the client has some relatively healthy relationships in her life, then *healing responses* can happen outside of group. Romantic relationships, friendships, and family relationships all provide an opportunity for healing. However, healing responses in outside relationships can be fraught with difficulties, especially in problematic relationships. The other person's issues may prevent him from offering healing responses. The client may cling to remnants of distancing behavior or have difficulty taking in the healing responses she does receive. When a client doesn't receive healing responses outside of group, it can be useful to explore why. Is she relating to the wrong people? Is she still engaging in problematic behavior that turns others off? Is there something different about the group that allows her to be more open and receptive than she can be outside?

Healing often becomes possible when, as a result of therapy, the client changes the behavior that has been distancing people and discouraging them from offering healing. *For example, in the above example with Marcy, if she realizes she is distancing herself from a man she is dating because of her "father issue," she might be able to see through her fear of rejection and reach out to him instead. This might allow him to respond to her in an open, loving way that would be healing for her.* In the advanced stages of therapy, the healing process happens more frequently outside the group, paving the way for the person to continue to grow after she has terminated.

3. *Experimenting* with healthy behavior is a step that must be done by the client outside of group in order to consolidate his therapeutic gains and integrate them into his everyday life. Often this occurs naturally after access and healing in the group. If it doesn't happen at all, this must be explored and understood. No matter how much a client experiments in group, he must also experiment outside group in order to effect meaningful therapeutic change. As a person experiments with healthy behavior outside of group, it becomes a natural part of his way of being. Then he is no longer experimenting but just living in a healthier way.

4. As the person continues to experiment with healthy behavior, *inner healing* should occur outside group. In fact, this is crucial to integrating the in-group healing into the person's life. The new healthy behavior and inner changes gradually become available in the wide range of activities and situations in the person's daily life. The long-term process of inner healing involves strengthening and solidifying the internal changes so that they also hold up in the face of occasional greater stresses or challenges.

☐ The Progression of Therapeutic Change

Therapeutic Progress

As a group member achieves inner healing on a specific core issue, you usually notice the following progress: (a) The core issues are activated less frequently and the person's reactions are less intense, and (b) the healthy capacities are liberated and developed, or they become available under a wider variety of conditions.

As a result, the person's symptoms will diminish or disappear and her character problems will improve because they are all related to the presence of core issues and deficiencies in healthy capacities. In addition, the client will improve her ability to relate to others in a way that reflects the culture of a healthy therapy group, which involves caring, vulnerability, responsibility, sharing of power, and appreciation of diversity. These changes will ultimately improve her ability to be an agent of social transformation, the kind of person who can contribute to building a healthier society.

Progression in the Change Process

In addition to these changes, the change process itself undergoes a progression in the following ways:

1. *Insight increases.* The person comes to understand more about how her issues play out in group and in her life, and their origins in childhood.

2. *Affect deepens.* The person is able to experience her reactions and defenses in a fuller way and access her pain more deeply.

3. *Healing responses tend to come more from the inside.* After access, the person is increasingly able to give herself the caring, protection, or acceptance she needs. *For example, Marcy may access the pain of her father's rejection and then provide internal caring and soothing, leading her to feel better about herself.*

4. *Access tends to become less necessary.* After accessing a particular issue repeatedly, the client may find it less necessary. Once she realizes she is using a particular defense, she can let go of it and move directly into experimenting with healthy behavior. *For example, once Marcy realizes that she is pulling back because of fear of closeness with Ben, she may spontaneously take the risk of connecting with him.*

5. *The therapeutic change process happens more frequently outside of therapy.* As the group member does more on her own, experimenting and healing responses naturally tend to occur during ordinary life situations.

6

CHAPTER

Transcript

This chapter presents a detailed transcript of a portion of a group session. It gives a real-life feel for the operation of a therapy group, but more important, it illustrates some concepts from the previous chapters. Throughout the transcript are comments explaining which concepts are called into play at each moment in the session.[7] This transcript focuses primarily on one person's access work. Chapter 13 contains another transcript that illustrates some other interactive processes.

In this session, Melissa accesses some deep and traumatic material and receives healing responses from the group members. This session occurred in a long-standing, cohesive group.

Melissa: I'd like to work today, and I don't really know what to do or where to go. There are times I've thought about leaving the group recently because it seems like all of this work uncovers things for me, and then I don't know how to deal with them. It seems like it gets very painful and I wonder, "Why am I doing this?"

Jay: You don't know how to …

Melissa: Well it seems like, when people do their work, I'm very touched by it, I'm very into it, but it stirs up things inside of me, and then it takes days for it to go away. And so I don't know what to do with it. So it feels like I need a break, a rest.

Melissa is voicing dissatisfaction with the group, always an important thing for clients to do. In this case, the difficulty relates to her internal process, and her voicing the dissatisfaction allows us to help her with it. Her empathy and identification with others' work seems to be triggering access to some of her core issues. However, she doesn't know how to make therapeutic use of this.

---

[7] Names and other identifying information have been changed to protect the confidentiality of the group members.

Sharon: You know, when things are stirred up for you we'd like to know about it. Why don't you bring it up? You said you don't know what to do with it. What about us? You've said you wanted to be more contactful.

Melissa: Yeah, but people don't want to hear about this kind of stuff.

Sharon: What else do we want to hear about?

Sarah: That's not true. I always want to hear about this kind of stuff. [general laughter]

Jay: We're not talking about people. We're talking about *these* people, right now. Do you think these people wouldn't want to hear about it?

Melissa tries to turn the discussion away from her relationships with the people in the group by talking about people in general (although she is probably thinking of people from her past). I keep her focused on the group.

Melissa: Well it feels like it wouldn't do it. I don't mean to be insulting, but it feels like talking about it wouldn't get rid of the pain.

Jay: Mm hmm. And that's what you want to do, get rid of the pain.

Melissa: Yes, of course I want to get rid of the pain. I can't imagine anybody wanting to stay with it. I mean, I'm not trying to push it away. I can go into it, but I get stuck there. And so it doesn't have value for me.

Sharon: Excuse me, can I say something here? All the pain you had in your life, there was nobody there, to just be with you while you hurt, to be a witness and to care, and to feel ... bad because you hurt.

Melissa: That's true.

Sharon: And just intellectually, don't you think it would be a healing experience to talk to somebody who understood where the pain came from and who cared about you?

Sharon is suggesting that Melissa could experiment with reaching out to other group members when she is vulnerable and in need. Melissa's needs were not met when she was a child, so she has a deficiency issue and assumes she won't get them met now. Sharon is pointing out that if Melissa could reach out and receive understanding and caring from the group members, this would be healing.

Melissa: I don't have that connection somehow. Unless I go into this very deep place ... [confused] I don't know what I'm saying.

Jay: Go ahead, keep going.

Melissa: There are times when I've gone into deep pain here and I've felt the connection. I've felt the connection ... [sounds surprised] I've only felt connected to Jay. I don't know why. I don't mean ... I'm so afraid of offending somebody here. What I mean is ... I just question why I keep doing this. Going into this pain. It's awful.

Jay: And when you've gone there and felt the connection. What's that been like?

Melissa: [pause] It felt healing, but … it seems like I have to go to this very young place to feel that. [pained]

Jay: To feel a connection?

Melissa: Yeah.

Melissa sees that she has accessed this core issue and received healing from her relationship with me, helping her develop a sense of connectedness. This is especially important because Melissa uses primarily a schizoid defense.

Sarah: And if you have to go to the very young place …

Melissa: When I have to go to the very young place, I lose my adult piece, and that's very shameful. When everybody else does it, I think it's wonderful. But for me it's very shameful.

She now realizes that there is a tremendous amount of shame associated with accessing this early childhood memory. In addition to the pain itself, she seems to feel shame about being this regressed or vulnerable.

Jay: I like the idea that Sharon brought up of being able to connect with people. That's really the key thing, because when you've done that, you felt some healing.

At this point I am emphasizing the possibility of healing.

Melissa: And I think that only happens with men. I can make a connection with men. I can make a connection on an adult level with women, but I certainly can't make a connection if I regress. That doesn't feel safe to me.

Jay: So it feels like the next step in the work would be to explore what that's about. To explore where that comes from in your relationship with your mother, so you can work that through … and make connections with …

I am suggesting a specific direction for her work, namely to access the core issue that seems to derive from Melissa's relationship with her mother.

Melissa: When I hear myself talk like this, I make judgments of myself … that I'm this cold person. What's the matter with me. This kind of thing.

Jay: You get into a lot of self-judgment.

Melissa: But it's hard. I can go into that place if I'm touched by somebody's work, and I'm touched by everybody's work. But I don't even want to go there.

All through this piece of work, Melissa keeps interrupting herself because of shame and self-judgment.

John: Do you want to stay in that place right now?

Melissa: Do I want to stay in that place? What do you mean?

John: You're in a very vulnerable place.

Melissa: Do I want to stay there?

John: Do you want us to be there with you?

Melissa: Umm, yes. I want you to be there, because it seems like the only way I can connect. I don't want to sit here and not connect. Because that's a violation to me.

Melissa is letting us know that to access this very core issue without a healing response would be a re-injury.

John: What do you need from us to help you?

John is reaching out to her and offering contact.

Melissa: And sometimes I resent the fact that I have to be in a vulnerable place to connect with anybody here. I resent that. It feels like I'm putting myself in a very weakened position. It's like I have to grovel, and I don't feel like groveling.

Because of Melissa's shame, she can't hear John at first. She begins to use her usual anger defense against shame.

John: I'm asking what you need from me to help you stay with that feeling. I'm not asking you to grovel, I'm asking what you need to feel safe to stay there.

Melissa: You know what I need. [moved] I need to hear your voice.

Now she recognizes that he is offering to connect with her, and she is moved. When Melissa takes in John's healing response, it allows her to go deeper into access.

Jay: Say more.

Melissa: [upset] I need the sound of your voice to know that you're there.

Jay: When you're in that vulnerable place.

Melissa: Right.

Jay: So that you know you're not alone.

Melissa: Right. That's what feels safe. I need to hear somebody's voice. I can't go there if I don't hear somebody's voice.

Melissa's core issue includes fear of abandonment and a deficiency in connectedness. Therefore the healing response is for someone to be there with her.

Melissa: And I hear his voice now. I can hear men's voices. And make a connection with a man. If I hear a woman's voice it doesn't feel safe.

Jay: It doesn't feel safe. What does it feel like if you hear a woman's voice?

I am moving her toward deeper access of the core issue related to her mother.

Melissa: It feels like they're going to get angry. [more upset]

Jay: They're going to get angry at you for being vulnerable?

Sharon: Like a judgment.

Melissa: They're not going to be there, or they're …

Sharon: They're going to make fun of you?

Melissa: No, it's worse. It's more traumatic. Like they're going to go berserk. [very upset]

Jay: You have a sense of going into that place and a woman going berserk on you. See what that stirs up.

Melissa: I had to protect myself somehow. It's like I'm phobic with bugs. If a bug comes near me I have to [makes brushing away motion]. And that's what it feels like. It's going to come at me. [ducks and protects head]

Jay: Something around your head. Like they're going to hit you?

Melissa: Yeah.

Melissa has accessed a memory of physical abuse. This is clearly derived from a harm issue in which the main element is the mother's rage and physical attack. There may also be a punishment issue, in which the attack is triggered by Melissa's being vulnerable, perhaps crying or being upset. But it isn't clear yet if this is the case.

Jay: If you get vulnerable, a woman is going to go berserk and hit you in the head … [Melissa noticeably changes her affect.] What just happened?

Melissa: So I stopped myself from going in there. [pause] I'm getting cold.

Jay: You're getting cold? Yeah. Feel scared?

Melissa: I guess so. And I'm aware that I'm still not interacting. I'm still not …

Melissa has done as much accessing as she can tolerate. The fear connected with the abuse does not allow her to go further. She uses a schizoid defense to come out of her regressed state. Then shame and self-judgment arise as she begins to criticize herself.

Penny: You are. You're fine

Sarah: That's not true, Melissa. You're interacting from a very young place.

Melissa: But it feels like … is this the way I have to connect with this group? I have to go to this …

Members: Today. For now. You may have to do that.

Ralph: And this is no worse than any other place of connection.

By reassuring her that they aren't judging her for being vulnerable, the group provides another form of healing. Instead of receiving anger or abuse for being vulnerable, she receives caring and support.

Jay: So how is it hearing these voices right now? Does that feel good?

I ask about her experience of receiving this healing response, to see if she is taking it in so that inner healing can occur.

Melissa: It feels good hearing the men's voices. You know what I mean, it's like I connect with the voice.

Jay: And where are you right now?

Melissa: It feels very sad right in this place.

Jay: And what about your connections with us right now?

I ask about connecting because she has said that she needs connection, and because I want to determine if inner healing is happening.

Melissa: I'm not connecting.

Jay: What's stopping you?

Melissa: Cause it's shameful to be in this place. Very shameful. I resent that I have to be in this place. I want to get angry. I'm angry to be in this place.

She isn't taking in the healing responses because of her shame. She typically has used anger as a defense against shame in the past, but today she just mentions it briefly and is able to stay with the shame.

Jay: Do you imagine that we feel ashamed of you in this place?

As a way of undercutting the shame, I ask her to focus on the group members, who are feeling accepting of her. Notice that I could also have facilitated more access of the shame issue. This issue may come from the abuse she uncovered earlier or it may have other origins as well. This merits further exploration in a future session.

Melissa: No I guess not. I don't know.

Jay: But in the shame, you close yourself off from us.

Melissa: Yeah.

Jay: So if you're willing I'd like you to look around and just take us in. Just see what you see.

If she can really experience the caring and love from the group members, this will be healing.

[She slowly looks at each person. At the end she becomes very upset.]

Jay: What just happened?

Melissa: Oh, this is awful. It felt so painful. I'm taking up a lot of time.

Members: No you're not Melissa. This is very important.

Melissa: I was connecting with Ralph and it felt very painful. [crying]

Jay: That's right. What was painful about connecting with Ralph?

Melissa: I think I got in touch with this yearning. Like a young part of me.

When she looked around the group, she took in that people really cared about her, allowing more inner healing. This opened up her yearning for connection. She accessed a very early aspect of her healthy capacity for connectedness. Though this also brought up shame, with the group's reassurance Melissa was able to stay with the yearning.

Jay: Keep going. And what was painful about feeling that yearning?

Melissa: When I'm in that young place, the pain is not having that, not ever having had that feeling, I guess. [more crying]

Jay: Not ever having had that connection?

Melissa: Right. So it's very painful to have it.

However, along with the yearning comes the experience of her painful deficiency issue.

Jay: So would you be willing to go back to Ralph? Just talk to him about the connection you felt.

I move her back to Ralph so she can experiment with the healthy behavior of connecting with someone from this vulnerable place and receive more healing responses.

Melissa: Ooo [moved]. You look a little like my father.

Jay: Tell him what that brings up for you.

Melissa: It brings up the illusion that I could have been protected, that my father could protect me. If he was there. I always had the illusion that if he was there … [sighs]

Melissa's father abandoned the family early in her life, and she constructed a fantasy father who would have protected her from her mother. This may be why she finds men's voices soothing.

Jay: Stay with Ralph.

           [Melissa tries to stop the work again.]

Jay: I don't want you to stop without having the connection that you need, and it looks like you're close to having it with Ralph, and I just want you to have that.

I believe that Melissa can gain more from the work, so I encourage her to continue.

Ralph: It feels like you're close and you want to leave now. Don't do that to your-self.

Melissa: Now I'm coming up. I need to make a connection with you on an adult level.

She can't tolerate any more regressed emotional access.

Ralph: Uh huh.

Melissa: [Memories come up about her father abandoning her.] I always had this fan-tasy about him, though.

John: What's your fantasy?

Melissa: That he would come and take me out of that house. [Talks about how she almost traced her father as an adult.]

She continues her access work at a more intellectual, less regressed level.

Jay: So how're you feeling with Ralph right now? Tell him.

I move her back to Ralph for continued healing.

Melissa: I'm feeling good with Ralph. But it's his eyes that remind me of my father. [amused]

Jay: Ralph, how are you responding?

It's important not to leave Ralph out altogether. Encouraging him to talk about his feeling response can make the interaction more real for Melissa. It can help her see that he isn't respond-ing like her parents did.

Ralph: I'm feeling very comfortable with you, and really identifying around that longing place. I know that space you're in right now, and I know how I used to be there. And I'm really glad you're there. You've sort of riveted us all. I want to kind of reach in and hold you in some way. I want to make your longing safe for you. [takes her hand]

Melissa: That would be nice to be comfortable with that. Instead of so scared of it. [Sighs] So that feels good. [Group laughter]

Melissa has taken in even more healing from Ralph, now at a more adult level.

Melissa: OK, so let's go folks. Now I'm connecting on an adult level.

Ralph: Even if you weren't on an adult level, it would feel good. It would feel like a privilege if you let me hold your kid, just with our eyes.

Ralph reminds her that she doesn't have to feel shame about being young.

Melissa: I find men so much more comfortable than women.

[Comments from women in the group and lighter discussion of her childhood]

Melissa: I'm still so worried about everybody. I need to hear from Sarah and Penny. The feeling is that I'm doing something wrong, letting everybody know how much more comfortable I feel with men than with women. I don't want to alienate anybody, you know. It's just a fact.

Melissa's core issue related to her abusive mother is now activated in a lighter way, so she checks out with the women in the group to make sure their responses don't match her fears.

Sarah: I want to give you some feedback. I felt privileged to witness your work. It felt wonderful to hear you say you felt connected to Jay. It just felt good that you could trust men. It all made so much sense.

[She gets similar genuine support and further discussion from Penny and everyone in group.]

Melissa finds out that the women aren't feeling anything remotely like what she fears. Their respect and appreciation for her provide further healing.

Melissa has done an excellent piece of work. There is no longer a question of her leaving the group. In the future, she could benefit from more access of the core issue(s) behind her shame. She could also further her healing by connecting more substantially with people while she is still in a regressed state. Notice that she made a little contact with Ralph in the young place and then came back to adult for the majority of the healing connection. In the future, it might be helpful for her to connect more from the young place. At some point it will also be important for her to make a healing connection with some of the women in the group.

II

CREATING A THERAPEUTIC GROUP CULTURE

A primary challenge facing the group leader is to help create a culture in the group that is optimally therapeutic, especially through appropriate group norms. Once a group has established a way of operating that encourages the work of therapy, much of the healing comes from the interactions between members. A good deal of the work of establishing a therapeutic group culture happens in the beginning stages of a group—during the first few weeks of a short-term group and the first 3 to 6 months of a long-term group. However, the group culture may need attention from time to time throughout a group's life.

Part II starts with a discussion of the proper structure for a group, including the selection and preparation of group members, covered in chapter 7. Chapter 8 deals with how to foster therapeutic norms and then introduces a variety of specific group norms. Chapter 9 discusses the responsibility norm and how to encourage motivation and self-direction in clients. Focusing on the norm of self-exploration, chapter 10 explains how to train clients in the skills of awareness and insight. Chapter 11 discusses the interactive norm and chapter 12 explains the value of contact and presence. Finally, chapter 13 contains a transcript of part of a group session, which illustrates some of these concepts.

In addition to the norms discussed here in Part II, there should be therapeutic group norms that support each of the four aspects of therapeutic change already discussed in Part I—access, healing response, experimenting, and inner healing.

7

CHAPTER

How to Structure a Group

This chapter discusses how to structure and prepare for a therapy group. It covers a wide range of practical issues including group format, rules, pre-group interview(s), screening, when group therapy is preferred and when it is not indicated, group composition, and preparing clients for group.

☐ Group Format

Location. The group should be held in a location that forms a good container. The setting should provide comfort and a feeling of privacy so members can experience the group as a "sacred space" apart from normal social interactions. Ideally, the room should just be large enough to hold the group and be arranged so that outside noise is eliminated. Except in emergencies, no interruptions from phone calls or other staff members should be allowed.

Size of Group. Ideally an interactive group contains 7 or 8 members (Salvendy, 1993, p. 79; Yalom, 1995, p. 276). If it is much larger, there is often not enough time for each person, and members end up competing for the group's attention. In addition it is important for a therapy group to encourage close, intimate connections among the members, and if it gets too large, this becomes difficult. If necessary, a group of 10 is workable, but any larger than this is problematic.

   If the group is much smaller than 7 members, it may lack variety in terms of personality structure. A group with 6 members is workable but not preferable. Five is too small for the long term but is acceptable on a temporary basis until more members can be found. Even 3 or 4 members can work temporarily. However, these small groups tend to become less interactive after a while because there simply aren't enough different relationships to provide material to work on. The leader often ends up doing more individual work in the group than is preferable.

Length of Meetings.   The standard in the field is for group meetings to last an hour and a half. I personally prefer 2 hours. The appropriate length of time, of course, depends on the number of group members. For a group of 5 or 6 members, an hour and a half would be adequate. However, in my experience, with a group of 8 members, 2 hours seems necessary to give each person enough time. This is not because everyone should take a turn in each meeting but rather so that over the long haul there is enough time for each person to participate sufficiently.

Frequency of Meetings.   The vast majority of psychotherapy groups meet once a week. Though I don't personally have experience with groups meeting two or more times a week, Yalom (1995, p. 268) suggests that such groups have increased intensity and, I assume, increased cohesiveness and importance to members. However, this is difficult to arrange because of the time commitment it requires from clients. Groups that meet less than weekly suffer because the group members lose their sense of connection with each other between meetings. They often have the experience of starting over at the beginning of each meeting. Members need time to reconnect with each other and to share what has happened in their lives since the last meeting. This leaves too little time for interactive work.

Length of Stay in Group.   Time-limited groups, also called short-term groups, have a fixed duration, usually spelled out in advance. This can range from 8 sessions to about 30, with groups of 12 to 20 sessions fairly common. It is expected that all members will stay for the entire length of the group. Some time-limited groups are run repeatedly; after one group has ended, some of the members can choose to continue in the next cycle of the group. This arrangement preserves the time-limited format while recognizing that some clients need more extensive treatment than one cycle of the group can provide.

Long-term ongoing groups continue even though their membership gradually changes. A new person can join a group whenever there is an opening and stay until she has achieved her therapeutic goals (or leaves for other reasons). This is called an "open group" because it is open to new members (at times). In contrast, "closed groups," which keep the same membership from the beginning, are almost always time-limited for reasons of attrition.

In a long-term group, it is advisable for members to stay for at least a year and often 2 or 3 years (or even longer). I don't require this because it is difficult to enforce long-term commitments, and also because sometimes new members realize after a while that a group is not appropriate for them. I only require new members to commit to a short trial period, which permits enough time to decide if the group is right for them. However, I don't accept group members who don't plan to stay for at least a year if the group does work out for them. If a new member stayed for only 3 or 6 months, it would be disruptive for the other group members who are expecting to form long-term relationships with each other. Rutan and Stone (1993) don't agree with the idea of using a trial period. Instead, to discourage drop outs, they ask their clients to agree to remain in the group until their presenting problems are solved. I don't use this approach because I don't believe that I am in a position to determine if a group is right for a client before she tries it out.

☐ **Group Rules**

Group rules are laid out explicitly by the leader and are expected to be followed unless there is a compelling reason to do otherwise. I distinguish group rules from group norms (see chapter 8), which are much less clear-cut and are often developed in collaboration between the leader and the group members.

Written Rules.   It is helpful to write up all the group rules. Table 7.1 contains the rules that I hand out to prospective members for my long-term ongoing groups.

Payment.   Specific payment arrangements will depend on the precise nature of your practice and clientele. What is relevant is that they be spelled out clearly, so clients know what is expected of them. Other arrangements for payment can be made if a client needs them, but she should ask you first, not just allow her payments to slide. Payment rules aren't just to ensure that you are receive your money; they also provide a framework for dealing with this potentially important treatment issue. If necessary, a client's handling of money should be explored in group or in a consultation because it may reflect significant underlying feelings about the group or the leader. The same applies to any breaches of group rules.

It is crucial that clients be required to pay for group meetings even if they are absent (and even when the absence is valid or unavoidable). There are two reasons for this.

1.   If a client cancels an individual session, the therapist can fill the space or take the time off. With a group, if someone is missing, the leader must still work during that time, and therefore deserves to be paid for it.

2.   Even more important, you don't want to set up a situation where clients are financially rewarded for missing group meetings. This can cause serious problems with attendance, which is very important for the proper functioning of a therapy group (see below).

Confidentiality.   The confidentiality of the group members should never be violated, by the leader or the members. Though you can make sure to uphold your part of this, group members can slip up. Therefore if a client is particularly concerned that a certain fact should be kept confidential, encourage her to explain why it is so important that the members not reveal it to anyone.

> For example, clients who have multiple personality disorder can be seriously stigmatized if the information gets out into the community. If a person with such a concern discusses it with the group, this will help to ensure her safety.

Make it clear to clients that they *can* discuss their group experiences with outsiders, because this is often important for assimilation and learning. However, they shouldn't reveal names or details about other group members that would make them identifiable.

TABLE 7.1. Group Information

Commitment

1.   You are committed to the first 4 weeks of the group as a trial period to determine if the group is right for you. You can take longer than 4 weeks to decide, but I ask you to allow at least 4 weeks.

2.   If you decide, during your initial 4-week trial period, that you don't want to continue in the group, you are expected to let the group know in person, so they can discuss it with you.

Payment

1.   At your first group meeting you pay for the 4-week trial period. After that you pay on a monthly basis.

2.   Your payment for the month is due at the beginning of each month. (Please note that some months have 5 meetings.) If you leave before the end of that month, you receive a prorated refund.

3.   Because of the nature of an ongoing group, when you miss meetings, the group still meets, and you can't be replaced. Therefore you are financially responsible for each group meeting even if you are not there because of illness or another commitment. Twice a year, however, you can be absent without paying.

4.   If you go on a long vacation and miss more than four group meetings, you have a choice of paying to keep your place in group or dropping out and returning. If you drop out, you are not guaranteed of being able to return to the group when your vacation is over. If the group is full at that time, you may have to wait until there is an opening.

5.   Payment for consultations is due at the time of the consultation.

Confidentiality

1.   Confidentiality between group members is very important. It is all right to discuss your group experiences with people outside the group, but it is very important that you respect each person's right to privacy by not identifying other group members by name or other specific details.

2.   I will keep in confidence anything that happens in group.

3.   I will also keep in confidence anything that is discussed in a consultation, though I may encourage you to share it with the group.

Attendance

1.   Because this is an ongoing group, your group will count on your being present as often as possible. If you need to miss a meeting please let me or someone in the group know. Let us know in advance whenever possible.

Table 7.1 continues on page 65.

TABLE 7.1. *Continued*

2. You are expected to arrive promptly at the beginning of each group meeting and stay until the end. If you are unable to be on time for a particular meeting, it is better to come late than not at all.

3. People are not to attend group under the influence of alcohol or other drugs.

Termination

1. If you are thinking about leaving group, I recommend that you talk to me or to the group about it before making a final decision.

2. People develop close relationships in these groups, so when you decide to leave, it is important for your sake and for the group's that there is enough time for everyone's feelings to be processed. This is often an important part of a person's group experience. Therefore you are required to give your group 4 full weeks notice of your intention (or 2 weeks if you have been in the group for fewer than 3 months). If you have been in the group longer than a year and have developed strong connections with other group members, I recommend that you allow even longer for your termination process.

Consultations

Group members consult with me individually once a month for a half hour to enhance your use of the group. You may request longer consultations or additional ones when needed.

The leader should keep confidential from the group anything that clients disclose in a consultation or individual session. This allows a group member to share something with you that he is not yet ready to broach in the group, and you can help him explore his fears about revealing it (see the *Consultations* section in chapter 27). It should ultimately be the client's choice about when to reveal an issue in group. Of course, you should make it clear that it is therapeutically important for him to share it with the group at some point, and if he procrastinates, work with him on his resistance. To ensure that you can remember what has been told to you in confidence versus openly in the group, ask clients to remind you when they want something kept confidential.

Some group leaders disagree with this policy (Rutan & Stone, 1993, p. 229). To discourage the keeping of secrets, they make a point of telling clients that anything shared in individual therapy is not confidential and the therapist can bring it up in group. This is only used as a last resort, of course—they prefer the client to bring it up himself.

Attendance and Punctuality.   It is important that group members take seriously their commitment to attend the group whenever possible and to arrive promptly. If group members consistently violate these rules, they will begin to feel that the group is not important and people don't care about each other. The group will lose its cohesion, undermining its therapeutic potency.

Attendance and punctuality rules can't be strictly enforced, of course, because people sometimes have valid reasons for being absent or late. Watch for a client's pattern of lateness or absence and challenge him before it goes too far. Even if someone has a seemingly valid reason each time, something else may be going on beneath the surface that should be explored. It is especially important to challenge such a pattern if it begins to spread to other group members. The danger is that patterns like this gradually increase over time if not stopped. If a few people are frequently late or absent, the other group members will begin to feel that attendance and promptness aren't important because this commitment isn't being honored. They will feel that they don't need to bother to be on time either, or they may feel that they can miss group when they feel like it. This kind of behavior can snowball and undermine the group.

It is better if a pattern such as this is challenged by the group members rather than by the leader, because then members see this as something of concern to each other, not just a rule being handed down by an authority. However, if the group members don't make the challenge, you must do it. This should be done with a concerned, caring manner, not in a judgmental, punitive way. You can express curiosity about why the client is willing to undermine his own therapy, and/or why he doesn't seem to care about his commitment to his peers. When relevant, he should be encouraged to explore the underlying reasons for his lateness or absence. If necessary, explain why punctuality and attendance are important for the proper functioning of the group.

Other Rules.   Clients aren't to attend group under the influence of alcohol or other drugs. This is important because drugs can alter a client's consciousness sufficiently so that psychotherapy won't be helpful. In addition, physical violence is not permitted,[8] for obvious reasons. It is also important to have clear rules about termination, so that group members allow enough time for this important process. (See chapter 22.)

Some group leaders write out a larger set of guidelines called a "group contract" or "group agreements" that includes much of what is discussed in the next chapter under group norms. (Rutan & Stone, 1993, pp. 117–125) I prefer to separate out the group rules because they are more clear cut. The group norms, which are worked out in the long term between the leader and the group members, are described in the other pre-group literature I hand out (see Appendix) and in the pre-group interview.

☐ Indications for Group Therapy

When Group Is Preferred

Interpersonal Issues.   Psychotherapy groups are especially indicated for people who have significant interpersonal problems, including isolation and loneliness, shyness and insecurity, difficulties with dating or intimacy, fear of conflict, lack of

---

[8] This is not included on my written rules because it is not necessary to spell it out with the population I work with.

assertiveness, interpersonal stiffness and rigidity, emotional deadness, too much anger or judgment toward others, lack of closeness, and fear of groups. Everyone has some interpersonal problems, but groups are especially valuable for people whose problems are severe or who are especially interested in improving the way they relate to others. Group therapy is especially helpful for people who have difficulty forming the kind of relationships they want but have no idea why. By getting feedback from others on their impact, they can begin to learn about their difficulties.

Interpersonal Stimulation.   Groups are also the method of choice for people who are prevented from making progress in individual therapy because they need more interpersonal stimulation to get to their issues and feelings. Some people flounder in individual therapy because they are blocked from accessing their emotions. In a therapy group, clients receive extra stimulation both from watching others work and being encountered by others. This additional spur brings up material that can power the therapy.

Need for Feedback.   Some clients relate to others in destructive ways without realizing this. In individual therapy, they may not act out these behaviors. Even if they do, a therapist may need to avoid being too confrontive in order to preserve the therapeutic alliance. In a group, such a person can be confronted by his peers and helped to understand the impact of his behavior on others.

Safety.   Even though many clients feel safer and more comfortable in the privacy of individual therapy, some feel just the opposite. Certain clients who have been controlled or otherwise harmed in close childhood relationships actually feel safer in a group setting where these fears are not activated as much as in the intimacy of individual therapy. These clients will allow themselves to be more vulnerable in a therapy group.

Transference and Countertransference.   Some authors recommend group therapy for certain borderline clients because they can develop intense regressive transferences in individual therapy. Group therapy can mitigate this potentially destructive situation by diluting the transference, partly because there are many people in the group with whom to develop transference, and partly because the setting isn't as intimate as individual therapy. Of course, some borderlines can also be difficult to handle in groups. I think for many of them, combined individual and group therapy works best. However, there can be problems with this arrangement, too (see the *Discussion* section in chapter 27). Sometimes the intense individual transference makes the client unmanageable in group. This is a difficult topic with no easy answers. See Porter (1993) for more discussion of this issue.

Some authors also recommend group therapy for people who "characteristically elicit strong negative countertransference from an individual therapist" (Yalom, 1995, p. 236).

Transition from Individual.   Therapy groups can also be an excellent transition from individual therapy to ordinary life. Groups are more like ordinary social settings and intimate relationships while retaining some of the safety and all of the therapeutic potential of the individual setting. When a person has progressed far enough in individual therapy, it is often appropriate for him to join a group, either while continuing individual therapy or after terminating. The client can thus experiment with the healthier ways of being that have been engendered by individual therapy, while remaining in a protected therapeutic learning environment.

Most of the above recommendations are shared by other group leaders and authors. (See Rutan & Stone, 1993, p. 87.)

When Group Can Be Valuable

All Issues are Ultimately Interpersonal.   In addition to those situations when group psychotherapy is especially indicated, it can be valuable for many other people and problems. Many psychological problems stem primarily from difficulties in the family of origin or other relationships, making them interpersonal in origin. Thus even when a person comes to therapy with a presenting problem that is not obviously interpersonal, such as anxiety or depression, he usually has significant interpersonal problems as well. He often has a childhood history of interpersonal difficulties in the family that are the origin of his current presenting problems. In group therapy a client will react to other group members based on core issues and defenses that derive from his family of origin, thereby giving him an opportunity to work through these issues and in the process resolve his (seemingly non-interpersonal) presenting problems.

When the client has presenting problems that aren't clearly interpersonal, he often doesn't believe that a group, especially an interactive group, is an appropriate method of treatment. Such people naturally think that to overcome their problem (e.g., their anxiety or depression), they need to spend most of their time in therapy talking about it. Joining a group to deal with their relationships with the other group members doesn't make sense to them. A good deal of education is required in such cases. For example, you might elicit the various interpersonal problems the person does have and then link them to his presenting problems.

Other Benefits.   Group therapy also offers support to clients who are isolated in their lives. Group members become educated about therapy by observing others work in group. New group members gain hope through hearing about the successes of long-term group members in overcoming their problems. A client can gain in self-esteem from learning that he isn't the only one with his difficulties. Clients also feel empowered through recognizing their ability to be helpful to others. These factors apply to all therapy groups, not just general purpose interpersonal groups. See Yalom (1995, chapter 1) for a fuller discussion of the special benefits of group therapy.

A Unique Growth Experience.   Group therapy offers clients a different kind of growth experience from individual therapy. They tend to improve their ability to relate to others and to function in groups, organizations, and communities. They often become more tolerant and appreciative of differences and the uniqueness of others. They tend to grow in their ability to empathize with, care for, and help others. They become more able to commit to and bond with a group of people. At the same time they learn how to assert their own individuality in the face of others' demands for conformity. These qualities not only improve clients' well-being but also help them become the kind of people who can bring about a healthier society.

When Group Is Not Indicated

Group therapy is not appropriate for those people who are too frightened of others, or lacking in trust, or full of shame to tolerate a group setting. It isn't appropriate for people who need the intimacy, privacy, or safety of the individual setting. In other words, group therapy is not appropriate for people who don't want to be in a group. Some clients must start out in a safer setting with just one other person, who will be consistently caring, understanding, and nonreactive. After enough time and growth from individual therapy, many of them can move on to a group if that is appropriate.

Attendance Problems.   Group is also not indicated for clients who can't meet the attendance requirements. If a prospective client is leaving the area within the year or will be away on an extended vacation, she should not begin a long-term, ongoing group. Neither should a person who will be forced to miss group meetings frequently because of a conflicting monthly meeting or because of a busy travel schedule at work. Be careful of people who live too far away or have extensive parenting responsibilities without enough help. If you stretch these boundaries by taking in a group member who is then absent frequently, you give the group the impression that attendance and commitment to the group aren't really important, thus undermining norms that are central to building group cohesiveness.

Other Reasons.   Salvendy (1993, p. 75) listed various other criteria for potentially excluding people from group therapy, including low intelligence, organicity, insufficient command of the language, severe stuttering, serious medical illness, paranoia, and acute psychosis or suicidal tendencies. Yalom (1995, p. 219) added to this list hypochondriasis and sociopathy. Some of these patients can be successfully treated in groups set up to deal with their specific problem.

Drop Outs.   One important way to understand what types of people should possibly be excluded from therapy groups is to examine those who prematurely drop out (i.e., leave soon after joining without receiving therapeutic benefit). Yalom (1995) discussed the research literature on this in some detail, concluding that "patients destined to drop out of groups are likely to have the following characteristics: lower psychological-mindedness; high denial; high somatization; lower motivation; more severe, psychotic pathology; less likability (at least according to therapists); lower socioeconomic class, social effectiveness, and IQ" (pp. 224–235). He also emphasized that dropouts are frequently deviants in the group or people who have great fears of intimacy or emotional contagion.

In some cases, it may be possible to predict that certain people will not be able to participate successfully in a group. However, it is better to be aware of clients with potential problems so that they can be given special help in overcoming them in the early stages of the group. You may need to be alert to protect them from destructive situations in the group or to provide extra help in the group and in individual consultations so they can negotiate the obstacles of the group situation.

Individual Therapy Failures.   Clients in individual therapy should not be referred for group therapy simply because they are not making progress. If there is a specific reason why group therapy is likely to be more successful than individual therapy, then such a referral is warranted, but it shouldn't be made simply to deal with an individual therapy failure. If a client is not making progress in individual therapy, the therapist should explore the reasons, preferably in consultation with a colleague or supervisor, to determine the best course of action.

When an Interactive Group Is Not Indicated

Specific Issues.   Clients who have pressing issues that need to be discussed in detail in therapy (e.g., drug addiction, AIDS, sexual abuse, problem children, eating disorders) are not appropriate for long-term general purpose groups. They should be referred for either a support group, a problem-focused group, or individual therapy. In many cases, such a person could *also* join a general-purpose group to deal with the deeper issues that underlie the obvious problem. However, such people often must start in individual therapy or a specialized group and then later be educated about the value of a general purpose group.

Crisis.   The same thing applies to people dealing with a crisis, such as a death, job loss, or physical illness. They should be referred for individual therapy or an appropriate crisis-oriented group because their first order of priority is to find a place to talk about the crisis. Once the crisis has passed, they may be interested in deeper, longer-term work, and then an interactive group is an option. If someone has already joined and become integrated into a group and then a crisis develops in her life, switching to another form of therapy isn't advisable. The person might add another modality in addition to the group, but she should remain in it. She will need the support of people she is already connected to. Within the interactive format, a client can occasionally spend time dealing with a crisis situation, as long as she has the overall commitment to the longer term interactive work. However, if a person starts a group when in a crisis, she won't have the emotional energy to deal with her relationships with the other group members and to sit through their work with each other.

Addictions.   People who are abusing alcohol or drugs are not appropriate for an interactive group. They should be referred to a group specifically designed to deal with sobriety issues, either a 12-step program or a professionally run addiction group. Individual therapy by itself is not usually effective with addictions. Clients in early recovery from alcohol or other drug addictions are also not appropriate candidates for interactive groups. They are still at the stage in their recovery where they need to focus on staying abstinent, and they aren't yet ready to deal with the deeper feelings and issues that are behind the addiction. In later stages of recovery, interactive groups can be very useful. If a client has already joined and become integrated into a group before the addiction is discovered, he should be encouraged to join an appropriate addiction program. You must evaluate whether it would be helpful for him to continue in the group as well, depending on whether the emotional impact of the group would disrupt his work on abstinence.

Lack of Interpersonal Motivation.   Because the primary material for group therapy arises in the interpersonal interactions among the group members, a prospective member needs to have some interest in developing relationships with others in the group. It is acceptable if he is terrified of, defended against, or otherwise incapable of relating, but he must have some *interest* in interacting with and relating to other group members, or at least the motivation to explore his lack of interest. If a client has no interest in relating to others, he won't participate in the work of an interactive group. Such a client must be referred to individual therapy or to a type of group that doesn't revolve around interpersonal issues—for example, a problem-focused group, a support group, or a group that uses primarily structured exercises or individual work in the group setting.

Inability to Tolerate Confrontation.   One other category of clients may have considerable difficulty with general purpose interactive groups—people who have such a fragile sense of personal value that they can't tolerate being confronted. Although many clients are afraid of being judged by others, these clients feels devastated by any anger or criticism directed at him. As a result, they can spend much of their time in group dealing with this pain and have no any energy to examine and benefit from the confrontations. This difficulty often occurs with people who have narcissistic issues, which frequently include extreme vulnerability to criticism. However, not all narcissistic clients have this problem; many have been successful in my groups. It is particularly a problem with certain clients who monopolize the group's attention or are insensitive to others. They can annoy other group members and elicit a great deal of confrontation, but they can't tolerate receiving it.

The best way to tell if a prospective group member will have problems with confrontation is to give him the information and let him decide. Make it clear that, even though the group is supportive, he will at times be confronted by other group members. People who have great difficulty with criticism almost always know it. If you explore how a person feels about being confronted, it usually becomes clear that group isn't appropriate for him. In most cases, he will tell you he doesn't want to join the group. He should be referred for either individual therapy or a self-psychology group (Bacal, 1990; Stone, 1992), which is specifically designed for clients with these vulnerabilities.

Protecting the Group.   In addition to determining the best treatment for the client, you must also take into account the well-being of the group you might place him in. Be especially careful with clients who may be extremely hostile. They can be very damaging to a group. Also be careful about putting a moderately angry or judgmental client in a group that isn't strong enough to handle him. The same goes for a client who tends to monopolize the group's time; make sure the group is strong enough to stand up to him.

Telling Someone You Exclude.   If you choose to exclude a person from your group, make every effort to tell him in such a way as to avoid shaming him. It is best to emphasize those reasons that won't be seen as his fault. You should even go so far as bending the truth in order not to traumatize a person who has come to you at a fragile, painful time in his life.

☐ Group Composition

What is a good combination of clients for a group to be therapeutic? Which combinations should be avoided? There is a simple rule of thumb that describes a good composition for an interactive group. *The group should be heterogeneous in terms of personality style and homogeneous in terms of level of functioning.* This is widely accepted in the field, except for Yalom (1995, pp. 262–264), who believes that homogeneity in all areas is most important for promoting group cohesiveness and heterogeneity is not particularly important.

The Advantage of Variety

Personality.   There is a great advantage to having a wide variety of personalities and interpersonal styles in a group. It offers each client the chance to develop transference with various kinds of people who will stimulate different core issues and defenses. It also means that a variety of people can provide support and healing responses and relationships. A client will react differently to a controlling man, a flirtatious woman, a dependent person, an aggressive fighter, a wall-flower, etc. A well-functioning group needs people to play a variety of roles, such as caretaking, confronting, understanding, risk-taking, stabilizing, feeling, encouraging, etc. That's why it isn't good for the group to be too small or homogeneous. It is also valuable, if possible, to have diversity in terms of race, culture, religion, and class, unless the surrounding community is seriously divided along such lines. Variety in a group also more accurately reflects the real world, especially today, where we are confronted with an incredible array of different people.

Problem-focused groups often benefit from being more homogeneous because clients can immediately connect with each other through their similarities. Because these groups aren't usually focused on interpersonal issues, variety isn't as important. They will be discussed in chapter 28.

Age.   Age is a complex issue. A wide age span provides variety, and group members can develop transference with each other as parents and children. However, a group can be successful even if it has a narrow age range. Most group members prefer to have at least a few other people their age because they are usually struggling with similar general life issues. Therefore it can be problematic to bring a person into a group if he is considerably older or younger than the rest of the group. Young adults (under 25) prefer to be in groups with their peers. They are often intensely involved with people of a similar age and not so interested in older people. Many are also not mature enough to explore themselves in the same way as those 25 and older. The same considerations hold, even more strongly, for teenagers and children.

Gender.   A relatively even mix of men and women in a group provides several advantages. Everyone has interpersonal issues with both men and women and transference with both father and mother. In addition, on the average, men tend toward one cluster of personality traits and women toward another, so a gender mix may also insure a personality mix. However, women's and men's groups have their own special advantages for those clients who desire them. They provide a unique opportunity to learn more about oneself as a man or woman, to discuss gender-related topics with a sympathetic group, and to develop one's ability to relate to people of the same gender (see chapter 26). It can be problematic, however, to have just one or two people of one gender in a group. One man in a group of women, for example, will often have to deal with all the transference toward men or fathers from the whole group (positive and negative). This can be daunting.

Differences in Level of Functioning

A group works better if there is relative homogeneity in terms of level of functioning or ego strength. Differences in level of functioning are problems only in the extreme. It doesn't matter so much if there are moderate differences in functioning in the group, with some high functioning people and some with moderate difficulties, for example. However if one person is functioning at a much lower level than the rest of the group, there will be problems: (a) The group members may ignore him. (b) They may treat him as a group "mascot," being nice to him but not really engaging in peer relationships with him. (c) If he is angry or monopolizing, he may become a group scapegoat (see chapter 23). (d) If his pathology is evident, he may scare the other group members, causing them to close down and stop taking risks. Of course, these last two dangers are present with any low functioning client in a group, even if he is not alone. However, a low functioning client may benefit from joining a group with similar clients. The group may be more difficult, but the members will accept him and relate to him as an equal. If he is the only low functioning person in a group, he will likely be isolated.

Responsibility.   Homogeneity is also preferable when it comes to responsibility. Gross differences among clients in their willingness to take responsibility for their work can prove disruptive. It is possible to run a group with mostly mandated clients, for example, who often have little sense of responsibility for their work, but this requires special treatment. It isn't advisable to have one or two low-responsibility clients in a group whose members have a much higher sense of responsibility. The higher responsibility clients will feel resentful and exasperated with those who avoid responsibility. As a result, the low responsibility clients may be forced out of the group, or the high responsibility clients may be tempted to give up on their commitment to working on themselves.

Too Many Difficult Clients.   Too many of the same kind of difficult client in a group can pose problems. For example, one angry, judgmental person can stimulate a group in positive ways. Three of them could make a group unsafe for any vulnerability. One monopolizer can usually be handled; two or three could be deadly. One person who isn't motivated to take responsibility for himself won't affect a group too much, but three could reduce it to trivialities. It is also wise not to have more than one or two borderlines in a group, unless the group is designed specifically for people functioning at that level.

Previous Relationships

There are many advantages to having a therapy group be composed of strangers. If clients feel anonymous in the group, they are less likely to hide certain facts or put on a fake persona. They are also less afraid of breaches of confidentiality. They won't be as encumbered by entrenched patterns of relating. Furthermore, if a client has a friend or relative in the group, he may feel less free to talk about difficulties in his life, because this person is part of his life. Of course, if you prefer that members not have contact outside of group, it wouldn't make sense for two members to have an existing outside relationship.

These problems are most severe with couples, so it isn't wise to take a couple into an interactive group, unless of course, it is a couples group. The same applies to parents and children. Because I recommend a structure that permits group members to have contact outside group (see chapter 20), it is possible to have two people in a group with a previous relationship. You can allow friends to join such a group if there is no better alternative and if it seems that they won't be inhibited by each other's presence. However, they both must be interested in dealing with all aspects of their relationship in the group, not just those issues that come up in group, because it is impossible to separate out feelings in that way. If a client has an emotional reaction to a friend in the group, it may derive from their history together so everything must be available for discussion.

If a person is interviewing to join a group that already contains a friend or acquaintance, then the existing group member should have the power to veto the prospective member if he feels that this would in any way disrupt his ability to benefit from the group. It is *his* group, and if he feels unsafe enough with the prospective member that it might impair his therapy, the new person should be referred to another group.

☐ Group Goals

Time-limited groups usually have significantly different goals for their clients than long-term groups. Some studies that are designed to compare the effectiveness of short-term versus long-term groups, but this is like comparing apples and oranges. They can't be compared because they don't have the same aims.

Comparison of Goals.   Long-term groups aim for fundamental character change. Their goal is to help a client radically alter fundamental core issues, develop new healthy capacities, and change the way the person feels about herself and lives in the world. Time-limited groups have much more modest goals, as they must. They aim to help clients get through a particular life crisis, reduce the intensity of certain symptoms, make certain circumscribed behavioral changes, or make some progress toward deeper character change.

Fundamental character change cannot be accomplished in a short time. Sometimes a client may appear to make a major breakthrough while attending a short-term group or workshop, but in all likelihood, he had already been making progress. It is an illusion that this change was all due to the short-term work. Fundamental change takes time.

Seeing the Group within the Larger Context.   It is useful to keep in mind that any given group should not be expected to solve all of a client's problems or do the complete job of personal growth. This is an important viewpoint in short-term therapy, and it applies to long-term as well. The group should be seen in the larger context of the person's ongoing life. If the client is involved in an ongoing program of therapeutic endeavor, this group is just one step in that process. It may help the person negotiate a crisis, improve functioning, or deepen insight in a particular area. The client's growth will hopefully continue after the group, both on his own and in other therapeutic settings (MacKenzie, 1993, p. 425).

Setting Goals for the Group.   Time-limited groups need to establish specific goals that can actually be accomplished in the time allotted (Yalom, 1995, pp. 451–452). By designing and structuring the group to meet these goals, you can ensure that the clients don't become frustrated or hopeless because of overly ambitious aims. *For example, in a bereavement group, the goal might be to complete a certain phase of the grieving process.*

☐   The Pre-Group Interview

Before a client joins a group, the leader should conduct at least one interview. In this meeting you should seek to give information about the group, learn about the person, decide on the best form of treatment and (if applicable) the best group for this person, screen him, develop rapport, and prepare him to join the group. (The following discussion assumes that the person is coming to you for the first time.)

Giving Information

A prospective group member needs information about how the therapy group functions and how it might benefit him, so he can decide whether to join the group and be prepared for entering the group. I like to give this information in both verbal and written form. I have written an article for prospective group members that describes what it is like to be in an interactive therapy group (see Appendix). If possible, I mail this article to a prospective member to read before he arrives for the pre-group interview. I then go over some of this information in the interview.

The most important idea to convey is the interactive nature of the group work, because this work is not for everyone and you want new members to be as fully informed as possible. First, give a general description of what happens in a group, but as the interview progresses and you find out more about this particular person, relate your discussion of the group to his specific issues and personality. *For example, if I learn that a person feels hurt and rejected easily, I might explain that when this happens in the group he can explore his feelings and learn about where the issue comes from.*

Obtaining Information and Making an Assessment

During the interview, you need to gain enough knowledge about the person to help you recommend the best form of treatment for him and to give you sufficient background data to guide your interventions if he does join your group. You need detailed information about his presenting problem, any current psychotherapy or medication, his previous experience with psychotherapy, especially groups, and any previous psychiatric medication or hospitalization. You also need detailed knowledge about his current life and some history. You may be aided in this by specific testing instruments. All this is standard for most forms of therapy, so it won't be discussed further here. Because the person will be joining a group, it is particularly useful to get interpersonal information, concerning the kind and quality of his current and past relationships—family, romantic, and work relationships and friendships. You might inquire about his history with groups, not just therapy groups, but all types of groups. A specific diagnosis is not nearly as helpful as an understanding of the person's psychodynamics and interpersonal functioning (Salvendy, 1993, p. 73).

Deciding on Treatment

The first order of business is to determine the best method of treatment for this person, given his particular personality, presenting problems, and financial resources. The criteria discussed previously in this chapter can help you decide whether to recommend group therapy. The treatment decision also depends on clarifying what the client's goals are for treatment, and if he is to join a group, what his goals are for the group.

If you are considering bringing the client into a short-term group, the two of you must develop specific, delimited goals, taking into account the client's presenting problem, psychodynamics and interpersonal patterns, and level of functioning. You are thus required to make a rapid assessment of the client, during the pre-group interview(s) and early in the group. Client goals are important in long-term groups as well, but these goals can sometimes be vague and may change over time. With a limited-time group, they must be quite specific because they provide the primary focus for the work.

These goals should be discussed and negotiated with the client, emerging from a collaboration between the two of you. You are the expert who can provide information, make recommendations, and help him explore options, but the final decision must be his. Because of the need for assessment and goal-setting, the preparation of clients for time-limited groups is even more important than for long-term groups and therefore may require more pre-group interviews.

For an interactive group, the goals should be formulated in interpersonal terms that are understandable to beginning clients rather than in terms of intrapsychic concepts (MacKenzie, 1993, pp. 437–442). *For example, a client might seek to become more comfortable with other people's anger and to assert herself even if it might cause conflict.*

If it seems that an interactive group would be a good form of treatment for this person, then you must decide which group would be best for him. Or, if you only have one group to offer, you must decide if this group would be appropriate for him. This is done using the guidelines on group composition.

Screening

Do the best you can to screen out people who will end up dropping out of the group. This can have negative consequences for both the client and the group. The client can feel hurt, ashamed, incompetent, or, worse, discouraged about the possibility of being helped in group therapy. The group can feel rejected, demoralized, and distracted from its own task of building cohesion and helping its members. Too many dropouts may cause a group to become excessively cautious whenever a new member joins.

The leader must be especially careful in screening clients for a time-limited group (Klein, 1993, p. 257). You want to avoid bringing clients into the group who might be harmed or who aren't likely to achieve their goals. Many of the exclusion criteria for long-term groups must be applied more stringently for short-term groups. Because time-limited groups must move faster, be especially careful that the clients can handle whatever work the group undertakes. If the group involves deep emotional work or conflict, it is important that the clients be able to handle these things early in the group. If the group involves personal disclosure, clients must be ready for this quickly. Clients who might disrupt the group must be more carefully screened, because there will be little time to recover from any upheaval.

For a time-limited group, a client's problems must be of the sort where something meaningful can be accomplished in a short time.

> For example, a client with a simple phobia and an otherwise intact personality can benefit from a short-term phobia group. However, a client with the same phobia who also has a borderline personality disorder may gain nothing at all from the phobia group. The phobia may not be amenable to symptomatic relief until the deeper issues have been resolved to some extent. This is not to say that borderlines can't benefit from time-limited group therapy, in fact there have been studies indicating they can (Clarkin et al., 1991). But the group must be geared toward the borderline disturbance and goals must be set that are reasonable for this population.

If a client is misplaced in a time-limited group, even if he isn't directly harmed by the group, he may have an experience of failure that could discourage him from trying other forms of therapy in the future.

Unfortunately, screening is not an exact science. Given that you are conducting at most two pre-group interviews, you can't always predict accurately how well someone will fare in a group. Many of a person's strengths and weaknesses as a group member show up only in the group setting.

Developing Rapport

The pre-group interview isn't just for giving and getting information and making decisions. It is also an important opportunity for personal connection between you and the client. Your therapeutic alliance with the client (see chapter 19) is an important supporting factor in his success in the group (Tschuschke & Csogalik, 1990), and the intimacy of the interview setting can help develop this rapport. The client needs to feel that you are interested in him and care about him, and he must have faith in your professional and technical abilities as a group leader. If you notice signs of mistrust or other problems between the two of you, bring them up right away, so that potential difficulties can be rectified. Of course, clients may have a wide variety of negative transference reactions to you during the course of the group, but these can be weathered more effectively if there is a good alliance.

☐   Preparing a Person for Group

Educating About Group Process.   The information you give the person in the pre-group interview and beforehand not only helps him decide about treatment, but also prepares him for entering the group. It is wise to begin educating clients about the group norms before they enter the group. In addition to the 20-page paper that I give to prospective group members, I give an expanded 50-page version of the same paper to clients once they have decided to join the group. It gives them a detailed idea of what it is like to be in an interactive group, how the therapeutic work happens, and what is necessary for a person to be successful in a group. Of course, I don't expect most people to read it all before they begin. It is something they can peruse during the first few months of group and refer to at other times. This handout isn't sufficient, however, because some people don't like to read, so I also go over much of this information verbally in the pre-group interview.

Group Rules.   It is also crucial to explain to the client the group structure and rules regarding time, length of stay, payment, confidentiality, consultations, termination, and so on. Hand out the group rules, go over them with the client, and ask if she agrees to abide by each rule. If she has any questions or objections, discuss them in the interview. Taking this time makes it more likely that the person will remember the rules and follow them.

Exploring Fears.   It is helpful to explore with the person his fears about what will happen in the group once he arrives. By learning what aspects of the group may be most difficult for him, you can help him with these concerns. If his fears are unrealistic, you can explain why that is so. *For example, he may be worried that the group members will reject him because of his symptoms, such as a sexual problem.* If his fears are common for a person first entering a group, he will be reassured to know that he is not alone with these concerns. Some fears will be particular to a client's character structure. If necessary, you can help him explore these fears briefly in the pre-group interview and explain how the group can be useful to him in working on them. You can also offer pointers on how to conduct himself in the first few sessions relative to his fears.

> For example, if he is an angry person, he may be afraid of blowing up at someone in the group. You can help him strategize about how best to contain his anger and explore it when it arises.

Multiple Interviews.   If you are having difficulty deciding whether to take someone into a group, or which group is best, it may be wise to schedule a second interview to get to know the person better. A second interview may also be necessary if the person needs more than the usual help in working on his fears about the group. Some group leaders routinely hold two or three pre-group sessions in which they take a more extensive history and/or work with the client therapeutically before bringing him into group. This allows you to screen more effectively, prepare the client more thoroughly, and develop better rapport. However, some people who are interested in joining a group may not be amenable to more than one pre-group session. It is possible to accomplish some of the work of the second or third interviews during early consultations after the client has joined the group (see chapter 27).

Preparing an Individual Client for Group. Although obtaining information and developing rapport are unnecessary for your current individual clients, most of the above discussion also applies. You have the advantage of being able to prepare the person for group gradually, if necessary.

When you are an experienced group leader and have worked for a while with a client individually, you can sometimes see how much he could benefit from being in one of your groups Be careful that your enthusiasm does not lead you to encourage him to join a group before he is ready. He may comply to please you. In this case, he may end up leaving the group abruptly and perhaps resisting joining a group later when he is ready.

CHAPTER

Therapeutic Group Norms

The next five chapters address the process of developing therapeutic group norms. In this chapter, we focus on a variety of therapeutic group norms and how to promote and protect them. The following four chapters each deal with an additional group norm that is important enough to warrant an entire chapter—responsibility, self-exploration, interaction, and presence/contact.

In this chapter, we first explain what group norms are and how they differ from social norms and group rules. Then there is a discussion about how to remove prohibitions that may have developed in the group against discussing certain topics or expressing certain feelings. Vulnerability is an important norm that can be promoted by developing a caring group environment and prohibiting certain actions that undermine safety. We explore when it is important to preserve the integrity of a piece of work and when interruption may be valuable. We see how group cohesiveness promotes an optimal therapeutic atmosphere, and how the individuality of each person and the diversity within the group also need to be respected and valued.

☐ Group Norms

Group norms specify those ways of being that are preferred or expected in the group and those that are frowned on or prohibited. Group norms can be explicit or implicit, consciously chosen by the leader or the group, or unconsciously arrived at without any explicit discussion.

Rules and Norms

Group norms are different from group rules. *Group rules* are explicit and are not to be broken without good reason. *Examples are the rules mentioned last chapter that prohibit violence or coming to group intoxicated.* Group norms, on the other hand, are looser because they constitute general behavioral guidelines.

> For example, a common norm stipulates that one must speak directly *to* other group members rather than *about* them. There are norms about when it is appropriate to interrupt someone who is working and what kind of material can be discussed in group.

How Norms Develop

Some norms are promulgated by the group leader, some come from the group, and some involve negotiation between the leader and group. A leader will need to establish certain therapeutic norms for the group to be effective in fostering healing and change. *For example, it is important that members talk about their feelings and explore their psychological issues. Without this norm, a group can easily lapse into idle chatter.* The leader should be conscious of therapeutic norms, so you can promote them, both explicitly and implicitly. It's best if they grow out of give and take between the leader and the group. If the group exerts too much influence, the norms may not be therapeutic. If the leader simply imposes norms, however, group members may feel powerless or resentful.

Many group norms come primarily from the group members, and as long as these norms aren't anti-therapeutic, the leader can allow each group to establish its own.

For example, some groups prefer longer and deeper pieces of work focused on one or two people at a time. Other groups prefer more open and spontaneous group interactions, which allow members to interrupt more frequently to express their feelings or opinions. As long as a group doesn't go too far in either direction, the leader can allow the group to develop its own balance. (See the Preserving Versus Interrupting Work section in chapter 8.) Some group norms derive primarily from the leader's style or even from the leader's countertransference difficulties. *For example, if the leader enjoys fast-paced, confrontive groups, he may unconsciously shape group norms to fit that mold. If the leader is afraid of aggression or sexuality, the group will tend to reflect this.* (See chapter 18 for more discussion of countertransference.)

Social Norms

Therapeutic group norms are considerably different from ordinary social norms. It generally isn't acceptable for people to express how they are reacting emotionally to each other in normal social interactions, especially negative reactions. It is also unusual for one person (the leader) to have the power to ask people to make themselves emotionally vulnerable. Keep this in mind when you are working to develop therapeutic group norms. You aren't simply asking the group members to accept one set of norms. You are also asking them to break some of the social norms to which they are accustomed.

Many of our social norms aren't particularly healthy. We avoid giving each other honest feedback and dealing directly with difficulties far more than is necessary. We value appearances and status rather than genuineness and vulnerability. We compete for domination rather than accepting each other and cooperating for optimal collective functioning. Though group therapy norms can't be adopted wholesale by society because some of them are appropriate only for a protected therapeutic environment, our culture could benefit enormously if people generally related to each other in a way that is closer to therapy group norms.

Types of Group Norms

Group norms come in two flavors: (a) prohibitions specify what behavior is not allowed in the group, and (b) positive norms specify what behavior is valued and preferred in the group.

☐   Removing Anti-Therapeutic Prohibitions

Prohibited Topics

One of your tasks as a group leader is to become aware of and remove prohibitions against behavior that is helpful to the therapy process. Often a group develops prohibitions against talking about certain topics. *For example, it's not unusual for groups to develop prohibitions against talking about sexuality, especially sexual attractions between group members.* This kind of norm usually develops implicitly. Initially the topic isn't talked about because of the potential shame or rejection involved, but after time has elapsed with no mention of the topic, group members begin to assume that it's out of bounds.

The leader's job is to become aware of the prohibition and find a way to end it. If the avoided topic is sexual attraction, you have a number of options: (a) Bring it directly to the group's attention that this issue isn't being talked about. (b) Be watchful for instances when there seems to be sexual energy between participants and mention it then. Do this in such a way that the persons involved don't feel shamed, perhaps by mentioning that sexual attraction is a common and important issue in group therapy. (c) Someone in the group may discuss a sexual attraction during a consultation or individual session. You can encourage her to bring it up in group and help her work through her fears of doing this.

Groups may also develop prohibitions against talking about jealousy, money, power, or other topics. Whenever a topic hasn't been broached for a while, it's likely that a prohibition has developed, and you should explore this with the group. In fact, some topics are difficult for group members to broach, so it is helpful for the leader to encourage these discussions. This means being on the lookout for hints of sexuality (or jealousy, etc.) and then actively trying to bring this out.

Prohibited Feelings

Sometimes a certain feeling is prohibited, rather than a topic. For example, some groups go through phases where there is a prohibition against anger and conflict. Other groups may shy away from vulnerability or dependency. Prohibitions may develop against expressing certain feelings toward the leader, such as anger or the desire for support. Prohibitions may also develop against talking about certain feelings toward the group as a whole, such as disappointment or closeness.

The same advice applies here. If it looks like a prohibition has developed, explore this with the group. Be on the lookout for evidence of these difficult feelings and encourage the group members to reveal them. It is especially important to do this the first few times. This helps to develop the group norm that these feelings are not shameful but instead are common and acceptable. After a norm is well-developed, the group members will take over this function. They will bring up their own feelings and encourage others to do the same.

☐ Vulnerability

The Value of Vulnerability

The ability to experience and show vulnerability is one of the most important factors in a successful therapy group, because it is crucial to the change process, especially access. Vulnerability means the capacity to be open to one's emotions and connections with other people, even when there is a risk of shame, fear, or hurt. Though the term *vulnerability* is sometimes used to mean the *presence* of these painful feelings, whether or not the person is open to experiencing or expressing them, I am using the word to refer to the actual interpersonal openness involved. The topic of vulnerability is more or less synonymous with safety, because when clients don't feel safe in a group, it usually means they don't feel safe to show their vulnerability.

The biggest block to vulnerability is the fear of being shamed. In our highly competitive society, vulnerability is not often welcomed or appreciated. We frequently take it as a sign of weakness and deficiency and looked on those who show it with contempt. Our clients often feel most vulnerable about issues and feelings they have been shamed for.

Paradoxically, vulnerability is intrinsically very appealing. When someone openly shows their most painful and tender feelings, this naturally engenders feelings of caring, warmth, appreciation, and closeness. This is one of the things that makes group therapy so effective. On the surface it might seem strange that one can bring together a group of strangers, many of whom have difficulty feeling positively about themselves and relating to others, and produce a group that is intimate and healing. However, because therapy groups value vulnerability, group members can show their pain and difficulties them and find that they are accepted and appreciated. The most healing part is that group members aren't accepted *despite* their problems but frequently they are appreciated *because* of them, or rather because of their ability to be open with their pain. Of course, the group leader must engender the right group climate for this to happen, but you have the advantage that vulnerability is naturally appealing.

In order for a group member to risk being vulnerable, he must have some internal support, trust in his ability to tolerate pain, and not too much fear of others' reactions. *For example, in the earlier transcript, Melissa had the inner strength to go deeply into her pain despite the considerable shame that it brought up.* In addition, the client must have a certain amount of trust in the group and the leader, based on their demonstrating caring for him and others. Thus vulnerability can be looked at from two perspectives—as a personal capacity and as a property of the group. This chapter explores vulnerability as a group factor and how the leader can foster it in the group.

The more group members trust you as leader and feel connected with you, the more they will feel safe enough to be vulnerable. The therapeutic alliance is discussed in chapter 19.

Caring

Vulnerability is fostered when clients receive caring from other members and the leader as a result of taking the risk to be vulnerable. Caring was discussed previously under healing responses. It is important that early demonstrations of vulnerability be met with appropriate expressions of caring, including empathy, identification, compassion, acceptance, appreciation, and understanding. Yalom (1995, p. 126) discussed the importance of developing a sense of safety and support in the beginning stages of a therapy group. Group members typically venture small amounts of vulnerability as a test to see if the group will respond well to them before going further.

> For example, a person may say that she is having marital difficulties but not share any of the details or her feelings. If the group responds in a caring way, then she may reveal more information. After a few more sessions, if she observes that other members are receiving empathy and compassion from the group, she may choose to express more of her pain.

If caring isn't forthcoming from the other members in response to vulnerability, then the leader must provide it, as often happens naturally as you work with someone. An experienced therapist usually conveys empathy and compassion, understanding and acceptance without even having to think about it.

Caring can come not only from the other group members and the leader, but also from the person who is being vulnerable. The more a person can give this to herself, the less she needs it from the group. However, most members of therapy groups have a hard time caring about themselves, so it is especially important to foster these attitudes in the group. It is much easier for most people to care for others than for themselves.

The simplest way for the group leader to promote caring is through modeling, by expressing the caring yourself. New group members also learn about caring by internalizing the behavior of the more experienced members. Actually, all aspects of group culture are disseminated in this way.

Encouraging Vulnerability

Vulnerability is also promoted by explicitly encouraging it as you work with people—by encouraging them to explore shameful issues and stay with pain that comes up. It is also helpful to express appreciation for a group member who takes the risk to be vulnerable.

As the group leader, you have an enormous impact on group norms in a variety of subtle ways, often without realizing it. In the case of vulnerability, you may show more interest when someone is being vulnerable. Your manner may become soft and caring when responding to someone in pain. You may frown or speak in a less accepting tone when someone doesn't respond to others' vulnerability in a caring manner. The same subtle process of reinforcement happens with other group norms as well. The group leader has the power to shape group norms without even intending to, because every small gesture and facial expression affects the group members. In fact, it is impossible for the group leader to avoid shaping group norms, as Yalom (1995, pp. 111–114) pointed out so cogently. Much of this goes on outside of the leader's awareness, which is acceptable as long as the proper norms are being established. However, if you become aware that there are problems with a group norm, you should examine the subtle messages you may be sending.

Occasionally someone will respond to vulnerability with judgment, ridicule, or attack. Then you must step in and ask him to explore where his reaction comes from. You help to promote his understanding, and you send a message to the member being attacked that this assault on her vulnerability wasn't appropriate. If a certain group member repeatedly undermines vulnerability, you need to work with him on this problem. This will not only help him but also serve to promote the correct group norm.

To summarize, there are six ways for a leader to encourage vulnerability (or any group norm): (a) respond positively to it, (b) show interest in it, (c) explicitly encourage it, (d) express appreciation for it, (e) challenge a client who undermines it, and (f) model it. Modeling vulnerability might not always be appropriate for the therapist because this might involve too much self-disclosure, but other qualities, such as caring or protectiveness, can easily be modeled by the leader. The following is an example.

A group I was leading got off to a bad start with respect to vulnerability and caring. The members experienced a considerable degree of conflict with each other during the first month of group, before they had developed enough connection and trust. When a member would make herself vulnerable, she would often get intellectual and critical responses rather than the caring she needed. I could see that people weren't feeling safe enough to reveal much about themselves in the group, especially their pain. In order to reverse this anti-therapeutic norm, I made a point of offering caring myself whenever anyone became vulnerable. I expressed appreciation when others were empathic and supportive. I challenged one man who repeatedly responded to others with intellectual interpretations and helped him discover that he was invested in being admired for his intelligence. I also helped the group to confront a woman who was frightening them with her aggression.

I asked the group members to examine whether they felt safe in group, whether they experienced enough support and caring to take risks and reveal their pain and shame. They confirmed that they didn't. We had a discussion about what the group members needed from each other in the way of caring and validation. We talked about the effects of the conflict and the lack of connection in the group. The group members took on the task of creating a safer, more caring group climate. They focused their energy on developing warm, supportive connections with each other. They occasionally held back on confrontations, but not in a way that fostered resentment. They made a point of showing appreciation to each other, despite the concern of one member that this was phony. After a couple of months, this paid off. The group became more supportive and cohesive; people began to feel safe to do their work. The proper group norm for caring and vulnerability had been established.

☐ Prohibitions for Protecting Vulnerability

Certain prohibitive group norms serve to protect vulnerability, trust, and group cohesiveness. Under most circumstances, the leader should discourage or prohibit the following behaviors.

Attacking When Vulnerable

Group members need to refrain from attacking or confronting someone when she is vulnerable. Suppose a client has just completed a piece of work in which she went into some painful feelings and left herself in an open, vulnerable state. Normally, the other group members will be feeling warmly toward her, but occasionally someone in the group may want to confront or even attack her (perhaps because of leftover feelings from previous interactions). This person may have perfectly valid reasons for doing so, and under other circumstances this might lead to good work. However, she is probably too raw to handle any confrontation right now. She might be overwhelmed or unnecessarily hurt. She might close up and defend against the confrontation. This badly timed confrontation might thus injure the client and undo some of the positive effects of the work she just completed.

The leader's job is to prevent this from happening and to help members understand why this isn't a good idea. In other words you need to establish a group norm that people don't confront others when they are vulnerable. The issue here is *timing*. There is nothing wrong with confronting someone. It just shouldn't be done when someone is especially vulnerable. Ask the person to remember the issue and bring it up at some time in the future.

Multiple Confrontations

When They Are Dangerous. It can be dangerous to allow more than one person to challenge or confront someone. The power of groups is awesome, both for healing and damage. A criticism that may be quite tolerable to hear from one person may be devastating to hear from three or four people. You must be careful to protect people who will feel deeply hurt or shamed when confronted by a number of people at once, what I colloquially call "ganging up" on someone. When this happens, such a person is likely to either be devastated or erect rigid defenses.

> For example, Sam accused Ellen of being sexually seductive with him while pretending that nothing was going on. She became upset and incensed at him and made a comment about always being misunderstood about her sexuality. At this point, Judy started to jump in to say that she also thought Ellen was seductive with Sam and other men. (I knew this because of a consultation I had done with Judy.) Though they were raising a valid issues, I felt that it would be too much for Ellen. When confronted by a number of people in the past about another issue, Ellen had been devastated and become closed off. So I stopped Judy before she could say much, commenting, "Let's just keep this interaction between Sam and Ellen for now."

When They Are Useful.   However, multiple confrontations can be quite useful at times. This group norm applies only under certain circumstances. Sometimes a client is resistant to a challenge from one person because he believes it is that person's problem. However, if challenged by many people in the group, he may be willing to own the problem, or at least look at himself seriously. If the person receiving the confrontations is strong enough to handle them or doesn't feel too much shame about this particular issue, then they can be helpful. You must use your clinical judgment about when to allow multiple confrontations and when to prohibit them.

When You're Not Sure.   When a number of group members do confront someone on an issue, you may not be sure how he is handling it. It is most dangerous when the client is feeling devastated inside but isn't aware of this and puts up a defensive front. This often spurs the group on to challenge him more vigorously in an attempt to reach him. In this case, it helps to ask the client, for example, "How does it feel emotionally to be getting all this difficult feedback?" If he is feeling very hurt and can acknowledge this, he will be able to process these feelings with your support, and the group will back off because they recognize that he is being affected. If he isn't in touch with any pain, but you suspect it is there, you might suggest that he explore his feelings after the group is over. This also alerts the group members to the possibility that he is being hurt unconsciously.

Discussing a Person Who Is Absent

Whenever a group member (call him Nate) is absent from a particular meeting, one of the members present (call her Eileen) may want to talk about her feelings toward Nate. This presents a dilemma. On the one hand, Eileen should be able to explore her feelings when they come up in group. On the other hand, you don't want her to say things about Sam that she wouldn't say to him in person for a number of reasons. The rest of the group may become uncomfortable, knowing Eileen's feelings about Nate which are hidden from him. If this comes out when Nate is present, he may feel mistrustful of Eileen and the group. When other people are absent, they may wonder what will be said behind their backs. Thus by developing a norm that people don't talk about someone who is absent, you can help to protect group trust and cohesiveness.

However, there are certain exceptions to this norm: (a) if Eileen is discussing something she has already said to Nate or will say to him; (b) if Eileen is clearly talking about her reactions to Nate in order to explore what it means to her as opposed to blaming him; (c) if Nate has already left the group so Eileen no longer has a chance to explore these feelings with him. Even then, encourage her to explore her reactions rather than Nate's character or behavior.

☐ Preserving Versus Interrupting Work

Preventing Work from Being Diverted.   Once a person initiates a piece of work or two people begin a dialogue, it is important that the work isn't interrupted casually. The norm should be established that an existing piece of work has precedence over other issues unless there is a compelling reason for interruption. This helps to preserve the integrity of the work that has been started. Other group members should not jump in with extraneous comments that divert the work or turn the group's attention to themselves without good reason. If this is allowed to happen, the group often becomes chaotic and not much real therapy can be accomplished. In addition, if people fear that they will be left in the middle of an emotionally important exploration, they won't risk becoming vulnerable. This prohibition doesn't cover all comments by other group members, only interruptions that turn the group's attention in an entirely different direction.

You can enforce this norm by stopping people who are interrupting inappropriately or encouraging the person who is working to do so. *You can say, "Wait, Bert is in the middle of some important work right now. Bring that up later." If two people are interacting, you might say, "Let's see if Bert and Jill are finished with each other before you start on something else."* If you do stop someone from interrupting, it is a good idea to check with her later to see if she was hurt by your action.

The Need for Silence.   In some situations, the leader needs to go even further than preventing members from diverting a piece of work. Sometimes a client can benefit from a few minutes of silence to get in touch with what she is feeling or allow her inner experience to deepen. A client may be struggling to get in touch with what she wants from the group or to find her own direction for her work. At these times the person shouldn't be interrupted even by comments that are relevant to her work. Any outside help can prevent the person from finding the deeper place inside where she knows herself more truly.

Interruption Can Be Appropriate.   Group members need to know, however, that it is acceptable to interrupt a piece of work if they have a compelling reason. For example, if someone is bored or impatient with a piece of work, she may need to say so. If someone has a strong emotional reaction to an interaction, she may need to express it right away despite the disruption it might cause. These kind of interruptions shouldn't be prohibited, but people shouldn't do this lightly. Because an interruption can stir up feelings in the person(s) working, it may become part of the existing work or lead to a new piece of work involving the person who interrupted. However, the person who was working may demand that she has the right to continue without interruption. All these reactions become grist for the mill in the interpersonal work of the group.

If someone does get interrupted in the middle of work, make sure to check with her later to see if she wants to continue. Ideally the person would take care of this herself, but many group members aren't assertive enough to do this and need the leader's help.

Some groups develop norms that are quite protective of existing work, whereas other groups prefer more permission for members to interrupt and express themselves. Problems occur only if the norms go too far in one direction or the other. If a group becomes too protective of existing work, members may engage in lengthy pieces of work that leave the rest of the group feeling excluded. This produces deadness and dissatisfaction with the group. A cohesive group requires a certain amount of freedom for open and spontaneous conversation and interaction. A client should not be encouraged to continue to take the group's attention after a piece of work has come to a natural conclusion or if he isn't accomplishing anything useful. Yalom (1995, p. 123) warned against groups developing the norm that whoever speaks first is allowed to dominate the group for a long time because other members are afraid to interrupt.

Group Exploration.   Under certain circumstances, it isn't necessary to preserve a piece of work. Sometimes it can be helpful for a number of group members to explore their feelings rather than focusing on one person's work. *For example, if the group leader announces an upcoming vacation, many of the group members may have an emotional reaction. Rather than working with one person in depth, each person might share and explore his or her feelings about the vacation.* I call this process *group exploration.* Some group methods favor this approach over working with one person and would therefore not have a norm about preserving a piece of work. Group exploration is discussed in more detail in chapter 25.

☐   Group Cohesiveness and Individuality

Cohesiveness

Group cohesiveness refers to the degree of closeness in the group, the degree to which the members value and like each other and the group. This well-known concept in the group therapy literature has been shown to correlate with positive outcomes in groups (Yalom, 1995, chap. 3). Cohesiveness in a group is similar to the sense of closeness in a healthy family and to the positive feeling of community that most of us yearn for in our lives. In today's fragmented world, though people may have individual friendships, a true sense of community among a group of people is rare. Interactive therapy groups can help people develop the skills for making community possible.

Cohesiveness is an implicit group norm in that the leader strives to create a group that is cohesive without directly telling members that it is their responsibility to connect with one another. Although the leader may encourage a client to explore her feelings or interact with other members, she herself needs to choose how much closeness she wants with the group. This is especially important for clients who are afraid of intimacy.

The Value of Cohesiveness.   Cohesiveness plays a role in group therapy that is similar to the therapeutic alliance in individual therapy. By supporting, promoting, and enhancing many aspects of the therapeutic change process, it forms a foundation on which the rest of the therapy rests.

Group cohesiveness is particularly valuable in fostering trust and caring and therefore the capacity for vulnerability. It also enhances safety and therefore the ability of group members to take necessary risks, such as experimenting with healthy behavior. It improves the likelihood that people will take seriously the feedback they get from each other. Group cohesiveness improves group attendance and reduces the likelihood of dropouts. In a cohesive group, members often look forward to coming to group and getting involved even if they are frightened of the feelings and issues they must deal with. Cohesiveness leads to deeper emotional involvement among the members, thereby providing the interpersonal juice that drives the therapy process. Increased involvement also leads to deeper access, thereby aiding the therapeutic change process.

In a cohesive group, responses from group members to each other are more likely to be healing rather than harmful. In fact, for many group members, especially those from dysfunctional families, the very experience of being in an intimate, caring group is a new experience and therefore healing in itself.

Fostering Cohesiveness.

Cohesiveness is fostered not only by caring and vulnerability but also through the group emphasis on interpersonal relationships. The quality of the trust and alliance between each member and the leader (see chapter 19) is also crucial to cohesiveness.

The leader can also promote cohesiveness by encouraging group members to take the group seriously. This means stressing the need for punctuality and regular attendance and treating lateness or frequent absence as a problem to be explored. When appropriate, remind people of the value of the group for bettering their lives and the importance of their bonds with each other for the proper functioning of the group.

In addition, cohesiveness is promoted when group members express their feelings about the group as a whole, especially positive feelings. Therefore it is important to encourage members in this direction. Surprisingly, even the expression of negative feelings toward the group, such as resentment, disappointment, or dissatisfaction, helps to build cohesiveness. If these feelings can be explored and worked through, members will feel more connected and committed to the group.

Time-limited groups need to develop cohesiveness quickly (MacKenzie, 1993, pp. 430–431) so they can move into work as fast as possible. This is aided by the fact that many limited-time groups are homogeneous in nature, which means that the participants are chosen because they all share a similar characteristic or problem. A homogeneous group develops trust and cohesiveness faster than a heterogeneous one. By focusing on the ways that clients are alike and encouraging them to relate to each other in positive, caring ways, the leader can help a group to bond quickly. In a homogenous, time-limited group, in contrast to an interactive group, the leader should avoid conflict and emphasize empathy, compassion, and support.

Expressing Dissatisfaction with the Group.

If the group is cohesive but one client feels disconnected from the group, she won't be able to use the group therapeutically, and she will probably leave eventually. The best way to avoid this is to encourage group members to express any dissatisfactions they have with the group. In fact, perhaps the greatest block to group cohesiveness is the avoidance of negative feelings toward the group. If someone is feeling unhappy with the group and doesn't express it, this will lead to trouble. If many people are avoiding their dissatisfactions, the group may become distant or hostile. Because clients may be reticent about bringing up their unhappy feelings, you must work to establish the norm that this is valuable. Notice signs of dissatisfaction such as withdrawal or surliness and ask about them. Give clients explicit permission to talk about negative feelings toward the group or the leader.

When these feelings are expressed, it usually leads to good work and more closeness in the group. If a client's negative feelings stem from her own intrapsychic issue, then voicing them gives her an opportunity to understand it and work it through.

For example, a woman felt hurt and angry after a group meeting in which she took the risk to confront someone. She assumed that no one else supported her action or felt as she did, and she was ready to leave the group. When she brought this up at the next meeting, it turned out that many people felt supportive of her but hadn't had a chance to express it. She had never felt supported in her family, and this work proved healing for her.

If the dissatisfaction is due to some problematic group dynamics, then other group members probably feel the same way. Bringing this out gives the group a chance to explore their various reactions, recognize what is going wrong, and change course.

For example, a man was feeling constricted in his group because he felt there was no room for him to express any anger or aggression. When he brought this up, three or four other people said they felt the same way. In the ensuing discussion, people acknowledged that they had been going out of their way to be "nice" to each other and avoid conflict. They resolved to begin dealing with their negative feelings toward each other. This interchange immediately brought the group to life, and people began to feel closer to each other.

Individuality and Diversity

Another implicit group norm supports each member's unique individuality and the diversity of the group. These, of course, are two sides of the same coin. If a group truly accepts each person in all her uniqueness, this also implies an openness to diversity. Though you should strive for diversity in choosing people for a new group whenever possible, any group will contain a wide variety of people. Diversity manifests not only in the demographic characteristics of race, religion, class, gender, age, sexual orientation, and ethnic group. It also shows in terms of personality, communication style, presenting problems or symptoms, childhood history, characteristic defenses, and so on. Therefore any group, even if it is homogeneous in some ways, will include considerable diversity.

A well-functioning group will accept and even appreciate each person's unique background and way of being while still challenging him to change those attributes that are problematic. The leader plays a big part in fostering this norm by modeling genuine interest in each person. When members express dissatisfactions with each other, there can be a fine line between legitimate challenge and non-acceptance of a person. Encourage people to express their negative emotional reactions rather than judgments. *For example, "When you don't give me a chance to have my say, I get frightened and angry," rather than, "You are a pushy bitch."* This approach supports each person's uniqueness while still allowing people to express their feelings toward each other.

Integrating Cohesiveness and Individuality

Perhaps the two most important things people want from a group are to belong to a close-knit community and to be completely accepted as they are. At the group level, these can be called cohesiveness and diversity. In terms of basic needs, these are connectedness and autonomy. On the surface, these two desires can appear to be in conflict. People sometimes feel they must give up their individuality in order to be accepted by the group. Alternatively someone may feel he must become an outcast in order to preserve his uniqueness and autonomy. However, in a healthy group this choice is not necessary. The leader must strive to establish the norm that both closeness and individuality are possible.

Ideally our society would also uphold this same norm, by creating community that is based on respect for each person's and each group's special uniqueness. Historically, we have suppressed individuality in favor of community. In today's society, we have gone to the opposite extreme. We place such a value on individuality that we are fragmented into isolated individuals and families. (As I noted elsewhere [Earley, 1997], this fragmentation occurs for a variety of reasons.) At the same time, we are struggling toward a fuller appreciation of diversity. A healthy society must find a way to have both community and diversity, connectedness and autonomy, and therapy groups can help train people in the attitudes and capacities that make this possible.

☐ Conclusions

Teaching About Group Norms

Under certain circumstances, the leader needs to teach clients explicitly about group norms or the therapy process in general—in the early stages of a group, when a new member joins, or when an important concept comes up for the first time. In these cases, it is appropriate to discuss the concept intellectually: *for example, explaining in detail the reasons why people shouldn't talk about someone who isn't present.* You can also accomplish this by repeated interventions with a client who doesn't understand an idea.

> For example, suppose I ask a new group member what she is feeling in response to another group member, and she responds by giving her perception of the other person. I then ask again and receive another perception rather than a feeling. I persist and ask a third time, this time explaining the difference between the two. I continue this until the person is able to identify her feelings, even though I don't think attach any clinical significance to her answer. I am doing it for the sake of the teaching, not only for this client but for the whole group.

If a client asks a question about why you do things in a certain way or how therapy works, choose your answer based on whether you think there is a need for teaching. If this topic hasn't been addressed before, or if it seems that the client doesn't understand this material conceptually, answer the question in as much detail as is necessary. However, if you sense that the question really represents resistance or defense, focus on that instead. Some clients who use intellectual defenses ask unnecessary questions just to keep the work on a rational level. Others will ask questions so as to engage the leader in debates about the process of therapy, or to avoid taking a risk that is especially frightening. Though it is important to teach when necessary, don't be fooled by questions that are being used as resistance.

Revising Group Norms

From time to time, group norms will naturally come up for discussion, revision, and expansion.

> For example, a client may say that he is dissatisfied with the group because members take turns in having the group's attention. He doesn't think there is room for people to speak up spontaneously when they want. He doesn't feel safe to jump in and say what is on his mind. This could stem from a misperception and his fear of being ostracized for expressing himself, or it could be an accurate assessment of a group norm that restrains free expression. Or it could be a mixture of the two. In any case, the best way to determine the truth is for the each group member to discuss her perceptions and feelings about this issue. Are people just taking turns? Do group members feel permission to express themselves when they want? Does the group feel stilted? How would the group members feel if they interrupted each other more often? When is it acceptable to interrupt?

On such questions, get as much input as possible from group members by helping each person air her opinion. If necessary, explain why certain norms are necessary for the group to be therapeutic. *In this case, suppose the group had become too dead because of excessive turn taking. You could explain how this was preventing a free flow of interaction and therefore stifling interactive work.* It isn't necessary for the group to arrive at an explicit decision about what to do. Once it has been discussed thoroughly, the group will naturally move toward norms that are conducive to therapeutic change.

CHAPTER

Responsibility, Motivation, and Direction

This chapter covers an important group norm—responsibility—and two related processes—motivation and self-direction.

☐ Responsibility

Responsibility means that a client recognizes that *she* is ultimately in charge of her progress in therapy and takes it upon herself to make her work successful (to the extent of her ability to do so). Let's look more closely at the meaning of responsibility. In ordinary usage, it has at least three different connotations—obligation, fault, and agency.

1. *Obligation.* In a therapy group, clients are obliged to hold up their part of the contractual bargain of therapy—to explore themselves, keep confidentiality, and maintain various other group norms and rules. They also have some obligations to the other group members, especially with respect to attendance, punctuality, and notice for termination. The group leader is responsible for fulfilling her obligation to perform ethical, effective therapy. However, the responsibility norm is not primarily about obligation. If clients followed group norms only because of a contractual obligation, they wouldn't make much therapeutic progress and many would rebel.

2. *Fault.* When a client is exhibiting problematic behavior, one could say that it is at least partly her responsibility (fault) for the difficulties that ensue. However, this attitude leads to blaming, which tends to be hurtful and counterproductive. The responsibility norm does not entail assigning blame. It is more useful for a client to

own her part in a problem without attacking herself. This leads to self-exploration and therapeutic change rather than guilt and shame.

3. *Agency.* The client is the agent of her own motivations and actions, and therefore she is the primary force behind her destiny, especially her ability to make the changes she wants in therapy. The more she realizes that she is responsible for the course of her therapy and acts from this knowledge, the more successful her therapy will be. The more she is an active author of her work in group and not a passive recipient of help, the better chance she has to make therapeutic progress. This is what I mean by the group norm of responsibility. Historically, existential approaches have emphasized responsibility (May, Angel, & Ellenberger, 1981; Perls et al., 1951; Yalom, 1980).

The Practice of Responsibility

In practice, responsibility means that the client is motivated to engage in the work of the group because of her hope of success. She actively explores herself, interacts with other group members, and takes therapeutic risks. She attempts to look at herself and acknowledge her part in interpersonal difficulties with other members. She attempts to understand herself and the direction of her therapy work and keeps track of her progress and what work still needs to be done to reach her goals. She decides what work she needs to do each week and takes responsibility for initiating it when appropriate. Of course, a responsible client doesn't attempt to do all this by herself. She uses the expertise of the leader and the feedback of the group in her work. In addition, the client's responsibility doesn't absolve the leader of his responsibility. The leader is still responsible for providing the highest quality therapy possible.

Difficulties with Responsibility

Though the above is the ideal of responsibility, we understand that no client will be fully responsible all the time, and many will fall far short of this standard. In the early stages of group, especially with inexperienced clients, the leader should expect that clients won't be able to take very much responsibility. The leader or group may need to temporarily supply the motivation or direction for the work. A group member's ability to take responsibility for her work develops gradually over time.

In addition, certain clients will have difficulty being responsible because of their character structure. Those who see themselves as helpless or the victims of other people's actions will be especially resistant to taking responsibility for themselves. The mandated client, who isn't even responsible for being in the therapy group, can cause serious problems for the work. However, we hope that even a mandated client will become involved with the group and ultimately be inspired to take responsibility for his work.

Despite the importance of responsibility, it may sometimes be valuable for a client to not be fully responsible. For example, a client might give some responsibility to the leader because of being so deeply involved emotionally that someone else needs to keep track of what is happening in the work. For a client who has been overly responsible in his life, it is healthy for him to learn to trust others to help him.

Promoting Responsibility

Nevertheless, the leader should promote responsibility as a group norm. At times he can explicitly state what clients are responsible for. (Examples of this are given through-out Part II.) Alternatively, he can refrain from providing direction or motivation when clients can do this themselves.

> For example, Dan asks the leader to tell him why he is feeling upset before he tries to come up with his own answer. The leader can refuse to answer, or she can suggest that maybe Dan knows more than he thinks. This forces him back on his own resources and develops responsibility.

At those times when a client isn't being fully responsible, the leader can make this explicit and help him explore what is behind this stance. *For example, the leader might ask Dan to explore why he asked her for help before trying to find the answer himself.* At those times when the group as a whole isn't taking responsibility, the leader can explicitly let them know that she won't take over what they should be doing themselves. She can challenge them to be responsible or to explore what makes them want her to run the show.

> For example, suppose a group is in conflict about who gets to work next and they look to the leader to decide. She can tell them that it isn't her job to direct traffic and they must work it out among themselves.

Active Leadership and Client Responsibility

In short-term groups especially, the leader should be directive when necessary (MacKenzie, 1993, pp. 442–443). The group should not be allowed to engage in general discussions or any activity that is not immediately useful therapeutically. Make it clear to clients what constitutes therapeutic work and keep them on track. Be explicit about group norms and active in promoting them and discouraging behavior that violates them. Whenever the discussion starts to wander, rather than allowing the process to unfold, intervene promptly to steer the dialogue back into a therapeutic direction.

However, let clients know that you expect them to take responsibility for their work rather than giving them the impression that you will do it for them. Clients should be expected to formulate their goals and means of working on them in collaboration with the leader, and to pursue these goals directly. *For example, if a client is discussing an issue that isn't directly related to his reason for being in the group and doesn't seem to be exploring himself, you could ask him why he is talking about that issue.*

It is useful to make an explicit distinction between story telling and self-explora-tion, as discussed in the next chapter, and vigorously promote self-exploration.

> For example, if a client seems to be telling a story, I will ask him to explore what he can learn about himself from the incident, giving examples of how to explore oneself. If he persists in story telling, I will ask him to look at why he is afraid of exploring himself or what he gets out of story telling. If even this doesn't have an effect, I may question whether he really wants to work on himself.

If handled properly, the time constraints in a short-term group can not only be navigated but also used for therapeutic advantage. The pressure of having a limited time to accomplish one's therapeutic goals can induce clients to take more responsibility and work harder in the group. The leader can foster this by keeping the group schedule in the minds of the members, for example, by reminding them when the group is halfway through and when there are only a few weeks left. This motivates clients to focus on their therapeutic goals and make the best use of their limited time.

☐ Motivation

Motivation and direction are two important processes that are related to responsibility. We will discuss each of them in turn and various ways that the group leader can foster them.

Motivation refers to a client's desire to change and willingness to do the work required to make change happen. People often come to therapy without being prepared to make the changes required for their pain to abate. *For example, someone may want his depression to vanish but not be willing to assert himself or express anger even though that's part of what is needed to lift the depression.* It isn't enough for a client to agree that he has a problem; he must be actively interested in changing. To enhance motivation, it is helpful to make a clear connection between a client's presenting problems and the work necessary to address them. *For example, you could explain that suppressing aggression is one of the causes of depression.* It also helps if other group members can validate the need for this work and how it has helped them.

Lack of Motivation.   Motivation can especially be difficult when a client's problems are ego-syntonic, that is, when her behavior affects other people adversely but doesn't directly cause her pain (and may even be gratifying). *For example, suppose Sandra takes up too much group time because she needs a lot of attention and is insensitive to other people's needs. It may not be easy to get her interested in changing this.* You might try to motivate this client by relating her problematic behavior to problems she is having in life, especially her original reasons for joining group. *For example, if you can relate Sandra's insensitivity to her isolation and lack of friends, she may become interested in changing it.* It is especially helpful for the client to get feedback from other group members about how her behavior affects them. *For example, if Sandra hears that people are turned off by her insensitivity to their needs, she may become motivated to look at her monopolizing.*

Some group members have difficulty being motivated to change because change itself is threatening to them. For some, this is because they are invested in certain core issues, perhaps because of secondary gain. Others, because of autonomy issues, may experience any change as a capitulation to the therapist's control. They must defeat you by failing in therapy. Still others may be frightened to make changes because of resistance from their spouse or family.

Supplying Motivation from the Outside.   With clients who are severely lacking in motivation, especially those who are depressed, frightened, or genuinely hopeless, the leader or group can sometimes motivate their work temporarily. Group members will often exhort someone to work on an issue and express their desires for the person to change his life for the better. The group leader can express a desire for the person to undertake certain work so he can feel better. In the best scenario, such a boost of concern and encouragement can be helpful in keeping the person working, and when he has made some progress, his own motivation will take over. However, with some clients encouragement will backfire. They will experience it as pressure and control, causing them to rebel, sometimes even sabotaging their own efforts.

Confidence in the Therapy Process.   Motivation is considerably enhanced when clients have some confidence in the therapy process and feel hopeful about achieving the changes they want. This is best fostered through testimonials from long-time group members. When people who have been in the group for a while share how much it has helped them, this is very encouraging for new group members. For this reason, as well as others, it is good to encourage group members to report on the successes in their own lives (as well as the problems) and especially the ways that the group has helped them change.

Confidence is also engendered when the leader is confident. You might tell a client directly that you are confident that he can make the changes he wants (if indeed you feel that way). It can also help to explain to new members how therapy works, so that a client gets a sense of your knowledge and belief in the process. We sometimes forget that clients don't really understand much about how therapy operates, and some teaching can be very useful for building confidence. However, even more important than anything you say explicitly, the group members should experience your confidence implicitly. If you have faith in the efficacy of the group therapy process from your experience leading groups and from your own personal therapy, this will emerge naturally in your manner of handling questions and insecurities. If you are an inexperienced leader, this confidence can be derived from your personal experience of growth in a therapy group. Clients also gain confidence gradually as they recognize the changes they are making in group. Therefore make sure to validate and clarify the ways that people are growing and encourage other group members to do so.

It takes courage to try out new behavior, to risk shame and rejection, to face pain and fear, in other words, to do the work required for success in group therapy. This courage is enhanced if the client has confidence in the therapy process and is motivated to work.

☐ Self-Direction

Self-direction is closely related to responsibility. Self-direction means that a client understands his issues and how he needs to work on them. It also means keeping track of his feelings toward other group members and the growth he has made. A person who provides his own direction is an active, interested participant in his own growth process, not a passive bystander, expecting to be "fixed" by the group leader.

Taking the Work Home

It is very helpful if clients actively think about the group and their work between sessions. After an important interchange in group or a remark that stirred up feelings, you hope that the client will ponder what happened during the week. Such reflection can help clients achieve a deeper understanding of the meaning of their feelings or the transferential origins of their reactions. Sometimes they recognize how their behavior in group reflects larger patterns in their lives. Sometimes they realize that they said something hurtful to someone else. The private time away from group can allow clients to understand things that they might avoid or deny in the heat of the group. Clients can also use this time to plan the next work they need to initiate.

However, all this can happen only if the client takes the time at home to ponder what happened in group and to explore himself. If he forgets about the group until the next time he steps into the leader's office, he loses the opportunity for much potentially valuable processing. If the client has an individual session or consultation with the leader between groups, then much of this can be done in that setting, with the leader's help. But this is often not possible, so the client's ability to work outside of group has a profound influence on the course of therapy.

Working outside of group can involve more than just thinking about the group. It also means consciously applying what has been learned in group to other situations in the person's life. By experimenting in ordinary life with new behavior learned in group, clients can enhance the effectiveness of the therapy process.

Fostering Self-Direction

The leader can foster an attitude of responsibility by asking each group member to reflect on the following questions:

1. *Group Goals.* Why is he in group, and what does he want to get from group in the long run, especially with regard to changes in his interpersonal functioning? *For example, a client might have joined the group because he feels isolated and lonely and wants friends or a love relationship. Or a client may have joined because he feels shy or because he is constantly in conflict with others.* Goals may also include relief from specific symptoms such as depression or anxiety.

2. *Issues.* What issues is he currently working on in group? What specific behaviors is he ready to change? *For example, a person might be working on being more involved with the people in the group, or being more assertive, or more vulnerable.*

3. *Strategy.* How does he plan to work on his issues? *For example, if someone is working on vulnerability, he might experiment with sharing painful things from his life in an open way. Or alternatively, he might decide to stop defending himself with anger when he feels rejected by others and instead let himself feel the hurt.*

4. *Work.* What particular work does he need to initiate with another member (or with the group as a whole)? This work may entail using a specific strategy that he has

chosen. *For example, if he is working on allowing his hurt to show, he might share with the group a recent situation when someone hurt him.* Alternatively, this work could emerge as a result of feelings towards a group member or towards the group. *For example, he may be feeling hurt by someone who seems to be ignoring him. He could decide to let this person know about the hurt in a vulnerable way.*

Consultations are an especially good place to bring up these questions, but they can also be discussed in group. The important thing is to let clients know that it is their responsibility to keep track of these issues. This is especially important in time-limited groups because of the need for focused and rapid movement.

Re-Evaluating Direction

Periodically, a client needs to re-evaluate his direction by discussing the above questions, particularly if he has been floundering or feeling dissatisfied with the group. Don't be afraid that this will encourage him to terminate. A re-evaluation only triggers termination when it is indeed appropriate. In fact, if a client doesn't re-evaluate when he is dissatisfied or needs to develop new goals, he is more likely to terminate prematurely.

Providing Direction

When direction is not provided by the client, it can sometimes be provided by the group leader or other group members on a temporary basis. However, this can backfire if the client doesn't want it. As with motivation, direction should be provided from outside only when needed and eventually needs to come from the client himself.

Example: As mentioned before, in the early stages of his group work, Harry was very responsible for directing his work. He knew what issues he wanted to work on, and he would frequently come to a group meeting having chosen someone to interact with. However, this attitude was related to his tendency to be overly responsible rather than free or spontaneous. As he grew and let go of being so responsible, he initially felt confused and helpless about what to do in group. He would begin a piece of work, and then not know what he wanted to do. Sometimes he would follow my directions, but often the group members would try to help him by providing direction. This backfired because, through the lens of his core issue, he perceived their attempt to help him as a judgment. He imagined that they weren't pleased with him for feeling confused and helpless. He responded in a passive-aggressive way by becoming even more unable to direct himself and by not accepting the help that was offered. He argued with the group members who offered suggestions. Even when he did good work in group, he rarely appreciated what he had done, expressing dissatisfaction with the group and with himself.

Eventually Harry was able to recognize that he resented any help that was offered. He told the group members that he wanted to be accepted just as he was. With my help in understanding what Harry needed, they responded well to this and backed off in a caring way. After a few weeks, he began to feel that he had carved out enough space to be himself, and he let go of the passive-aggressive defense. He gradually began to take charge of his work again, but now in a more spontaneous way by noticing what was happening in the moment rather than planning it out ahead of time. For example, in one group he noticed that he was holding back on his passion in an interaction with another group member and connected this to a lack of passion in his life. When he took a significant risk by challenging someone in group, he validated himself for this. He thus had regained his ability to direct his own work, but now in a healthier way.

Contracts

Sometimes it is useful for a group member to take responsibility for undertaking certain work as the group proceeds. Once an issue has been identified and the client is interested in working on it, the leader can suggest a particular contract. This can be done in consultations or in the group, in which case other group members are available to help.

Awareness Contracts.   In an awareness contract, the person tries to notice whenever a certain issue arises for her in the group. *For example, Kate realized that when she perceives someone as controlling, she gets frightened and withdraws emotionally. So she agreed to an awareness contract where she would try to notice when this happens in the group and talk about it.* Once a person brings up such an issue, then you can work with her further to achieve more access or to experiment with new behavior.

Access Contracts.   Sometimes an issue comes up when someone else is working and it is inappropriate to interrupt. *For example, if Kate becomes frightened when one person is exerting power over another, she may need to wait until the end of the work to bring it up.* In this case, you may want to suggest an access contract, where the person not only becomes aware of an issue but explores what is behind it. *While Kate is waiting, she could explore what gets triggered in her when she observes someone being controlling.*

Other reasons may prevent a person from mentioning an issue at the moment he is aware of it.

For example, remember Richard has difficulty in speaking in group. You might suggest an awareness contract in which he will notice when he has something to say and is holding it back. However, because of his fears, he may not be able to tell the group when he is resisting speaking. Then Richard could silently explore what scares him about speaking in group.

Experimenting Contracts.   Sometimes a person's issue is clear enough that you know he needs to experiment with new behavior. This can be included in an experimenting contract. *For example, a man tends to refrain from expressing any discomfort or annoyance with anyone in group. It would be useful to set up a contract where he will try to express his negative feelings when they come up.*

Feedback Contracts.   Sometimes when a person is given feedback on problematic behavior, he doesn't know what people are referring to. *For example, the group may tell Eric that he acts arrogant at certain times, but he isn't aware of this. Eric could agree to a feedback contract with the group members where they will point out to him when they think he* *is doing this.* A feedback contract can also be useful between two people. *If it is only Sally who experiences Eric as arrogant, then he could ask her to tell him when she perceives this. The feedback can help Eric find out what he is feeling and doing that is perceived as arrogant. It remains to be seen if he will agree with this perception or want to change.*

A feedback contract can also be useful when a person is sure he wants to change certain behavior but doesn't know when he is doing it. *For example, Eric might realize that he is arrogant and want to be different, but he may have trouble being aware of when he is doing it. Therefore he could ask the group to help him by telling him when he is being arrogant.*

Clarifying Motivation.
Whenever a contract is being set up, make sure that the group member really wants to do it. Otherwise he can feel that something is being imposed on him, leading to resentment and resistance. Especially with feedback contracts, the person must be truly interested in working on the issue or at least finding out what is bothering people. Otherwise the client may experience the feedback as judgmental and hurtful, and no useful work will result. *For example, if Eric is not interested in hearing about his arrogance and someone gives him feedback about it, this may simply start an argument.*

10

CHAPTER

Self-Exploration—Awareness and Insight

This chapter deals with the important group norm of self-exploration. Clients are in the group to explore their feelings and reactions for therapeutic purposes, not simply to express themselves or form friendships. We look at two important skills that clients learn to help them explore themselves—awareness and insight.

☐ Self-Exploration

Self-exploration means that, in talking about himself or interacting with someone, a client has the intention to understand more about himself psychologically. He isn't just telling a story about himself or seeking practical advice. He isn't simply interested in expressing his opinion or venting his feelings. He doesn't just want to tell other members what's wrong with them or help them change. Whenever a group member engages in these activities without using them for exploring himself, you might ask him what he intends to gain from them in order to point him in the direction of self-exploration. If a client repeatedly avoids self-exploration, you should challenge him explicitly. *For example, the leader might say, "I notice that you are telling the group another story without exploring what you can learn from it."* You should make clear to the group members that they are in the group to explore themselves, and they should learn to recognize when someone is exploring himself versus engaging in other behavior. If repeated suggestion does not induce a client to explore himself, help him explore this resistance.

Problem Ownership. Clients may avoid self-exploration because they don't want to own responsibility for a problem. When two people are interacting, self-exploration often gets sidetracked when one person blames the other person rather than exploring his own reaction to her. *For example, one member says to another, "That was a controlling, obnoxious thing to say." Because this is about the other person, you might ask, "What is your emotional reaction to what was said?" or "What is going on with you that you needed to say that right now?" If the person realizes it, he might say, "I felt intimidated when she said that."*

It can be helpful to explain that confrontations can often benefit both parties. The feedback given to the person being confronted often contains some truth, and the person who is confronting can often learn about the core issue that was behind his need to confront. This is an important norm to establish because people so readily assume that any difficulty is due to the other person.

Helping Others.   Self-exploration can also get sidetracked in the name of helping others—for example, facilitating or offering comfort or advice. Helping isn't always a defense, but if you sense that more is going on than a simple desire to be of assistance, ask the helper to explore his investment in the process. He may realize that he strongly identifies with her, or that he is really annoyed at her, or feels sorry for her, and so on. Then he can explore what this means to him psychologically.

Exhibiting Problematic Behavior

Suppressing Problematic Behavior.   In most cases, engaging in interactive work brings out a client's problematic interpersonal style. He shows his tendency to be combative, self-effacing, mistrustful, or judgmental, for example. In some cases, however, a client realizes that certain behavior of his is problematic, and therefore he suppresses it in group in the hopes of being liked.

> For example, a man who is critical of powerful women may hide these judgments from the group when they come up. A woman who tends to mistrust other women may conceal her suspicions under a veneer of politeness.

This is understandable. If a person is aware of problematic behavior, it is natural to attempt to suppress it. Fearful of being criticized or even ostracized from the group, the person will do his best to fit in. Some clients even believe that suppressing their negative actions constitutes good therapeutic work. Because the group is a place to learn new healthier behavior, they think they should suppress their problematic behavior. If a client were actually able to work through his difficulties and substitute healthy ways of relating, then this could be healing; however, he usually ends up simply adding another layer of defenses on top of those he was already using.

> For example, if a man has a tendency to get angry and competitive with other men, he would need to work this through and replace it with the healthy behavior of connecting with men. If he only suppressed his anger and was distantly polite with the other men in the group, this wouldn't be a step toward therapeutic change but toward greater defense.

The Value of Exhibiting Problematic Behavior.   Therefore the self-exploration norm requires clients to demonstrate their problematic behavior and feelings in group. Group members should expect that they are going to have the same kinds of interpersonal problems in group that they do in their lives, at least initially. Whatever problems they have in relating to people in their lives will likely show up in group. In fact, we hope that this is true. If one of a person's problems doesn't emerge in group, he won't be able to explore it. *Suppose a client has a certain way of relating that emerges only in intimate love relationships, for example, jealous rage.* Usually there will be an analogue of this behavior that occurs with other people, so it can be worked on in group. *For instance, the person may get angry when two people in group are connecting and he feels left out.*

In rare instances, a client may have certain problematic behavior that only happens with a spouse or lover, for example, and not in group. Then he can work on this problem only by talking about how it happens outside group, which is far less effective than through group interaction.

When a core issue is activated in group, the client doesn't always have to act out the problematic behavior; talking about the feelings can be enough.

> For example, a client who is feeling judgmental toward other group members may be reluctant to express these judgments for fear of alienating the group. This is understandable, but he needs to tell the group that he is feeling judgmental, even if he doesn't go into the details. Thus he can work on understanding and accessing the issues behind the judgments.

Encouraging the Norm.   Often group members hide their difficult behavior at first, gradually letting it show as they become more comfortable and trusting in the group. The leader can encourage the norm of exhibiting problematic behavior in the following ways.

1. As part of their preparation for group, new group members should be told about the value of showing their problems in group.

2. If a client acts out behavior that is noxious for the other group members, and they criticize him, the leader can remind the group that the client is only doing what they all must do in order to heal, showing his difficulties in group. This also helps to reduce the shame the client might be feeling.

3. Sometimes a client complains that the same problems are occurring in group as in his life and therefore questions the value of the group.

    > For example, Paul came to the group partly because he lived an isolated, lonely existence. After a few months in the group, he was feeling left out and rejected by the group members. He complained that he had come to group to solve this problem and it was happening here, too. He was considering leaving the group. The leader reminded Paul that, as could be expected, he had brought his customary ways of relating into the group, and this is a necessary first step in the therapy process. Paul was both alienating the other members by being overly critical and perceiving himself as more excluded than he really was. Now that he had acted out the issue, Paul could begin to explore it.

4. In an individual consultation, you may realize that a client hasn't been able to work on a presenting issue because he isn't showing it in group. Explain the value of doing this and work with him on his fears of showing this part of himself.

Acting Out Versus Experimenting

Let's discuss here one way that the self-exploration norm is promoted in many psychodynamic groups. Clients are encouraged to talk about their feelings rather than acting on them. "Acting out" typically refers to a client acting on a feeling to avoid experiencing and exploring it. I recognize that sometimes group members act out their feelings instead of exploring them, hence my discussion in chapter 3 on the difference between healing and gratification. However, there are many valid reasons for expressing or acting on feelings and these should not be prohibited.

Different Views of the Change Process.   My disagreement with the psychoanalytic view of acting out derives, I think, from fundamentally different views of the therapeutic change process. The traditional psychodynamic view of change focuses primarily on access, on making the unconscious conscious. In group work, this means that group members notice their emotional reactions to each other, the leader, and the group, and explore the meaning and origins of these reactions. Change is believed to come from understanding one's reactions and their sources and not from trying out new healthy behavior or from the healing possibilities of group relationships. At least this is the perspective of analytic theory. I suspect that many psychodynamic group leaders sense that there is more to therapeutic change than this.

By allowing and encouraging clients to act on their needs and feelings in the context of a strong norm favoring self-exploration, we have a chance to see the operation of their core issues and defenses in interpersonal interactions, providing much material for exploration.

> For example, suppose a client has a tendency to reassure other people through touch in order to unconsciously get her own needs met. If a group norm prohibits touching (because it is considered acting out), this client won't show this kind of problematic behavior and therefore won't be able to explore it.

Experimenting.   There is a fine line between acting out and experimenting with new healthy behavior. Both involve taking action, and it isn't always clear at first when an action is healthy and when it is an avoidance of self-exploration. Experimenting is much too important a part of the therapeutic change process to risk restricting it by prohibiting all acting out. The leader must certainly challenge clients who are acting out rather than exploring themselves, but this must be tailored to each particular situation rather than having a blanket rule against acting out, which might inhibit healthy experimenting.

> For example, if a client feels a need for support and comfort from the group and has a tendency to deny her needs, then it is important for her to ask for what she needs, not just talk about her feelings. She might thus request nurturing physical contact, which is considered acting out by some therapists. However, experimenting with this need could lead to explore her fears about asking for support. A rule against acting out would short-circuit this work, which could be an important part of her healing.

The Value of Holding Back on Experimenting.   In some situations experimenting may be premature in the change process, and holding back on it can open up deeper material to be accessed.

> For example, Marty was working on his fear of reaching out to women he was attracted to sexually. In talking to such a woman in group, he overcame his fears enough to tell her about his attraction and reach out to hold her hand. On the one hand, this was healthy experimenting. On the other hand, Marty was bypassing access and therefore the healing that followed wasn't as deep as it could have been. The group leader asked him to hold back on reaching out to the woman while he explored more deeply the origins of his fears. Marty got in touch with how he expected to be ridiculed for showing his sexuality and connected this with a couple of incidents from his childhood. This increased access led to a deeper kind of therapeutic change.

However, despite the value of holding back in some cases, it isn't wise to have a group norm specifying that clients should always hold back. Each particular situation must be evaluated on its own merit.

☐ Levels of Communication

In teaching clients about self-exploration, it helps to bring their attention to levels of communication that go beyond content. I find it useful to distinguish three levels of any statement. The *content level* refers to the explicit meaning of the words. The *emotional level* pertains to the emotions being expressed. The *relational level* refers to what the statement says implicitly about the relationship between the people involved—closeness, power, boundaries, and so on.

> Let's look at an example. Suppose Andy says to Jake, "I can't stand the way you are so judgmental." The content of this statement is about Jake's being judgmental. He could respond to this by discussing whether he thinks he is judgmental. The emotional level of this statement has to do with Andy's anger at Jake. Jake could respond to this by talking about his emotional response to Andy's anger. He might feel hurt or threatened or angry in return. At the relational level, what does this statement say about the relationship between Andy and Jake? This level isn't so obvious from the words, though it might be plain from Andy's tone of voice, facial expression, or body language. Maybe he is implying that he doesn't want anything more to do with Jake. Maybe he is saying that Jake should stop being judgmental. Possibly he is making this statement because he wants to work through this problem so he can be closer to Jake.

As a group leader it is important to be aware of all three levels of communication. Though the emotional and relational levels may be expressed in words, they are often apparent only by paying attention to non-verbal clues. It is also important to train group members to notice and be able to communicate at each of these levels. Most people are used to paying attention almost entirely to the content level and notice the other levels only when things get heated emotionally. In the beginning of a group, direct people's attention continually to the emotional and relational levels, not because they are more important than the content, but because they are usually ignored. People frequently react to each other's emotional and relational communications but aren't aware of this because they are focused on content. A good way to help clients understand these other levels and learn how to explore themselves is through teaching them awareness skills.

☐ Awareness

In an interactive therapy group, the vast majority of the therapeutic material is derived from what happens in the group in the moment. Therefore, group members need to learn how to become aware of what they are feeling and experiencing at the moment it is happening. The concept of awareness goes beyond the usual meaning of "here and now," which often just refers to events that occur inside the group rather than outside. Borrowed from Gestalt therapy,[9] *awareness* refers to the experiencing and labeling of what a person is feeling *at the moment* it is happening, including emotions, thoughts, images, body sensations, motivations, actions, and anything else that can be experienced.

The Value of Awareness

Awareness is useful for a number of reasons:

1. It gives group members the most information about their inner experience, reactions, and conflicts, because they don't have to rely on memory (other than very short term memory) but can investigate their experience at the time it occurs.

2. Many interesting reactions pass quickly and can be missed if attention isn't paid to them at the time they happen.

3. Awareness often takes a person deeper into her experience. Paying conscious attention to an experience at the moment it is happening invites it to open further. If the person is feeling an emotion that is partially hidden or blocked, becoming aware of it often leads to a deeper, fuller experience of the emotion. If the emotion contains hidden meaning, awareness may encourage the meaning to unfold. If the emotion is based on memories or transference, awareness makes it more likely that the memories will surface.

---

[9] Because I have a background in Gestalt therapy and use its concepts in various places in this book, I will provide here a brief introduction to this approach for those who are not familiar with it. Gestalt therapy emphasizes awareness of what one is experiencing in the moment as the most important aspect of therapy. A Gestalt therapist has an understanding of good functioning and notices when a client is blocking his natural, healthy way of relating to others. This is brought to the client's attention so he can experience how he is doing this in the moment and his underlying feelings and motivation. He can then experiment with new healthier behavior. The Gestalt approach values body awareness, emotional expression, spontaneity, contact with others, and the ability to mobilize healthy aggression in the service of getting one's needs met. Because of its existential orientation, importance is placed on the client's being responsible for herself and the therapist not being overly supportive.

4. By becoming aware of what's happening at the time it is happening, the person has the option to get immediate feedback from other group members that is relevant to this awareness. *For example, if Lisa becomes aware of feeling weak and needy, she can find out if that is indeed what she is showing to other people.*

5. The person can also experiment with new behavior based on her awareness of the moment. *For example, Lisa could experiment with asserting herself in order to develop her strength. While experimenting with assertiveness, she could also notice how the new behavior feels to her and use that awareness to modify her experiment.*

6. Awareness is the primary means of achieving access. Even access to the childhood origins of transference reactions derives from a person's experience in the moment. If a client remembers an event or speculatively reconstructs an event without experiencing his immediate emotions, he can only gain intellectual understanding. The aliveness of the here-and-now experience leads to the deepest access. Being aware of one's experience in the moment with an intent to access its origins often leads to reliving childhood experiences in an emotionally vivid way. This deepest level of access can lead to the most enduring therapeutic change.

7. Awareness can lead to presence, as described in chapter 12.

Awareness as a Skill

Awareness is a skill that group members develop gradually. There are many levels of awareness. At first a client may only be able to notice thoughts and strong emotions, while as her skill improves she will be able to sense defended feelings, additional reactions, hidden conflicts, and other repressed material. In addition, it requires considerable skill for a client to be aware when under stress, especially the stress of an intense interpersonal dialogue with another group member.

Promoting Awareness.   One of the primary ways to help clients develop awareness is to ask about it. In various situations, the leader can ask a group member what she is experiencing right in the moment. It is especially useful to ask this question when someone is reacting to something said to her.

If a client is not in touch with her experience at the moment, the leader (or other group members) can suggest what she may be experiencing, based on observing facial expression, tone of voice, gestures, and posture. The leader should highlight the tentative nature of these comments. *You might say, "You look sad right now. Does that fit your experience?"* The client is the ultimate judge of what she is experiencing, even though she might be defending against it. When a client isn't in touch, you could suggest what you might be feeling in the same situation.

> For example, "I would probably feel some hurt right now if I were receiving all of the criticism you've gotten." It can also be helpful to list some alternatives for the confused person to choose from. "You might be feeling rejected or dismissed or resentful or disappointed."

Body Awareness.   If a client is having difficulty getting in touch with what she is feeling at a given moment, it helps to ask her to notice what sensations she is feeling in her body. Emotions frequently have a bodily component that can be sensed. For example, sadness can be felt as a burning in the eyes, anger as a clenching of the jaws or a feeling of power in the arms, fear as a trembling in the chest, love as a melting sensation in the heart. Defenses against feelings can also be experienced in the body. A defense against anger might be experienced as shoulder tension, a defense against sadness as tightness in the chest, and so on. Sleepiness or restlessness might indicate feelings that are being suppressed. By exploring her somatic reactions, a client can not only identify emotions more easily, but also experience them more fully.

Insight from Awareness.   Often when a new group member is invited to explore what he is feeling, he will take an observer stance with respect to his own experience. He will look at his behavior as if he were another person and try to figure out what is happening using logic and his knowledge of psychology. This means ignoring the most important source of information about himself—his own internal experience. This approach is common because of the overly intellectual orientation of our society. Trained to use their intellect in an abstract, alienated way, people are given no education in self-awareness and introspection. Though purely intellectual analysis has its benefits, they are of limited value in psychotherapy.

When working with a person who is theorizing about his own experience, explain that he will get more accurate and useful information if he goes into his emotions, allowing insight to emerge spontaneously from his experience rather than from intellectual analysis. Especially for people with little skill in awareness, this kind of learning requires considerable practice, but it develops more quickly in a group setting where clients can learn from watching others.

Questions Versus Interpretations

Many approaches to therapy use interpretation as the main form of intervention. Although it is useful to have in mind a deeper understanding of a client's patterns and psychodynamics, I don't recommend leading with this insight. By doing this, you take the responsibility for the therapy process away from the group member and place it with the group leader. You foster the idea that clients only need to express themselves and you will figure out what is going on. This disempowers group members and encourages passivity and dependence. By asking questions about awareness, you make it clear that clients are in charge of noticing and understanding their experience. Even when you are looking for childhood origins, it's preferable to ask questions, thereby encouraging clients to come up with their own insights into the roots of their current reactions.

It is valuable to have an understanding, or at least a hypothesis, about each client's deeper psychodynamics, but I prefer to use this as a guide for my facilitations rather than stating it directly in an interpretation. Understanding childhood origins is especially necessary when you are working with more troubled clients with personality disorders. They often have such deep and intense unconscious reactions that awareness skills aren't enough to access this material. It is crucial to have a framework for understanding underlying dynamics to guide your work with these clients. I am indebted to object relations theory and self psychology for providing much of this information.

If you ask a question and a client is unable to access their current experience or deeper dynamics, then it may be useful to offer an interpretation. When it is done in this way, as a last resort, the interpretation can help educate the person about how to be aware of her internal process without disempowering her.

Facilitating Awareness

The next few sections illustrate how a group leader can facilitate awareness in clients by asking certain questions. At any given moment, a person's consciousness includes a number of thoughts, emotions, and sensations, and therefore different questions may be required to uncover all that is relevant. In the three most common situations, you may be trying to facilitate a client's awareness of (a) her response to another group member, (b) a certain behavior of hers, and (c) how she is avoiding taking a certain action.

Awareness of Response. Let's examine the situation where one person (let's call her Joanne) is responding to something said by another (let's call him Jason). Suppose Jason tells Joanne that he thinks she is wrong about something. It might be useful for Joanne to be aware of her emotional reaction, what Jason did that elicited this feeling, and the meaning Joanne attributed to Jason's behavior. Joanne might also have another feeling underlying the first one she is aware of. Let's look at each of these possibilities in turn.

1. *Feeling.* What Joanne is feeling emotionally in response to Jason. You might elicit this by asking the following question (therapist to Joanne): "How are you responding to what Jason just said?" This might produce the following awareness (Joanne to Jason): "I'm aware that I'm angry at you." Notice that the leader asks questions, but the members respond to each other. This style of unobtrusive facilitation is a simple norm that group members pick up relatively easily. At first you may have to say, "Tell Jason how you are responding to what he just said."

The above can be summarized as follows:

Question: "How are you responding to what Jason just said?"

Awareness (to Jason): "I'm aware that I'm angry at you."

2. *Perception.* What Joanne perceived in Jason's behavior that elicited her response. In other words, what did Jason do that triggered this feeling in Joanne?

Question: "What are you angry about?"

Awareness (to Jason): "I'm angry because you told me I was wrong."

3. *Meaning.* The meaning Joanne attributed to Jason's action, which elicited her response. In other words, what did Jason's behavior mean to Joanne, especially what did it say about his relationship with her?

Question: "What does that mean to you?"

Awareness (to Jason): "I feel like you are attacking me and putting me down."

Because this meaning may come from a core issue, it is occasionally useful to ask further questions that elicit information about the self- and other-representations involved (see chapter 1, Basic Concepts).

The image of Jason that contributes to the meaning (other-representation).

Question: "How do you see Jason in this interaction?"

Awareness: "I see him as a powerful authority figure who wants to make me feel bad."

The self-image of Joanne that contributes to the meaning (self-representation).

Question: "How do you see yourself in this interaction?"

Awareness: "I see myself as a person being unfairly attacked who must protect herself."

4. *Underlying feeling (and meaning).* Often one emotional reaction defends against or covers a second one.

Question: "What more vulnerable feelings might be underneath your anger?"

Awareness: "I feel frightened and bad about myself."

The above quotes are ideal responses given for illustrative purposes. In actual group work, most clients won't have such an easy time knowing exactly what your questions mean or being aware of their experience. You will often have to explain more carefully and perhaps dialogue with a client for her to fully understand what you are inquiring about.

Awareness of Behavior.   A second situation involves a person's awareness of her behavior, usually a verbal communication. Suppose Joanne makes a provocative remark to Jason.

1. *Behavior.* The actual behavior, especially its interpersonal ramifications.

Question: "Are you aware of what you just did?"

In this case, a question is often insufficient, so feedback is necessary, from the leader or a group member.

Feedback: "That remark seemed pretty provocative."

Awareness: "Yes, I see that my comment was provocative."

2. *Motivation.* Joanne's underlying motivation for making the remark.

    Question: "Do you have any sense of why you made that remark in that way just now?" or "Do you sense what response you may have wanted to produce in Jason?"

    Awareness: "I now realize that I wanted to get him riled up" or "I'm not aware of any hidden agenda. I was just expressing my anger."

Awareness of Avoidance.   A third situation is one in which a person is avoiding some action. Suppose Elizabeth is being unusually silent in group.

1. *Avoided action.* The action or communication that Elizabeth is avoiding.

    Question: "Is there anything you are avoiding doing or saying right now?"

    Awareness: "I'm avoiding telling about a success of mine."

2. *Feared response and feeling.* The response that Elizabeth is afraid of receiving and the feeling that would bring up in her.

    Question: "If you mentioned your success, what are you afraid would happen?"

    Awareness: "I'm afraid of being ridiculed and feeling ashamed."

Ideally as group members learn awareness skills, they increasingly examine their experience in the moment without needing to be asked. Then these specific questions need to be used only when someone has missed something important or is so emotionally involved that she needs outside guidance.

Following Process

An important way of teaching and working with awareness is to follow the client's moment-to-moment process closely during a piece of work. Pay careful attention to the person's constantly changing experience, as revealed by his reports on his awareness and your observations of him. You can feed back what you see and hear of the person's experience, to let him know you are with him and to encourage him to stay with his awareness. When you aren't sure where he is, you can ask him to report on his experience at that moment. Clients can learn to do this without taking themselves out of the experiential flow.

In following process, it is especially helpful to point out any striking affective responses you notice that the person may not be aware of.

> For example, a client shows a fleeting fearful reaction in her face while challenging you. Therapist: "You looked frightened just then. What happened inside?" Another example: A client is speaking about not liking something another group member said, and you see the beginnings of sadness and tears. Therapist: "This seems to be bringing up pain for you."

Many therapists focus their attention on the content of what a client is saying and its possible unconscious implications. Although this is important, tracking a person's process yields large rewards in the aliveness and relevance of what is uncovered, especially in a group setting.

Bringing Attention Back to the Moment.   Another important awareness intervention involves bringing a client's attention back to what is actually happening in the moment.

> For example, Sherry has a reaction to something Joe said, and then she explores what this means to her, how it operates in her life, and possibly its origins in childhood. At some point in this process, you might bring her attention back to what she is experiencing now. How does she feel now toward Joe? How is she feeling about exploring this in front of the group? Sometimes two people will begin with some difficult feelings toward each other and proceed to explore their relationship. After they seem to have made some progress, you might ask how they are feeling toward each other now.

Parallel Process.   Sometimes the content a person is exploring is actually being played out in the moment in her process, that is, the content level is being enacted at the emotional or relational levels. This is called *parallel process.*

> Let's take the example above where Sherry is feeling upset because of something Joe said to her. This brings up her fears of being exposed and judged. However, in her exploring these feelings, she is further exposing herself and is probably afraid of being judged about the work she is doing. Her process is parallel to the content of her exploration. At some point you might ask if she is feeling afraid of being judged about this. If not, then she has probably made some important progress, which can be appreciated. If she is afraid, this fear might be preventing her from exploring herself freely. Bringing it out into the open gives her a chance to examine this issue with the group as it is happening. She might get more clearly in touch with her fears and where they come from. She might get feedback about how people in the group are really feeling toward her.

Any time a piece of work involves parallel process, the client has an opportunity to use awareness for deeper and more vital work. And parallel process is a surprisingly common occurrence.

☐ Insight

When a person enters psychotherapy for the first time, he begins to learn how to think in psychological terms—how to look for underlying motivation, the meaning of emotions, internal conflicts, and so on. A group is particularly well-suited for this task because each person learns not only from their own work but from observing everyone else's. New group members can learn about how people work psychologically and interpersonally by watching others struggle with their feelings and conflicts. They can especially gain from other group members who are more psychologically sophisticated, who know how to explore themselves and gain insight into their issues. Clients can sometimes learn more easily from observing others' work because they aren't sidetracked by their own emotional and transferential reactions. They can often see a pattern clearly in others that they miss in themselves.

Types of Insight.   Insight is the cognitive component of self-exploration. Even though affect and intellectual understanding ideally go together as a unitary process, clients often block one or the other. In addition, it is useful to separate them for descriptive and theoretical purposes. There are three kinds of insight:

1. Understanding the current group interaction. *For example, Marcy might recognize that she feels hurt in reaction to what Ben said because she interpreted his statement as a rejection of her.*

2. Insight into how this pattern plays out in the person's life. *Marcy might realize that she frequently feels hurt by men.*

3. Insight into its childhood origins. *Marcy might understand that this pattern comes from her father's rejection of her as a child.*

Facilitating Insight

The most useful insights grow directly out of emotional experience, as discussed in the *Awareness* section. If a client stays with his moment-to-moment experience with the intention of understanding all aspects of it, insight usually arises spontaneously.

If a client seems to need help in gaining insight, the leader can ask certain questions to stimulate it. "When has this issue come up before in group?" "Is this a pattern that shows up frequently in your life?" "When do you remember feeling this way as a child?" "Who did something like this to you when you were young?"

As the person explores himself, if you empathically validate what he is saying about himself, you can encourage him to go further. If necessary, you might also gently steer him in the direction he needs to go.

If these methods fail, interpretations can also be used. These should be pitched to a depth of insight that is close to what the person senses consciously. A client can't make use of deep interpretations that go far beyond his current understanding of himself, even when they are accurate. Because most therapists are trained in how to work with people to gain insight, I won't discuss this in much detail.

The following two kinds of interpretations are particularly useful in groups.

Clarifying Interpersonal Process.

At times, two clients engage in a dialogue that becomes bogged down because of interlocking defenses or a lack of clarity. Then you should interpret what is happening so the participants can learn from it and improve their communication. Yalom (1995, p. 150) called this "process illumination." It can also come from other group members. *For example, you might say, "It seems to me that the reason this interaction has become strained is that the two of you are feeling competitive with each other over the attention of the men."* You might also ask the group members if they have ideas about what the difficulty is. *One of them might say, "I think both of you are feeling hurt about not being seen by the other, and the more you talk about this the more you each feel ignored."*

The feedback can be even more detailed. *For example, "I think that at one point Sara felt shamed by a comment of Burt's and pulled away from him. Afterwards he became more demanding that she be present with him."* If possible, make these comments at the moment that an incident occurs so that the clients can become aware of their feelings and motivations right then. However, this isn't always possible because the interpretation may involve an overall tone or pattern to the interaction rather than a single incident. *"It seems that you are both interested in understanding what the other person did wrong."*

Clarifying What Is Healthy.

One of the group leader's main jobs is framing work for clients so they understand what they are working on and what they have accomplished. This can precede an interaction as a way of directing the work; it can happen during work to stimulate insight; or it can come after a piece of work. When someone has finished work, the leader can explain what has been accomplished that was healthy or therapeutic (e.g., the client's new understanding, the access achieved, the healing accomplished, the new healthy behavior). People often make progress without realizing exactly what they have accomplished.

> For example, a man was afraid of allowing vulnerability or closeness with the group. His usual pattern was to be distant or angry or to address his issues in a way that was responsible but emotionally closed. One day he talked about his sadness at feeling disconnected from people in the group in a somewhat vulnerable way. After this work, the leader pointed out that his vulnerability was a sign of progress. The client needed to hear this because he could only see that he still wasn't feeling connected in group.

Sometimes a client acts in a way that is growthful without even being aware of this, so the leader should validate and frame her behavior as a healthy step forward.

> For example, a woman had a tendency to be pleasing and compliant, especially with the group leader. In one group, I suggested a way of understanding her process in the moment and she disagreed with me. She didn't realize that thinking for herself and disagreeing with me was an important growth step for her. So I pointed this out and expressed my appreciation for this new healthy behavior.

When a client is experimenting with behavior that is a mix of healthy and problematic, he should be supported for the healthy part, and this may require an interpretation from the leader.

For example, one group member was terrified of other people's anger, especially men's anger because his father had been so abusive and frightening. After working on this in group for a while, he began to be able to express his own anger. It came out inappropriately at times, especially when someone would remind him of his father. He needed the group's support for his newly developing and fragile anger, yet sometimes people were bewildered at his angry overreactions. It was important for the leader to interpret his anger as new healthy behavior that was being exaggerated. Then the group members could understand his process and support him.

Review

You may have noticed some similarity and overlap among the terms *access, self-exploration, awareness, insight,* and *self-direction.* Let me clarify the meanings of each of these concepts relative to each other. Self-exploration and access refer to almost the same process, looked at from different points of view. Self-exploration is a group norm valuing a certain process that involves especially awareness and insight. Awareness is both a skill that clients develop (how to know what one is experiencing in the moment) and the result of using that skill (knowing that particular experience). Insight also refers to a client skill (how to achieve intellectual understanding of psychological processes) and the result of using that skill (what one learns about oneself). Access refers to the degree or depth that one achieves in doing self-exploration, both cognitively and emotionally, and how this relates to the therapeutic change process. Self-direction involves using previously gained insight to take responsibility for directing one's own therapy process.

CHAPTER

Interactive Work

This chapter covers the important group norm that stipulates that members should focus on their interpersonal interactions and relationships with each other. First I discuss the three levels of dynamics operating in groups, highlighting the importance of the interpersonal level. After I define the interactive norm and its relationship to outside issues, I discuss various ways to foster interactive work.

☐ Levels of Dynamics

There are three types of dynamics operating in a therapy group: (a) intrapsychic (the usual psychological dynamics therapists normally explore in individual therapy, including motivation, emotions, defenses, childhood origins); (b) interpersonal (the dynamics that go on in the relationship between any two or more people in the group, including emotional reactions, closeness, assertiveness, boundaries); and (c) group as a whole (the dynamics of the group taken as a unit, including stages of development, group norms, group roles, emergent leadership, scapegoating, group-level resistance).

> Let's look at an example: Jill returned to group after missing a session. Though she gave a somewhat plausible excuse, she clearly could have chosen to come to group. Jeff was angry at her because she had missed a number of sessions recently, and he wondered about her commitment to group. Jill felt hurt but didn't show it; she tried to placate him by apologizing without really dealing with what was upsetting him. (a) At the intrapsychic level, Jeff was emotionally abandoned by his mother, and the intensity of his reaction to Jill came from this transference. (b) At the interpersonal level, Jill has a pattern of dealing with hurt by trying to placate people in a superficial way, rather than showing her hurt, or standing up for herself, or dealing directly with the content of the confrontation. (c) At the group-as-a-whole level, there had been too much absence and lateness in group, which was probably due to hidden hostility that was poisoning the group atmosphere.

At any given moment, the leader can choose to address a particular level. *For example, if you felt that absences and lateness were seriously hampering the group, you might focus on that group-level problem. You might choose instead to focus on Jill's communication pattern or Jeff's transference.*

The Value of Various Levels.   I believe that the interpersonal interactions among the members provide the greatest therapeutic leverage in a group setting. The interpersonal level stimulates the reactions and transferences that are the lifeblood of the therapy and also allows for experimenting and healing responses. The intrapsychic level is equally important because it is the domain of access.

Group-as-a-whole dynamics provide the context in which the other levels occur. The leader must monitor this level to prevent or to remedy problems in the overall operation of the group. When the group dynamics are operating smoothly the leader is free to focus on the other two levels, which provide the greatest opportunity for therapeutic healing. When the group is not working well, serious attention must be paid to the group level of operation. In Part IV, I will explore the group-as-a-whole level in more detail and discuss how other group leaders and theorists conceptualize these levels.

☐ Interactive Work

Because of the potency of the interpersonal level, the leader needs to establish early in a group that work will focus on the relationships between group members and their interpersonal interactions. The leader should strive in a variety of ways to establish the norm that interactive work is the primary focus of the group. If you are leading a group that combines interactive work with another group modality, it is especially important to establish the interactive norm, even though it isn't the only norm for the group. Otherwise group members may give short shrift to interpersonal work in favor of less threatening modalities.

Guidance at the Beginning of a Group.   Some group leaders prefer to give little guidance at the beginning of a group. In their view, it is best to allow the group to evolve in its own way with only subtle nudging from the leader in therapeutic directions. They believe that this is more natural and helps people to show their true selves for reflection and interpretation. I disagree with this approach for two reasons: (a) I don't believe there is anything natural about bringing together a group of strangers who need psychological help and offering them little guidance at first. Though this brings up powerful anxieties and interesting transference reactions, it is no more natural than starting with more guidance. (b) People will show their true selves in any group that is relatively unstructured, safe, and has good therapeutic norms. Clients carry with them their ways of interacting with others, and these naturally come out in the group setting, even when the leader provides clear guidance.

Defining Interactive Work.   Therefore, I recommend giving beginning group members as much guidance as possible on the purpose and style of group work. This is especially valuable in limited-time groups because it moves the group quickly into the most productive work. I explain to prospective members ahead of time that the group will be "interactive" and discuss what this means, making a clear distinction between interactive work and outside issues. *Interactive work* involves "Talking to someone in group about your feelings toward each other or about your relationship, or bringing up what you feel in the group or in the moment." *Outside issues* mean "Bringing up issues from your current life outside group or your past, or discussing your psychological issues in general or other topics." I explain this in the pre-group interview and in written material given to members before they join. I emphasize this distinction whenever necessary during the formative stages of a new group. No matter how much you explain beforehand what interactive work is, some people won't really get it until they have seen it in vivo a number of times and initiated interactive work themselves.

☐   Honesty

The interactive norm emphasizes the importance of clients being honest about their feelings toward others. This can be difficult for many group members because of the fear of hurting people. However, in promoting this norm, don't directly challenge a member on his honesty because this could be experienced as intrusive and undermining, thereby sabotaging the therapeutic alliance. You could say that you wonder if the person isn't saying all that he is feeling.

In general, it helps to encourage group members to challenge each other when they don't completely believe what is being said to them. Clients need permission to bring up challenges of this nature. Otherwise the group remains polite and vaguely mistrustful. If a client doesn't believe someone, she may be reluctant to speak up because she knows other members are supposed to be honest and to question someone's veracity feels like slandering his character. In addition, a person sometimes knows intellectually that someone is being truthful but feels mistrustful anyway. These feelings need to come out in the open to be explored and resolved. If you sense that a client isn't trusting what someone says to her, it can be useful to ask, "Do you believe what ———— just said to you?" Even if the client did, this intervention helps to establish the norm that challenges of honesty are acceptable.

Challenges such as these often lead to useful dialogue, in one of two ways: (a) The person acknowledges that he wasn't being fully honest and reveals his true feelings, thus clearing the air and leading to a more therapeutically useful interaction. (b) The person reasserts his honesty and explains himself more fully and emphatically. The challenger may ask more questions to clarify what seemed suspicious, and eventually she is able to believe him. This is helpful even if she knew intellectually that he was being honest. It is especially important if she was having trouble believing his positive feelings toward her. After such a dialogue, she can take this in emotionally, thus enabling inner healing to occur.

☐ The Value of Outside Issues

Though interactive work is the focus of the group, work on outside issues should not be ruled out. After all, if the group members are to develop close relationships, they must get to know each other's lives. Under the following circumstances, the leader should actually encourage work on outside issues:

1. If a client has strong feelings about an issue, especially if he is so caught in it that he can't be present in group on a particular day, then talking about the issue may relieve the emotional pressure and include the group in the person's struggle. He then can let go of it for the evening and get involved in the group.

2. If sharing the issue will help the group to know the person at a deeper level. This is especially important for new members.

3. If the outside issue is related to something happening in group. *For example, if a man is having difficulty with intimacy in the group, he might discuss intimacy issues in his marriage.*

4. If sharing the issue with the group constitutes an interpersonal challenge for the person, so that it is really interactive work. *For example, suppose a woman has difficulty asking for emotional support, and she needs help with an outside issue. Talking to the group about this issue will bring up her difficulty with support so it can be worked on interactively.*

Short-Term Groups.   Because of the need to develop cohesiveness quickly, there may not be room to explore conflict between group members in a time-limited group. Instead they focus on outside issues rather than interactions between members (Klein, 1993, p. 265), using sharing and support, psychoeducational work, or homework assignments. Experimenting can be accomplished through role playing in the group or by trying out new behavior in one's outside life rather than through encounters between group members.

> For example, if a client has difficulty saying "No" to people, rather than looking for a real situation in the group where she needs to say "No," I might have her describe a typical outside situation where this is a problem and set up a role playing exercise for her to practice this. I also might ask her to notice during the week whenever she is about to agree to something that she really doesn't want to do.

When something important is learned in the group, the client should be encouraged to think about how it can be generalized to her outside life. Clients should also be encouraged to share with the group those positive changes in their lives that are the result of the group work. Limited-time groups often start with a brief check-in where each group member shares what has happened in his life during the last week that is relevant to the focus of the group.

☐   Initiating Interactive Work

In keeping with the emphasis on responsibility, encourage group members to initiate interactive work. There are two general ways for a client to do this:

1. Express her reactions *in the moment* to an event in group or to something another group member said or did.

2. Bring up work that relates to *previous meetings or longer term issues,* especially feelings toward another member or her concerns about their relationship. Encourage her to reflect on what work needs to be done on a given night, and come to group with an idea of what to initiate.

Ways of Initiating

To be more specific, there are five ways to begin interactive work. A group member can:

1. Talk about what he is experiencing in the moment. This provides practice in awareness and can lead to any of the other possibilities below.

2. Bring up an issue with someone in group or with the leader—a reaction or feeling toward that person. This typically leads to a dialogue between the two people.

3. Reach out to someone in group or to the leader—to get to know her better or to become closer to her. Emphasize that clients don't need to have an "issue" with someone to initiate work on the relationship. Group members sometimes think they can initiate interactive work only if they have a problem with someone. In fact, they can also initiate work with people they like as a way of becoming closer. A good way to begin such work is for one person to tell the other what he likes about her.

4. Bring up an issue with the group as a whole. This could be something happening in the moment, such as feeling close to the group or angry at the group. It could also be a longer standing issue, such as feeling left out of the group or perceiving cliques in the group.

5. Ask for feedback from someone or from the group as a whole. This feedback could revolve around a specific issue, such as wanting to know if people feel intimidated by him. Or, as is common for new members, it could concern something general such as how other members are responding to him.

Spell out these possibilities so members can take responsibility for initiating interactive work.

☐ Ways of Relating

To further clarify the interactive norm, let's look at four different ways that one group member can relate to another.

Facilitation

A client attempts to help another group member (without becoming personally involved, as a group leader might) by asking questions, making interpretations, giving advice, and making suggestions.

Facilitating can occasionally be useful in a group if the person receiving it really wants it at the time. Group members with low self-esteem can benefit from discovering that their facilitations are really helpful to others. Facilitation can also be valuable when it is experienced as a sign of caring; this is often more important than the content of the help. However, if the client doesn't want facilitation or doesn't find it helpful, it can be experienced as intrusive, controlling, or insensitive. Especially if the person offering it can't let go when it isn't received. In this case, you may want to work with the person offering the facilitation on his reason for needing to give it or his lack of sensitivity to other people's needs.

The danger of a facilitation is that it can hide the real feelings of the person offering the help. Sometimes a facilitation simply comes from a desire to help, but other feelings or agendas may also be at work. *For example, Stan makes an interpretation about a woman's anger that sounds plausible, but she is put off by it. On further exploration it turns out that Stan has felt hurt by her anger in the past, and his interpretation was an attempt to get back at her.* It is especially important to prevent a client from regularly using facilitations to avoid dealing with his own feelings and issues. In this case, you can turn a facilitation back to the person by asking, "What are you feeling toward (member) right now?" or "Is there anything coming up for you that prompted you to offer that interpretation (question, etc.)?"

Some methods of group therapy encourage facilitations in the form of interpretations. Ormont (1992) calls this "bridging" and values the fact that group members become more involved with each other than if interpretations come only from the therapist. Although this is certainly true, I think it is more valuable to encourage group members to get directly involved with each other through giving feeling responses. Otherwise they can hide their own feelings behind interpretations of others.

Empathy and Identification

These are ways of responding in a parallel way to another person, resonating with the person.

For example, suppose Mary says, "I feel sad because it seems that I don't belong in this group." (a) Empathy means feeling some of Mary's sadness in resonance with her. This might be expressed as follows: "I really feel what you're going through." (b) Identification means knowing what it is like to feel what Mary is feeling you have had a similar experience or struggled with the same issue. This might be expressed as "I feel that way at work sometimes. It's a real bummer."

Empathy and identification play an important role in promoting caring, vulnerability, and group cohesiveness. They help connect people with each other and promote a sense of safety in the group. People also learn from each other's issues through identification. As one person is working on an issue, others should be encouraged to notice how the work resonates with them. They can gain valuable insight into themselves by paying attention to their reactions. In addition, if one person has a powerful experience of access, this may trigger other group members into accessing their own deeper material. Then they can each work on accessing the feelings that were brought up. However, if you are working with a group of more disturbed clients with fragile defenses, this process of contagion can be dangerous and chaotic because they may not be able to hold their feelings until they can get the leader's attention. Then you must help them learn more effective defenses and ways to contain their feelings so that the group doesn't get out of hand.

Empathy and identification can also be used to avoid confrontation or differences. Watch out for a client who relates to others only through resonating with their feelings and never by expressing his own direct feeling responses.

Perception

This means talking about one's view or understanding of another person. *For example, as a response to Mary, "It seems like you keep yourself from being part of the group."* A perception contains elements of both facilitation and feeling response. It can be useful as feedback, but make sure the person giving the perception isn't using it to avoid a feeling response. People often state perceptions as if they were feelings. *For example, "I feel like you keep yourself from being part of the group."* Make a clear distinction between perceptions and feelings, and ask for the person's feeling response when that is called for. *For example, you might say, "That's your perception about Mary. How do you feel toward her?"* For the most part, clients should be talking about themselves, not the other person. Feedback in the form of perceptions of others is certainly a valid way of responding, but not if it is used to avoid expressing one's own reactions. When you sense that there is something peculiar about the way a person expresses a perception, ask him to explore his feeling response to the other. Often instead of just a neutral observation, there is a hidden feeling response.

Feeling Response

This means expressing an emotional reaction to the other person. This could be a positive reaction, such as caring, appreciation, or support. *For example, as a response to Mary, "I want you to belong here. I care about you."* Notice that this is not the same as empathy or identification. Here the person is expressing his emotional response to Mary, not how he feels similar to her. Alternatively, it could be a negative reaction such as anger or judgment.

For example, to Mary: "I'm annoyed. There you go again feeling sorry for yourself." It also could involve a wide variety of other emotions, including envy, fear, shock, amusement, and admiration. In an interactive group, I emphasize feeling responses because they lead directly to interactive work.

☐ Fostering Interactive Work

Interactive work tends to build on itself. As group members begin to talk about their emotional reactions to each other, this generates additional emotional reactions and therefore provides more interpersonal material to work with. This positive snowball effect leads the group members more and more deeply into interpersonal work with each other. On the other hand, if group members emphasize individual work on outside issues and ignore their feelings toward each other, then over time, they have fewer feeling reactions to work with because the focus of the group has shifted elsewhere. If this happens, encourage the group members to return to interacting with each other. If they claim that they don't have many feelings toward each other to work with, this is both because they are ignoring their feelings toward each other because of the shift away from interaction. There are always some feelings among group members to work with, and once the group shifts back to interactive work, the interpersonal material will gradually increase.

Encouraging Interactive Work

Here are some suggestions for encouraging group members to do interactive work.

1. *Ask for it explicitly.* When a group has focused on outside issues for a while, it can be helpful to point this out and suggest that the next work be interactive. In the early stages of a group, you can teach group members about initiating interactive work using a simple exercise as follows: Suggest that each member think of one other person in the group toward whom she has feelings which haven't yet been expressed. Then ask someone to volunteer to begin by expressing these feelings to the person she picked. If appropriate, allow this to expand into an interaction between the two people. Then ask for another volunteer, and so on.

2. *Set up interactive work in consultations.* This is especially useful during the first few months of a person's being in the group. In the safe setting of a consultation or individual session in which only you will hear them, clients are often able to access feelings toward others in the group that do not come up in the more threatening group setting. During this consultation, ask the client to consider each group member in turn and tell you her initial impressions or feelings toward that member. After she has described her feelings, explain that she could bring out these feelings in group as a way of initiating interactive work. If she is too frightened to do this, you can work with her on her fears to help prepare her to do the work. In any case, the client should be allowed to choose when she is ready to tackle this work.

3. *Encourage people to explore their blocks.* If you notice that people seem to be avoiding interactive work, you can ask them to explore what's behind their reluctance. They might discover that they are afraid of stirring up conflict or being judged or dealing with intimacy issues. Make it clear that they can do this exploration without having to initiate the work that they are afraid of. They don't even have to divulge what it is. If this provides enough freedom for them to explore what is stopping them, they are usually quite willing to initiate the work.

4. *Point out emotional reactions.* Be on the lookout for signs of any subtle emotional reaction that one member may be having toward another or toward the group. If you point it out at the moment and ask him about what he was feeling, this will often get things rolling.

   For example, suppose the group is discussing a topic and you notice that someone rolls her eyes in response to Mary's comment. You can say, "I noticed you had a reaction just then to what Mary was saying. What was it?"

Facilitating Outside Issues

Previously we discussed those circumstances under which it is advisable to encourage clients to share outside issues. Here we look at different ways to facilitate this work.

1. In most cases, even when an outside issue is appropriate, focus your facilitation on how the client is relating to the group (and they to him) rather than on the issue itself. It is surprising how often what looks like purely outside work has important interpersonal ramifications. I discuss how to do this below.

2. In some cases if the outside issue seems particularly poignant and resonant with the group, you may want to foster group involvement by encouraging others to share similar issues they have in their lives.

   For example, if one member is dealing with the death of a parent, and others seem to have strong feelings of empathy, you might inquire if other group members are dealing with similar issues, such as other losses or similar feelings about parents.

3. While a client is sharing an outside issue, it is often useful to work with him on becoming more present while talking about it. If someone talks about an emotional issue in a matter-of-fact voice or as an entertaining story, you can help him to identify the underlying feelings and to express them to the group. Once this brings him more into contact with himself and the group, he is likely to explore the issue more deeply or interact with someone.

   For example, if a client is talking about the death of a parent by telling a story about how the family dealt with the funeral, you might say, "Check inside and see what you are feeling right now as you talk about this."

4. In certain situations, you may decide to work with the group member on the issue itself, as you would do in individual therapy. How often you do this will depend on

your personal preferences and the needs of the group members. Occasional pieces of individual work, especially if they allow deeper than usual access, can benefit the group by giving people a chance to know different parts of each other. However, you must be careful. If you allow too much individual work, most group members will begin bringing in more and more outside issues. Because interactive work is the most threatening kind of group work for most people, groups tend to slide into doing outside work if you allow this.

Moving from Outside to Interactive Work

When a person is sharing an outside issue, there are a number of interventions that can move the work in a more interactive direction:

1. Ask the group member if he has that issue with anyone in group. *For example, suppose Hank is saying that he gets intimidated by certain kinds of women. You can ask him if he has felt intimidated by any of the women in the group.* Or if you have noticed this issue in group, point it out. *For example, you could mention that Hank seemed to be intimidated by a certain woman in an earlier group meeting.*

2. Ask the person to sign an awareness contract where he will notice when he has that reaction in group and bring it up right away. *For example, ask Hank to pay attention to his interactions with women in the group and notice if he feels intimidated at any point.*

3. If the issue involves difficulties in reaching out or connecting with others, suggest that the member pick someone in group that he would like to connect with.

   For example, a man talks about how isolated and lonely he feels and how difficult it is for him to make friends. In exploring this, it emerges that he is frightened to initiate connections with people for fear they won't be interested in him. You could suggest that he pick someone in the group that he would like to get to know better (or become closer to) and experiment with connecting with that person. Of course, even picking someone and revealing this to the group may be terrifying, but he doesn't actually have to do this in order to benefit from this work. Even if he only gets as far as feeling the fear, you can then work with him on accessing the fear and learning more about it. If he is then able to reach out to the person, you can work with him on the way he expresses himself or the way he reacts to the person's response.

4. Ask how it feels to be sharing this issue with the group. How is the client feeling about the way the group is responding to him? Is it meeting his needs? This focuses the person on his interactive process with the group rather than only on the content of the outside issue.

   For example, the client might say, "Oh, it's a great relief to be saying this, because I can see that people don't think I'm ridiculous." This reveals a fear he was struggling with. On the other hand, if the client's response indicates that he is self-absorbed and out of contact with the group, you can explore this with him.

5. Ask what the group member needs or wants from the group in sharing the issue.

Typically a person will need one or more of the kinds of caring—empathy, compassion, identification, appreciation, acceptance, understanding. He may also need advice, permission, or encouragement. Often people have a hard time identifying what they need, so you may need to suggest possible alternatives. The process of struggling to identify needs can be very helpful. It also prevents the person from just telling stories without making contact with the group.

> For example, Melissa shared with the group that her daughter was having a baby as a single mother and Jamie was excited about helping her but didn't want to be too intrusive. When I asked Melissa what she wanted from the group in sharing this, she realized that it was very important for her to tell the group that she was excited and proud. The group knew that Melissa had been born out of wedlock and was made to feel tremendous shame about this as a child. She knew that the group would understand how important it was that she didn't feel any shame about her daughter's plans.

Once the person's needs are identified, you can explore the dynamics between the person and the group: (a) Is the group meeting the person's needs? (b) If so, is he taking it in? (c) Is he sharing in such a way as to keep the group from meeting his needs? He may be boring, out of contact, playing victim, and so on. (d) Is he afraid to let the group know what he needs? Does he think he doesn't deserve it, or that he will be shamed for having needs?

6. Have the client pick one group member to share the outside issue with, and explore the emotional contact between them. This is another way to explore the dynamics of the sharing, but in this case, there is a greater opportunity for the other to respond (because it isn't a whole group), and this makes the dynamics clearer and easier to work with. For example, it highlights the degree to which the client actually makes himself vulnerable to the other. And if the other person responds in a caring way, how does the client deal with that?

12
CHAPTER

Presence and Contact

This chapter covers the therapeutic group norm involving presence and contact. Through sample interventions, I illustrate how a client can move to greater degrees of presence and contact.

☐ Presence

Presence is a term that is difficult to explain and little understood in most forms of therapy. It is central to the Diamond approach (Almaas, 1988) and familiar to Gestalt therapists who sometimes refer to its as "aliveness." Presence refers to being vital, embodied, and in touch with oneself, whereas awareness refers to the ability to perceive one's experience in the moment. Presence goes beyond awareness to include a full experiential inhabiting of one's experience. Presence doesn't only mean being in touch with one's emotions or even fully expressing them. For one thing, presence doesn't just involve emotions. One can be present (or not present) for many other experiences that aren't usually called emotions—being relaxed or agitated, centered or scattered, solid or empty, or feeling vulnerable, grateful, passionate, touched. Presence sometimes has a spiritual or sacred quality to it.

Presence is valuable in itself as a healthy way of being in the world. It also leads to deeper access and facilitates inner healing. The more a person is present while they are accessing pain and receiving a healing response, the greater the chance for an inner shift. One reason is that presence enhances a person's inner experience of his healthy capacities. For example, connectedness is an inner experience that includes more than any particular emotion or experience of closeness in a relationship. A person who truly feels connected (to self and others), experiences an inner sense of warmth, trust in relating, solidity, and value to others. This is an experience of a certain kind of presence.

When a group member has a healing experience in group that could increase his sense of inner connectedness, it is crucial to know whether he is allowing this inner experience to happen or blocking it in some way. Working with the person on his blocks can lead to a sense of presence in experiencing connectedness, promoting inner healing. The same holds true for developing value, autonomy, and other capacities.

☐ Contact

Contact refers to the quality of presence in interpersonal meeting, the directness of relating in the moment. It is a concept from Gestalt therapy (Perls et al., 1951) that refers to the active engagement of a person with her environment. This meaning of contact isn't restricted to warm, intimate contact. It can also include anger, challenge, curiosity, nurturing, or any other kind of relating. Contact moves beyond facades to true interaction, thereby bringing out the most useful interpersonal material to be explored. In addition, contact facilitates healing. When two people are in contact, a healing response from one will more likely translate into inner healing for the other. Contact can be facilitated in a similar way to presence, by pointing out when it is being blocked and suggesting experiments to increase it.

The following examples show how a client can move from being less present or contactful to being more so. Each example includes a statement that shows evidence of limited presence or contact (1), the therapist's intervention (Th), and a second statement that reflects increased presence or contact (2).

☐ Being Interactive

This way of relating, which was covered in the previous chapter under the interactive norm, can also help increase contact.

In-Group Statements. Discussing how one feels in the group rather than in general is a step toward being more interactive.

(1) "I have a hard time asserting myself when I'm afraid of not being liked."

(Th) "Does that happen to you in this group?"

(2) "Yes, I'm afraid to confront people in group because I'm afraid they won't like me."

Relational Statements. Contact is enhanced even more when a client talks to a group member (or the leader) about his relationship with her or feelings toward her.

(1) "I'm afraid to confront people in group because I'm afraid they won't like me."

(Th)   "How about saying that directly to someone?"

(2)   "Jane, I am afraid to confront you because I'm afraid you'll dislike me."

The client should also talk about her feelings toward the group as long as the feelings really apply to the group as a whole and she isn't simply trying to avoid interacting with a particular person. *For example, "I feel like I don't belong in this group." or "I'm afraid to commit myself to the group. I feel like I'll be trapped."* If the person has a feeling that applies to each of the members of the group rather than to the group as a whole, then she should pick one person to work with. Then that person can respond and the leader can work with their dialogue. It is more difficult, but not impossible, for a whole group to interact with a person. In the cases where the person's feelings really are about the group as a whole, she will need to get responses from several group members.

Sometimes when a person is exploring his feelings toward one person or toward the group, his work will focus primarily on accessing his feelings and gaining insight, and so a response from others is not necessary. In this case there's no need for him to be interactive.

☐ Directness

Unqualified Statements.   Presence and contact are enhanced by making succinct statements without qualifiers that dilute the impact.

(1)   "Now, of course, this is my stuff, but sometimes I feel like you're a little defensive. Not enough to bother me. And of course, I admire how you can stand up for yourself."

(Th)   "How about saying that again without all the qualifiers that undermine the impact of what you're saying."

(2)   "I think you often get defensive."

Directness facilitates interactive work because the person's true feelings are apparent; the recipient gets the full impact; and the work is clear. However, directness is not always best. Occasionally it is healthier for a person to qualify and soften what he has to say, especially if he is very angry or the other person is fragile. This is particularly called for if the person is characteralogically hostile or has a pattern of being overly blunt and insensitive to the impact of his statements on others. Then he will need to learn tact rather than directness.

Focus.   Directness is also facilitated by encouraging a client to stay focused, to avoid bringing up tangential topics or more than one topic at once, and to keep from being distracted by other things in the room. When a client is distractible, it helps to repeatedly and gently bring her back to the task at hand, so she can complete the work. I sometimes think of this as "corralling" the person. However, you don't want her to become dependent on you to keep her focused. If focus is a repeated problem for her, bring it up as a issue, investigate its origins, and encourage her to become interested in changing it.

Statements Rather than Questions.   Sometimes questions are a way of avoiding making direct statements, so the leader can also foster directness by encouraging a person to make a statement rather than asking a question.

(1)   "Why do you think you needed to defend yourself just then?"

(Th)   "What's the statement behind your question?"

(2)   "I don't like your defensiveness."

I–You Statements.   Group members sometimes have a tendency to use "we" statements when talking about their relationships with each other. This can be confusing because it avoids responsibility for feelings and intentions. Contact is enhanced by asking people to use "I–you" statements instead.

(1)   "There is a barrier between us that keeps us from getting close."

(Th)   "Who is responsible for this barrier?"

(2)   "I perceive you as putting up a barrier to closeness with me."

Contactful Statements.   A client who is characteristically distant and intellectual may discuss his feelings toward another group member as if he were an uninterested observer rather than someone emotionally involved. If you ask him to talk directly "to" the person, rather than "about" their relationship, this heightens the contact and leads to deeper work.

☐ Emotions

Emotions and Inner Experience.   Talking about one's emotional reactions and other experiences enhances presence and contact. This is, of course, what we're looking for when we ask awareness questions. However, if the person gives an answer that doesn't really describe an emotion or other experience, you must ask for it.

(1)   "Sarah, I have a hard time with you because you're so strong."

(Th)   "What is your emotional reaction to Sarah's strength?"

(2)   "Sarah, I'm intimidated by your strength."

You can facilitate presence by asking a person to report on the details of her here-and-now experience. In addition to noticing that she feels sad, a client might also notice the quality of the sadness (e.g., wistful, stabbing pain, feeling bereft, heaviness). If you ask a client to notice where in her body she feels an emotion, this helps to increase presence. In addition, the client should have time to be with a feeling and allow it to deepen and develop.

Emotional Reactions Rather than Judgments.   It is especially important to encourage people to express their emotional reactions to others rather than their judgments. This opens up dialogue by focusing on how the people are relating to each other rather than who is right or wrong.

(1)   "You're so cold and distant."

(Th)   "How does that make you feel toward him?"

(2)   "I feel hurt because it seems like you don't like me."

It is common for people to need help moving from judgments to feelings. People who are quick to blame others whenever they feel hurt or angry need to take more responsibility for their own emotional reactions. Other people are uncomfortable about expressing anything negative to other group members. It helps them to understand that you aren't asking them to pass judgment on others but to express their own reactions. In most cases both people have something to learn from such a confrontation. *For example, there may be some truth in the perception of the other as being cold and distant, but the perceiver may also be unusually sensitive to rejection.*

Emotional Expressiveness.   Group members often block presence when they block the natural and full expression of emotions in voice, facial expression, and body language. You can point out blocks to emotional expression and suggest experiments where clients express what they are feeling in a fuller or more forceful or more vulnerable way. Someone may be able to talk about his feelings only in a detached mechanical way. A person might say he is hurt but not show any vulnerability. Someone else might talk about feeling anger, but not show any aggression. Expressing these feelings often leads to deeper insight and more vital interactions. Of course, in some cases people need to move in the opposite direction. A group member might be so emotionally liable that she needs to work on being able to talk about her feelings in a measured way, without getting carried away by them.

Congruence.   It is also useful to watch for congruence, which means a match between a person's feelings, expression, and the content of her statements. Incongruence is often an indicator of hidden feelings. It frequently manifests as inappropriate humor or smiling.

(Th)   "See what it would be like to say that without smiling."

☐ Responsiveness

Sometimes people deflect contact by not responding directly to a communication and instead pursuing their own agenda.

Gail: "I'm upset with you for not being sensitive to my pain."

Ruth (1): "It's true. We haven't connected well recently."

(Th)   "You didn't really respond to the specifics of what Jill said."

Ruth (2): "What makes you think I'm not sensitive to you?"

Sometimes people give a short, polite answer that is not really responsive.

Gail: "I admire the way you zero in on your vulnerable feelings and express them so clearly."

Ruth (1): "Thank you."

(Th)   "Say more about your emotional response."

Ruth (2): "That makes me feel close to you because I feel like you're really seeing me."

☐ Eye Contact

In addition, the presence or absence of eye contact is important. At first, you may simply need to ask someone to look at the person he is addressing, especially at the moment she is expressing feelings. Does she look down when expressing anger or look away when talking about closeness? At more advanced levels you can watch for the degree of directness of gaze and aliveness in meeting. This is particularly relevant during intimate connections. Does the person become mechanical or somewhat dissociated during close contact?

☐ Conclusions

Our society is primarily oriented toward accomplishment, control, and results. There is little appreciation of experiences like presence and contact, which really make life worth living. This overemphasis on instrumental values has contributed to many of the problems our world faces today. A therapy group can help people appreciate these other ways of being.

☐ Perspectives

Many of the group norms that have been discussed in the last five chapters can also be seen from several other perspectives:

1. Client skills. Many of them are skills that group members gradually learn to increase their ability to work effectively in group. This is especially true of awareness, insight, presence, and contact.

2. Many of them are healthy capacities that may be more available for some clients than others. Any given client will be blocked in certain of these capacities because of his history and psychodynamic issues. *For example, presence may be especially hard for someone who was punished for being direct or expressive as a child.* He will need to work specifically on these underlying issues in order to develop or liberate that capacity.

3. Social skill. All these norms or capacities are useful not only in a therapy group but also in ordinary life situations. However, some of them must be used carefully. For example, only in certain situations is it appropriate to tell someone exactly how you feel toward them. Some clients may believe that they can indiscriminately use the skills they are learning in group in their outside lives. They may express anger injudiciously or reveal their deepest secrets to the wrong people. Because group norms are not the same as social norms, group skills don't automatically carry over to ordinary interactions. These clients must work on learning how to be sensitive to the situations in their lives and the people they are communicating with, so as to determine when an action is appropriate.

The following is a list of the main therapeutic group norms covered in the last five chapters:

1. No anti-therapeutic prohibitions against certain topics or feelings

2. Vulnerability and caring

3. Group cohesiveness and individuality

4. Responsibility

5. Self-exploration

6. Interpersonal work

7. Presence and contact

CHAPTER

Transcript

This chapter contains a transcript that illustrates some concepts from the last few chapters, especially presence and contact.

Ralph and John are members of a mature group that has been meeting for over four years. John has been in the group for about three years, Ralph for a year. They have wanted to be closer to each other but had difficulties making it happen. Ralph is notorious in group for analyzing other people's unconscious process in a provocative way.

The transcript occurs near the end of a group meeting. Ralph has just made a comment about wanting to say things to people to evoke their "essence."

John: I have a hard time with your saying that. The whole concept that you see yourself as here to help or produce people's essence or to be the lightning rod. It just irritates me.

Ralph: Uh huh.

John: It makes me uncomfortable with you. Cause I'm not sure if you're seeing me, or you're seeing me-as-you-think-I-should-be, or me as you, in your divine position of essence as understanding [sarcastic]. So I get very defensive.

Ralph: Uh huh.

John: I don't know why you carry that on. I was curious about why you take that on. Why do you have to be the guy who dredges it up?

John has been making some very direct, contactful statements about his feeling toward Ralph, operating at the emotional and relational levels, but now he switches to the content level by asking Ralph to figure himself out. He ostensibly begins asking Ralph for insight, but at the emotional level, he is still expressing anger.

Ralph: Well, it's worked for me, to whatever degree …

John: It doesn't work with me.

John switches back to being direct.

Ralph: Yeah, that's true.

John: I don't see how it works for you. I don't see how it gets you closer to people.

Jay: (to John) Hold it. Let's not get into "people." It doesn't work with *you.* That's what's important right now.

I focus John on being interactive by talking about their relationship, not Ralph's pattern in general.

Jay: How are you responding to that, Ralph?

I ask Ralph for his awareness of his emotional response to John.

Ralph: Well, I mean I just watch myself dealing with it all, and there's a defensive part of me that says, "Yeah, well, you know … "

Jay: You're feeling defensive with John right now?

Ralph responded with a general statement about his feelings rather than a direct statement of feelings in the moment, so I translated his general statement into the present and asked him if he was feeling defensive now.

Ralph: Yeah, well, with him in particular, but around the theme, there is this part of me that …

Jay: Wait a minute. Stay with John, not the theme.

Ralph frequently uses insight as a defense against contact by analyzing himself endlessly. Therefore I try to keep him in the here-and-now interaction by focusing on the relational level rather than the content.

Ralph: Part of me says, "Yes, that's true. That doesn't work with John," and there's this angry part that says, "What the fuck does work with John, anyway." You know, you're a tough nut. Even that might not work with you. You're here today, but will you be here tomorrow, which is probably a piece of my stuff. I mean, you're really on today. You're really centered, and I thought you were really great with Jay. And I feel that you're really here and letting all your shit hang out. But will you be here tomorrow, but that's another issue.

Ralph is referring to two things: (a) John's being present in the group, because John tends to be absent from group without having a really compelling reason, and (b) John's being emotionally present, because often he is very quiet in group.

John: Yeah, you're going back into that shit-stirring stuff with me right now. I'm saying that I don't like it when you stir the shit with me. It pushes me away.

Ralph: Uh huh.

Jay   (to Ralph): Wait a minute. You're not just stirring shit. You have your own feelings about …

John is accusing Ralph of his usual provocative behavior, and though he may be accurate, I am more interested in helping Ralph to be more present in the interaction. I attempt to do this by focusing on the emotional response evoked in him when John is not consistently available.

Ralph: Uh huh.

Jay: So tell him what your feelings are about whether he's going to be here to-morrow or not.

Ralph: That's a separate … I mean, I think he's right …

John: I don't think it is separate. I think maybe that's why you stir the shit. You get angry at me, and you don't say that, and then you try to figure me out.

My intervention doesn't work, and they continue to struggle at the content level.

Ralph: Everything you say adds another thing. So I can only deal with so many things at once. I'm not sure that everything I do is about you not being here tomorrow. Sometimes it's about you not being here today, and I do feel you here today, and I've actually been really excited about feeling you here the last month.

John: I hate this place. I feel, right now, and I get this from the group, like if I'm here or not, it's almost … I feel judged somehow in this place. Right now. "You're not here right now, John, so somehow you're less-than." That's how I'm hearing it. Somehow you're not good enough cause you're not here today.

John is bringing up a very important issue, his fear of being judged by Ralph. As often happens, this interaction touches on core issues for both of them. John has an issue about being judged and Ralph has one that leads him to judge others. Even though the two of them are interacting, and both clearly have issues that could be investigated, my focus is primarily on Ralph. I am particularly interested in his lack of contact and presence because that seems to be the bottleneck in the interaction (see Bottleneck Issues in chapter 17).

Ralph: That's your piece, because …

John: I know that's my piece.

Here they are struggling about problem ownership, about who is to blame for their difficulty in connecting.

Ralph: ... that's not the way I felt. The way I feel is: I feel like all along, at different times we've tried to connect, and I fear some of what you say to me about what makes me difficult for you to be around. But I also feel like you've disengaged, and you've gone off and decided that you want to connect with others, and that's it, and ...

John: You're right, all those things I have done.

Ralph: Right, and ...

Jay: And how does that make you feel, Ralph.

Again I'm asking focus on his feelings rather than the other person's behavior.

Ralph: How does that make me feel? It makes me feel ... sad. I never really give up, so I don't think the full impact is there. I don't feel like the last word has been spoken.

Ralph answered my question about his feelings, a step in the right direction, but then immediately went back to intellectualizing.

Jay: It makes you feel sad ... Keep going with how it makes you feel.

I try to keep him focused on his feelings long enough to allow something deeper to evolve.

Ralph: I mean that isn't a real strong feeling, because I don't feel like it's over. So I don't want to feel sad and start grieving it, because I don't feel hopeless.

Jay: So what are you feeling?

Ralph: I also feel relieved because ... sometimes I feel like you use your vulnerability like a weapon, and ...

Now Ralph is not only avoiding his feelings, but he has gone back to his favorite tactic, guessing about the other person's underlying motives. This tends to annoy people and make them defensive unless they have asked for help of this nature, which is certainly not the case here.

Jay: Wait, Ralph ...

Ralph: But, but, I'm ...

Members: Wait. Mmm. That's the place you go, Ralph. Yeah. Don't do that.

The group has seen Ralph do this enough that they try to help him stop. He is quite resistant.

Jay: See you're back into his underlying motives. Can you stay with …

Ralph: Well, I don't know how to reference my feelings without bringing out that piece.

Jay: Reference your feelings to his behavior but not to his underlying motives.

Ralph: Well, that's the behavior.

Jay: What's the behavior?

Ralph: That his vulnerability becomes a weapon.

Jay: That's not his behavior. That's your interpretation.

I am trying to explain the difference between talking about someone else's behavior and his motives, but Ralph isn't getting it. I let it go for now.

Ralph: Well, I don't believe he always does that, but it can happen.

John: So.

Ralph: So I really feel frustrated with that because … talk about feeling bad, it's like you're bringing out all this vulnerability, but it feels like a weapon, rather than a statement.

Jay: That's all about him. The only thing you said about yourself was that you felt frustrated.

"Frustrated" is not a very useful description of a feeling. Ralph is emphasizing what John did rather than how it affected Ralph emotionally and what it meant to him.

Ralph: Right. Well, it makes me feel badly because … Well, gee, if I were more vulnerable, then I could be John's friend. But there's this part of me that says, no, that's not true.

Jay: You feel bad.

I am attempting to focus on what seems like the feeling part of Ralph's statement.

Ralph: It's like I'm not enough. I'm not doing it your way.

Ralph is opening up a little. He describes feeling judged, but then in the statement below, he goes right back into his head.

Ralph: I mean I feel a mirror with you sometimes. A lot of the things you say to me, I also feel toward you … And I also do feel judged by you, in that same way. And evaluated by you.

John: I don't accept that. I don't think I judge you. I think I tell you what I'm feeling. I don't try to analyze who you are. I see what you do, and I tell you how I respond to it. I don't really judge you. It's not a really big piece of it.

[They continue to argue. Ralph claims that John judges him, and John claims that Ralph analyzes his underlying feelings without being asked. Ralph claims that he can't count on John being there. They are stuck in blaming each other.]

They thus perpetuate the power struggle about problem ownership and blame. I call this a blame cycle (see chapter 15).

Ralph: There's something … There's just more here …

John: I agree that there's more here …

Ralph: And again, I don't want to make it about you, but it seems like you keep slipping away. And I think it was great you took a break from group last week. I missed you, but I really felt … But there's this quality of you vanishing that I find really … I can't start until I feel that you're committed to being in the room.

Jay: So when you experience that quality in him, how does that make you feel?

I try to help Ralph focus on his emotional reaction to John. This will move him away from focusing on John's issues and help him own his reaction.

Ralph: Well, I guess the end product has been that I've basically given up for the time being. I feel frustrated …

Jay: I don't want to know the end product. I want to know the inner process.

Ralph: The inner process is that I feel angry, frustrated, then I get philosophical …

Ralph has now given one aspect of his feeling response, his angry, protective response, and he also reveals his intellectual defense. Now I ask him for the underlying vulnerable feeling that is behind the anger.

Jay: What happens before angry and frustrated? There's another, vulnerable, feeling there before angry and frustrated.

Ralph: Well, I … rejected …

Jay: OK, so just hang out with that for a moment. Let yourself feel that … and see if you can find a way to talk to John about that.

Ralph: [pause] Well I have this irrational desire for you to be more durable.

Ralph is beginning to focus on his emotional response, and to become aware of the meaning that John's inconsistency has for him. This material could provide insight into Ralph's fear of emotional abandonment, but Ralph isn't yet present enough for insight to be a useful direction. Therefore, I ask him to bring the vulnerable feeling into the interaction, hoping to increase contact and therefore presence. Notice that Ralph revealed material even earlier that could have led me to make an interpretation about abandonment, but this would have simply led to intellectual insight, which Ralph characteristically uses as a defense. With another client who was more feeling oriented, I might have chosen to focus on insight.

Jay: I wonder if you can find a way to talk to John about your feeling of rejection, when you feel like he's not there.

Ralph: Well, I guess when I feel I have to walk on eggshells around you, it feels impossible to me, it feels impossible to …

Jay: That doesn't sound like rejection.

Ralph: Well, I guess I flashed on my father, and having to do it his way, or no way. Like there's no give and take.

Ralph has switched to a different aspect of his difficulties with John, probably to avoid the vulnerable feeling. I separate them out and focus him again on the vulnerability.

Jay: You know it feels to me like there are two issues with John. One is the feeling that you have to do it his way, and the other is feeling rejected when you feel like he's not there. And it seems that it's very hard for you to stay with the rejection one. You keep going off in other directions.

Ralph: Well I think my mother was very energetically abandoning. She would just go off, and she was very rarely there at all. I experience when people's energy tails off as very rejecting.

Ralph is beginning to have insight into the childhood origins of his issue, and he is more present. However, because Ralph in particular could easily lose this through intellectual analysis, I encourage him to focus on his awareness of his inner experience in the moment.

Jay: And just take a moment to be with what happens inside you when that happens.

Ralph: It feels very motherless. [softly] I feel like a motherless child. [pause]

Jay: Like really left, really abandoned.

He is now present, so I respond empathically.

Ralph: Uh huh. A real, kind of negative emptiness.

Jay: Uh huh. [pause] What's it like to be in touch with that? Is that OK?

I'm checking to see how he feels about being so vulnerable, and he seems to be handling it OK. Notice that Ralph is working on two issues here. One is a defense that leads him to analyze and criticize others, and the other is a core issue about abandonment. I have encouraged him to deal with the first issue by experimenting with the healthier behavior of being direct, emotional, and vulnerable. This has led to his accessing the pain of the second issue. Both issues have to do with deficiencies in connectedness.

Ralph: Yeah. It's an awful feeling. [vulnerable] It feels a little bit like solitary confinement, a sense of isolation in myself … It's like not being able to do anything that changes the situation.

Jay: Not being able to do anything to get this person to be present with you?

Ralph: Right. Right.

Jay: See if there's a way now to bring this feeling into connecting with John. I'm not sure how to do that. It may feel very vulnerable to do that, and I don't even know if you want to, but see what happens if you try to.

I ask him, somewhat awkwardly, to move from presence to contact.

Ralph: Well, I guess maybe you are mirroring a part of me that I don't want to see.

Jay: You switched into figuring it out. See if you can be with him, with the feeling itself.

Perhaps because of my awkward intervention, Ralph went back into intellectualization, so I steer him back to presence and contact.

Ralph: [contactful] Well, I guess it's a terrible feeling to feel excited about having contact with you, and not being able to count on that being there the next time …

Jay: Good. It feels like you really … did that.

Ralph has achieved good contact, so now I check in with John.

Jay: What's happening John?

John: [soft and present] What's happening is that I'm looking into his eyes. That's what's happening. And I feel very sad that that's how it feels. I guess I know that … and there's truth in that. [long pause as they make eye contact]

Jay: And where are you, Ralph?

Ralph: [very softly] Um, not knowing ... There's got to be a next step, but not knowing what that is. [pause]

Ralph is making contact with John, but as is often the case in these situations, he wants to figure out what to do next. I encourage them to continue the contact by reporting on their awareness of the moment.

Jay: Why don't you each say what you're feeling in the moment, as you're in contact with each other?

Ralph: To me it feels like I'd rather have you dish out anything than leave me. I'll duke it out with you, but don't leave.

John: [pause] In the moment I was feeling very close to you, but also afraid of that.

When John feels close to Ralph and makes such a good connection with him, he is giving Ralph what he really wanted all along, but couldn't easily get. This healing response reinforces Ralph for making healthy contact rather than being judgmental. The core issue, which has to do with abandonment, cannot be healed in one session because consistency is needed. That will have to come over time as their relationship develops.

Jay: Afraid of what?

John: Afraid of being close to Ralph.

Jay: Mm ... And what about that is scary?

Ralph has made a significant therapeutic step, and John presents something to work with, so I have now switched to working with John.

John: I don't know what about that's scary. It's scary. It's scary to look. It's scary to see what's going on. You know it also feels ... like an old place to be. I've done this a lot. We've done this a lot. It happens a lot.

Ralph: Not necessarily like this, though.

Here Ralph confirms the importance for him of this work. He has clearly taken in John's healing response and inner healing has occurred.

John: I didn't go to the next step. I just stayed here. [pause] In thinking how, for me, it's very hard for me to stay in my body. That's a lot of what my process is. I don't generally look and see the world, I look down. [thoughtful] And I don't stay in my body, so I'm not present.

John is exploring his blocks to being in contact.

John: And I need to tell myself that that's not something to be ashamed of, that's a process. It's a reaction to something, and I'm responsible to change it if I want to be in the world, which I want to be.

John is struggling with his inner critic, which shames him for having any blocks. This is probably why he was sensitive to being criticized by Ralph earlier in the session.

John: For a long time I haven't been here ... The whole concept of wanting and desiring and having a choice ... It's so new and foreign, and I'm not even sure if I want certain things. It's hard to say I don't want, too.

John was sexually abused as a child and consequently blocked off his needs and desires, as well as his connection with his body.

Ralph: Uh huh.

John: It gets mixed up in this relationship all the time.

Ralph: [very empathic] So I'm sorry if there is something about the way I approach you that makes you wrong or shamed for not being present. You know, I'm sure I do it to myself.

Ralph is now so open and connected that he can easily own his part in their difficulties and want to change.

John: You know, it doesn't matter. When I hear your quality of acceptance, it doesn't matter if I don't take care of it. I don't want to be in the position of setting myself up to be a victim. So if that's your response to me ...

John is now stuck in criticizing himself for being a victim.

Jay: That's not being a victim.

John: For me it is. It's my shame. If I want to jump into that ... It's me. It's nothing you do.

Ralph: Right, but you don't have to see yourself that way.

Jay: But it's not being a victim to tell him how his behavior affects you, and it's OK for him to say that he wants to change that. You don't have to push that away. That's not being a victim. That's part of a relationship, you know. It's not something you're just doing alone.

Ralph and I give John feedback that he wasn't acting like a victim, and I do some teaching about the give and take of being in a relationship.

John: I still haven't learned that. I have a hard time with ... telling people what they do. It feels uncomfortable for me, you know. And even having the expectation that they can change ... for me, because they want to have a relationship with me. To me that feels controlling, unnecessary ... I'm still not thinking it through yet.

Jay: It could be done in a controlling way, but you didn't. Ralph came to that on his own.

Ralph: Yeah. That was an offering.

Jay: He came to that in himself …

Ralph: For myself as much as anything else.

John: I accept that.

John takes in the feedback that he didn't adopt a victim stance to control Ralph.

I might have explored with John the origins of the inner critic that judges him for being a victim. I could also have worked further with him on the block to contact that he brought up, but the work between the two of the them had gone on for quite a while, and it was nearing the end of the group. Therefore, I just allowed the work to come to an end and then the group members gave feedback to Ralph and John.

III

FACILITATING THE PROCESS

So far we have discussed the change process and how to foster a therapeutic group culture. In Part III we discuss other aspects of the group leader's task in facilitating the group. Chapter 14 deals with understanding and working with defenses and resistance. Chapter 15 covers how to help clients own their part in interpersonal problems in group, and chapter 16 discusses aggression as both a healthy and defensive process. Chapter 17 explores the choices a leader faces in making interventions and also the issues of support and forgiveness. Chapter 18 discusses the optimal attitude for a group leader and how problems with the leader's attitude can affect the group. Chapter 19 covers various aspects of the leader–client relationship, including the therapeutic alliance and countertransference. Chapter 21 addresses the question of group members having contact outside group sessions.

CHAPTER

Defenses and Resistance

This chapter deals with defenses and resistance to the therapy process. We discuss the value of defenses and how to work with defenses and resistance.

Pain-Driven or Defensive Behavior.　When you see that a group member is exhibiting a problematic reaction, how can she tell if it is pain-driven or defensive? A *pain-driven reaction* derives directly from a core issue without defense. In other words, though the person may be reacting in a rigid, exaggerated, or inappropriate way, his pain will not be hidden or distorted. He will be feeling the pain of the core issue, even if he isn't conscious of where it comes from. In this case, you don't need to deal with defenses but can move directly into access or experimenting. In contrast, when a client is reacting from a defense, you usually must work with this first to get to the core issue beneath.

☐ The Value of Defenses

The Original Value of Defenses.　Defenses must be treated with respect. Originally constructed when the person was young and vulnerable, they have served to ward off unbearable pain that couldn't be assimilated. In many cases, they helped the child deal with harmful interactions and relationships. Now that the person is an adult with more resources (both inner and outer) she can explore letting go of her defenses. However, defenses should be respected as "old friends" who helped the client in the past but may no longer be needed.

> For example, Molly was abused as a child and developed a defense of dissociation to hide from the intense pain of that experience. Without the dissociative defense, Molly might have been completely overwhelmed by the trauma she suffered as a child. As an adult, her

149

dissociation is no longer adaptive and prevents her from being strong, clear, and present in many situations. Therefore, though she now needs to explore letting go of it, the defense served her well as a child and should be honored for that.

Protection from Overwhelming Pain.

Even in adulthood, a person's pain can sometimes be intense and potentially overwhelming, so defenses may still be needed to prevent retraumatization and possible loss of functioning. Often a client needs to maintain some of her defenses until she becomes strong enough through therapy to tolerate experiencing the underlying trauma.

> For example, Molly can begin to let go of her dissociative defense only when she feels connected enough to the group leader and the group to feel safe in doing so. She also needs to develop enough inner strength to tolerate the extreme pain that will emerge. It will also help if she has other defenses available, such as the ability to suppress the pain when a group meeting is over.

Defenses should be approached gradually, caringly, and respectfully. It is especially important to avoid any judgment in approaching a person's defenses. Given that much of people's pain derives from parental judgments, any criticism from the group leader may exacerbate this problem.

Protection from Others.

In many situations it isn't particularly safe or wise for a person to be vulnerable, because she might be harmed. *For example, if a person feels insecure about her ability to perform well at work, it might not be wise to show this to competitive coworkers or a supervisor who might use it against her. In other more supportive work settings, however, showing her vulnerability might be helpful.* In unsafe situations, choosing to rely on defenses may be healthy.

Personal Strengths as Defenses.

In addition, people frequently use personal strengths as defenses. *A witty client may use her sense of humor to distract from doing serious work. An assertive client may control others as a defense. A caring person may nurture others in order to defend against feeling her own needs.* Though these personal qualities are sometimes used as defenses, they are positive attributes that should be appreciated when used appropriately.

Honoring Defenses.

To summarize, defenses should be honored for at least four reasons: (a) At one time, they saved the child from unbearable pain or dysfunction. (b) They may defend against pain that a person cannot handle now. (c) They may protect a person from harmful responses from others. (d) A defense may be a personal strength that is only used defensively in some situations.

It is important to let clients know that you don't want them to give up the behavior they use as a defense. The same behavior may be healthy in one situation and defensive in another. Therapy aims to help clients bring these behaviors under conscious control, so they can be used when appropriate and relaxed when not needed. We want clients to expand their repertoire of healthy responses, so these can be used instead of defenses whenever possible. This attitude is reassuring to clients. They understand that you aren't trying to take away something that has value to them.

☐ Defense Versus Resistance

In the psychotherapy literature, defense and resistance are more or less equated. Frequently resistance is defined as defense; in psychoanalysis, resistance is seen as a defense against instinctual strivings. This is based on the assumption that whenever a client is resisting the therapy or therapist, it is because he is defending against whatever the therapist is trying to uncover. This is not always true, so I distinguish carefully between the two terms.

I define *defense* according to the person's internal psychodynamics and *resistance* according to the person's response to therapy. A *defense* is any behavior or internal process that attempts to avoid experiencing or activating a core issue. *Resistance* is any behavior that doesn't cooperate with the therapy process or the therapist. What's important about this distinction is that resistance can be for reasons other than defense. If you as group leader suggest (directly or indirectly) that a client engage in a certain process (e.g., explore a feeling reaction, take a risk, own a problem) and she resists you (consciously or unconsciously), this could be because of a defense or a variety of other reasons. For example, your suggestion might be wrong, mistimed, or too much for the client to handle at that time. The client might be feeling blamed or pressured or controlled or otherwise reacting to her feelings about you rather than your suggestion.

Resistance should be explored, but without assuming that it constitutes a defense against the underlying pain you are trying to get to. The situation is sometimes more complex than that.

☐ Working with Resistance

When you recognize that a group member is using a defense, the natural urge is to point it out and encourage her to let go of it and explore the pain or experiment with healthy behavior. This is often successful, but sometimes the client resists. She may deny that she is defending, or react emotionally to having it pointed out, or be unable or unwilling to let go of the defense. In these cases, it is important for the leader to work with the resistance rather than simply trying to get past it. This is an important principle in both psychoanalysis and Gestalt therapy. You must let go of seeing the resistance as an impediment to the real work and instead become interested in working with it. There is as much to gain therapeutically by exploring the resistance as there would be if the client had not resisted to begin with.

Reasons for Resistance

There are many possible reasons for resistance other than the straightforward one of defense:

1. Your suggestion may have been based on an incorrect understanding of the client, or it may have been partially right and the client needs to modify it to fit her expe-

rience. In this case, you need to encourage the client to disagree with you and present her own point of view. You should take her perspective seriously, while at the same time looking for what she may be avoiding.

2.   Your suggestion may have been accurate but too threatening for the client at the time. If you suggested an experiment, it may involve too big a leap for the person.

For example, suppose that Joyce has difficulty asking for and receiving nurturing from others. You might suggest that she pick a group member and ask him or her for what she needs. This might be too much risk for Joyce at her current stage of working on this problem. Maybe she first needs to simply feel her needs without taking any further risks. Maybe she needs to learn how to receive caring before taking the additional risk of asking. It might be better to let the group members offer support and nurturing and work with Joyce on her ability to receive.

3.   Your suggestion may be accurate, but it may bring up other issues that must be dealt with before it can be acted on. *For example, asking for nurturing might bring up shame, and this must be explored before the client can actually ask.* If the two of you explore the resistance openly (i.e., without pressure from the leader or defensiveness from the client) issues that need to be explore will arise naturally. This has just as much value as if the client had taken your suggestion, perhaps more.

4.   The client may be resisting *you* rather than the content of your suggestion. She may be reacting to dynamics in the therapist–client relationship; for example, she might be feeling controlled or judged by you. This is very common. It might be something in your tone of voice or timing that triggered the resistance. She may have negative transference with you. If you sense that she is reacting to you, ask her directly while conveying the message that it is OK if she is. We will deal with leader–member interactions in chapter 19.

5.   You may see a client's behavior as a defense, and she may feel bad about her behavior being seen this way.

For example, suppose you are exploring a person's need to express anger instead of showing vulnerability. She feels that the anger makes her feel strong so she can protect herself from negative people. This is ego-syntonic; it seems like healthy behavior to her. If you suggest that her anger is a defense, this may upset her. She might be willing to access the underlying hurt or shame as long as she doesn't feel judged for her anger. This can be a delicate line to walk.

6.   The client may not want to explore what you have in mind, or she may not be sure whether she wants to. There isn't necessarily anything wrong with this. Each client should have the right to decide when she wants to deal with each of her issues. *You* may think that she should deal with it now, but it is *her* therapy. In a case like this, it is very useful to ask the client if she would like to explore a certain issue or take a certain risk. If she says "No," then this clarifies things. You can explore why she doesn't want to or simply move on, supporting her autonomy in making this choice. If she says "Yes," then she is much more likely to cooperate in the work. Whatever her answer, she has benefitted from pondering this question and making her own choice. Therefore she is more likely to commit herself to this piece of work.

Pushing Versus Respecting Resistance

Respecting Limits.   When you are working with a client, it can be valuable at times to encourage her to move past certain resistances, taking her deeper into access or further into risky experimenting. People often need to experience areas of discomfort and anxiety (as long as it isn't too great) in order to grow. However, make sure that the client is able to set a limit when she can't or doesn't want to go further. If a client allows you to take her further than she is ready to go, she may be overwhelmed by fear or pain, causing fragmentation or brittle defenses and undoing the good work that has already been accomplished. Alternatively, a client may go along with you compliantly without really being engaged emotionally. In either case, this is destructive to the work. If you are unsure about whether a client is capable of saying "No" to you, make sure to specify clearly that she can stop when she wants and look for signs that she needs to.

> Suppose a client suddenly feels very afraid in group when someone gets angry at her. You naturally begin to explore with her where the fear comes from. This could lead to very painful memories of physical abuse, for example, and clients who have been abused in this way often don't have the ability to set limits, including limits on the therapy going too deeply. You must watch for signs that the client is becoming emotionally overloaded or is dissociating. You also need to check in with her frequently to see if it is all right to continue.

Watch for a situation where group members may be pushing a client past where it is safe for her to go, so you can support the client in setting a clear limit. It is wise to foster a group norm that specifies that members have the right to end a piece of work at any time and have this limit respected. This makes it easier for clients to say when they don't want to go further, and easier to stop members from pushing a client too far.

Transference Dynamics.   Be watchful for transference when working with resistant clients. Many had parents who controlled or pushed them to achieve or perform in various ways. Other clients had parents who did not treat them as separate people with their own needs. If you try to encourage or push such a person, it usually backfires. She often gets caught between wanting to please you and defy you. The negative transference takes over and the work becomes about control, submission, and defiance. If the client defies you directly, this is the easiest to handle. The client might also become frozen in her conflict between pleasing and defying. She might unconsciously fail at what you suggest in order to retain her autonomy, to keep you from controlling her.

Passive–Aggressive Clients.   With a client like this, be careful of using suggestions or directions. Not only should you not encourage her or push past her resistance, be careful about even ordinary suggestions. Make sure a passive–aggressive client is ready to take suggestions you offer. It is helpful to ask the client if she is interested in working on something before proceeding, and don't accept a yes answer unless it seems genuine to you. Before making specific suggestions, you might ask if she would like to go further with the work at this time. Let her know that you aren't invested in her doing this, that you are just offering an opportunity and she is perfectly welcome to refuse. Of course, this must be sincere; you can't pretend.

If you aren't sure if a passive–aggressive client is open to your suggestions, err on the side of not suggesting and let her find her own way if necessary. Make sure the motivation comes from her. Even then such clients may run into internal conflict between the part that wants to go ahead and the part that is resisting. However, at least you won't be identified with one side of this conflict and can therefore work with her on it. Be prepared for progress to occur in very small increments, and understand and appreciate it when the client takes a small risk. Praise her for each step forward without expecting her to accept your praise.

When to Push.   There is one situation where it may be advisable to push a client past where he asks to stop. This is when he is feeling very ashamed and wants to end the work, but you know that if he is willing to get feedback from the group, it will be healing and he will feel much better. In this case, I often say, in a personal way, that I would feel bad about leaving him in such a painful place because I know a resolution is possible, and I want him to feel better.

> For example, a client was challenged by a couple of group members about something he had done. He became so upset and ashamed that he wanted to leave the room or at least shift the group's attention away from himself. However, I knew that most members liked him, even the two people who had challenged him. A core issue of his had been activated that resulted in his feeling rejected by the entire group. I didn't want him to end the work feeling so bad when I knew that a little reality feedback would alleviate his distress.

This kind of personal caring from the leader can often give a client the boost he needs to continue. It may also encourage some group members to offer the healing responses they are feeling, thus softening his resistance. However, if the client insists on stopping, you should always respect this.

Clarifying Intent.   Sometimes when a client will say that he feels like stopping his work, you may not know whether he is expressing a feeling but is willing to continue, or if he is really saying that he wants to stop. In this case, spell out these two possibilities clearly and ask which one he means. This clarification is sometimes crucial in helping the client figure out where he stands.

One Step at a Time.   Whenever you are actively working with someone on access or experimenting, it is important not to expect her to take more than one step at a time. By a "step" I mean any move toward deeper access or greater risk. Because any such step takes the person into unknown and potentially frightening territory, it is important to go gradually.

> For example, if Marcy is frightened to reach out to Ben at all, then when she finally does take the risk to reach out, it is unlikely that she will do it in the most direct, open, vulnerable way. She will probably still need to use some defenses. You may be tempted to point out the ways she is still defending and ask her to reach out in a healthier way, or a group member might do this.

This is usually a mistake. Since the client is taking a big risk to do the experiment at all, it's not a good idea to ask her to take an even greater risk. She might defend again or retreat altogether. She might feel ashamed because she didn't do it well enough to please people. Make sure that the client has had the time to see the results of the step she took, to receive appreciation for it and integrate it. Then if it seems appropriate you might suggest that she go even further or allow the group to do so.

In addition, be careful about expecting clients to take too many steps over the course of a piece of work. If a client has already taken a step or two, be careful about asking her to do any more. Even if you are quite willing for her to say no to further work, the suggestion can leave a person feeling inadequate because she didn't do more. You don't want to leave a client with a sense of failure because the last thing you suggested was beyond her capacity. It is especially important to avoid this with a client who has a harsh inner critic.

In the example with Joyce above, suppose she does some work involving pain and risk that results in her getting in touch with her need for nurturing and her fear of feeling this need. This is already a big step for Joyce. In most cases, it wouldn't be a good idea to then suggest that she ask for or receive nurturing from the group. People can usually only take one significant step at a time. If you suggest a second big step, Joyce won't be able to do it and may feel like a failure.

☐ Working with Defenses

There are a variety of approaches to exploring defenses:

1. *What is the person defending against?* This is usually the first line of inquiry and is often fruitful. When the client is defending against taking a certain action, then he can explore his fear without taking the action.

For example, if a client is afraid of expressing affection, you can explore his fears of what would happen if he expressed it. This isn't too threatening because he can do the exploring without actually expressing affection to anyone. Make sure that he feels free to avoid revealing anything that might trigger the fear and therefore make it impossible to do the exploring. For example, he may not want to reveal which group members he feels affection toward.

When a client's fear has to do with shame and exposure, then the act of exploring the fear is usually tantamount to taking the action he is afraid of. This makes the exploring more difficult.

For example, suppose Richard is quiet and reserved and doesn't share much of himself, especially his pain and insecurity. This is clearly because of a defense, and you can ask Richard what he is afraid would happen if he did share more. If he is able to explore that, it is a step toward letting go of the defense, because the act of exploring is, in fact, a sharing of his insecurity. However, Richard's fear of this sharing may make it difficult for him to do the exploring. This situation must be handled delicately.

When the client is defending against feeling pain, then he may be able to explore his fears without triggering the pain, or triggering only a small amount of pain. However, in some cases this won't be possible, and the exploring itself may bring on the pain. This situation must also be handled with great care.

2. *How is the person defending?*

You can explore with Richard exactly how the defense operates. Does he think of things he would like to share but find himself unable to speak because of his fears? Does sharing not even come up? Does he imagine that he has doesn't have anything worthwhile to share? Does he recognize that he has pain and fear, but can't think of anything to say about it when he is in group? If he feels pain, how does he keep himself from expressing it in group? Does he think of other things? Does he withdraw emotionally?

Exploring the method of defending helps a client to understand his process better, and may give him increased choices about when to defend and when to be open. It provides information that could clarify what he is afraid of. *In Richard's case, this exploration also gives you (and the group) a chance to show interest in him without it being too threatening.*

When the client is defending against feeling pain, it can be helpful to explore exactly how the defense operates, both mentally and in terms of bodily sensations and tensions. This is commonly done in Gestalt therapy. *For example, suppose Richard reports a mild feeling of sadness that soon disappears. He might notice where he feels the sadness in his body and what happens in that place when it disappears. He might notice a hardness or a coldness or a tension in his heart. It helps to be aware of the thoughts that occurred right before the sadness disappeared.* Exploring how a defense operates can, in some cases, lead to the loosening of the defense.

3. *What is the origin of the defense?* With defenses that are recalcitrant, it can help to explore not only what is being defended and how, but also the possible origins in childhood. Notice that the origin of the defense may be quite different from the origin of the core issue. *For example, the pain behind Richard's reserve may have originated when his parents showed little interest in him and actively discouraged him from going to them for help when in trouble. What about the defense itself? If Richard uses an aloofness defense, pretending that he doesn't need anything from anyone, where did this originate? Maybe it was internalized from one of his parents or a teacher or friend. Maybe it was rewarded by his family or subculture as a sign of strength.* Understanding the origins of a defense makes it less ego-syntonic and therefore may help to loosen it.

4. *Is the defense also a compensation?* When a client seems particularly reluctant to give up a defense, it may be a compensation. This means it not only protects against an experience of pain but also compensates for a deficiency in a basic need. *For example, James was overly prideful about his intelligence. This was a defense against underlying feelings of shame and worthlessness. However, in addition to defending against this pain, his pride also gave him a feeling of self-worth; it compensated for a deficiency in his sense of inner value.* Compensations are incomplete or flawed attempts to have an experience of a healthy capacity that is missing. Because the compensation may be the only way the person can experience the missing capacity, the client will often cling to it stubbornly. He is getting a secondary gain from the defense, so it especially hard to relinquish. *For example, James was very invested in his intelligence. It was difficult to work with him on his intellectualization defense, not only because it served to defend against his feelings, but primarily because his pride in his intellect was the only way he could feel good about himself.*

When you sense that a defense may be a compensation, ask the client to explore what he gets from using it, or what he would lose it he gave it up. *For example, rather than encouraging James to stop intellectualizing, you could ask him to explore what he gets from seeing himself as intelligent or what he would lose if he gave up his intellectual focus.*

The Value of Exploring Defenses.   It isn't always best for a client to let go of a defense and engage in experimenting. Sometimes it is better to hold back on experimenting to allow for deeper processing of material. Sometimes even access should be postponed until a defense has been explored thoroughly. If the defense was erected for an important reason and the client bypasses it, he may miss out on exploring the defense itself, and this may be necessary for a full resolution of the issue.

Problem Ownership

This chapter deals with one important manifestation of defense and resistance—a client's difficulties in owning his problematic behavior. I discuss various dynamics that cause difficulties in problem ownership—including blame cycles and defense cycles—and practical interventions to help clients through this roadblock.

☐ Definition of Problem Ownership

One of the potential stumbling blocks in therapy is when a group member fails to recognize that certain behavior of his is contributing to a problem—either a problem in group or a problem in his life.

> For example, suppose Peter has an angry overreaction to Sandra[10] stemming from a misperception of her. He may initially be convinced that his reaction is a completely natural response to what she said, and it will be an important therapeutic step for Peter to acknowledge the overreaction and misperception. Of course, Sandra's action may also have come from an issue of hers, so they may both have responsibility for the difficulties between them.

Owning a problem is similar to making a symptom or behavior "ego-dystonic." Piaget (1969) called this *decentering*.

---

[10] In this section and other places where I discuss an interaction between two people, I almost always use examples where two people of opposite genders are relating to each other. This is only because it makes it easy to distinguish one person from the other by the gender pronoun references. It unfortunately gives the impression that men don't relate to men or women to women as much as women to men in groups. This is not true.

Forms of Problem Ownership

Problem ownership can take the following forms:

1. The person is interested in exploring *his* reaction rather than the *other's* behavior.

   In this example, Peter would look for the reason for his reaction in his psyche rather than in Sandra's behavior. For instance, suppose that Sandra is acting confused and helpless, and Peter responds to this with anger. It would be helpful for Peter to explore what it is about his makeup that causes him to get so angry at someone who is confused and helpless. Maybe his mother acted helpless at times when he really needed her to be strong for him. It is the attitude of self-exploration on Peter's part that will lead to constructive work.

2. The person recognizes that his perception of another is distorted or his reaction extreme.

   Let's say that Sandra asked for help in a way that *was* appropriate, but Peter saw her as playing a helpless victim. Peter might get feedback that others saw her behavior as appropriate, and this might prompt him to consider that his perception of her (and his subsequent reaction) may have been derived from his own issues.

3. The person recognizes that his reaction is a defense.

   For example, suppose that Peter doesn't show his anger but instead defends against it by becoming cold and aloof toward Sandra. Problem ownership would mean Peter recognizing that his aloofness is really a defense against his anger, rather than claiming that he simply isn't interested in Sandra.

4. The person recognizes that his reaction is transference. *For example, Peter might recognize that his anger at Sandra reflects anger at his mother for being too confused and helpless to take care of him when he needed it.*

5. The person recognizes that his reaction is one instance of a repeated pattern of behavior that is a problem for him. *For example, Peter realizes that he frequently gets angry at people who are in pain and ask for help.* Here the client is owning an issue he has in general, not just a particular reaction in the moment.

There are degrees of problem ownership. A group member may acknowledge an issue of his or attain insight into some transference, but then soon after he may defensively claim that his reaction was completely normal. This means that the problem ownership he achieved was fragile and easily lost. When a client has a higher degree of problem ownership, he not only acknowledges an issue of his when someone else points it out, but he also notices it on his own, both in group and in his outside life, and he actively tries to change it.

The Value of Problem Ownership

Owning a problem makes it much easier to move deeper into the therapeutic process. The client will look further at his part of the problem and cooperate more effectively with the therapist. He will be interested in seeing how this problem manifests and understanding its role in his life. He will be willing to work on accessing more deeply the feelings and origins of the issue and experimenting with new healthy behavior.

Often when two group members are in conflict, they each become locked into thinking that their problems are due to the other person, and no real therapy can happen until they are willing to explore themselves. One way to achieve this is to establish the norm that self-exploration has top priority in the group. Then a client should treat any reaction to another person as material to be explored regardless of who is responsible. This helps to break cycles of blame. However, this approach deals only with part of the story. Group members learn not only from their reactions to others, but also from other people's reactions to them, so the person being reacted to also may have exploring to do. In addition, the relationships between the group members shouldn't be treated as only a means to stimulate self-exploration. They are also important sources of healing, so two clients in conflict must not only explore themselves, but also work through their relationship. This makes it impossible to avoid the issue of problem responsibility, but it is worth it because of the increased therapeutic richness of the clients' full relationships with each other.

> For example, Lawrence frequently criticized the other group members for not being clear enough and being too emotional. He was generally resistant to examining himself and exploring his own reactions. When I would suggest that he explore the emotional meaning of a judgmental reaction of his, he would demand to know if I thought he had done something wrong. He would then construct an argument to prove that his reaction was completely natural, and he had nothing to look at.

> We eventually realized that much of his resistance to owning problems really had to do with his feelings toward me. Because of father transference, Lawrence often felt quite angry with me and had a strong need to differentiate himself from me to develop his autonomy. He didn't have permission to express these negative feelings directly to me so he displaced them onto the group. He couldn't accept any of my help in exploring himself or his problematic reactions, because that would have put him in a subordinate position relative to me, stirring up shame and anger. He wasn't really satisfied with the group, but he couldn't just leave because he very much wanted my approval.

> As we began to deal directly with our relationship, he gradually came to understand these dynamics, and I responded in such a way that he felt seen and accepted by me. This led him to soften his criticisms of the group and become a more cooperative member. He was also able to accept more help from me and own his problematic behavior more easily.

☐ Shame and the Resistance to Problem Ownership

The greatest difficulty with problem ownership is that it often gets entangled with blame and engenders shame. Frequently clients were blamed severely by their parents and are therefore sensitive about it happening in group. When the leader or a group member suggests that someone own a problem, it is often experienced as a judgment or attack (and of course, sometimes it is). This is a particularly difficult problem for clients with narcissistic issues.

Let's use the example of Peter becoming angry at Sandra for being helpless. If Sandra responds by accusing him of distortion, he is liable to get defensive. Even if she challenges him in a caring way, he could experience it negatively. If the challenge comes from a third party, he might feel that people are taking sides against him. For example, if you, as the leader, ask Peter to explore where his anger is coming from, he may wonder why you are focusing on him when Sandra is the one with the problem.

Problem ownership can be harder to achieve in a group than in individual therapy because when a client reacts to others, he usually assumes that his reaction is natural and the other person is at fault. Of course, this happens in individual therapy, too, but unless the client is reacting to the therapist, it is easier to persuade the client to explore himself because there is no one else to focus on. If the client does react to the therapist, however, problem ownership can be easier to achieve in a group because of the feedback from other members.

Problem ownership can be particularly difficult for paranoid clients and other clients with character disorders, who avoid looking into themselves while blaming problems on others. You may have to forego any attempt to help these clients own their problems until they have been in the group long enough to make meaningful connections with others. Then the feedback from other group members may have enough impact on them to stimulate self-investigation.

Minimizing Shame.   Be sensitive to issues of shame in bringing up problem ownership.

For example, if you see that a person has a pattern of taking up too much group time and attention, you must be careful how you bring this to her attention in the group. This issue can be shameful for most people and therefore must be approached sensitively. Sometimes it is best to bring this up in a consultation (or individual session) so the person doesn't have to deal with the humiliation of having it aired in front of the group. This could cause her to be deeply wounded or to defend so rigidly that there would be no benefit.

☐ Feedback

The group setting has advantages for achieving problem ownership. The client can get feedback from other group members that helps him to see his distortions and overreactions, and he may trust this feedback more than facilitations from the leader. *In the example with Peter, if he balks at your suggestion to explore his anger, other group members may agree that his anger seemed out of proportion to what Sandra did.*

Feedback in a group is more likely to be taken seriously because it comes from people who have witnessed the actual event. In individual therapy, feedback from the therapist is frequently about an event from the person's life not witnessed by the therapist, so the client can always conclude that the therapist doesn't understand because he wasn't there. However in group, the event in question usually happens right before everyone's eyes, and so the feedback has enhanced credibility.

Who Gives the Feedback.   Even then, the group member must trust that the other group members (or the leader) aren't trying to hurt him, and that they have his best interests at heart, before he will take the feedback seriously. This kind of trust is enhanced if the group is cohesive, and also if the member receives the feedback from people whom he perceives as caring about him. *For example, if Peter gets feedback about his anger being exaggerated from two people in group whom he trusts care for him, he is likely to listen to it.* In receiving feedback from the leader, it helps if there is a good therapeutic alliance. If the client feels touchy about problem ownership, it is advisable to forestall feedback from people who are angry at him and encourage it from people whom he trusts.

Sometimes you must decide whether it will be easier for a client to hear a challenge from you or from the group. If there are some group members who aren't feeling angry and are trusted by the person, it is better if the feedback comes from them. This is especially true if the person has difficulty with authority figures or if your therapeutic alliance with her is shaky, especially if you have unresolved countertransference feelings toward her. On the other hand, if the group seems angry at the client or if she is particularly fragile, then it may be better if the feedback comes from you. The leader has a better chance of giving the feedback in a neutral, helpful way. The group members are there to express themselves, not necessarily to be therapeutic for others, so they may not exercise as much care as the person needs.

Considering Feedback.   It is possible that a client will get feedback about his behavior that isn't accurate or helpful, that comes more from the bias of the person giving the feedback. Therefore it is important that the client not automatically assume that the feedback is correct and it is indeed his problem. Not only might the feedback be wrong, but if he accepts the feedback without checking it against his experience, he won't benefit much from it. It is important that the client consider carefully what he thinks about the feedback, explore himself, check with other group members, and engage in further dialogue about it, if necessary.

☐   Skipping Problem Ownership

Continuing with the Interaction

If a group member is particularly resistant to problem ownership, or you suspect he will be, it may be advisable to move on with the interaction without making an issue of problem ownership. Maybe the client can gain something from the interaction without admitting his part. *For example, if you allow the interaction between Sandra and Peter to continue, and she is hurt by Peter's anger, he may learn to be compassionate about her feelings.* Maybe his responsibility will become clearer as the dialogue proceeds. *For example, in clarifying what she meant, it may become obvious that Sandra wasn't feeling that helpless and therefore it was Peter's distortion.*

Even if the client doesn't benefit from the continued interaction, the other person may learn something from the exchange. *For example, even if Peter doesn't learn anything, Sandra may gain in her ability to deal with other people's anger.*

The client may need some distance from the emotional heat of the moment to consider his behavior and realize that he has something to work on, or he may need to act out the problematic behavior a few more times before his part becomes clear to him and to the group.

> For example, suppose a few weeks later, Peter gets angry with someone who is expressing pain in a childlike way, and later he becomes upset with someone who is having trouble being strong in a situation. It will start to become clear to the group that Peter has a pattern of responses that must come from a issue. Almost everyone will see it and will be able to marshal considerable evidence in convincing Peter. It will be much harder for Peter to avoid owning the problem.

Continuing with the Therapy Process

Sometimes you can proceed to other aspects of the therapeutic process without dealing with problem ownership.

> For example, suppose someone feels excessively hurt over something a group member says to him, and you sense he will be resistant to owning this as an overreaction. You can simply ask him to explore his hurt and what it means to him without first getting him to admit that his response was exaggerated. This may lead to access without a prior need for problem ownership.

Some clients are willing to explore transference without admitting that their reactions are distorted. *For example, one group member resisted acknowledging that his reactions to men in the group were distorted in any way, but he was interested in transference and therefore willing to free associate to childhood memories about his father and brothers.*

Another way to bypass problem ownership is to suggest that the group member experiment with different behavior without suggesting that there was anything wrong with his original behavior. *For example, suppose a group member is beating around the bush, and you know this is an indirect expression of his distrust of the group. Sensing that he would become defensive if you pointed out his indirectness, you could simply suggest, "Let's try an experiment. Try telling the group that you don't trust them."* This allows you to move on to the step of experimenting directly without getting stuck in problem ownership.

☐ Working with Resistance to Problem Ownership

When a client is defensive about owning a problem, one approach is to let go of any attempt to get him to own it and instead work directly on his resistance. This is usually just as valuable as if the client had owned the problem because you may learn something quite valuable about where this defensiveness comes from. Focus on the resistance by asking the group member non-judgmental questions about his reluctance to own the problem. *For example, if Peter heatedly denies that there is any problem with his anger, you might say, "What feelings came up when people made comments about your anger?"* or *"It seems that maybe you felt judged or reprimanded just now."*

Perhaps the client doesn't trust the group in some way or feels insecure about being accepted, and this challenge feels like more rejection. Perhaps he doesn't feel safe with you because he felt hurt by something you said to him in the past. *In this case, you could say, "I wonder if you don't feel that my comment about your anger was intended to help you. Maybe it felt like I wanted to make you feel bad. Has this happened before between us?"* Perhaps this issue is loaded for him. *For example, Peter has deep pain about his mother's not being strong for him, which is behind his anger at Sandra. If he is challenged about this anger, it may stir up this pain.* Perhaps being blamed is a major childhood issue for the client, which is now being inflamed. *For example, Peter's father may have repeatedly blamed him when things went wrong in the family.*

Whatever the resistance is about can be explored as a valid issue in itself. Once it diminishes, return to the original issue of problem ownership if that seems appropriate.

☐ Other Problems

Compliance

The leader should also be watchful for the opposite of resistance—compliance. Some clients accept everything that is said about them without even checking with themselves to see if it fits or not. Such a person has a core issue that requires that she be "confluent" with other people, meaning that she isn't allowed to be separate. When someone suggests that she has a problem, she automatically assumes that the other person is right. She may go out of her way to find some aspect of her internal process that matches the accusation, even if it is mostly off the mark. *For example, Janine has a tendency to be pleasing to others and lighten up the group with humor. Michael suggested that she was doing this as a way to get people to like her because she was afraid of being rejected. In fact, Janine's main motivation was to prevent people from being angry at her, but in an attempt to comply with Michael's interpretation, she found a small part of her that was also afraid of rejection. This allowed her to agree with him.* A client like this needs to learn how to check inside herself to decide what is really going on, even if it doesn't fit the interpretation.

It is easier to spot compliance when it occurs with other group members or with your co-leader. It is more difficult to see it when a client is being compliant with you. After all, you assume your opinion is right. It is helpful to notice whether the person seems to consider your opinion and check it against her experience before agreeing, or whether she seem to agree automatically without any elaboration of the material.

Self-Judgment

Once a person owns a problem or acknowledges a defense, it is not uncommon for her to become harsh and judgmental with herself for having this problem. This can be very painful and also prevent the person from effectively addressing the problem. Make sure that *you* aren't feeling judgmental toward the client, and convey caring and compassion in your statements. Make it clear to clients that your goal is to promote awareness and ownership *with* self-acceptance. You don't want them to condemn themselves but rather to be curious about self-exploration. Of course, this is hard for many people to do. They must deal with a harmful inner critic and work through a deficiency in their sense of value.

☐ Blame Cycles

One of the most common ways for clients to defend against problem ownership is to blame the person they are having difficulty with: "Since it isn't my fault that something went wrong in our interaction, it must be yours." This often leads to a cycle of blame, where two people go back and forth arguing about whose fault their problem is. *The transcript in chapter 13 showing an interaction between Ralph and John illustrates a blame cycle.* Blame cycles are very common among couples and other close family members. They frequently pose a problem in marriage and family therapy.

Technique

Once such a cycle is established, it can be hard to stop. The first step is to point out to both people that they are in a blaming contest. It is surprising how often people don't even realize that their main intention in a dialogue is to lay the fault on the other person so they don't have to feel wrong. It is usually necessary to work with each person separately on his part in the interaction. You may have to be forceful in preventing them from continuing to argue with each other or snipe at each other. Explore with each client the feelings that were triggered in him by the other person, and especially try to get to the vulnerable feelings of hurt or fear or shame that are behind the more aggressive feelings. If feasible, help the client to understand the transference behind the reaction. This tends to diminish anger, and it also helps the other person to take the blame less personally. Sometimes the drive to blame the other person derives from transference toward a parent who rarely admitted any fault and avoided taking responsibility for problems in the home. Even if the client can't fully see his part in the problem, just getting some emotional distance from the angry interchange will help to calm him down and foster understanding.

It is especially helpful in such a situation if the rest of the group doesn't get caught in taking sides. If even a few group members can see both sides of the struggle and empathize with both people, it tends to defuse the anger. Each antagonist begins to realize that the other person isn't an ogre. On the other hand, if the group polarizes, with members siding with one person or the other, this can exacerbate the problem. If this starts to happen, ask the members to see if they can relate to both sides of the conflict.

Once one or both people have successfully explored themselves, they are much more likely to be able to work through their difficulties. Even if they can't completely resolve them at that time, they are less likely to get into trouble. However, you should decide whether you think they can continue the dialogue without attacking each other.

If they can, let them work more on their relationship, possibly leading to some valuable resolution. If things are still tense between them, it may be best not to encourage any more dialogue at that time. Make sure that both people have had a chance to explore as much as possible, and then move on to getting supportive feedback from the group. This often helps each embattled person to feel better about himself. The members who are at odds can continue the work with each other in the future. Express confidence that they will be able to work it out in time.

In extreme cases, where two members remain stuck in a blame cycle, it can be helpful to arrange individual consultations with them. This allows you to help them explore their reactions in a safe, calm situation that is removed from any inflaming stimuli.

☐ Defense Cycles

A *defense cycle* is an even more entrenched version of a blame cycle. This happens when two people get locked in a vicious cycle of defensive reactions to each other. The first person has a core issue activated and reacts with a characteristic defense. This defense triggers an issue in the second person, who reacts with her own characteristic defense. This then triggers the same defense in the first person, producing further rounds of defensive reactions.

> For example, suppose that Donna and Phil are working on their relationship with each other. Donna is especially afraid of being judged by people and Phil is afraid of being abandoned by women. Donna defends against her fear of being judged by acting a little aloof and withdrawn around Phil. This triggers Phil's fear of being abandoned, and he reacts by telling her that she is avoiding connection with him and demanding that she stop being withdrawn. Since this is a judgment of her, this exacerbates her fear of him and her withdrawal defense. This makes him feel even more abandoned and therefore increases his demands and judgments. And around and around they go.

Technique. This kind of pattern is common in couples therapy as well as therapy groups. When a defense cycle happens, first spell out the entire dynamics of the cycle for both people, and make it clear how they are pushing each other's buttons. This can help to loosen the entrenched quality of the dialogue. It is especially helpful to point out any commonalities in the struggles of the two people. *For example, sometimes both people are feeling unseen or both are struggling not to by taken over by the other.* It usually helps to work with each person separately, as in a blame cycle, to access the pain and transference behind the defenses. You can also ask each person what he or she could do to break the cycle. Allow the group to offer suggestions if necessary.

Deeper Access and Healing. A defense cycle can be difficult and frustrating to work with, but it also offers an opportunity for a great deal of inner healing because of the access involved. Defense cycles tend to happen when both people have strong transference with each other. Because they repeatedly activate each other's issues, they tend to get very involved with each other, even though it is a primarily negative involvement. If the leader is able to help them access the pain behind the defenses, the degree of access will be great because of the mutual transference and triggering. There-fore when two people in a defense cycle finally work through their conflicts with each other and establish a close, positive relationship, enormous change takes place. This process can take months, but if both people are willing to stay with this difficult work, it can be very productive.

> For example, if Donna and Phil each explore the deep fears and pain behind their defenses and then gradually form a close bond, Donna will not only have the experience of being close to a man without being judged, she will have this relationship with a man who was a powerful transference figure for her. Therefore this will produce in Donna a level of thera-peutic change that wouldn't have been possible without such a high degree of access, and similarly for Phil.

16

CHAPTER

Aggression

Handling aggression can require subtle discriminations because it can be used in both healthy and defensive ways. This chapter develops a theoretical understanding of aggression and explains how it relates to the therapeutic change process. This is followed by a discussion of specific techniques for working with aggression.

☐ Definition of Aggression

Aggression is a healthy capacity that plays an important role in the operation of autonomy and safety and in providing healing for core issues that derive from attack, domination, violation, or other types of harm. However, aggression can also be used as a defense against a core issue, in which form it can sometimes be quite destructive. The psychological literature has a mixed view of aggression. In Gestalt therapy (Perls et al., 1951), aggression refers to the positive capacity to contact others in a way that attempts to get what one needs to grow. "Modern psychoanalysis" has a similar view of aggression (Spotnitz, 1996). In assertiveness training, on the other hand, aggression has a negative connotation because it refers to attacking others in order to get one's needs met. In classical psychoanalysis, aggression is seen as a basic drive that can be destructive or constructive depending on how the ego handles it. While I recognize that aggression can be quite destructive in certain forms, I find it useful to understand it as a healthy capacity.

I define *aggression* as the ability to mobilize oneself energetically to exert power and autonomy, especially in the face of others who are also exerting power, and to protect oneself from attack or intrusion. Aggression can be mobilized in extreme forms, such as verbal abuse or violence. Of course, this isn't healthy unless it is done in a therapeutic role-playing situation where no one will be harmed or in self-defense in a life-threatening situation. Aggression is ideally channeled in interpersonally constructive ways that assert and protect oneself while maintaining a respectful stance toward others.

☐ Vulnerable and Aggressive Reactions

Vulnerable and Aggressive Responses

Let's look at core issues in more detail. They are typically rooted in a childhood experience of harm. To understand this better, let's examine healthy adult responses to such a situation. Whenever a person encounters behavior from another person that feels harmful, for example, attacking or rejecting, there are two types of natural, healthy responses—vulnerable and aggressive.

A vulnerable response involves feeling the pain that has been invoked, such as hurt, shame, or fear. If this pain is an appropriate response to the moment and is not conditioned by a core issue, then it is healthy to feel and show this pain.

> For example, if one group member makes a judgmental comment about another, the recipient may feel some shame. Allowing herself to experience and show the hurt or shame is healthy, unless the amount of hurt or shame is exaggerated because of the activation of a core issue or is a response to something that wasn't really harmful.

An aggressive response is when a client stands up for herself or protects herself from the harmful behavior. If someone attacks a client, an aggressive response could mean defending herself, challenging the manner of the attack, expressing anger, and so on. It means protecting the client's integrity, boundaries, or sense of value from an unconstructive attack. If the aggression is an appropriate response to what happened in the moment rather than being conditioned by a core issue, it is healthy. If the client overreacts, counterattacks, or reacts with protection when none is needed, then this is a problematic reaction.

The vulnerable response comes first and is more basic than the aggressive one. The aggressive response is an attempt to protect the person from the harmful behavior of the other or the resulting pain. Sometimes the aggressive response is a natural response to being hurt or an attempt to correct the situation, but frequently it is a defense against the pain.

Vulnerability is the healthy capacity to be open in the face of pain or danger. If a person has developed her capacity for both vulnerability and aggression, she will be able to respond with one or the other or some combination of the two, depending on the situation.

> For example, if a woman's husband tells her something hurtful in a constructive way, then it would be healthy to show her hurt and also to consider the content of his complaint without defensiveness. On the other hand, if he is vicious and demeaning, it would be healthy to challenge this behavior in a firm and possibly angry way.

Aggression and Core Issues

The same thing applies to a child. When a child is treated in a way so as to cause pain, she will have both vulnerable and aggressive responses to this. If these become structured into a core issue, the adult will have both vulnerable and aggressive reactions when that issue is activated.

> For example, when Marcy was shamed and rejected by her father, she felt ashamed and worthless, and she also felt angry and judgmental toward her father. Since this happened repeatedly during Marcy's childhood, she developed a core issue that involved both reactions. When, as an adult, Marcy experiences a man as rejecting or shaming her, she will react from this core issue in both ways. She will have a vulnerable reaction of hurt and humiliation and an aggressive reaction of anger and judgment.

☐ Aggression and Healing

Accessing Both Reactions

How does this understanding of aggression affect our view of the therapeutic change process? Even though aggressive reactions are frequently used as defenses, they can also be a legitimate response to harm. A client who is defending through aggression must learn to let go of the defense so he can access the underlying pain, but he may later need the aggression as part of his healing.

When working toward accessing a core issue, the client may access either the aggressive or the vulnerable reaction, or both. Over time it will be valuable for the person to fully access both reactions. The vulnerable reaction is important for opening up the core issue for healing because it is the more basic one. If it isn't accessed, the healing with be limited. The aggressive reaction can be useful, however, in leading to the vulnerable one. After expressing her anger or rage, a client often spontaneously moves into the pain beneath it, thereby allowing fuller access.

Protective Healing

In addition, the aggressive reaction may lead in the direction of protective healing. When a person is dealing with a harm issue, she often needs healing in the form of protection from the original harm or from something similar in the present. The aggressive reaction is a natural response that can provide this protection. If a person's aggressive reaction is blocked, then she will need to receive protection from others at first, but eventually she should provide the protection herself. Her aggressive reaction is the source of that ability to protect herself.

> For example, suppose Marcy has already explored the shame that derives from her father's mistreatment of her, but she has difficulty being aggressive and standing up for herself.

Let's say she is triggered once again by Barry in the group, who is indeed shaming her. You could encourage her to protect herself by expressing her anger toward Barry. Once she has acknowledged feeling angry at him, you might say, "See what it would be like to express that anger directly to Barry."

Sometimes a person's aggressive reaction is not powerful enough to be truly healing. She may feel ineffectual anger or impotent rage. However, by accessing more fully the aggression that is blocked, the person can move toward a more powerful expression of the self-protective urge, which can be truly healing.

This brings up the question of what makes an aggressive response healing. The most important criterion is that the response gives the client an experience of personal power. Let's look at this in terms of the basic needs involved. If the harm issue produces primarily a deficiency in autonomy, then the protective response must restore the person's experience of autonomy. The aggression must help her to feel that she can take charge of her life, know her own desires and opinions, make her own choices, protect herself from being controlled by others, etc. If the harm issue deals with safety, then a healing response must restore the person's feeling of being protected from attack or intrusion. She must feel that she has the right to and the power to defend her own boundaries and integrity. If the harm issue undermines her sense of value, the aggressive response must be an assertion that this is wrong because she is a person of worth.

For example, with Marcy and Barry, suppose Barry had said, "There you go. Another weak, manipulating female, crying all the time." She might need to assert to him that she isn't weak, that her crying is an appropriate way of expressing her feelings, and that she resents being judged and shamed in that way. If he responds with a further assertion of his position or with anger, she might start to back down or collapse. Then she would need the leader's and the group's support to stand her ground and fight back Regardless of how Barry responded, it would still be important to support Marcy's aggression as a protective healing response. In some cases, even if Barry were being reasonable and Marcy erroneously perceived him as shaming, you might choose to support her anger, as long as Barry could tolerate it and knew that you supported him, too.

☐ Technique

Many people have only one of these two possible responses available to them. They respond characteristically with either aggression or with vulnerability. In working with someone about such responses, it is important to see his patterns. Is he capable of both aggression and vulnerability? Does he almost always respond with anger? Does he avoid standing up for himself? If he rarely expresses aggression and is always feeling hurt or ashamed, for example, it may mean that his aggressive responses were punished as a child and he never developed them. He may not be capable of healthy aggression. It can be helpful to question him about these feelings during an interaction. Did he feel any anger in response to what was just said to him? How did he undermine the anger he might have felt? Did he feel frightened of being angry? Did he try to understand the other person as a way of avoiding feeling angry?

In the opposite situation, when a client reacts aggressively in a interaction there are four possibilities.

1. *Healthy.* It is a healthy self-protective response; no core issue is involved. The response is constructive and appropriate to the stimulus. The other person was actually attacking, and an angry response was called for. Or the other person's statement was milder and the client channeled his aggression in a constructive way.

   For example, if Barry tells Marcy, in a reasonable tone of voice, that he has difficulty with her when she cries, she might tell him why her tears are important for her and ask what bothers him. This involves some aggression, but Marcy is using an amount that is constructive and appropriate to Barry's statement.

2. *Defense.* It is an aggressive reaction, and this client frequently gets angry in inappropriate ways, so he is using his aggression as a defense against feeling his pain. In this case, ask him about the vulnerable feeling behind the anger. You can even explain that everyone has both reactions. The vulnerable one comes first and the aggressive one follows. He may only be aware of the anger. Ask him to remember back to the split second before he got angry. What did he feel? Shame, pain, fear, hurt? Help him explore why it is so difficult for him to feel or express the vulnerable feeling. Does he feel that he'll be opening himself up for more hurt? Is he afraid it will be used against him? Does he want revenge?

   When you are first getting to know a client and aren't yet sure of his pattern, start by asking for the vulnerable feeling. This usually yields information about what triggered the core issue, material that can be therapeutically useful. *For example, if the client is feeling hurt about loss, then he may have an underlying issue around abandonment. In contrast, if he is feeling fear, he may have underlying issues around abuse or intrusion.* The aggressive feeling doesn't produce as much therapeutic information. Even if the aggressive response is healthy, it is still important to access the vulnerable feeling underneath. Then the person can exercise her aggression afterward, when it will be more healing.

3. *Misperception.* It is an aggressive reaction, based on a core issue and the other person is perceived as being vicious (or demeaning or something similar) when he really isn't. The client reacts in a way that would have been appropriate if this perception were accurate. *For example, Marcy expresses a degree of anger that is exaggerated for the situation but would have been appropriate if she were really being attacked unfairly.*

   It is tempting to explore the client's transference and help her to see the irrationality of her anger, and in some cases this is completely appropriate. However, if this client tends to block her aggression, you don't want to squelch her anger even though it is misdirected. Instead you may want to support the anger as healing aggression. However, it isn't appropriate for the client to direct the anger toward the other group member because he is not responsible of her reaction. The way around this dilemma is to help the client to access where the anger came from in her childhood, and encourage her to express it to the person it really belongs to, perhaps a parent. She can either talk about her anger at the parent or engage in role-playing, as in Gestalt therapy or psychodrama. This supports her ability to be aggressive and self-protective while helping her to clarify the real meaning of the anger, and it also protects the other group member. The rest of the group will also be able to support her anger, while otherwise they might have felt a need to protect the other person from her.

For example, you could move Marcy away from Barry and ask her when she felt angry like this as a child, thus helping her to realize that her anger derives from her relationship with her father. Then she could be encouraged to express her anger at her father through role-playing. She would imagine that her father was sitting in a chair in the room and express her feelings to the chair (or pick a group member to role play her father and express her feelings to him). In this way, she wouldn't have to worry about her father's response, so she could concentrate on feeling and expressing her aggression. This would be healing for her with respect to the shame issue with her father, and it wouldn't alienate Barry or the rest of the group.

4. *Overreaction.* It is an aggressive reaction, and it is so extreme as to be inappropriate for any situation, for example, uncontrolled rage or nasty counterattack. In this case, you need to help the person explore the underlying core issue, which probably involves a great deal of pain. In the future, when she has worked through much of the underlying pain, you may want to help her learn how to express aggression in a constructive way.

This pattern of aggressive overreaction, rooted in past trauma, fuels the rampant violence in the world today. People who have been traumatized by abuse, war, oppression, or terrorism harbor tremendous pain inside, and some of them react to relatively minor frustrations with violence, thereby perpetuating the cycle. In addition to promoting international understanding, conflict resolution, democracy, and rule by law, we also need to heal people from the wounds of violence so they can move beyond their hatred and reconcile with their perceived enemies.

17
CHAPTER

Intervention Choices

This chapter examines the choices a leader faces in making interventions. It also discusses some other issues not covered previously—internal and external support and the role of forgiveness in the therapeutic change process. It ends with a detailed example illustrating some of the concepts from the last four chapters.

☐ Intervention Choices

Let's examine some of the different types of work that can occur in an interactive group and the intervention choices presented to a leader. The following are four possibilities: (a) an interactive dialogue between two people; (b) one person engages in self-exploration; (c) a person receives feedback on her behavior from the leader or group members; and (d) a person explores her feelings about being in the group. When a client begins a piece of work, she will usually begin with one of these modalities, but sometimes the leader needs to direct her toward a different one as the work proceeds.

Dialogue

Who Is the Focus of the Work?   When working with a dialogue between two people, pay attention to who is the primary focus of your interventions. You may work for a while with both people on the communication between them, and then you may become interested in one person's issues. Sometimes you will keep your therapeutic focus mostly on one of the two people in a dialogue, even though it is not individual work. This is often appropriate, but don't forget about the other person. It is easy to let the other person slide into the background and become almost a co-therapist in the interaction. This may lead you to miss reactions that this person needs to work on. It is useful to make sure the other person occasionally expresses her feeling reactions. This keeps her more present and gives the client doing the work someone more authentic to interact with.

For example, Celia and Mandy are talking about their relationship. Celia is feeling insecure about her value to Mandy, and you focus on helping Celia access her fears about self-worth and learn to be assertive in relating to Mandy. However, during this process Mandy is not exploring herself. She is conversing with Celia about their relationship and occasionally expressing her feelings, but she isn't doing any self-exploration. This is fine while Celia needs your full attention, but the danger is that it can reinforce the very pattern that Celia is working on. She is feeling insecure and not as "together" as Mandy, and focusing on Celia alone perpetuates this perception. At some point it is necessary to ask Mandy to explore her feeling response to Celia in more depth and include her as a full emotional participant in the dialogue.

Switching to Another Modality.   When two group members are interacting, the leader constantly faces a choice between continuing the dialogue, focusing on individual exploration, or providing feedback to one person.

Suppose Adrian is angry with Tom about his withdrawal. There are three choices: (a) *individual* (you could focus on Adrian and encourage her to explore exactly what she is feeling, what Tom's withdrawal means to her, and where her emotional charge comes from); (b) *dialogue* (you could ask Tom how he is reacting to Adrian's anger and encourage the two of them to dialogue about this, paying attention to communication, how they each deal with anger, power, and other issues that emerge); and (c) *feedback* (you might decide that Tom needs to look at his withdrawal, so you give him feedback about that or encourage other group members to do so).

Often work will move back and forth among these three options.

For example, suppose you focus on Adrian individually at first. Then when she has achieved some insight, you might ask how she is feeling toward Tom in order to re-engage the dialogue. On the other hand, if you encourage the dialogue and they get stuck in anger and blame, you will need to work with each individually before the dialogue can be fruitful. You might start with the dialogue and then move toward feedback to one of the people. Feedback from the group might lead to deeper individual work or trigger feelings that lead back to a dialogue.

Feedback.   Feedback should be encouraged when the work is stuck because one of the people isn't owning a problem of his that is derailing progress. This, however, can only be done if the person is strong enough to make use of the feedback. Sometimes a person is too fragile or too vulnerable at that moment, and feedback will just stir up pain or defense. This is especially true for clients with narcissistic issues. Then it is best not to focus on problem ownership, but rather explore something else, perhaps the person's vulnerability. When he is stronger or has better support in the group, problem ownership can be tackled.

☐   When to Work Individually

Notice that "individual work" is not the opposite of "interactive work." Interactive work includes anything that grows out of a response to someone in the group or to being in the group. Thus all of the modalities considered in this section are considered interactive work. "Outside work" is the opposite of interactive work.

There are certain situations when it may be necessary to focus on individual work. Some of these have been discussed in the last chapter—blame cycles, defense cycles, and healing mismatches. In addition, individual work is called for when an intense transference reaction is derailing the communication. This must be explored before the person will be able to make headway in the dialogue

Avoiding Dangerous Confrontation

Be on the lookout for dangerous confrontations, especially when the group is in an early stage or one of the members involved is new to the group. It is not wise to let the level of confrontation at any given moment get beyond the level of support in the group. It is amazing to realize that a certain degree of anger and conflict, which might be perfectly safe in a seasoned group that had been meeting for a year or more, could completely destroy a group in its first or second meeting. Similarly, once a group member has been in the group long enough to know that there are people who care about him and feel connected to him, he can tolerate a higher level of conflict than at the beginning. If this same level of conflict happened in his first month, it might be too frightening for him to return. The crucial variable here is *perceived* support. Even if the support is there, if the group member doesn't feel it, then too much confrontation is dangerous.

A confrontation might also be too dangerous because of the fragility of one or both members in the confrontation. Narcissistic clients are particularly vulnerable in this way, especially when they are new in group.

When you sense a confrontation is dangerous, defuse the situation before it starts, if possible. As soon as any anger is expressed, move in and work with the angry person on what is behind the anger, and do not allow a dialogue to develop.

> For example, suppose in the first meeting of a group, Adrian tells Tom that she is angry at him for being so cold. If you sense that this is too much for Tom, you can immediately work with Adrian on her anger, perhaps discovering its childhood origins. When you are finished with her, you may want to check with Tom to see if he needs to process any feelings that arose.

Deciding on Modality

The choice of modality should be governed by your clinical intuition and knowledge of group members and their issues. When a client reacts to another member, if you think she should spend time exploring this reaction individually before she interacts with the person, then you can suggest this. Since most therapists are trained primarily in doing individual therapy, beware of focusing too much attention on in-dividual work and access. Make sure to take the other person's needs (and the group's needs) into account in making this decision. Remember that you don't need to achieve the deepest possible access in each piece of work. You can achieve a small amount of access and then allow the interaction to continue, trusting that the person will learn more from the interaction and from others in the weeks ahead. The group process can be trusted to bring up any issues that the person hasn't fully explored.

☐ The Group

It is important to keep the group in the back of your mind at all times. No matter what is going on with one or two people, it always takes place in a group context. Any work can be affected profoundly by what is happening in the group, even if nothing is being said. A piece of work can also be significantly affected by what the person working imagines is going on in the group. At these moments, it is necessary to explore where the person's reaction is coming from and get feedback from the group, if appropriate.

> For example, in the interaction between Adrian and Tom, if Tom reacts very defensively to Adrian's anger, it might be because he has been confronted by other group members recently and doesn't feel safe in the group. If so, he may need to explore this with the group before continuing his work with Adrian.

Furthermore the group is affected by each person's work. No matter how valuable a piece of work is to an individual, it shouldn't go on too long. If the group is feeling bored or irritated for one reason or another, this needs to be taken into account. Of course, you don't have to do all this yourself. The group members are responsible for bringing up their reactions. If someone has a strong reaction of any kind to a piece of work, she may need to interrupt the work to express herself. If people don't feel that they can do this, important feelings will get buried and the group process will suffer. In addition, after any piece of work, group members need to express their reactions, both their feelings toward the person who was working and the personal issues that her work may have triggered in them.

☐ One Member Interacting with the Group

Almost half of the interactive work that happens in a group takes the form of an interaction between one person and the group rather than a dialogue between two members. One group member will explore how she relates to the group as a whole or the feelings that are brought up by being in the group.

Types of Issues

Let's examine the types of issues that come up in relating to the group as a whole. Clients frequently deal with feelings of being excluded from the group, not belonging to the group, and feeling different from others. They struggle with shame about various kinds of self-disclosure. They deal with their fears of trusting others to accept them and care for them. They struggle with the fear of being judged or ridiculed by others.

Clients sometimes experiment with expressing aspects of themselves that have been blocked. A client may experiment with expressing anger, sadness, love, or self-assertion to see if the group can accept and appreciate that side of herself. She may try out taking a stand that seems unpopular in the group. She may risk being herself even if she fears that she will be ostracized for this. As time goes on, people take the risk to allow the group to be important to them and to allow the other members to really matter. They make an emotional investment in the group.

Exploration and Access

In working with a client on any of these issues, first help him to explore the issue as it is arising in the group for him. What feelings are being evoked, what behavior is being blocked, what deeper meaning does this have for him? If appropriate, encourage him to access the childhood origins of the issue.

Make sure, however, that the client doesn't focus on feelings toward the group as a whole in order to avoid dealing directly with one person. Some clients will say that an issue involves the whole group because they are too frightened to face a specific person.

> For example, a man said that he felt afraid of being rejected by the group because of the weakness he felt he had shown. However, in exploring this fear, he realized that it was primarily directed toward one particular woman, whom he was attracted to. She was the one he was afraid would reject him.

Interacting with the Group or One Person

If a client needs to experiment with new behavior or receive healing responses, he can do this either with the group as a whole or with one other person. Though I usually favor interacting with one person, in some cases, it is appropriate to do this with the whole group. For example, a client may take the risk to show her sadness in the group and then get feedback from various people about their responses. If a client is genuinely angry with the group, this can sometimes be expressed to the whole group. However, when anger is expressed, the people receiving it often feel a need to respond. Expressing generalized anger to a group is dangerous because most members won't have a chance to deal with their responses and may end up feeling alienated and resentful. The client might also be using this as a way of avoiding confronting certain people directly. When in doubt, make sure that the client addresses her anger to specific individuals and they have a chance to respond.

> For example, Dora felt hurt and angry because she perceived the group as judging her, especially when she had made herself vulnerable. She dealt with this by making hostile comments about the group and then breaking into tears. Since these statements weren't directed to anyone in particular and she seemed fragile, no one challenged her or reassured

her. Most of the group felt confused and resentful toward her for judging them, and this reinforced the very feeling of alienation that Dora started with. In a later group, the leader encouraged Dora to pick one person to interact with. She told Elinor that she felt that Elinor looked bored and uninterested when Dora was expressing intense pain. Elinor explained that she felt empathy for Dora but had a hard time expressing it because Dora didn't leave much room for anyone to relate to her at those times. This was the kind of interaction Dora needed. She needed to discover the support she did have in the group and also to learn how she made it hard for people to be close to her.

Even if a client feels a certain way (e.g., angry) toward most of the group members, it is often valuable for her to pick one person to interact with. Usually a dialogue is necessary to work through an issue, so it is best if a client deals with one person at a time. She may interact with one person this week and pick another in a future session.

Preventing Overgeneralizing

Picking one person to dialogue with also prevents clients from overgeneralizing. When a client is judged or rejected by a couple of group members, she may generalize this so that she believes the whole group feels this way toward her. By picking individuals to talk to, this illusion is dispelled. If you think that the client needs to get feedback on her behavior or learn to work through conflict, have her pick one of the people who feel negatively toward her. If you feel that it is more important for her to recognize that she has support in the group, have her pick one of the other group members to talk to.

For example, Dora found out that she had support from Elinor in the example above. In another group meeting, she interacted with Damon, who really did have negative feelings toward her. He was annoyed at her for needing reassurance from him but then running away when he tried to reach out to her. This feedback was also useful for her.

Even though a group member realizes that most of the group feels good about her, she may still become obsessed with one problem person. Then her work is to take in the support she has in the group rather than focusing only on the one negative voice.

☐ Bottleneck Issues

A *bottleneck issue* is one that seriously impedes the flow of the therapy process. When the bottleneck is blocked, not only is work on that particular issue halted, but nothing else can move through either. It is important to identify bottleneck issues so that they can be given top priority. Bottleneck issues can be of three types:

1. *Individual bottleneck.* A particular client has an unresolved issue that blocks his ability to work on any other issues. *For example, his mistrust of the leader may be so strong that he won't allow the leader to facilitate him.* If a client is blocked with a bottleneck issue, this issue must receive top priority whenever you are working with this client because until it is resolved, the client can't make progress on anything else.

2. *Interpersonal bottleneck.* When two people are in a dialogue, one of them may be blocked in such a way that the work between them can't move further until her issue is resolved. *For example, one client may be so irrationally angry at another that her anger must be worked on before any dialogue would be fruitful.* Another possibility is that an interpersonal dynamic exists between two people that must be addressed before anything else. *For example, one person may need the other's approval and the other may be frightened of the need. Whenever they try to deal with anything else between them, this issue causes hurt and misunderstanding, especially if it isn't brought out in the open.*

3. *Group bottleneck.* A problem in group dynamics may be preventing therapeutic work from happening in the group. *For example, there may be so much conflict that group members don't feel safe enough to let themselves be vulnerable.* If a group is stuck with a bottleneck issue, this should be given the highest priority, because until the group issue is resolved, nothing much therapeutic can happen for anyone.

☐ Responsibility for the Flow of Work

There are often issues about the flow of attention in the group—who gets to work next, whether it's OK for someone to interrupt a piece of work, what to do when a person loses the group's attention before he is finished, and so on. Unless there is a compelling clinical reason for the leader to make such a decision, these should be left to the group. This puts the group members more in charge of their own fate, helping to empower them. These issues can also generate interesting interpersonal material between group members.

Whenever there is a difficulty in the group, the question arises of who should be responsible for bringing it up, the group members or the leader. Sometimes there will be an important reason why you should bring it out into the open, perhaps your neutral stance will help you to be heard. Otherwise, it is better if the group members do it. It teaches them responsibility for their lives and generates good interactive material for the group. However, when you see a problem and the group members aren't saying anything, what do you do? If you hold back, the problem may get worse. If you intervene, you deprive the group members of the chance to do it themselves. Fortunately, there is a third alternative. You can ask the members why they aren't saying anything. This brings the problem out but leaves the responsibility with the group.

> For example, if someone is monopolizing the group time and you see that people are getting bored and irritated, you could say, "I notice that most people have been pretty quiet for a while. I wonder what you are feeling?"

☐ Support

Support, a key concept in working with group members, refers to the underpinnings that allow them to take risks in a group. Drawing from Gestalt therapy concepts, *support* means the various ways that a client feels internal strength and receives help and healing from others. It is important to distinguish between self-support (inner support) and external support. *Inner support* includes a client taking responsibility for her work, especially self-direction and motivation, and the development and availability of healthy capacities, especially connectedness, autonomy, value, and safety. *External support* includes the facilitation from the group leader and possibly other group members, and healing responses, including caring, affection, encouragement, and protection.

Monitoring External Support

When using a relatively active leadership style, it is important to monitor the degree of support you offer. The general rule of thumb is to provide as much external support as needed but not more. This includes both support from the leader and the group. This means that sometimes you will need to encourage support from the group and at other times discourage them. External support should be given when it is needed to continue with a therapeutic task or when it will be healing for the person. It should not be given if the person has the internal support to proceed on his own or if he doesn't want the support. Let's look at this in more detail.

In general, group leaders should strive to do as little as possible while still enabling the group to be maximally therapeutic. Avoid facilitation that comes solely from your need to be running things. In the early stages of a group or with new group members, you may need to be quite active. Later in a group or with sophisticated group members, you can afford to intervene much less, allowing clients to set the direction for the work (except when they move in non-therapeutic directions). When one person is exploring, he should be allowed to find his own way if he can. Interpretation should usually be offered only after the client has failed to achieve insight by his own devices. As discussed earlier, healing responses should usually be given after access.

Refraining from Giving Unnecessary External Support

Some clients will ask for or induce support that they don't really need. They may look for direction and insight from the leader or group when they could discover it on their own. They may look for nurturing or reassurance when they could find it inside themselves. At these times, refrain from giving this support, and perhaps suggest that the person can proceed on his own. It may also be necessary to point this out to the group and stop them from providing support. This forces the person back on his own resources, which can be empowering.

For example, Katherine had a habit of throwing open a question about herself to the group, getting them excited about her dilemma, and eliciting ideas, interpretations, and advice from everyone. Then she would then sift through the group members' responses to see what she liked. On the surface it looked productive, except that it had the flavor of an enjoyable conversation rather than a self-exploration process. Katherine never really took the time to look inside and explore herself. When I pointed out her process and stopped the group from offering their input, Katherine was able to discover herself at a deeper level. She got more in touch with her own feelings and opinions about the best way to handle her difficulties.

At times a client will elicit support that he doesn't really want. Sometimes he unconsciously wants to induce the support and sometimes he does it inadvertently. The well-known "Yes-but" game (Berne, 1964) is an example of induced support that is then pushed away. In other cases, a person may elicit support simply because he is confused or stuck or floundering in his self-exploration and the group members want to help. However, if he doesn't really want the support, he may sabotage it in an active or passive–aggressive manner. This can be frustrating and confusing for a group. In this case, the leader must point out that the person isn't receptive to the support and stop the group from offering it. You can also work with the person on his underlying reason for refusing the support.

> For example, when Harry let go of his pattern of his goal-directed manner of exploring himself, he had a tendency to get stuck. The group members would get impatient and offer good insights and suggestions. However, Harry experienced this as pressure to perform, which he hated and rejected. However, since he wasn't allowed to be aggressive, he pushed away the help in subtle ways. I gradually worked with him to understand this process, and he was eventually able to tell the group directly to back off. This was an important step forward for him.

Providing External Support

Sometimes you must move in the opposite direction because *more* external support is needed for work to be successful. If you suggest an experiment or encourage deeper access and the client is too frightened to take the risk, it may be due to lack of support. The person may not have the inner support (in the form of basic capacities) or feel enough support from the group to be able to attempt something difficult. Although in many cases, such work will have to wait until later, sometimes the person will be able to do it if more external support is offered.

> For example, Toni was working on accessing intense pain about childhood abandonment when she became too frightened to continue. The development of her capacities for connectedness and value was not high enough to tolerate the disrupting effect of the emerging pain. Noticing that her pain was about abandonment, the leader asked how connected Toni felt to the group at that moment. She said she felt completely isolated, so the leader suggested, "Try looking around at each group member and notice what you see." By doing this, she was able to tell that the group members were really tuned into her struggle, and some people also told her how interested and caring they felt. This provided the extra level of support she needed to go further with her work.

☐ Example

The following detailed example illustrates some of the concepts from the last four chapters.

A Blame Cycle

Penny was in a lot of pain and especially wanted support from Melissa. This was because a couple of members were absent, and Melissa was the only other woman in the group. Melissa was preoccupied with her own feelings and didn't respond in a very supportive way. At the next group meeting Penny expressed anger at Melissa about this, and Melissa became extremely angry and defensive. She blamed Penny for expecting too much, and Penny blamed her for being cold and self-involved.

An Aggressive Reaction That Was Mixed Experimenting

As we untangled the transference, it all began to make sense. Penny had been severely neglected by her mother, and in response had completely closed off her needs for nurturing or caring, especially from women. Recently because of the progress of her therapy, she was beginning to open up these needs. Therefore, when she asked for something from Melissa that wasn't forthcoming, her anger at her mother spilled out onto Melissa. This is an example of an aggressive reaction to a painful deprivation issue. A mild angry or hurt response might have been appropriate to Melissa's lack of support, but Penny's reaction was much more intense than that because it was distorted by the issue. However, the degree of anger she expressed would have been appropriate had it been directed at her mother, and Penny characteralogically had difficulty expressing aggression. Therefore her expression of anger to Melissa is an example of mixed experimenting, because it had elements of both health and dysfunction.

An Aggressive Reaction as a Defense

As a child, Melissa had repeatedly been blamed by her brother for things that she didn't do, and her grandmother had accepted his word and punished her. Melissa felt deeply wronged and humiliated by this. Penny's exaggerated blaming of her brought up this transference, and Melissa responded with an exaggerated degree of retaliation and blame. She felt that she had to protect herself at all costs. This reaction also derived from the fact that she never received the protection she needed as a child. She was physically abused by her mother when she was young and there was no one to protect her because her father had abandoned the family. Her mother also never protected her from her abusive and rejecting stepfather, so she had to develop her own aggression to protect herself. Therefore there was an element of healthy aggression in Melissa's reaction, but her aggression had always been available to her as an adult, so she wasn't experimenting with new behavior. Melissa's aggressive reaction was primarily a defense against the pain of being blamed.

A Defense Cycle

The blame cycle between them was aggravated by the fact that Penny had also been blamed by her mother for many things that weren't her responsibility. Penny responded to Melissa's defensiveness and blaming with retaliatory blaming of her own. Thus they were triggering each other's defenses, resulting in a defense cycle.

Healing Mismatch and Healing Response

In one sense, this interaction represents a healing mismatch for Penny. She was asking to have her needs met, which was an experiment with new healthy behavior for her, and she didn't get a healing response from Melissa. However, this gave her a chance to experiment with a different kind of healthy behavior—her anger and aggression. Even though Melissa responded negatively to Penny's anger, it wasn't enough to stop Penny, and most of the rest of the group supported her anger, though without taking sides against Melissa. Thus Penny received enough of a healing, accepting response to her aggression to reinforce it.

One member, Jill, had a negative reaction to Penny's needs, but by the time she spoke, I had framed Penny's work clearly for her and the group, so Jill could see that it was good work for Penny to be expressing her needs. This enabled Jill to explore her own transference that caused her to have a negative reaction to Penny. She did this rather than dumping her reaction on Penny, so in this way we avoided a healing mismatch.

Individual Work, Dialogue, and Feedback

It took work over three group meetings to resolve the conflict. Once the dialogue between Penny and Melissa degenerated into a defense cycle, there was nothing more therapeutic to be gained from dialogue until the underlying feelings had been explored. Therefore I did everything I could to keep them from attacking each other and instead moved them each into doing individual work on uncovering and accessing their transferences. The group members helped by stopping them when they started fighting with each other. Once when it was necessary to stop Melissa from exacerbating the blaming, the group gave her feedback about the destructiveness of this behavior, and this encouraged her to access her transference instead. The group also supported and understood both of them, without taking sides. This was especially important for Penny, who had always been abandoned as a child when she attempted to assert herself.

Healing for Melissa

Once when I was trying to help Melissa see how stuck she was in blaming and defending, she got angry at me because my intervention felt like more blame. However, we were able to get past that, and she accessed the pain of being unfairly blamed again. I then told her that I felt like holding her and protecting her from that ever happening again. This healing response allowed us to make an important connection. It seemed appropriate that this come from me because we had had difficulties just before that, and also because her father had abandoned the family when she was young so she needed this kind of response from a male authority figure.

The Resolution

By the end of the third meeting, after Penny had accessed some very painful feelings about her mother, Melissa spontaneously and genuinely went over and hugged her. This was healthy experimenting for her to let go of her anger and reach out for connection, and it was also a healing response for Penny. After that session, they were resolved with each other and over time developed a close, loving connection.

The Group Leader's Attitude

This chapter contains recommendations for the optimal group leader attitude—about using the resources of the group, mistakes, self-disclosure, and integrating intellect with intuition and various other complementary leadership qualities. I discuss certain problematic attitudes of leaders that can cause difficulties for a group. Finally, we explore the personal issues involved when an action-oriented leader shifts from leader-centered to group-centered groups.

☐ Using the Resources of the Group

Even though you are responsible for the success of any group you are leading, it is a mistake to try to do it all yourself. In a therapy group, the group members have immense resources to contribute. Allow yourself to rely on them. They can give feedback that you can't, provide support than you shouldn't or don't want to, and see things you miss. They can identify with each other's feelings, model how to explore and interact, and provide balance and a healthy container for the work. When a person is in trouble and you don't know what to do, ask for their help. When the group is having difficulty, ask for their insights and use their skills. Of course, this doesn't absolve you of the responsibility for figuring out what is happening and intervening appropriately. The group is not always helpful; sometimes it can be therapeutically destructive, and then you must take charge. But never underestimate the power of the group to help, especially a mature group.

> For example, sometimes when two clients are engaged in an intractable conflict and I'm not sure what to do, I will ask the group for their suggestions. If it is a mature group, I can usually trust them not to polarize around the conflict, so their input often is very helpful. They usually give useful feedback about what each person is contributing to the fight,

though not everyone may see it in the same way. The very fact that the group members are concerned and caring about both people in the conflict helps to loosen the bottleneck and foster a more cooperative attitude. Sometimes a group member will provide an insight I had missed that helps to move things along. Sometimes a group member provides a certain kind of support (e.g., acceptance or identification) that helps one of the combatants to feel cared for and soften his defenses.

☐ Mistakes

In thinking about leadership of a group, don't assume that there is only one right intervention at each point in the action. At any given moment, there are a number of different interventions that would be helpful and therapeutic. Just because you didn't choose the one your supervisor or colleague favors, don't assume that you have made a mistake.

Mistakes Are Common

All group leaders, even experienced ones, make many therapeutic mistakes. All therapists make errors from time to time, but in a group, there is so much going on at any moment and events happen so quickly that it is especially easy to miss something. Groups are very complex, much more than individual therapy, and therefore there are many more chances to slip up. Don't expect yourself to be infallible, and don't be afraid that making a mistake means you aren't a good group leader. It isn't necessary or possible to avoid mistakes, and expecting it of yourself can get you into trouble (Yalom, 1995, pp. 116–117). This attitude can lead you to hide behind a wall and be afraid to admit errors, making it hard for clients to trust you. In fact, if you can comfortably admit mistakes, especially ones that have caused clients to feel angry with you, it paradoxically gives clients faith in you. They appreciate your humanity and humility and your caring enough about them to look at yourself. They also sense that you know you are competent because you don't have to hide your errors.

Handling Mistakes

In fact, a mistake rarely causes any harm unless its effects remain hidden or it is poorly handled. Usually a mistake will cause no lasting problems for a group member if, when it is brought out, the leader can admit it, help the client to explore his reaction, and do what is necessary to correct it. This may mean working to repair your therapeutic alliance. It may mean helping the client to explore the pain it triggered and then providing a healing response. In fact, the ability of the leader to admit a mistake can be an important healing response for many clients whose parents could never do that. Notice that all these suggestions for handling a mistake are a normal part of the ongoing therapy process. Usually the best way to deal with a mistake is to admit it and then work with it using the normal processes of the group.

For example, Dotty and Matt were in the middle of working on a conflict when Jane's anger at Matt was triggered. She interrupted with an attack on him. Matt and Dotty both indicated that they wanted to continue their interaction rather than dealing with Jane right then. When Jane interrupted again with a judgmental comment, I told her to be quiet, letting some anger slip out in the process. I thought Jane was comfortable enough with anger that I could do this, but I judged incorrectly. The next session, she said she was very upset with me and didn't trust me to be on her side in conflicts with men. My leaking anger was clearly a mistake. However, it provided an opportunity for us to work explicitly on our relationship. Even though my mistake had disrupted our therapeutic alliance, Jane had been feeling somewhat mistrustful of me anyway, and this gave us a chance to work on it. I apologized for spilling my anger onto her, and we explored in depth the issues around her mistrust of me and worked on improving our therapeutic alliance (see chapter 19). This eventually led to a trusting connection between us. Because I handled the mistake well, it didn't lead to any long-term problems.

It can sometimes be helpful to acknowledge that you have made a mistake even when this may not be the major issue. As long as your response was short of the therapeutic ideal, you can admit a mistake if this will help the client trust you. *For example, a woman is extremely hurt by something you said in a situation where you didn't completely see how vulnerable she was. Perhaps 90% of the problem stems from her extreme sensitivity and the fact that this was largely hidden. Nevertheless, you didn't make an ideal therapeutic intervention, which would have meant sensing her degree of vulnerability and speaking accordingly. It might be best for you to acknowledge that you didn't fully see her and apologize.*

Your objective is not to apportion responsibility fairly, but rather to do what is most therapeutic. In some cases, apologizing is best; in others, the most therapeutic thing would be to challenge the client to own her part in the problem.

☐ Leader Self-Disclosure

How much the leader reveals him or herself to the group is an issue with important therapeutic ramifications. The traditional psychodynamic position of neutrality specifies that the leader/therapist should show little of herself so that the client's transference isn't contaminated by the reality of the therapist, thereby making it easier to see and understand transference reactions. This certainly has validity in forms of individual therapy where the main focus is on the transference relationship, as is the case in psychoanalysis. If you are working with someone who has strong transference and serious deficiencies in basic needs, there are significant advantages to limited self-disclosure. Some clients have a tendency to react intensely to small nuances in the therapeutic relationship, so it is better to keep potentially provocative stimuli to a minimum. Rather than complete neutrality, I prefer the empathic stance (Kohut, 1971, 1977) taken by many contemporary psychodynamic leaders.

In group therapy, if the leader is using a method that relies primarily on the analysis of the leader–client relationship, then similar considerations might hold. However, I don't think this is the best use of a group. The leader–client relationship is just one of many that are important in a group, so it rarely generates the same intensity as in individual therapy. The transference to any one person is diluted in the group setting. In addition, there are so many varied interpersonal stimuli in a group that it isn't possible to limit them as much as in individual therapy. Group members can observe the therapist while she is working with others, and over time they often get to know quite a bit about her, even if only from nonverbal cues. The leader can't really be a blank screen in a group. For all these reasons, there is more room in group therapy for the leader to reveal herself when it is appropriate (Rutan & Stone, 1993, p. 131). I agree with Yalom (1995, pp. 202–216) that leader self-disclosure can significantly enhance the therapy process if handled properly.

Revealing Facts

Let's make a distinction between disclosing facts and feeling reactions. For you as the leader to reveal facts about yourself is less problematic than revealing feelings, but also less potentially valuable. It shouldn't be done very often, but casual revealing of facts about the leader's life is normally not a problem and sometimes it can be therapeutic. *For example, if a group member is perceiving the leader as socially confident and herself as unbearably shy and socially inept, this self-denigration can be therapeutically challenged if the leader shares briefly that she has also had to deal with social fears.* Remember, however, that you are in a group, so even if your disclosure is appropriate for the person it is directed toward, you also must take in account its effect on other group members. Any self-disclosure should be made only when you are fairly sure that it won't stir up difficult feelings in a vulnerable group member. If there is someone else in the group who might be adversely affected by hearing about a problem of yours, such as a client who needs to idealize you for a while, it might be better to remain silent.

The degree of concern that is needed about self-disclosure varies depending on the level of functioning of a group. In a fairly high-functioning group, you need not be as careful about self-disclosure as with a group with some low-functioning members.

As long as it is not dangerous for the group members, revealing facts can help make the group leader more human and accessible, thereby enhancing trust. It also undercuts the notion of the healthy doctor treating the poor disturbed patient, and thus recognizes that we are all human and dealing with roughly similar life issues. This is especially empowering for clients who are struggling with low self-esteem.

Revealing Positive Feelings

The more interesting and difficult question concerns when to reveal your feeling reactions to a client or the group. It is usually not dangerous to reveal positive feelings, especially if they aren't intense. *For example, it is often helpful for the leader to express appreciation for some aspect of a client's behavior or work in group, or to talk about feeling touched by a client's vulnerability.* In fact, it is very important to reveal your positive reactions to group members from time to time. Many clients haven't received much appreciation and affection in their families of origin, and as group leader, you are an important transference figure. Your genuine expression of warmth, caring, and respect will provide important healing for some of your clients.

In most cases it is better to reveal your positive reactions to specific behaviors rather than personal feelings of warmth toward a client. You need to be concerned about whether you might stir up feelings of jealousy or hurt in other group members who don't receive such positive expression of feelings from you. For this reason, you should never compare your feelings toward one client with those toward another, even if asked. The same thing applies to your feelings about one group versus another.

A general rule that applies to any type of self-disclosure by the leader is that it should always be in the interest of the client's growth. If you don't hold to this rule, you take the chance of slipping into talking about yourself in order to gratify your needs, to the detriment of the group. The group setting, especially, lends itself to narcissistic gratification of the leader's needs for attention and admiration, so group therapists must be especially careful of this lure.

Revealing Negative Feelings

It is usually dangerous for the leader to reveal negative feeling reactions to a group member. This can seriously damage your therapeutic alliance with that client and perhaps with others as well. It is crucial for each group member to feel that you really care for her and have her best interests at heart. The disclosure of even mildly negative feelings could undermine this trust. In addition, as group leader, you have enormous power in the group, so the expression of negative feelings toward a group member could be deeply hurtful and perhaps damaging to her sense of personal value.

When It Can Be Helpful.   In some cases, however, it can be helpful to reveal a negative reaction to a client. If the person is strong enough to handle it and your therapeutic alliance is reasonably solid, then there are times when it is valuable to tell a client a negative reaction. Clients certainly learn from negative feedback from other group members, and the same can apply to feedback from the leader. But this should be given only if the person is not getting this feedback from others, or if she is involved in an interaction with you and this feedback seems critical to resolving the relationship. *For example, Lawrence was constantly criticizing the way the group was being run, and yet at the same time he hungered for my approval. I revealed that I felt frustrated with him for his criticism of my leadership and the way he disrupted the group, and this made it difficult for me to give him the approval he needed. I felt it would be valuable for Lawrence to understand the consequences of his actions and that he could handle hearing this from me.* If you do choose to reveal negative feelings toward someone, the feelings should be only talked about, not expressed in an angry or judgmental way.

When It May Be Necessary.   It may be necessary to reveal negative feelings when a client senses your negative reaction toward her and asks you about it. *For example, suppose that in talking to a client, you use a harsh tone of voice. The client says, "Why did you say that to me? Are you mad at me for what I did?"* If you were indeed angry with her and it slipped out, then you must make a hard choice. In most cases like this, I will be honest and acknowledge that I was feeling angry, and also apologize for letting my personal feelings get in the way of my job as group leader. To lie about it is to undermine the client's ability to perceive others accurately. You could avoid answering the question by asking the client to explore her reaction to perceiving you as angry. However, even this is potentially undermining because it implies that this is her problem rather than a natural reaction to your anger. Many clients were given double messages as children. They were told one thing about the parent's feeling toward them while they sensed or saw another. This can result in the person being confused and not trusting her own feelings and perceptions. In the extreme, this is the famous double bind, which can undermine a person's reality testing. As a leader, you don't want to contribute to this if at all possible, so honesty is usually the best policy.

However, you must also evaluate the possible harm to the client (or your alliance with the client) if you admit the truth. If the client is very fragile or her trust of you is tenuous and she might leave the group, it might be better to avoid answering the question directly. In this case, you would simply explore her fantasy of what you felt toward her and what that means to her. There is no easy answer here. If you do decide to acknowledge the negative feeling, make sure that the client has a chance to work through the feelings that this brings up for her.

☐ The Leader Stance

Caring and Compassion.   The above discussion may give the impression that I am encouraging you as leader to hide or suppress a variety of feelings that are erupting in you during group. I must admit that sometimes this must be done, but it should be rare. Groups can be intense hothouses of feeling and the leader is not immune to being strongly affected. However, one of the reasons for refraining from self-disclosure and from personal involvement in the relationships of the group is so that you can minimize the chances that negative feelings will be stirred up in you. Your aim is to take a leadership stance where you are involved in the group emotionally in a caring, compassionate way but not as an interactive participant who is working on your own issues and feelings. Your stance is one in which you are interested and caring about each group member and the group as a whole. Therefore you may occasionally be triggered by a client or an interaction, but most of the time you naturally remain in an appreciative, compassionate place. You don't have to suppress or hide difficult feelings because most of the time you don't have them. The stance you assume makes these feelings less likely.

Not Being Too Involved.   If you were a *member* of a similar group and were getting involved with the other members, working on your emotional issues, and expressing your feeling reactions, you might have a whole host of strong reactions to the very same stimuli that don't affect you very much when you are in a leader stance.

> For example, suppose Henry is arrogant and insensitive to others. If you were a group member, you might get angry at him and express it. This would then trigger feelings in Henry and the two of you would interact, potentially producing hurt, rage, shame, or fear in both of you and other group members. In your leader stance, however, you can become interested in what pain is behind Henry's insensitivity and remain in an understanding place with him. You would work with him from that place, and he would sense your caring and therefore trust you. His trust would help you to feel more warmly toward him, thus making it easier for you to be compassionate with him rather than angry.

An important part of the leader stance is that you don't seek to meet your own emotional needs from the group members (except for normal professional satisfaction). This means that you must be getting enough interpersonal connection and satisfaction in your personal life. Otherwise, you may become too involved in your groups because your own needs are at stake. This makes you vulnerable to having your personal feelings triggered if a client becomes angry at you or distances himself from you, for example. This could throw you off in a way that would prevent you from being empathic with that person.

In the leader stance, you are removed from the group, but not entirely. You are empathic and compassionate; you are caring and accepting toward others. But you aren't overly involved, and therefore you don't have problematic reactions very often. Most of the time you don't have to suppress or hide feeling reactions to maintain your neutrality. This occurs naturally because of the emotional stance you take. This is similar to the stance an individual therapist takes.

Watch for Countertransference.   For a variety of reasons, this stance can sometimes be more difficult to maintain in a group. Therefore, you must be careful not to overlook negative reactions you have toward clients despite the leader stance. Even though you don't often have problematic feelings, they do occur, and it is especially dangerous to have such a reaction without realizing it. Be on the look out for countertransference (see chapter 19).

☐ Integration of Leader Attitudes

The best group leadership comes from a therapist who has integrated various aspects of her personality that may seem like opposites. Here I discuss four specific integrations—intuition and intellect, authority and responsiveness, caring and challenging, empathy and perceptiveness.

Intuition and Intellect

Using Your Intuition.   Don't expect to lead a therapy group from your intellect. Even though this book presents a theory and many practical suggestions for group leading, it isn't possible to make interventions by using this information in a purely cognitive way. Almost all facilitations in a group emerge intuitively and spontaneously. There is frequently too much happening at once for a leader to be able to rely on intellectual reflection and analysis of each situation. You must simply take the action that seems best at the moment. Theory and intellectual understanding of technique are crucial for good group leading, but they don't usually come into play at the moment of an intervention. They are very useful for learning the craft of group leading, but over time, this understanding becomes gradually embedded in your personality and your being. Therefore, when you make leadership decisions on the spur of the moment in group, they reflect both this knowledge and your experience, and therefore they are usually therapeutic.

When to Use Your Intellect.   Cognitive understanding is especially important when something is going wrong in the group, and your normal intuition is leading you astray. Then you need to reflect more deeply about the situation, sometimes during a group, often between groups. This can be done by yourself or with a supervisor or consultant. Here theory and intellectual comprehension of technique are useful for communicating about the situation, understanding the problem, and strategizing about how to handle it. For example, for each group member, it can be useful to formulate an understanding of the person's interpersonal patterns, core issues, defenses, strengths and deficiencies in healthy capacities, childhood traumas and relationships, group goals, and relationships with other group members. Similarly it can be useful to understand the developmental stage of the group and any group dynamics that might be causing difficulties. Of course, you may also have to explore possible countertransference reactions. All this information can be brought back into the next group meeting to help inform your leadership, but your choices in each moment will still be largely intuitive.

Power

It is important to have available the following two leadership abilities: (a) taking charge, suggesting experiments, and sometimes pushing a client in the direction she needs to go; and (b) following a client's process and encouraging her autonomy. These two capacities may seem like opposites, but both are needed. It is helpful for a leader to know when it is best to take charge and when to follow, when to push the client and when to empower her, and when to use these two sides together in a synergistic way.

You may need to assert your authority when a client is in trouble emotionally or when the group is in serious conflict or chaos. It is helpful to take charge more in the beginning of a group and less as the group members can take over this task themselves. It is useful to push a client at certain times when she is resisting work she is really able to do, or when she will be unnecessarily hurt if you don't. It is valuable to suggest risky work that a client wouldn't think of or wouldn't initiate on her own because of fear.

It is important to follow a client's process when she needs to be accepted just as she is, or when she needs to have the experience of discovering herself. You need to be purely responsive when a client would react to any exertion of power by you. You should also follow a client's process when she is handling it fine on her own. You should encourage autonomy when a client or a group is ready for it, and especially if they are avoiding it. It is especially important to empower a person or group when they were disempowered in the past.

These two leadership capacities can sometimes be combined. Sometimes you must take charge to empower a client or encourage her autonomy. Sometimes you assert your authority by being silent. Sometimes you follow a person's process by actively empathizing and asking questions. Sometimes you encourage autonomy by challenging a client on her compliance.

Emotional Integration

It is important to achieve an emotional integration between (a) caring deeply about a client's feelings, and (b) challenging her to own and explore her problematic behavior. It is always valuable to care about your group members and especially to feel compassion for their pain. However, it is also necessary at times to challenge someone to look at behavior that causes problems for herself and others, even when this may be painful for the person. Such a challenge should come from a caring place in you, but it can be experienced by the client as something very different from caring. The client sometimes feels that if you really loved her unconditionally, you would accept her just as she is; you wouldn't challenge her in any way. However, in your caring you may need to challenge her. Can you communicate that caring as part of the challenge? As a leader, you need to have both caring and challenge available to you, and the ability to use them together.

> For example, after Jerome challenges Dana on something, she tells Jerome that she wants to connect better with him, but she couches her communication in a subtly superior tone, a characteristic way of relating for her. He reacts by withdrawing but doesn't seem to know exactly why. The group leader wants to give Dana feedback on her behavior. He says, "You know, when you said that to Jerome, I think you unconsciously did something that caused him to withdraw. Are you interested in hearing what I saw?" Dana indicates that she is, and the leader says, "It seems that part of you wanted to connect with Jerome, and you said that, but in your tone of voice and certain words, you gave the impression that you felt superior to him. My guess is that he withdrew because of that. Does any of that fit your experience?" Notice that the leader's caring is not expressed explicitly but rather in the way he approaches her gently and without judgment. He also doesn't lead with an interpretation about why Dana acted superior, and he checks out his perception with her. This is an example of a challenge presented in a caring way.

Perceptual Integration

It is important to achieve a perceptual integration between (a) empathizing with the client's immediate conscious experience, and (b) understanding the client's patterns of underlying issues and defenses. When you empathize with a client, you are tuning into what she is aware of consciously. If she is aware of feeling ashamed of being a "failure," then that is what you empathize with. If she is conscious of feeling excited and aggressive, then that is what you resonate with. This kind of empathy is extremely important for building trust and helping a client to explore her feelings more deeply (Rogers, 1951). However, these conscious experiences are rarely all that is going on. The client who feels like a failure may be unconsciously failing in order to spite you; the real issue may be autonomy, not success. The client who feels excited and aggressive may be using this to hide her fear. It is part of your job to be able to see or guess at what is going on beneath the surface. This is different from straightforward empathy, because you are tuning into parts of the client that she isn't in touch with. Your deeper understanding of the client may derive partly from intuition and partly from theoretical understanding. However you do it, this deeper insight into the client is very important, even if you don't spell it out explicitly by interpretation. Even if you want the client to uncover this insight herself, it is very helpful if you have an understanding or at least a hypothesis about the deeper dynamics.

However, insight into the client without empathy is also not very helpful. The client will often perceive you as distant and judgmental or this may cause her to feel inferior to you. She may rebel against you because she doesn't feel your caring for her.

Sometimes empathy with the client's conscious experience will lead her into the deeper issues. Sometimes it won't, and you must attempt to take her there. If you do this from a clearly empathic place, the client will be more likely to trust you to facilitate her. This is one of the contributions of self-psychology. Kohut (1977) used the term *empathy* to refer to empathic interpretation, which addresses deeper issues but is framed in a way that is experienced as safe and supportive by the client.

> In the above example with Dana, the leader might say, "I'm guessing that maybe Jerome's challenge made you feel ashamed, and perhaps your superior tone was an unconscious way to try to make up for this." This is an interpretation, but it is done in a caring, empathic manner.

☐ Problematic Leader Attitudes

The Leader's Phobic Areas

There may be certain topics or feelings or interactions that cause you discomfort, and even if you intellectually know that they are good for the group, your discomfort may cause you to unconsciously discourage the group from exploring these areas. For example, you might be uncomfortable with anger and conflict, sexuality, money issues, or very deep levels of pain. You might have difficulty with anger directed at you or warm feelings toward you. You might want to avoid jealousy, rejection, or competition and power struggles among group members. You might be uncomfortable with clients being very close to each other or clients leaving the group. These feelings could lead you to avoid making these issues explicit when they arise or to subtly prevent group members from bringing them up.

You may become aware of this only when the unconscious prohibition is violated, when a group member tries to deal with one of these issues. Then you must be aware enough of your difficulties to avoid acting on them, to help the client bring out the issue rather than squelching her. Such a problem might come to your awareness when you are reviewing the topics and issues that have emerged over the course of a group, and you realize that a certain issue, say sexuality, has never come up. Then you need to ask yourself if you are uncomfortable with sexuality and if you may have inadvertently discouraged it. If so, you can try to notice how you communicate this message and work on changing that. You can also point out the absence of sexuality in the group and make a conscious effort to encourage clients to discuss it. Of course, it will also be important to work in your own therapy on the issues that cause you discomfort with sexuality.

Too Much Leader Gratification

It is important to make sure that your group leading isn't distorted by your own needs for gratification. You can expect to derive specific satisfactions from leading a therapy group—connecting with people, helping others to grow, exercising professional competence, being part of a close community, and so on. However, most of these needs should be met in your personal life. If your personal life is not satisfying enough or if your needs are too great in one of these areas, you may find yourself using the group in a way that is harmful.

You might have a strong need for personal contact and connection, leading you to become too attached to certain clients at the expense of others, to have favorites. You might have a need to be the source of caring and nurturing, or the center of attention, or to be in control of the group. These needs can cause you to play too dominant a role and not allow the members enough space to relate enough to each other. This is discussed further in the next section.

If you realize that any of these things are happening, you must make a conscious effort to pull back from your overinvolvement and to explore what is preventing you from obtaining more satisfaction in your personal life.

Shifting from Leader-Centered to Group-Centered

If you are an action-oriented therapist, you may have to make an internal shift in attitude in order to lead an interactive group, especially if you are already running leader-centered groups. A *leader-centered group* is one in which most transactions happen between the leader and the group members with little interaction between members. A *group-centered group* is one in which most transactions happen between members. The leader still has tremendous influence, but much of the initiative, the interactions, and the healing process derive from the group. An interactive group is a group-centered group even though the leader may at times be fairly active. The leader's activity is primarily aimed at facilitating members interactions with each other or with the group as a whole. Occasionally there may be an interaction that is primarily between the leader and one member, but this is the exception rather than the rule. It tends to happens when a member is in trouble that requires the leader's focused help or when there is interactive work between a member and the leader.

I advocate a higher degree of leader activity than that of many psychodynamic or interpersonal leaders, because both these styles rely primarily on occasional interpretations. However, I prefer a lower activity level than most action-oriented leaders who tend to be at the center of things. I believe that it is important to be active when group members need the help, while at other times you may be quiet for long periods of time.

Giving Members Responsibility

In making the shift from a leader-centered to group-centered style of leading, one of the first things to remember is that you don't have to make the work happen. That is the responsibility of the members. Make it clear to them that they are in charge of initiating work and make sure that they know how to do it—then back off and allow them to take over. If a group is not doing much interactive work, don't be fooled into thinking that you must do something to enliven the group. At this point, some leaders introduce group exercises or do individual work in the group. This is usually a mistake. It gives the group members the idea that you are responsible for making things happen in the group rather than *they*. If a group is stagnating, focus on how the group members are avoiding their work with each other. There is always interactive work to be done. If it isn't happening, help the members to explore what is blocking it. Perhaps there is passivity that needs to be looked at. Maybe some of them are looking for a strong leader to run things. Perhaps they are afraid of confronting each other.

Exploring Your Blocks

You may need to explore personal issues of yours that make it hard for you to give up being the center of the group. Some leaders need to control their groups. In a leader-centered group, you get to direct everything, while in a group-centered group, you have much less control over what happens. You might have a need to be the one who makes things happen, causing you to take charge and facilitate at times when clients should be doing it themselves. This could make it hard for you to let go of control when the group develops to the point where the members need to take more power in the running of the group (see chapter 21).

Some leaders are attached to being involved in everything that happens in the group. You may have a need to be the center of attention, which leads you to talk too much in group or to be overly involved in every interaction. It may be hard for you to sit back and allow things to unfold without being able to say very much. To lead a group-centered group, you must let go of this need.

Some leaders need to be needed by their group members. It may be hard for you not to be the primary source of nurturing and love in the group, leading you to set things up so that too many of the clients' interactions involve you rather than each other. It may be difficult for you to allow the group members to work with each other and give to each other at times when you are not involved, when you are not the giver. If you are having trouble allowing a group to be group-centered, explore yourself to see if any of these issues may be influencing you in an unconscious way.

Changing an Existing Group from Leader-Centered to Group-Centered

If you are already leading a group which is leader-centered and you want to change it to be more group-centered, you will have to modify group norms that are already developed. The group members are already expecting you to be the center of things. They aren't used to looking to each other for feeling responses or help. You will have to work hard to undo the existing norms as well as to foster group-centered norms. The first thing that is necessary is to make the transition explicit. Tell the members exactly how you want to change the group format and why. Ask how they feel about this change and what issues it brings up for them. Get them as involved as possible in the process so they will work with you to make the change rather than resisting you.

Make it clear what their responsibilities are under the new structure. If you are introducing interactive work for the first time, spend as much time as necessary discussing the interactive norm and how the members can initiate interactive work. Be prepared to remind them frequently. Watch for your own tendency to slip back into the old group patterns. When they look to you too much for guidance, refrain from responding or suggest that they interact with each other. Changing group norms is a challenging job that requires time and patience.

19 CHAPTER

The Leader–Client Relationship

This chapter discusses various aspects of the relationship between the group leader and group members—the therapeutic alliance, how to work with interactions between a group member and the leader, and countertransference.

☐ The Therapeutic Alliance

The therapeutic alliance is a well-known concept from psychoanalysis (Greenson, 1967) that refers to the working relationship between therapist and client. It has also been studied extensively by Carl Rogers (1951) and his students as one of the conditions for successful therapy. If you have a good therapeutic alliance with a client, the client trusts you to have her best interests at heart. The two of you can collaborate on the joint project of helping her to grow and change. The client, in spite of any transference reactions, can work with you well enough for the therapy to proceed. She can listen to and make therapeutic use of your feedback, interpretations, questions, suggestions, and other interventions. It also means that your countertransference reactions don't prevent you from acting caringly and intelligently on the client's behalf. This section deals with the client's side of the therapeutic alliance. Later, I discuss countertransference.

To work well in a psychotherapy group means revealing some of the most precious, vulnerable, and potentially shameful aspects of yourself. It means taking risks and trusting that someone will care about you and understand you enough to make this worthwhile and healing. It means believing that someone will be strong and competent enough to help you grow rather than injuring you again. While the group can provide aspects of what a client needs, the leader is very important. Each client must feel that the leader really understands and accepts her and is competent enough to handle whatever comes up in her. Even when the group members are working primarily on their relationships with each other, each one needs to have an alliance with the leader that is strong (even if it is sometimes invisible).

Since limited-time groups need to proceed quickly, it is wise for the leader to try to foster a good therapeutic alliance as fast as possible by being warm and understanding without worrying about the danger of gratifying clients.

When the Alliance Is Important

This is especially true when the leader has to challenge a client, to help her look into an issue of hers. If she trusts that you are perceptive and care for her, she is more likely to be able to examine painful or shameful parts of herself. In some cases such a challenge needs to come from the leader because you can give it in a caring way. When a client is unusually sensitive to being shamed or group members are angry at her, it is better if the challenge comes from you. You aren't in the group to express your feelings; you are there to help. Therefore you can give difficult feedback from a caring place that maximizes the chances of being its heard by the client. However, this is only true if the two of you have a good therapeutic alliance—if you do care for her and if she trusts you.

The quality of the therapeutic alliance is especially important when two group members are in a conflict and you need to challenge or work with one of them on her role in the problem. Under these circumstances, the client can easily feel that you are siding with the other person against her. A strong therapeutic alliance makes this reaction less likely.

> For example, Jordan and Samantha were arguing about whose fault it was that Samantha felt so deeply hurt by him. The leader gave Jordan the feedback that he was responding in an arrogant way that was inflaming Samantha. If their therapeutic alliance had been shaky, Jordan might have felt that the leader was siding with Samantha. However, he trusted the leader and was therefore able to take the feedback seriously and examine his behavior.

The therapeutic alliance also assumes importance when a client has negative transference with the leader, for example when she feels hurt or angry at you, or when she experiences you as judging, dismissing, ridiculing, or betraying her. If the therapeutic alliance is strong, she will be willing to consider that her reaction is transference, and therefore explore herself to understand her deeper feelings. She can trust that you do care, and use that trust to access the underlying pain. If the therapeutic alliance is not so strong, a negative transference reaction can undermine it so that the client won't be able to work with you. She won't trust you enough to consider that her perception of you might not be accurate. She may not even trust you enough to allow you to facilitate her. Then the first order of business must be repairing the alliance. This is discussed in more detail later in this chapter.

Characteristics of the Alliance

There can be various degrees of trust in the therapist–client relationship. In addition, an alliance that is basically solid may occasionally be disrupted by an incident that triggers the client's fears. When this happens, it is important that the client and therapist not only repair the alliance, but also explore what triggered the break. In this way, the alliance is strengthened.

A therapeutic alliance doesn't have to be perfect, just solid enough to permit the client to work in the group and to heal breaks that occur. The strength of a therapeutic alliance can be limited by the level of functioning of the client. Clients who are severely deficient in value and connectedness can manage only a shaky alliance at best. For such a person, working through inevitable breaks in the alliance may constitute a significant part of the therapy. Rather than the alliance being a support for the rest of the therapy, the alliance in some sense becomes the focal point of the therapy. This is true for many borderline and narcissistic clients (Kohut 1971, 1977). In a group setting, such clients must continually work on their experience of wounding and their trust issues with the group as well as the leader.

☐ Client Interactions with the Leader

Bringing out a Client's Reactions to the Leader.   So far this book has only discussed how to facilitate interactions among group members. However, it is also important for group members to interact with the leader. Clients should be encouraged to bring up any feeling reactions they have toward you as well as toward each other. It is often difficult for clients to feel that it is acceptable for them to have reactions to the leader, let alone express them. Be on the lookout for any signs of a client reacting to you, so you can help him to talk about his reaction. You may notice unusual resistance to your facilitations, a hurt look, a distancing stance, surreptitious bids for reassurance, and so on. Mention these and ask the person to explore their meaning, and be on the lookout for client's displacing anger they feel toward you onto each other. If a group member doesn't feel safe enough to express anger to the leader, he may unconsciously direct it toward another member or the group as a whole. If you suspect this is the case, explore what resentment the client might be feeling toward you.

If the client does talk about an emotional response to you, make sure to welcome it, and say so explicitly, if necessary. The most important thing is that a client's feelings toward you are expressed. You don't want a client's negative reaction toward you to go underground, where it is either not consciously recognized or not expressed.

Two Roles.   Facilitating a client's interaction with the leader is similar in some ways to facilitating an interaction between two clients, but there are important differences. In this situation, the leader must play two roles—facilitator and responder. If you have a co-leader, it is best to let her do most of the facilitating so that you can take on only one role, that of responder. If you are leading the group alone, you will need to wear two hats at once, which is not an easy task. Even in your role as responder, you don't respond to the client as you would if you were a group member. That degree of involvement and self-disclosure for the group leader would be inappropriate and dangerous, as discussed above. Your primary task is to facilitate the client's exploring his feelings toward you and experimenting with new behavior, and to respond selectively with those feelings that will be most therapeutic for the client. This is similar to what is required of an individual therapist in a similar situation.

Exploring the Client's Feelings

Is the Alliance Intact?   When a client expresses a negative feeling toward you, such as hurt or anger, first ask yourself whether the client is so mistrustful of you that this constitutes a threat to the therapeutic alliance. *For example, Mike says with considerable hurt and anger, "There you go again, passing over me, not paying attention to me. You don't really care about me. That's clear."* There is a good chance that this signals a disruption of the therapeutic alliance. In this case, you need to focus on repairing and strengthening the alliance. In cases where the alliance is still intact, you can simply focus on helping the client with the work that emerges from the interaction.

Exploring Feelings.   In either case, the best initial approach is to show interest in the client's feelings and help him continue expressing and exploring his reaction to you. It is most helpful if you genuinely feel empathy and compassion for him.

> For example, with Mike you might say, "You feel that I pass over you because I'm more interested in other group members. Is that right?" You might then explore what happened to make him feel that and who he thinks you are more interested in. Is it everyone? Is it women? Does Mike feel that he isn't worthy of your interest or caring? Does he feel that you are cold and indifferent? To him or to everyone? What is it in him that is particularly sensitive to being passed over or to people not being interested? Has this happened to him a lot in his life, in his childhood?

Sometimes a client has a strong feeling reaction to you based on a fear of what you might do, even though she knows intellectually that you wouldn't really do such a thing. In this case, it can be helpful to explain to her the difference between her intellectual understanding and her emotional reactions. Explain that you want to help her explore her emotional response even though her mind knows better.

> For example, suppose Maureen said, "I'm really afraid that you are judging me as being a weak cry-baby for all these tears, but I know that isn't true. You're always encouraging us to go into our feelings." She is starting to talk herself out of her feelings, so you might say, "Don't be concerned right now with what you know about me. Let yourself feel the fear that I see you as a cry-baby." If necessary, explain the difference between feelings and intellectual understanding.

Defensiveness.   Watch out for your defensiveness. When a client feels hurt or angry because he misperceived your behavior, it is very easy to lapse into defending yourself. You may rationalize this as giving the client reality feedback so he won't feel bad, to correct his distortion. *For example, you might be tempted to tell Mike that you actually care for him and explain the reason why you did what appeared to him as passing him over.* However, even if your motivation for correcting a client's perception is not coming from defensiveness, it often sounds that way to the client. It is much better at first to hear him out and to encourage the full exploration of his feelings toward you. This also gives you a chance to tell whether there is a rupture in the alliance. Later it may be the right time to correct his perception of you.

Criticism of Leadership.   Defensiveness is especially a problem when the client expresses a criticism of your leadership rather than her feelings. *For example, Melissa said, "I don't like the way you spend long amounts of time working with two people and keeping everyone else out of the interaction. I think we should be able to speak up when we want."*

Be careful not to get caught up in a discussion of the quality of your leadership unless you have no other option. Try your best to reframe the client's criticism in feeling terms or to elicit the feelings that are behind the criticism. Invariably the client really needs something personal and relational from you, rather than simply wanting you to be a better leader. Try to help her uncover this.

> For example, you could get caught up in a discussion with Melissa about when it is appropriate for members to interrupt each other, but the crux of the matter was that Melissa felt that you didn't want to hear from her. As she explored this reaction, she realized it went back to her relationship with her father, who typically dismissed what she had to say. Of course, if the client's alliance with you has been seriously ruptured, she may not allow you to facilitate her in this exploration until it has been repaired.

When a Client's Challenge Is Valid

Sometimes a client will challenge you about something you did (or failed to do) that stems from a mistake of yours. If the client doesn't seem to have any additional emotional charge in her challenge, then it is best to simply own your mistake and apologize, if that is called for. Don't fall into the trap of being afraid to admit a mistake, of having to be perfect. Acknowledge your mistake with regret but without losing confidence in yourself, knowing that we all make mistakes and this is not necessarily a reflection of your competence as a group leader. When you do this, group members are usually relieved and reassured about your sincerity, and not worried about your competence.

> For example, suppose that after Mike challenged you, you became defensive. He then became angry at you for not listening to him. As soon as you realize that you have become defensive, it is best to acknowledge this and apologize for it.

Even if there is significant transference mixed in with the challenge, it is important to acknowledge your mistake. However, don't do so prematurely. Allow the client to explore his feelings and transference first. Otherwise you may short-circuit his work.

Sometimes a client challenges you about something you may need to explore before you can tell if it has any validity. In cases like this, you might ask for feedback from other group members. This can be valuable for you in recognizing mistakes, and it also empowers the group members. You also may need to think about the issue and explore it outside of group. Always take the client's feedback seriously (Yalom, 1995, p. 309), but make sure he gets the opportunity to explore his reaction as well.

When the Alliance Is Intact

If the therapeutic alliance is not in danger, then all you need to consider is the client's primary issue in her work with you. There are two main possibilities:

1. *Access.* The person may need to explore the meaning, the deeper feelings, and the transference behind her reaction to you. In this case you would work with her individually, as described previously. If the work progresses to the point where a healing response is called for and you genuinely want to give it, then go ahead, but make sure it is not premature.

2. *Experimenting.* Alternatively, the client's main work may involve expressing herself to you—expressing her anger or hurt or other feeling—or in asking for what she wants from you. If expressing anger to an authority figure is an issue for her, then this may be the focus of the work. Your job then is to accept her anger or to help her express it more fully. The same applies to other feelings such as hurt, betrayal, mistrust, and so on.

> For example, in the case where Melissa felt that you didn't want to hear from her, it might be important for her to express her anger to you or to allow herself to reveal how hurt she was. You might say, "I wonder if you have really let me know how angry you are with me?"

What the Client Needs from the Leader.   In some cases, the client may need to ask you for something such as caring, empathy, respect, approval, or liking. This might also include asking you to change in some way. You may need to facilitate her doing this. In some cases, you may sense that she needs to do this but is having trouble, so you may have to suggest what it is she needs or wants from you. And of course, you may have to help her explore her blocks against asking for what she needs. *For example, Melissa may want to ask you to pay more attention to her, and this might be terrifying for her.* Once the person's feelings or needs have been expressed, ask her to reflect on what that experience was like for her. This may unearth additional material related to saying this to an authority figure, and this exploration can then lead to deeper access.

> For example, Melissa may have been afraid you would abandon her because she asked for something from you (because that is what her father did). Someone else might be afraid you would be overwhelmed by her needs or retaliate with rage.

The Leader's Response.   Often it is sufficient for the client to say what she needs, explore how that feels, and know that you accept her feelings. However, sometimes the client needs a response to her request, perhaps a direct expression of caring, respect, and so on. If you genuinely feel this toward her, certainly express it. This can be an important healing response. However, make sure to pay attention to whether she can take it in, and work with her on this if necessary. If you don't really feel as positively toward her as she seems to need, then just accept her expression of the need and allow your relationship with her to develop over time in group. As you get to know her better and she grows and changes, your positive feelings toward her are likely to grow.

In many cases, the client won't believe explicit words of reassurance from you. She will only be able to receive from you through your actions and your presence.

> For example, suppose a client feels that you don't care for her. If you simply tell her you do, this may not make any impact. However, if you are genuinely caring about her at that moment, it will show in the way you work with her.

This is the best healing response a client can get and is often more effective than anything you could say explicitly.

> For example, suppose a client is concerned about your strength or competence. If you attempt to reassure her, she will probably perceive you as defensive. However, if you handle her challenge with insight and skill, this implicitly demonstrates your capability in the only way she could believe.

When the Alliance Is Disrupted

If the alliance is in danger, you should focus on repairing it rather than therapeutic change. A disrupted therapeutic alliance is a bottleneck issue; until it is resolved, the client won't be able to work on any other issues. Therefore it must be given top priority.

In this situation, you want to help the client understand his feeling reaction to you, but be careful not to suggest that he explore his transference too quickly. It can appear as if you are blaming him for his reaction and therefore discounting his feelings. It can actually be helpful to discover anything that you did as a group leader that was less than optimal, and admit it. Even if you believe it plays only a small part in the client's reaction, if you acknowledge your part in the problem, it helps to rebuild trust.

> For example, Nelson told me that he didn't trust me to protect him from the women in the group because he saw me taking care of them and not him. Even though I did care about protecting him, I admitted that I have an easier time being supportive and protective when clients shows their vulnerability in obvious ways, as many of the women did, and that I sometimes missed seeing Nelson's vulnerability.

Making Contact About the Therapist–Client Relationship.   Make it clear to the client that you value your relationship with him and want to restore the connection. You can say what you intend to do to help this happen or ask him what he needs from you. *For example, you could tell Nelson that you are glad he brought this up because now you will be more sensitive to situations where he needs your support or protection.* It can be very helpful to access a feeling place where you genuinely care about the client and express that directly to him in a contactful way. This should not be done in order to refute what the client has accused you of, but as a genuine human response to his pain and need. *For example, you might say to Nelson, "I really care about you, and I don't want you to be hurt."* After making some connection with the client, you may also want to suggest what he could do to help this process of re-establishing your alliance. *For example, you might ask Nelson to tell you when he needs your protection.*

When the Leader Reacts.   If the client is attacking you harshly, this may make it difficult for you to take any of the constructive actions that have been suggested. In this case, you may have to gently point out his attack and try to help him approach you in a more constructive way. The group can also be helpful in this.

It is dangerous to do this, because it can exacerbate the client's mistrust, but if the attack is seriously throwing you off, you may have no other choice. Make it clear that you are having trouble being receptive to the client's message because of the way it is being presented.

For example, if Nelson attacks you viciously and you feel angry and defensive, you might say, "You know, I think there is something valuable in what you are bringing up, but your anger is so intense that I am having trouble hearing you."

Clarifying Distortions and Exploring Transference.

Once you sense that the client is feeling heard and starting to trust you again, then it may be a good time to clarify any distortions in her perception of you. *For example, you might say to Maureen, "I wasn't seeing you as a weak cry-baby. I saw you as someone in pain who needed comfort."* Remember to be careful of defensiveness.

You can now also gently encourage the client to look into her transference. Do this in a way that doesn't invalidate her reaction to you.

For example, you might say to Maureen, "I wonder if you've been put down for crying before." Or to Nelson, "Even though I did miss the fact that you needed protection, I wonder if the intensity of your reaction relates to being dominated by your mother and sisters."

Throughout the entire interaction, check in periodically to see how the client is feeling toward you. This gives you a way of gauging the effectiveness of your approach and telling how much more needs to be done to restore the alliance.

Positive Feelings Toward the Leader

In addition to negative feelings, clients often have a variety of other feelings that are just as important to express and explore. They may feel close to you, dependent on you, trusting of you, proud of you, or protective toward you. They may idealize you or need you or love you. They may gradually come to see you as a person and care about you. Any of these feelings may have important significance with regard to both transference and healing, and so should be explored in full. Just as in the discussion above, the primary work can be either accessing the meaning of the feelings or experimenting with expressing them. And as before, you must judge if a healing response is called for from you and how best to provide it. Positive feelings sometimes indicate that a healing relationship has developed between you and the client, and for the healing to continue and deepen, the feelings need to be acknowledged and expressed.

For example, Melissa had developed a life-long defense of isolating herself from deep connections with people and closing her heart. She had been in a group of mine for a long time. Early on, she had expressed and worked through some intense negative transference toward me stemming from her stepfather. As our work progressed, she grew to trust me and allowed me to help her access some very deep, vulnerable places. We developed a healing relationship in which I became the father she never had. As she began to open her heart and allow deeper connections in her life, she let herself feel loving toward people (including me) but without telling them. This was a good intermediate step because it allowed her to be open and connect with people without too much fear. When she was ready to go further by acknowledging her connections with people, she began by letting me know how important I was to her and that she cared about me as a person. This led to a deeper connection between us and further healing.

☐   Countertransference

The central challenge with countertransference is to realize that it is happening at all. Once a leader is alert to the presence of emotional reactions that are detrimental to her job as group therapist, then she can do something about this. For this reason, it is imperative that a group leader be aware of her own emotional reactions and have the ability to engage in deep and probing self-exploration. This often means having significant experience in her own therapy, including group therapy (Yalom, 1995, p. 526).

Kinds of Countertransference

Many authors recommend that group leaders pay close attention to their feelings as they lead a group, not only to monitor their countertransference, but also because the leader's emotional reactions can provide important information about the group members (Rutan & Stone, 1993, pp. 183–188; Tuttman, 1993). For example, you may find yourself feeling an emotion that you have picked up empathically from a client who wasn't even aware of it.

Countertransference has been defined in at least three different ways in the literature: (a) any feeling that the therapist (group leader) has toward a client; (b) a feeling toward a client that causes the leader to have difficulty doing her job properly; and (c) a problematic feeling toward a client that is based on the leader's personal history and unresolved transference. I prefer to reserve the term *countertransference* for meanings (b) and (c).

I find it useful, as do a number of other authors, to distinguish between meaning (c), in which the leader's feelings are based on her own history, and other problematic reactions the leader has to the client that are elicited by the client's behavior. Different terms have been used to make this distinction—"countertransference" versus "objective countertransference," or "therapist's transference" versus "countertransference." At the risk of complicating the issue, I prefer to introduce my own terms which seem to be more intuitive: *Personal countertransference* is a reaction the group leader has to a client (or the group) that derives primarily from a core issue of the leader's. The underlying issue that causes this should be explored by the leader on her own or in her personal therapy. *Elicited countertransference* is a reaction of the leader that is elicited by certain behavior of a client (i.e., this client tends to elicit this reaction from almost everyone). One way to tell the difference between the two kinds of countertransference is to notice how the group members seem to be responding. If they seem to have the same reaction as the leader, then it is probably elicited countertransference; if not, it is probably personal.

Countertransference is often a mix of these two types, and sometimes it is hard to tell how much it derives from one versus the other. For example, in the case of elicited countertransference, even though most therapists react to the client in a certain negative way, there will always be a few who don't.

> For example, Faye was whiny and manipulative, always playing the helpless victim and pulling for special favors from her group leaders. They responded to this by feeling annoyed and disgusted with her. This was largely elicited countertransference, as evidenced

by the fact that over the course of three different groups, Faye's behavior caused four different leaders to react to her in a similar manner. However, in addition, each leader was influenced by his or her own issues. One leader, who had difficulty acting on his needs, envied Faye's ability to ask for what she needed and justified his resentment because she did it in an underhanded way. Therefore, some of this leader's countertransference was personal. However, there was another group leader who didn't have a negative reaction to Faye. Instead, his countertransference took a different form; he became overly involved with helping her.

In the case of elicited countertransference, the leader has two jobs: To use her awareness of her reaction to learn more about the client's behavior patterns and how they affect others, and to work through her reaction so she can be in an emotional position to help the client therapeutically.

Reactions to Clients' Confrontations

Next we discuss two of the most common types of countertransference problems that come up in groups.

The Leader's Reaction.   It is never easy for a therapist to be the recipient of a client's confrontation or negative feelings. This can bring up hurt, shame, fear, or aggressive reactions of anger and judgment. However, in the group setting, these reactions can be magnified. If a client attacks you or implies that you are an incompetent leader or an uncaring person, this can be especially hard to deal with because it is done publicly. If an individual client does this, you don't have to be concerned about who else is hearing this and what they might think of you. In a group setting, feelings of shame can emerge because of the more public setting.

In addition, sometimes more than one member will confront you about the same issue. When one person brings it up, others who feel similarly may join in, emboldened by the first. The whole group may even challenge you at times. This can be extremely difficult to handle emotionally. Just as it is hard for a group member to deal with multiple confrontations, so is it hard for a leader. You may be able to handle this better than some clients, but it nevertheless stirs up painful feelings and defensive reactions.

> For example, Sandy says to the leader, "You are so cold and distant. I don't feel like you care about us at all." Then a couple of other group members join in and agree, saying they feel they can't trust you."

These kinds of confrontations can threaten the leader's sense of competence, bringing up fears of professional inadequacy. This is especially a danger for relatively inexperienced group leaders. *You may begin to doubt yourself. Maybe you are really incapable of caring for clients. Maybe you have chosen the wrong profession.*

When you are confronted, you may react by becoming defensive or by leaking anger. Your attempts to facilitate may become tinged with a punitive or judgmental tone. You may be thrown off emotionally, becoming upset and internally self-judging, and this could cause you to be withdrawn and distracted in the group and to miss important clues about what is going on.

Looking at Yourself.   The tricky part of handling a confrontation is considering how it might be accurate. It is important to look carefully at the client's accusation for what you can learn about yourself. *In the above example, you might question Sandy and the other group members more about what makes them feel you don't care. Maybe there is something you are (or aren't) doing that conveys this message. You also need to look inside yourself, at that time or perhaps after the group is over, and ask if you do really care about them, or examine what might be blocking you from caring or from showing your caring.* If you think you did contribute to the problem, acknowledge this explicitly to the clients.

However, don't get caught up in worrying about whether you are a good group therapist. Too much focus on this will undermine your functioning as a leader. You must be able to look at yourself honestly and without judgment. You need to be able to see any mistakes you have made without condemning yourself. The goal is to see and acknowledge any flaws in your group leading while retaining your confidence in yourself.

> For example, you may realize that you have been overly afraid of encouraging dependency and have therefore refrained from expressing enough caring in the group. Or perhaps you realize that you didn't see how much caring Sandy needed from you because she didn't show it very directly.

Looking at the Clients.   If you are blaming yourself, remember that this confrontation is an opportunity for good work for this client and may be exactly what she needs. *Maybe it is important work for Sandy to confront you because she wasn't allow to be angry at her depriving mother. It also might be important work for the group. Maybe they need to test your ability to handle confrontation before they feel safe to confront each other.* When a client confronts you, it may reflect the fact that you are doing a good job as a leader rather than the reverse. The client trusts you enough to challenge you, and she has progressed to the point where she is strong enough to do this.

How to Avoid Reacting Negatively.   Once I have looked at my part, I often make a conscious choice to identify with the facilitator/therapist part of me rather than with the part that is being confronted. I focus on the fact that I am here to help this person (or people) understand, express, and learn from her feelings toward me. I figuratively step aside and allow the person's anger to be directed at a different part of me while I assume the role of helper. This usually allows me to stay in a place where I am open to the client and interested in her issues and needs, rather than reacting from the part of me that might be hurt, ashamed, or angry. By focusing my attention and energy on assisting the client therapeutically, I rarely get caught up in negative reactions. This is a more specific application of the leader stance I discussed earlier. *In the above example, I would help Sandy to express her anger at me and to access the maternal transference that is behind it.*

In doing this, however, I must be aware that reactive feelings could unconsciously contaminate my therapeutic interventions. I must watch for this possibility, so if it happens, I can back up and make corrections or acknowledge that I was thrown off.

> For example, if I realize that I am pushing Sandy toward accessing her transference to absolve myself of any blame for not being caring, I will back off and allow her process to unfold in a more natural way.

Repeated Confrontations. If a client repeatedly confronts the leader with negative feelings, this can cause the leader to pull away from the client emotionally or develop ongoing resentment. This is especially true with borderline clients, who may express intense anger repeatedly. This can cause the therapeutic alliance to be disrupted on the leader's side as well as the client's. To resolve this, you must focus your energy on working through this difficulty with the client, even to the point of initiating work with her if necessary. It is important to repair this alliance as soon as possible. You may need to investigate whether your own issues are being triggered by the client's attacks, causing you to act in ways that make the client feel more unsafe. A defense cycle may have developed between you and the client. *For example, Sandy accuses you of not caring in a way that makes you feel guilty, and you react by withdrawing from her. This causes her to feel even less cared for, and she accuses you even more vociferously.* If you can see what is transpiring, you may want to make this explicit to the client if she can handle your self-disclosure. Then you can work toward changing your behavior and reconnecting with the client.

Anger with a Client

Feeling Protective of Other Clients. Another common countertransference problem involves feeling angry with a client for behavior that hurts other people. This is a particular problem in group therapy because a client's negative ways of relating may directly affect other people whom you care about. In individual therapy, you only hear about your client's destructive behavior (and possibly experience it directed at you). In a group, you see him hurting others, and the danger is that this may cause you to become angry or judgmental toward him. This can happen during a dialogue between two people when one of them says something that is insensitive or hostile or manipulative and ends up wounding the other. It can also happen if a client does something that disrupts the safety of the group or threatens to undermine an important therapeutic group norm. *For example, Lawrence may become judgmental of Pat for being weak just when she is accessing some important pain from childhood.*

In these situations, your aggressive, protective responses may be triggered in a way that renders you incapable, for that moment, of caring about the attacker. You may unwittingly focus only on protecting others from this person and forget that you are also there to help him. This can especially be a problem if a client repeatedly acts like this; you may have ongoing resentment toward him that can seriously hamper your ability to work with him. *For example, if Lawrence repeatedly shames people during important work, you may develop such resentment toward him that you wish he would leave the group.*

How to Handle This Reaction. The first step in handling this, as with any countertransference problem, is to be aware of it. Once you realize you are having a negative reaction to a client, your desire to help may naturally reassert itself. If some cases, more processing may be needed. You may need to examine what issues of yours are being activated by this person, and work on these issues yourself.

In this situation it is very helpful to take time to focus your attention on the attacking client's underlying pain. Whenever, a client is acting in a destructive manner, it always derives from underlying core issues, though they may be hidden. If you only look at the outward, harmful behavior, it is easy to be annoyed. However, if you take the time to remind yourself that this client is acting this way because he was abused or neglected as a child, or because he was abandoned or exploited by his parents, this makes it easy to feel more compassion and caring, even when he is attacking others. Even if you don't verbalize this to the client, just remembering can help to shift your attitude toward him. You can see the hurt, frightened, or shamed child that is hidden beneath the condescension or manipulation.

> For instance, Lawrence's mother was weak and overly emotional when he needed her to be strong, and this left him vulnerable and unprotected. Now he attacks women who seem to act the same way, because their behavior triggers his old pain, but now he can be strong and protect himself by attacking the women.

If you don't know exactly what the client's history is, it helps to hypothesize. Based on your intuition and theoretical understanding, you can make some educated guesses about what might be driving him to be harmful. Even if you aren't completely right, this will help you to take a more caring, understanding attitude toward the client.

20

CHAPTER

Outside Contact Between Group Members

In many types of psychotherapy groups, particularly in psychodynamic groups, there are rules explicitly prohibiting contact between group members outside group meetings. In fact, this is a given in psychodynamic groups. This restriction is primarily to avoid the problem that outside interactions may not be dealt with in the group and clients can form divisive subgroups. Some leaders prefer not to make rules against outside contact because group members often don't obey them. These leaders prefer to deal with the issue in a more cooperative way by explaining to their members how outside contact can lead to trouble.

On the other hand, in my experience group members can gain a great deal having outside contact if it is handled properly. I have discovered ways to minimize the chances of negative consequences. In this chapter, I discuss the advantages of outside contact and how to avoid the dangers.

☐ The Advantages of Outside Contact

Healing Relationships. Probably the biggest advantage of outside contact between group members is that it allows for richer and more involved healing relationships. As I have already noted, the relationships between group members can provide healing for core issues. When these relationships extend outside the group, there is an opportunity for greater healing. People can develop a deeper level of intimacy and carry their relationships into more realistic aspects of their daily lives.

> For example, Denny and Stephanie talked on the phone fairly often. Denny was quite needy and often talked to Stephanie about the pain he was in. Stephanie had difficulty in setting limits, especially with men, so she allowed him to spend more time on his problems than

she wanted, and she felt that he ignored her needs and interests. She brought this up in group, and they discussed their feelings and positions. Denny had no idea she wanted to talk more about herself and was quite interested in having her do this. She, however, didn't trust him and refused to have outside contact for a while. This seemed like a good experiment for her in limit setting, so I supported it.

After a while, they took up their phone relationship again, and this time it worked out well for both of them. Stephanie was able to assert herself, and Denny paid more attention to her needs. It was healing for her to stand up for herself with a man and have him be responsive. Because there was little sexual attraction on either side, this relationship was healing for Stephanie in another way. She had had few relationships with men that didn't involve sex, and she knew that Denny really cared for her as a person, not a sex object. Denny had intimacy fears derived from rejection and abandonment by his alcoholic mother, so when Stephanie was willing to hang in and work through their difficulties, this was healing for him.

Their relationship developed into one of genuine mutual caring and respect, which included lunches, parties, and get-togethers with a third group member who was close to both of them. Because of the level of connection they could achieve outside of group, this relationship provided a more profound level of healing than would have been possible if it had been restricted to group meetings.

Socially Inept Clients.   For clients who are socially inept, outside contact provides another opportunity to develop social skills because they can get feedback on this process from the group members they are relating to. For clients who are socially isolated, outside contact can allow them the experience of developing real-life supportive relationships and friendships while still being able to work in group on the difficulties that arise in doing this. In their ordinary lives, making connections may be too difficult; they may be too frightened to initiate contact or too interpersonally dysfunctional to maintain it. However, with other group members they can be helped to overcome these problems through work in the group, making the outside connection possible. For certain clients, the ability to develop outside friendships can be a crucial part of the therapeutic change process.

Evoking Realistic Issues.   Another advantage is that outside relationships tend to evoke a wider range of interpersonal issues. For example, clients have a chance to deal with their fears about calling people when in emotional trouble, their difficulties in reaching out to initiate friendships, their inconsistency in maintaining connections with others, and their fear of losing themselves in a close relationship. They have an opportunity to get feedback on their social personas and their interpersonal patterns in ordinary conversation (as opposed to group work). A wider range of psychodynamic issues are activated by the greater variety of social and interpersonal situations clients are confronted with. They also have an opportunity to experiment with a greater range of interpersonal behaviors.

Transfer of Learning.   Whenever group members carry their relationships outside of the group into more everyday circumstances, they are taking a step toward transferring to ordinary life the learning and therapeutic change that has happened in the group. It encourages clients to build healthy aspects of the group culture into their outside lives. They have an opportunity to work therapeutically on interpersonal situations that are closer to ordinary life, not just those that occur in the group setting. Just as group therapy is closer to ordinary life than individual therapy, a group that includes outside relationships is even closer. As clients learn healthier behavior in the group, they have a chance to try this out in other situations with their fellow group members. When things go wrong or clients revert to old patterns, they can bring this directly into group and explore what happened. This makes it much easier to transfer group learning to ordinary life.

When group members relate to each other outside of the group, this encourages them to go beyond intrapsychic resolution of psychological difficulties and begin to create a healthier way of life in their circles of family and friends. This facilitates bringing the healthy group culture into the larger society, thus making the group an agent of social change as well as individual growth. This is discussed further in chapter 29.

Group Involvement.   Because of the possibility of developing real-life connections, more is at stake in the relationships between group members, and therefore there is greater involvement and intensity. This is more likely to activate deep issues to be explored in the group. The group often becomes more important to the members, thereby increasing cohesiveness.

Handling Problems with Outside Contact.   It is common for group members to connect outside of group even in groups where this is discouraged or prohibited. And when they do, they are not likely to tell the group about it because they have gone against the leader's recommendations. This makes it more likely that if something goes wrong, the leader will have no way to work it through or correct it, because it is hidden. In fact, I suspect that this is the reason outside contact has gotten such a bad reputation among some group leaders. In my view, the problem doesn't lie in the outside contact itself, but in severing the outside relationship from the purview of the group. In my groups I actually encourage members to have outside contact if they want to. This is considered part of the group experience; the group boundaries include not only the group meetings but also any other contacts between group members. Therefore I have the right to provide guidelines about these connections, and this helps me to prevent most problems with outside contact from arising and to handle those that do.

☐ The Dangers of Outside Contact and How to Minimize Them

There are a number of inherent dangers when group members see each other outside of group.

Avoiding Problems.   Probably the most serious danger is that two group members will encounter interpersonal difficulties between them outside of group that they can't resolve, and they will avoid dealing with these issues in group. This may happen if one of the people feels embarrassed by what has transpired and asks the other not to talk about it in group. It can also happen if both people become afraid of a conflict and keep it hidden from the group. If this happens, it is likely to poison the relationship between the two group members, and, in addition, it may distract them so they won't be able to work on anything else in group very effectively.

I have handled this danger by providing clear guidelines that specify that members are not to avoid such issues. Even more important, I work to establish group norms where the members see the value of bringing in outside difficulties. Because I don't discourage members from having outside contact, I am free to help them learn how to handle it in a therapeutic manner. Often in a new group, this starts out with two people getting together for coffee or chatting on the phone. One of them may be left with uncomfortable feelings about their contact. *"Why did Sarah not seem interested in me? Did I appear insecure or insensitive? Did I seem too eager for more contact and therefore turn her off?"* Another possibility is that one group member may be disappointed or angry with the other. In either case, because of my guidelines or my direct encouragement, the two people will have a dialogue in the group about their outside contact. They will probably work through their difficulty, and the other members will see that they both gained something. This helps to establish the norm that it is valuable to bring in outside difficulties.

Because I do individual consultations with each group member periodically, if two people are avoiding difficult feelings that came up outside, one of them is likely to talk to me about it in a consultation. Then I can encourage him to bring it into the group.

It is important to encourage clients to talk about outside contact soon after if happens rather than waiting weeks to bring it into group. This makes it less likely that problems will fester or that two people will develop an intense outside relationship that becomes separate from the group work. It also means that you can provide guidelines or help them work through any difficulties with the contact.

Avoiding Challenge. If two group members develop a positive outside relationship without significant problems, there are a couple of dangers. One is that they will avoid challenging each other in group for fear of rocking the boat. I handle this with a clear guideline that encourages members not to avoid confronting someone because one feels close to them outside of the group. I also watch for this problem. If there are two members with an outside connection who always support each other in group, then I question whether they are avoiding challenging each other.

Avoiding Intimacy Work. Another danger with group members who have a good outside relationship is that they may avoid working on intimacy with each other in the group. They may feel close to each other outside but not actually work on deepening their connection. Even if they do work on this outside the group, they are missing the benefits of a therapist who could help them explore the intimacy issues that are being evoked. I handle this problem by encouraging people with outside connections to explore intimacy issues in group.

Subgrouping. There is a danger that people may form subgroups of two or three that exclude other group members. This, of course, can also happen in the group, but it can be more serious if it happens outside. I don't believe that subgrouping itself is necessarily bad for a group. The reality is that each group member will be drawn to certain people more than others, and this needs to be allowed and expressed. If a subgroup forms, other group members may feel hurt or excluded, but this is valuable grist for the mill. These feelings of envy or jealousy should be expressed and explored. Subgrouping becomes non-therapeutic only when members form alliances against other members or try to relate only to the people in their subgroup. As long as the subgrouping is discussed openly and each member is willing to relate to all other group members, then subgrouping is not destructive for the group. I have a guideline that specifies that two group members are not to gossip negatively about a third member outside of group. This helps to minimize destructive subgrouping.

Diluting the Group Energy.   When people have outside relationships, there is a possibility that too much of their energy goes into their outside contact and too little is focused on the group, where the main therapeutic work is done. However, the guidelines I have already discussed tend to prevent this. If members bring in work from outside relationships and avoid gossip, this keeps their energy focused in the group. If anything, people tend to be more involved in relationships that also extend outside the group, so if these relationships are worked on in the group setting, this can intensify the group energy. In those rare cases where it seems that group energy is being diluted, I bring this up for discussion in the group.

Compliance.   Some group members have a tendency to comply with what others want them to do or be. They have trouble knowing what they want, setting limits, or standing up for themselves. When this happens in the group, they can be helped to realize when they are being compliant and to set limits and take care of themselves. Outside of group, this help is not available, so compliant clients can give themselves away without realizing that this needs to be dealt with in group. A compliant client might even be exploited by another group member, sexually, financially, or in other ways. This is, of course, very dangerous and could result in abrupt, inappropriate termination. If, as leader, you sense that something like this may be happening, bring it up for exploration. The compliant client may need to forego outside relationships until she has become strong enough to take care of herself outside the group. Clients with this issue who recognize their vulnerability and refuse to make outside contact should be supported in this. Others may not realize they need this protection or may not be strong enough to ask for it. Then you must suggest it.

Occasionally one group member may make excessive demands on other members for outside contact, and they may not be strong enough to set the limits they need, perhaps because the group is new or because of their low level of functioning. In this case, you may need to restrict the demanding client in his outside contacts. Otherwise some members may leave the group to get away from him.

Other Problematic Relating.   In general, outside contact can stir up more difficult problems than those that occur in group, and so you must be careful to protect vulnerable clients. Compliance is not the only interpersonal problem that may require restrictions on outside relationships. A client might have a tendency toward withdrawal, angry outbursts, sexual acting out, or other difficulties. If the person is not capable of handling these impulses in a satisfactory way outside of group and doesn't bring them into the group for work, this could cause serious problems in his relationships with other group members. It is probably better for him to restrict his relationships to the group sessions until he has grown enough to handle outside problems. You may need to suggest this restriction to certain clients to protect them from these dangers.

Sexual Relationships.   It isn't a good idea for group members to become involved sexually or romantically. This can introduce a level of intensity and preoccupation that might preclude any real therapy from happening in the group. Furthermore, if they break up, the hurt and anger is often so intense that one of them will leave the group. Therefore I recommend that clients not become sexually involved with each other, and, in fact, this has rarely happened in my groups.

However, if it does occur, it is especially important to require the members involved to tell the group what has happened and to work on their relationship openly in the group. Otherwise it can lead to disaster. The guidelines about outside relationships should be spelled out in the written group rules so you can use this leverage to make sure that the members do this.

Professional or Business Relationships.   It can be problematic for group members to form professional or business relationships with each other. If you have therapists in your group, they might decide to co-lead a group or form a supervisory relationship. Other members might engage in bodywork, legal work, hairdressing, or other kinds of financial involvements with each other. These kind of relationships aren't necessarily destructive, but there is a potential for problems, so each situation should be considered carefully before the members proceed. It definitely isn't a good idea for one group member to enter into therapy with another because the therapist would then be restricted from being him or herself in the group.

Other Members Not Present.   When two people work on an outside incident in group, the other group members may lose interest in what is happening because they didn't witness what is being discussed. More important, they can't give feedback on the incident. However, this problem can often be circumvented by focusing as much as possible on the interaction the members are having at the moment in the group. Don't let them get too focused on hashing out the details of exactly what happened outside of group. There is usually something important happening between them as they discuss what happened outside, and this is a source of rich information for feedback and therapeutic intervention.

This chapter may leave the reader with the impression that most work in my groups involves outside connections. This is not true. No matter how involved people become with each other on the outside, the vast majority of the interactions in group relate to incidents from group sessions.

☐ Pros and Cons

Given the number of potential problems with allowing outside contact between group members, it is certainly understandable that some group leaders have a rule against this. If such a rule can truly be enforced, this may be best for some client populations. However, I hear from many group leaders that clients tend to disregard this kind of rule. I find it preferable to encourage outside contact and then use my leadership to ensure that it is therapeutic. A colleague reports that instead of having a rule against outside contact, she discusses problems with outside contact as they arise and gradually encourages the members to forego it. With this approach, since the group members are involved in making the decision, they are more likely to abide by it.

The stance you take regarding outside contact may depend on the level of functioning of your group members and also possibly their character structure. For relatively high-functioning clients, outside contact poses few problems. They are able to follow guidelines about outside contact, and they aren't as likely to get in serious trouble outside of the group. Low-functioning clients are much more likely to act out sexually, fall into compliance, or avoid dealing with difficulties. Therefore they are much more at risk in having outside relationships. However, many of them are socially isolated when they join a therapy group, and therefore they have the most to gain from having outside relationships if the problems can be handled. I have had many low-functioning clients in my groups, and there have been few problems with outside contact. However, I haven't personally run a group consisting entirely of low-functioning clients. Handling outside relationships in this situation might be more difficult.

In case you are leading a problem-focused group with a population that especially needs support, it is mandatory that outside contact be encouraged (see chapter 28).

IV

GROUP-RELATED ISSUES

Part IV discusses issues that are specifically related to the group as a whole. Chapter 21 covers the developmental stages of group process, and chapter 22 deals with termination. Chapter 23 explores group roles and positions, and chapter 24 discusses how to handle difficult group members. Chapter 25 covers a variety of other group-as-a-whole issues.

Developmental Stages of Group Process

This chapter deals with the stages of development that a group traverses. In an ongoing group where new members join periodically, these stages also apply to the experience of each new member. There have been many studies of the developmental stages of therapy groups (Beck, 1974; Bennis & Shepard, 1956; Levine, 1979; MacKenzie, 1990; Tuckman, 1965), most of them based on time-limited groups. Overall, researchers tend to agree about the stages, but differ about some details. In this chapter, I present my understanding of the development of interactive groups, which is basically consistent with these previous studies. I have divided this process into six stages—entrance, inclusion, conflict, working, intimacy, and termination. The termination process is covered in the next chapter.

As we look at the stages, keep in mind that in reality groups don't have such clear delineation between stages and straightforward sequencing of events. The following description is only a rough approximation of the order in which significant issues emerge in groups, which are always messier than any conceptual scheme. There is often some overlap between stages and even some circling back to earlier stages. Furthermore, the issues that are most prominent in each stage also matter to a lesser degree during other stages.

☐ The Entrance Stage: Starting A New Group

The First Meeting

The Beginning.   At the beginning of a new group, the six to eight members will have met the leader at least once but won't know each other. Your main job as leader is to ease them into group work and begin building a therapeutic group culture. It is

219

probably wise to begin by discussing group rules and norms, thus reminding them how the group is supposed to operate, even though you have already done this in the pre-group interviews. Go over the written rules for the group, making sure to discuss confidentiality. Discuss how the group functions, with an emphasis on self-exploration and interactive work.

Then it is time for members to begin to get to know each other. This can be done using a structured exercise or by just starting the open-ended group process. In an interactive group I rarely use exercises of any sort, but I sometimes start with a simple exercise in pairs in the first meeting, so that each group member gets to know one other person a little, providing an extra sense of safety and connection. However, an exercise is not necessary. I have also begun groups by plunging right into the group process. Some psychodynamic leaders begin with an unstructured process, believing that leaders should provide little in the way of guidelines for the members. I prefer to provide quite a lot of orientation while still encouraging the members to take responsibility for their own work.

Initial Guidelines and Interventions.   When the unstructured group process begins, it is helpful to suggest that members discuss what brought them to the group and what they want to get from being there. I also encourage them to talk about what they are feeling in the moment, as a beginning training in awareness. However, make it clear that they can say whatever they want. You are not dictating exactly what should happen, just providing general guidelines. At first, group members tend to direct their statements to the leader rather than to each other, but if you don't respond too much but rather encourage them to talk to each other, they will quickly begin to do so.

Initial interventions are usually aimed at helping group members become aware of their feelings in the moment. Some people will be anxious, some excited, some concerned about their ability to speak up in the group. It is important to have everyone involved in the group interaction, even if only in small ways. Therefore, don't spend much time working with any one person; leave room for light interactions involving many of the group members. If necessary, call on silent members to get them involved.

Most of the members will be feeling anxiety, but many will not realize that others are anxious too. If people don't spontaneously talk about this, it is good to mention it. It helps for a client to realize that he is not alone in his fears and for the group members to discuss their tensions together. This is good practice at being aware of here-and-now experience, and sharing common feelings builds group cohesion. Many members are concerned about being judged, but when they show their initial anxieties, the group appreciates their taking the risk to reveal themselves.

Subsequent Meetings

Balanced Risk.   Don't encourage anyone to go too deeply into her material at the beginning. You don't want the amount of risk and exposure to become lopsided at this early stage. If one person exposes too much or gets into deep feelings too quickly, she may become frightened or ashamed and not return to the group. Ideally all the members will take risks in a gradual way, one step at a time, thereby maximizing the sense of safety in the room. If someone dives into deep material too quickly, encourage her to be more cautious. Ask her if she really wants to open up so quickly in a new group, and if she has considered how she may feel later. Also make an effort to steer the group away from potentially intense conflict at this stage when there isn't enough cohesiveness to handle it.

Checking Out the Group.
During the entrance stage, new members are checking the group out to see if it is right for them. They may be sizing up the leader to see if you seem competent and caring. They want to see if the style of the group meets their needs and if they can open up in this setting. They may also be observing the other group members to see if they want to become involved with them. Group members who are your individual clients may already be committed, but for everyone this early period is a time of caution and testing. During this stage many members prefer to observe and make only tentative forays into the group.

It is useful to schedule consultations with new members after the first or second meeting, especially with anyone who seems to be having trouble. In an early consultation you can teach the client about group norms and how to initiate interactive work (see chapter 11). You can explain how the therapy process works and deal with various fears and difficulties that have arisen. These first consultations are important in helping members adjust to the group and preventing drop-outs.

Beginning Interactive Dialogues.
When the group seems ready, it helps to move the group toward doing interactive work. They may begin this work on their own, but often they need your encouragement because of the extra risk involved in directly encountering each other. One way to do this is as follows: "Each person pick one other group member and become aware of your initial impressions of and feelings toward this person." Then ask someone to start by expressing these feelings to the person she picked. Encourage this person to respond and allow an interaction to develop if that is appropriate. When they are finished, and other group members have had a chance to express their reactions to what happened, ask for another person to do the same. If one of these interactions stimulates further work in other members, allow that to unfold. It isn't important that everyone get a turn in doing this exercise. This is just a way to get the ball rolling in an interactive direction. It is fine if these initial reactions are not terribly significant. The main objective is to teach members how to initiate this kind of work. This exercise can also be used in later in the group if members have gotten away from doing interactive work.

Moving On.
The entrance stage lasts until most group members decide that the group is right for them and begin taking the risk to do some real work. Then the group moves on to the inclusion stage. This generally takes a week or two in a short-term group. In a long-term group, it can take from several weeks to several months.

☐ Adding a New Member to a Group

The stages described in this chapter apply to both the unfolding of a group over time and also to the developmental process of each new member who is added to an existing group. In a closed group, no new members are added, so the developmental stages unfold in a more straightforward manner. However, this is possible only with limited-time groups. In an open-ended group, new members must be added from time to time or the group will gradually die as people leave. Each time a new member joins, that person goes through a sequence of stages in her integration into the group that is similar in many ways to the stages the overall group goes through. Therefore, the descriptions of stages in this chapter apply to both individuals and groups.

I have divided the description of the entrance stage into two parts. Because starting a new group is quite different from adding one member to an existing group, these are discussed separately.

Impact on the Stage of the Group.   The addition of a new member (or members) affects the current stage of the group. It exerts a pull on the group backward to an earlier stage, with the result that sometimes a group partakes of two stages at the same time. For example, if a group is in the conflict stage (Stage 3) and two new members are added, this will pull the group back toward the entrance stage. The group probably won't fully revert to Stage 1 but will exist in a state that somehow combines the entrance and conflict stages (1 and 3). The more new members that are added, the greater the pull, and if the group is still fairly new, it will be pulled back more easily. However, with a mature group, adding one new member may not affect the stage of the group at all.

It can be advantageous to add two new members to a group at the same time whenever this is possible. This reduces the number of times that the group must be disrupted by the addition of a member. It often makes it easier for the new members because they have a companion in the awkward experience of entering a group, and if the group is slow to accept them, they may be able to connect with each other.

Reactions to a New Member

Group Reactions.   When a new person is added, the group members can have a wide variety of reactions, from welcoming the person to excluding her. Groups that are still in the process of forming themselves (in the inclusion or conflict stages) tend to be less welcoming of new members. However, if a group is small, it may be eager for more people. Groups that are stable sometimes want new members to add extra spice to a process that has gotten somewhat stale. Some groups that are well-established with close bonds can be frightened of or resentful toward anyone new. This is especially true when a new group first stabilizes its membership, achieves the intimacy stage, and then loses its first member to graduation. When the next person is added to replace this member, this is a usually big jolt for the group, and they may resist accepting the new person.

> For example, one group had been meeting for 2½ years and had become quite close. However, over a period of 6 months, three members left, bringing the group down to four people. They knew they needed new members but were reluctant to accept them. When two new members joined at roughly the same time, the existing group members focused mostly on interactions among themselves, giving the newcomers little time and attention. One of the new members was perfectly happy with this because she liked to move into new situations gradually and carefully. The group appreciated her coming into the group slowly because they felt she was respecting what they had developed with each other, and eventually they

accepted her completely. The other new member, Lori, had very different needs. Because she felt insecure in any situation where she didn't feel fully accepted, she attempted to get involved quickly. When she reached out to connect with the old group member, they weren't receptive to her doing this so soon and told her so. Lori was very hurt, and when she confronted them in a demanding way, they rebuffed her. The leader challenged the group on their resistance to new members, but this didn't prevent them from excluding her. The situation escalated, and she ended up leaving the group in anger. This might have been prevented if the leader had also worked with Lori on her need to get in so quickly and the way she expressed it.

Make sure to give your group members enough time before a new person enters to get used to the idea and to explore their feelings about it. This is especially important if the group may be resistant. If the group is in the middle of an unusually conflictual or embarrassing process, put off the new person for a few weeks so that when she arrives they will be more open to her.

Individual Reactions.   Each person will react to the idea of having a new member according to his own issues. Clients who are frightened or suspicious and have achieved some trust with the existing group will be resistant or even hostile to anyone new. Clients who enjoy novelty and perhaps fear commitment may welcome new energy. It can be helpful to view the group as a family and the new member as a baby who was just born. Some clients have had negative experiences with a younger sibling. Those who had their place with the mother usurped by a baby brother or sister may be especially resistant to new members.

The First Meeting.   At the first meeting with the new member, encourage the group to introduce themselves to the new person and vice versa. Even though this may be awkward, it helps to ease the new client into the group process. If it seems that the addition has disrupted the member's normal ease with each other, comment on this and encourage them to examine their reactions to having a new person there. Notice how each reacts according to his particular character structure. Clients who are caretakers will be more concerned about the new person's feelings than their own. Clients who are shy and wary of strangers will clam up. Outgoing clients may be eager to know the new member and therefore quiz her. Encourage the new person to talk about her reactions to being in the group and the way she is being welcomed. The most important thing is that everyone's reactions be expressed and explored.

Supporting the New Member

Speed of Involvement.   It is important to let the new person take her time in adjusting to the group; she should feel free to participate only as much as she feels comfortable. However, don't allow her to sit for too long being completely silent. If she says nothing, call on her during the first meeting so she can at least give some reaction. If necessary, help her to get somewhat involved during the first month, because she must make a decision about whether the group is right for her, and this is hard to judge if she doesn't participate. On the other hand, respect any fears she has that require her to move slowly. Don't push a new person faster than she can handle safely.

Some new members will feel a need to become included in the group quickly. This can be positive if it doesn't go too far. If the person becomes pushy and demanding that the group accept her before it has had time to get to know her, help her to explore what is behind her rush. This often comes from intense early needs for nurturing. If the new member is present for some emotionally intense work, make sure she talks about how this affected her. If she was frightened and doesn't talk about this, she may not come back to the next meeting. Make sure to offer extra support, such as a phone call or consultation before the next meeting, if she seems to need it.

Deciding Whether to Stay. If the new person is not clear on whether she wants to stay in the group, make sure she explores this in group (or in a consultation) before very many meetings have transpired. Otherwise, she may just decide on her own not to stay without getting other input, and therefore she may miss getting feedback that might lead her to make a better choice.

Teaching New Members. New members often don't understand how the group process really works, although this may not be apparent from what they say in group. Consultations can be very helpful by providing you with an opportunity to teach the new person about group norms and how therapeutic change happens. *For example, if a client confuses the group with a social setting, he may not be able to imagine why he should bring up negative feelings toward a member he doesn't care about. You can explain that though it might not be worth dealing with these negative feelings if he knew this person in a social setting, he can learn a great deal by working on them in a therapy group.* This kind of teaching can go on in the group if you realize the need for it, but sometimes this only becomes apparent in consultations. They can be crucial in keeping some new members from terminating prematurely.

☐ The Inclusion Stage

Once a new member (or in the case of a group, most members) decides the group is right for her, she moves into the inclusion stage. However, this doesn't mean that the member (or members) is now truly committed to the group. That involves a deeper level of emotional involvement and therefore comes later, at the end of the inclusion or conflict stage.

The major tasks for a client in the inclusion stage are (a) understanding group norms and learning how to work in the group, (b) becoming involved with the group, (c) self-disclosure and acceptance by the group, and (d) commitment to the group. MacKenzie (1990) delineated a single stage, which he called the "entrance stage," that includes my entrance and inclusion stages.

Group Norms. The inclusion stage is the time during which most group norms are laid down. Members learn how to be aware of their experience in the moment and how to explore themselves intrapsychically. They learn something about how people operate psychologically and how to make sense of their motivations and defenses. They learn how to connect their reactions in the group to issues in their current life and in childhood. They learn how to tune into their feelings and how to be honest and direct with each other. They learn about being responsible for their own work and caring for others. All of the therapeutic norms should be promoted during this stage.

Becoming Involved.   An early task for each group member is to become involved with the group—to participate verbally in the group process and especially to become personally involved, by sharing meaningful material and by having emotional encounters with other group members. A client does this first by talking about small reactions to other members and sharing basic information about his life. Then if the group responds well to a client's first tentative forays and if other clients take comparable risks, the group will feel safer, and the client will gradually risk more.

Some clients tend to avoid becoming involved, because of fears of being engulfed or betrayed or because of a habitual stance of distance from people. They must be helped to explore these fears without being pressured to go further than they are ready. However, make it clear to them that they must eventually become involved if they are to get much from the group therapy process. Some clients, on the other hand, will need involvement to feel OK and so they will lead the way.

Self-Disclosure and Acceptance

Self-Disclosure and Shame.   As time goes on, group members begin to reveal themselves to each other in deeper ways. They especially disclose things about themselves that they feel ashamed of, that they imagine will make them unacceptable to others. This happens because they begin to sense that the group is different from other situations in their lives, that maybe here they can finally be themselves and be accepted. This fosters a hope of healing, and gradually they take the risk to reveal painful and potentially shameful facts about themselves.

> For example, a young man might reveal that he is still a virgin or that he is HIV-positive. A person might share that she was sexually abused, or is currently bulimic, or is having an extramarital affair

Clients also begin to show parts of themselves that they think aren't OK—their tears, their anger, their insecurity. They let down their guard and allow their real selves to show.

> For example, Penny revealed to the group how much she needed their caring and nurturing. This was particularly terrifying to her because Penny's mother had responded to her needs with disgust, and so Penny had internalized the feeling that her needs were bad. When she let the group know how much she needed them, she felt mortified, and when they responded with love and caring, she was greatly relieved and took the healing in deeply.

Acceptance.   If the group is functioning well, when a client takes this kind of self-disclosure risk, she will be accepted by the other group members. In fact, they often appreciate her more for having revealed herself in a deeper way, and this is an important source of healing. Of course, since this is not just a support group, people sometimes do react negatively to these disclosures, but this can usually be worked through in a way that feels satisfying to all concerned (see chapter 4).

Clients who have loose boundaries and feel at ease with public disclosure often lead the way during the inclusion stage. Those who are shy or secretive have the most difficulty with this stage, but in the end they have the most to gain. Their revelations are very big risks and have greater healing potential.

Stages and Group Issues.   Self-disclosure is at the height of its significance during the inclusion stage (MacKenzie, 1990), but it continues to be important after that. As each member's work and trust deepen, they gradually risk revealing material with a greater potential for shame. This pattern is true of all issues. There is a stage during which a given issue is paramount—for example, power during the conflict stage—but that issue is also important before and after that stage as well. For example, power issues between group members also occur during the inclusion stage, and power continues to have importance even after the conflict stage is completed.

Trust.   Trust is an important issue during the inclusion stage, particularly for those clients who have trouble trusting that their revelations will not be used against them. Actually, trust can be an issue during other stages as well. For example, some clients have trouble trusting that self-assertion or aggression will not lead to retaliation or abandonment. This comes up primarily during the conflict stage.

Toning Down Conflict

During the inclusion stage, it is often a good idea to guide the group in the direction of sharing rather than conflict. One of the key cautions in the early stages of an interactive group is related to conflict; you don't want the level of conflict to exceed the level of support. When a group has been meeting for about a year and has passed through the conflict stage, there is a sense of mutual support and caring. Each member knows that the others accept her and like her, so if she gets embroiled in a difficult conflict with one person, she trusts that the rest of the group cares for her (as well as the other person). An intense conflict between two people can be easily handled in such a group, whereas if the same confrontation happened in a group that was only a month old, it could destroy the group.

Therefore it is OK to allow people in the inclusion stage to share a lot of outside material with each other. Even though this is not necessarily interactive, it provides a way for them to get to know each other without too much risk. In fact, the members need to learn background information about each other and discover what each person is struggling with in her life. You don't want the group to engage in too much outside sharing, however, because that would establish the wrong norm concerning interactive work. Try to strike a balance between outside sharing and interactive work. You don't need to avoid all conflict; a certain amount is appropriate as long as it doesn't become too intense.

If an interaction between two people threatens to get out of hand, step in and work with each of them separately. For example, if one person is becoming very angry, rather than allowing the other to respond, work with the first person on exploring where his anger is coming from. By keeping them working individually on the deeper material, you are doing valuable therapeutic work without risking a dangerous explosion. (See chapter 17 for more discussion of how to handle confrontations.)

Belonging

Key questions for group members during this stage are, "Do I belong in this group? Do the other members accept me?" This brings up acceptance issues from the family of origin, school groups, and other peer groups.

> For example, Melanie felt excluded from peer groups as a child until she learned to be entertaining and charming to gain people's interest. At the point when she joined a therapy group, she had become aware of her entertaining defense, and so she largely let go of it in the group and experimented with being her authentic self. However, this brought up fears that she wouldn't be accepted into the group. She had joined a long-standing, cohesive group, and she missed quite a few meetings because of sickness at first, so even after being in the group for quite a while, she still wasn't as close to the other group members as they were to each other. She experienced this as rejection and exclusion, though the group members really did accept her. Melanie worked on the childhood issues underlying her feeling of rejection and experimented with reaching out to individual group members. Over time she became fully integrated into the group.

In addition to the question of being accepted by the group, there are other belonging issues. Does the client accept the other members? Does he want to be a part of this group of people? Does he deserve to be part of it? Some clients will deal with this issue by pushing their way into the group, whether or not this is necessary. Others will stay on the sidelines, assuming they are being rejected, whether this is true or not. Some will do various things to alienate themselves from the group, without realizing that they are causing their exclusion. Some will keep themselves apart from the group, as a way of acting out their feeling of separateness, inferiority, or superiority. All of these issues must be brought out and explored.

Dropouts and Group Formation

It is usual for a few members of the original group to drop out during the entrance and inclusion stages, though if all group members are also your individual clients, there may be fewer dropouts because of their existing connection with you. For one reason or another, a few clients will decide that group therapy isn't right for them, or they need a different kind of group, or they aren't yet ready for a group. People also may leave because of relocation, illness, or financial issues. Therefore it is wise to have a potential source of more group members when starting a new group.

Sometimes a client's decision to drop out will be correct for him, and sometimes the person is running away from difficulties that could be handled. Some clients can be helped to stay in group if they get enough support, either in the group or through consults or individual therapy. If a member is in therapy with someone else, confer with the other therapist about the client so the two of you can work on helping him to make it in the group. If a client needs individual therapy to be able to handle group, offer to see the person yourself or find a good individual therapist for him.

A long-term group may go through a period of instability, losing some members and gaining some replacements. This is disruptive for many members and also for the group's development. It may mean the group will take longer to move through the inclusion stage. If members are upset and fear that the group is falling apart or will never be solid, sympathize with their feelings and explore what deeper meaning it may have for each person. However, also take the fear seriously and express confidence that the group will come together.

Conflict and Inclusion Stages

There is often a great deal of overlap between the inclusion and conflict stages; some writers see them as just one stage (Levine, 1979). In fact, conflict issues often arise as early as inclusion issues. I have chosen to conceptualize them as separate stages because of the importance of delaying intense conflict until the inclusion process is further along. In other words, I am not saying that conflict naturally comes after inclusion; I am saying that as a leader, you should strive to make this so. What's most important is not the natural course a group would take if left on its own but the best order of development that is possible. Although the leader can't completely change the natural order of things, you do have some leverage, and this is a good place to apply it. Work toward having the inclusion process mostly precede the conflict process.

Commitment.   At some point, each member feels that he does belong in the group and begins experiencing deeper emotional ties to the other members. He becomes truly invested in being part of this group of people for some time to come. This feeling of commitment emerges for some clients during the inclusion stage and for others at the resolution of the conflict stage.

This issue often brings with it fears of being trapped or engulfed. Clients who have a fear of commitment in love relationships are often afraid of committing themselves to the group. The danger for these members is that they will terminate at this point in the process rather than working through this fear. They may signal this by becoming judgmental of the group or the leader. They may make other excuses for leaving, such as a lack of money or time. The best safeguard against this outcome is to help the client see that this desire to leave comes from a commitment fear. If you know early in the group that a person has such issues, it might be wise to predict that he will want to run after 3 or 4 months. If you sense that a member may drop out, bring it up in group or schedule a consultation to help him explore these fears. The important thing is to involve the person in exploring his desire to leave before he makes a premature decision to do so.

Moving On.   When most members of the group are involved and feel acceptance and belonging, the inclusion stage has ended. This usually happens in the first month of a short-term group and after 3 to 9 months in a long-term group. You may ask, if a short-term group can accomplish this so quickly, why should it ever have to take longer? The answer is that short-term groups move through these stages in a more superficial way. At the inclusion stage, the level of acceptance and belonging is not as deep as can be achieved in a long-term group. In a short-term group, the speed of group development is accelerated because of the more active leadership and the time pressure on the clients, but the level of character change that is possible is not nearly as profound.

Time-limited or problem-focused groups that do not deal with conflict between group members can't develop into the conflict phase. These groups tend to move quickly into and through the inclusion phase and stay at that level of development. Those limited-time groups that are interactive and therefore do explore conflict may have time to move through the conflict stage into the working stage.

☐ The Conflict Stage

In addition to acceptance and belonging, group members also have to differentiate, to become separate individuals. During the entrance and inclusion stages, there is often some illusion of sameness and agreement among the group members. They are just getting to know each other and need a sense of safety. One way to achieve this is to pretend they are all pretty much alike. They can understand each other, agree with each other, and be nice to each other. This is a natural pretense that makes it easier to navigate the early stages of a new group. However, by the conflict stage they are ready to let go of this illusion and test out their differences. They need to be able to express all their feelings, including negative feelings, toward the group, toward each other, and toward the leader. They need to assert who they are as individuals. They need to learn to work through conflict and to take more power in the running of the group. These are the tasks of the conflict stage. MacKenzie (1990) calls this the "differentiation stage"; he sees the major task for clients as self-definition.

Confrontation

In this stage, group members find the courage to confront each other and the leader. They take the risk to be fully themselves and discover that this is OK. Many group members come from families where conflicts were never resolved. Conflict may have been avoided, or there may have been occasional blow-ups or constant fighting, but conflict always led to distance or resentment, never to understanding and connection. Therefore, clients often fear open conflict because they assume that things will get worse. One of the important lessons from a good therapy group is that conflict can not only be resolved, but it can actually lead to greater closeness and trust. This requires that the leader work with clients on dealing with and working through confrontations in all the ways discussed earlier in the book, and that conflicts not be left hanging too long. When two people are in the middle of a conflict, it is important for the leader to demonstrate confidence that things can be worked out.

If a client shows signs of having negative feelings toward you, make sure to encourage him to express them. You have even more power to ensure that conflicts with you are worked out, and in this way you give the message that anger and difficult feelings are workable. This may then help group members to have the courage to confront each other as well. It is especially important to recognize that when the group is in the conflict stage, many members will seem to be having trouble with you. This doesn't mean that you have done something wrong. It is probably just the opposite. You have created an atmosphere where they feel safe enough to confront you. In fact, if no one has confronted you by the time the group has reached this stage, then you need to consider if you are doing something unconsciously to discourage them.

Autonomy

Conflict and confrontation are the means for a person to differentiate herself from others and assert her autonomy. Thus separation and individuality are key issues during the conflict stage. Group members have developed enough cohesion during the inclusion stage that they can now differentiate without the group fragmenting. They also *need* to differentiate for both their growth and the group's development. Whereas in the inclusion stage the biggest question may be, "Can I be accepted with my weaknesses?" during the conflict stage it is, "Can I be accepted despite being different from others?"

Clients who have a tendency to be defiant will often lead the way in this stage. They may be the first to challenge the leader or the group or to confront another group member. Those who have a tendency toward compliance will have the most difficulty with this stage and also the most to gain. They will be afraid to assert themselves and express anger, but when they do, it will be important growth.

Interpersonal Power

We previously discussed three levels of communication—the content, emotional, and interpersonal levels. The interpersonal level involves communication about relationship. Within this level, some communications are about power, about one person trying to affect what the other does. *In the previous example, Andy said to Jake, "I can't stand the way you are so judgmental." This could be simply a statement about Andy's feelings, which is the emotional level, or Andy could be implying that Jake should stop being judgmental. In the latter case, this is a communication about power because Andy is trying to change Jake's actions.* This isn't necessarily a problem; we have the right to try to influence other people. However, communication about power can become problematic if one or both people do not recognize what is happening, or if power is exercised manipulatively or coercively.

When working with a dialogue between two members, be aware of the possible power dynamics, and bring them out when you see them getting in the way of clear communication. You may see that one person is being bullied or manipulated by another, or that the two are in a power struggle. One person may be unconsciously sabotaging things to preserve some autonomy in the face of a power move by the other person. Comment on whatever you see without judgment, and be especially careful not to take sides against the person whose power is more obvious. It is easy to assume that the problems between them are all her fault; however, the other person usually has just as much work to do on their power issues.

For example, Joan and Jack were disagreeing about something that had happened between them outside of group. However, Joan stated her opinion as if it were *the* truth and implied that Jack would catch on eventually and change his ways. Jack tried to be as accommodating as possible without actually agreeing with her. I pointed out these power dynamics, making sure to describe each person's part in the interaction so Joan wouldn't feel attacked by me.

Once the clients see their dynamics, help them to experiment with healthier behavior. If a person tends to comply with others, help him to experiment with assertiveness. If a person tends toward competition and domination, help him to see the negative consequences of this approach and to understand his need for control. Ultimately he will need to risk allowing others to share the power.

Power Issues with the Leader

Notice which clients seem to have power issues with you. One client may always agree with your ideas and suggestions. Another may always rebel against you. Maybe a third vies for leadership with you. Point out these reactions at the moment they occur, making sure that the client knows you are doing this to help him, not to stop him from doing something "bad." Be especially on the lookout for your countertransference reactions to power maneuvers by group members. You may find yourself becoming angry, seductive, overpowering, argumentative, or pleasing in response.

> For example, Lawrence tended to resist my feedback and interpretations with intellectual arguments. For a while, I responded by trying to convince him of the merit of my point of view, but I was rarely successful. Then I stepped back and realized what was going on. I pointed out the cycle we were in and acknowledged my part in it. I then encouraged him to explore what was behind his need to resist my attempts to help him. Lawrence realized that he felt discounted and unappreciated by me, and he experienced my interventions as confirmation that I thought he wasn't doing things right.

The conflict stage provides a chance for clients to begin to take more power in the working of the group. For a person to feel a part of things and committed to a group, he must feel that he has some input into shaping the group. So in this stage, clients should occasionally confront the leader, or the group, or other members about things they are dissatisfied with. This stage also allows clients to work on the difficult process of learning to share power with each other—being simultaneously true to their own needs and sensitive to the needs of others.

Transfer of Power

When clients confront you, this begins to transfer power from the leader to group members. This is a gradual process that accelerates during the conflict phase. In the beginning, the leader should take a good deal of authority and power. The group members have little knowledge of psychotherapy and the workings of a therapy group. Many of them are in considerable pain and are dependent on the leader to show them how they can be helped. As the group develops, this changes. The members learn more about themselves and the therapy process. They understand the group norms and begin to have a sense of how therapeutic change happens. They start to grow as individuals and become more responsible and powerful. They connect as a group and begin to be able to work together. All this means that they gradually become capable of taking on much more of the responsibility for directing their own therapeutic work and making the group effective.

As the members become more able to take charge of the workings of the group, the leader should encourage this. The members are flexing their muscles and challenging the leader (as well as each other). Be careful not to hold on to your power because of your own need for control. This can either retard the growth of your group or cause unnecessary rebellion.

> For example, suppose one member challenges the group by saying that the norms are too restrictive. You could respond with your view of what the group norms should be, and early in the group, this might be appropriate. However, at this stage it might be better to encourage the other group members to respond to the challenge, fostering a group discussion of the issue. You should contribute your view only if specifically asked or if things are going in an anti-therapeutic direction.

On the other hand, don't abdicate your authority before the group is ready to take it. This could allow them to set up non-therapeutic norms or leave them floundering, which might undermine their faith in their own abilities.

Moving On

A goal for this stage is that group members discover that their negative feelings can be expressed, they can be confronted by others, and conflicts can be worked out. They can exert influence on the course the group takes. They can be themselves fully and still part of a cohesive group. They feel committed to the group. As this stage ends, group members often feel closer than ever because the intimacy is not built only on support or false politeness. The members know that they have shown their anger and been confronted on their weaknesses and they are still accepted by the group. Short-term groups typically complete the conflict stage in a couple of months, whereas long-term groups can take 6 to 18 months.

☐ The Working Stage

At this point the preliminaries are over and the group has entered the ordinary working stage of its development. The members are connected, the norms are established, and the work of the group proceeds. Of course, significant work has already been accomplished during these earlier stages, but now a solid group foundation has been built for the continuing individual and interpersonal work of the group. In MacKenzie's system (1990), the stage that most closely corresponds to this is his "individuation stage," in which each client explores herself more deeply.

This doesn't mean, however, that things cannot deviate from this ideal situation; they often do. A snag may develop in the group process that doesn't have to do with its developmental stage (see chapter 22). This must be attended to in order to keep the group functioning in a therapeutic manner. In a long-term group, terminations and new members may upset the group's cohesion, causing it to regress to an earlier stage of development. This is not necessarily bad unless there is too much coming and going or the group becomes too small. Although you should do your best to keep the group stable, cohesive, and full, each change can serve as another opportunity for group members to deal with the issues that are activated.

☐ The Intimacy Stage

There is another stage of development in my long-term groups, when the members become more deeply involved with each other. In addition to caring for each other and feeling connected in their group work, each client develops close relationships with some other members of the group, and a deeper level of overall group bonding happens. This usually begins after the group has been meeting for 9 months to 2 years. On the surface, this seems to correspond to MacKenzie's (1990) stages of "intimacy" and "mutuality," but these stages of his are probably different from mine because short-term groups would not have the time it takes to reach what I mean by the intimacy stage.

In my groups, this stage is frequently related to the outside relationships that group members are developing. These relationships often progress beyond what can happen within the limits of group meetings, and this enhances the level of work that occurs within the group. However, even for those members choosing not to relate outside the group, there comes a time when their relationships must deepen.

Resistance

This stage becomes particularly apparent when a group is resisting it. When the group has been at the working stage for long enough, a need arises for members to become more intimate with each other, and if they are not taking this risk, the group begins to feel flat and uninteresting. Despite the fact that good work may still be happening, members begin to wonder why they are in the group and may consider terminating. At this point, you need to challenge them to explore their avoidance of developing deeper connections with each other. The group needs to move on to the intimacy stage.

Resistance can happen at any stage. A beginning group may keep their interactions at a very superficial level, resisting entering the inclusion stage. A group may avoid anger and confrontation, thereby resisting the conflict stage. A group may get stuck in unresolved conflict as it resists finishing the conflict stage and entering the working stage. Your job as leader is to point out these resistances and help the group resolve them so it can move on in its development. This means exploring with members their fears of dealing with belonging or conflict or whatever the next stage involves. It also means exploring any dynamics at the group level (see chapter 25) that are blocking the group's progression. *For example, there may have been an intense confrontation very early in a group that caused a member to leave prematurely. This might make this group phobic about dealing with conflict.*

Bringing in Outside Relationships

In the intimacy stage, it is important that relationships that have developed between members outside of the group be brought in for intimacy work. Even if two members are feeling good about each other and not encountering problems in their outside contact, they should be encouraged to work on their relationship in the group. In fact, when members feel close is an especially good time to work on deepening their connection in the group. Many group members have profound difficulties with intimacy. They may be frightened of becoming engulfed, they may be afraid of deep contact, intense dependency needs may come up, and sexual feeling may arise. An interactive group is an ideal place to work on these issues, but if a relationship is kept outside the group, this can be avoided. Your job as leader is to ensure that intimacy issues are explored.

> For example, Philip and Elena gradually developed a friendship outside of group. They had lunch together and sometimes called each other for support. They felt good about each other without any romantic involvement. At some point Elena realized that she used the genuine acceptance that she felt toward Philip as an excuse to avoid telling him things she didn't like about the way he acted in group. She was afraid of losing what they had. Philip realized that he often felt a need for more contact with Elena in group but was afraid to reach out for it. He rationalized this by saying that he could always see her outside of group.
>
> At one group meeting, Philip decided to risk discussing their relationship in group. Elena had missed a couple of meetings, and Philip began to tell her that he had missed her in group and was annoyed at her for being absent. Elena replied by explaining why she had to miss group. Philip then realized that he wasn't really saying what he needed to say. He wanted to tell her how important she was to him. With the leader's help, he said this in a way that really conveyed his feelings, and there followed a moment of close contact between them. Elena was very moved and felt warm and connected, but she became scared of the intensity and started to change the subject. The leader kept her in the present with Philip, and she let him know how she felt toward him. As a result, they deepened their relationship, and each of them grew in their ability to make contact and tolerate intimacy.

In the intimacy stage, interactive work between two people sometimes takes this form, where the focus is on the contact between the people—their ability to be present with each other in the moment and to be in touch with their feelings for each other. This may or may not be expressed in words. Sometimes it just comes through in the eye contact. If words are used, the expression is often more important than the content. Contact was discussed in chapter 12.

Working at a Deeper Level

As relationships in group become more important, many issues that were seemingly worked through before come up again because of the increased intimacy. This doesn't really mean that the previous growth wasn't real. In most cases, the client had indeed resolved the issue at the previous level, but now the increased intimacy activates the issue at a new depth, and it must be worked through at this level. For example, dependency needs can come up in more intense ways now that the group is more connected.

If a client unconsciously senses that her needs could be met in a deeper way with the increased closeness of the group, a more primary level of need may surface. This provides an opportunity for more complete healing of the associated core issue.

Clients may find that it is more frightening to express negative feelings because they now have more to lose if they are rejected. In the intimacy stage, watch for a sudden absence of negative reactions in group. It is easy to attribute this to the increased closeness, but often it is because of a renewed fear of conflict. The opposite can also be true. Some clients may find that it is now more difficult to express positive feelings because of the closeness involved. They can be more deeply hurt by people who mean a lot to them. If clients become aware of these resistances and take the risk to express with their feelings in the context of the increased intimacy, the work of the group can proceed to a deeper level of access and healing.

CHAPTER

Termination

The final stage of group development is termination, and this topic is important enough to deserve its own chapter. First I discuss the termination process for one member. This process has two components—the decision of whether to leave and the work that is activated by the termination. This chapter describes how to help a client explore her reasons for wanting to terminate and how to deal with group members' emotional responses. We also look at the issues that are stirred up by the termination process—autonomy, decision-making, and loss, and I discuss how to help clients terminate in a therapeutic way.

At the end of the chapter, I mention additional issues that arise when an entire group terminates. In ongoing, open-ended groups, it is rare for an entire group to terminate, but this is the rule in time-limited groups.

☐ Deciding Whether to Leave

Considering Leaving.   It is not unusual for a group member to be thinking about leaving. This happens far more frequently than actual terminations. It is not necessarily a sign that anything is wrong, though the client may feel that way. It is very important that the client talk to the group (or the leader in a consultation) about his feelings before making a decision. This gives you a chance to help him understand why he is dissatisfied so he can make as informed a decision as possible. Therefore strive to establish a group norm about this and include it in your group rules. It is also helpful to tell beginning members that they are likely to feel dissatisfied with the group at times and may feel like leaving, but this is normal and should be explored before acting on it.

In many cases, when a member is considering leaving, the real issue isn't termination at all, but the process of considering it opens up significant work for the person. There are two common possibilities.

Dissatisfaction with the Group.   A client is dissatisfied with the group, and he is thinking of leaving because he doesn't believe he can change things. When such a client expresses and explores his dissatisfaction, this may lead in two possible directions.

1. Some group members agree with what he is unhappy about, and therefore he has an impact on the group that propels it to change in the direction he wants. (See *Revising Group Norms* at the end of chapter 8 for an example.)

2. The client explores what is happening inside him that is causing the dissatisfaction, and this leads to insight, access, or experimenting, thus furthering his work in group.

    For example, a client was unhappy with the group because she felt there was no room for her to be powerful. She felt that whenever she asserted herself she was criticized. In exploring this, she got the feedback from the group that it wasn't her power but her demeaning attitude that caused the criticism. In fact, the group members told her that they appreciated her strength. This helped her to formulate a goal for her group work—to be powerful without putting others down.

Re-Evaluating Goals.   The client has met his initial goals for the group and doesn't understand what further work is possible. When a client brings this up, it is useful for him to re-evaluate his direction in the group (see chapter 9). The person should be encouraged to review his initial reasons for joining the group and consider if he has accomplished these goals. If not, this points out his next work. If he has reached his initial goals, then encourage him to think about what new goals he might want to formulate. First help the client explore the changes he would like to see in himself, in terms of interpersonal growth (or other work that can be done in the group). If he comes up with goals he wants to pursue that are appropriate for the group, then it makes sense for him to continue rather than terminate. At this point, it might be useful for him to also discuss what work he should initiate to reach the goals. If he can't think of new goals that are important to him, this may be a sign that it is time for him to leave. In either case, the client ends up with a clearer sense of his next step.

When Is Termination Appropriate?   Any discussion of termination brings up the thorny question of how to decide when a group member is finished with his therapy. It isn't a good idea for a group leader to hold an ideal of what clients should accomplish before it is appropriate to terminate. This sets you up as an authority on others' lives, and although this may be necessary for a beginning client, someone nearing completion needs to decide for himself when to terminate, as long as he uses your input and seriously explores his reasons. It is certainly important for you to help a client see what he can gain from continuing in the group, but I believe that there is no clear-cut end to therapy, especially group therapy. A client can always continue longer in a group and grow further. A person's growth is usually gradual, and his goals often change over the course of therapy, so there usually are no simple criteria for deciding if a client has fulfilled his original contract by resolving his presenting problems. Furthermore, the end of this group is not necessarily the end of the person's therapy or growth. He may continue to grow on his own, in other therapy, or through other means (Yalom, 1995, pp. 361–362).

I believe the right question to ask is whether the client wants to leave because he is avoiding something in the therapy. If he is, this should be challenged and explored. If not, then he has a right to leave whatever his reasons are, whether he has "completed therapy" or not. However, it is important that the client consider and know his real reasons for leaving, and he may need your help in doing this.

Exploring Reasons for Leaving.
Make sure to have the client explore in depth his reasons for wanting to terminate even if he gives clear, cut-and-dried reasons such as money or scheduling difficulties. There are often deeper, psychological reasons for the decision, which emerge only after much exploration. If you believe that the client is leaving for the wrong reasons, it is your therapeutic responsibility to help him discover this, and if necessary to tell him directly, though of course, this should be done in as supportive a way as possible. Do your best to avoid taking an adversarial stance, and help the client to realize that you want to explore what will be best for him. It is easy for a client to feel that you are trying to convince him to stay, and he has to prove to you that it is OK for him to leave.

Make sure that you don't try to get the client to stay for your own reasons—perhaps you don't want to lose the income, or you would miss him, or the group needs him. You should consider only the client's welfare. Make sure to process your own feelings about losing a client so you don't distort his process with your countertransference. The group members should also realize this. They have the right to express any feelings about his leaving and to try to convince him to stay, but both he and they should know that it isn't his job to take care of them by staying.

Inappropriate Reasons for Leaving.
The following are common reasons why a group member might want to leave inappropriately.

1. He feels rejected or excluded by the group, and he can't tolerate the pain and shame. This experience of exclusion may not be true, and the client needs to find this out. When the group members express their feelings about his leaving, he may be shocked to discover that they really want him to stay. The client may not even realize that he is leaving because he feels rejected, and this insight alone may help him to stay. In some cases, the group may indeed be excluding the client, especially if he has become a scapegoat. Some members of the group may be rejecting the client, and he may experience it as if the whole group is. In these cases, he can learn a lot by exploring what has caused his rejection and working through the issues underlying his part in it.

2. A painful or frightening issue is coming up for the client that he wants to avoid facing. It might be an intense conflict with another member. It could be that he is frightened of the intimacy that is developing in the group. Personal material of some sort may be arising that he is afraid of—rage, memories of abuse, jealousy, shame, and so on. Frequently this is completely unconscious. If you can help the client discover exactly what is frightening him, he is likely to be willing to face it, especially with the group's support. Then he won't have to terminate.

The Group Members' Reactions.
In addition to helping the client explore his reasons for leaving, encourage the group members to express their personal reac-

tions to his possible termination. They may try to focus on his issues rather than dealing with what is being triggered in them by his announcement. This can initiate valuable work for them, and it also may have an important impact on his decision about leaving. Especially if a client is leaving because of feeling excluded, he may change his mind when he discovers that the group members indeed like him.

Some members may try to convince the client to stay. This is all right as long as they explore their reasons for doing so. On the other hand, some clients may go out of their way to avoid putting any pressure on the client, taking the stance that they will support whatever he decides is best for him. This is also fine if it is their real feeling. However, some clients use this stance to defend against strong feelings of anger or abandonment and to avoid asserting themselves in asking him to stay. It helps to question any client who seems to have no emotional reaction to the termination announcement.

> For example, Renee joined the group for the summer and then announced she was leaving when the fall came. This had been her plan all along. (I had no idea she would do this or I wouldn't have accepted her into the group.) As the group members discussed their reactions to her termination, no one mentioned any strong feelings until the last person to speak expressed her outrage and sense of betrayal. This stimulated the rest of the group to recognize that they also had some of these feelings but had repressed them. The ensuing work was valuable for both Renee and the group.

On the other hand, sometimes a group may push a member to leave, subtly or not so subtly, because they have made him a scapegoat (see chapter 23). If you sense this is happening, challenge the group members to explore what they are avoiding in themselves by trying to get rid of this person.

Autonomy and Decision-Making.   Being challenged and hearing other people's reactions can cause a client to be in conflict about leaving. This opens up the question of how he makes decisions in general. Does he constantly vacillate from one option to another? Does he make a decision and hold to it unflinchingly no matter what? Can he be open to changing his mind without being swayed too much by other people's needs?

Being challenged about termination also brings up autonomy issues. Does he have the right to make and carry through his own decision? How much should he try to take care of the other group members? If he empathizes with their feelings, will he give in and stay? Some clients react to this with defiance, others with compliance, others with flexible self-assertion. Your job is twofold: to help the client explore to see if his reasons for leaving are valid, and to support him in making his own decision (with input from others) and carrying it through.

> For example, during Judd's first month in the group, he announced that he was leaving, primarily because he was the only man in the group, and he didn't feel ready to deal with his difficult feelings toward women in such a situation. The women in the group responded to this by letting him know that they appreciated him as a person and how much they would miss him if he left. This was a surprise to him, and he reconsidered his decision. However, because Judd had a tendency to ignore his own needs in order to take care of others, especially women, it wasn't clear what his real motive was in reconsidering his decision to leave. Was he moved by learning how much the women cared for him, or did he feel compelled to stay in order to avoid hurting their feelings? Eventually he decided that it was right for him to leave.

Support for Leaving as a Healing Response.   Some clients had parents who made them feel guilty about separating and leaving home. When such a client terminates, he needs support from the leader and the group in his leaving; this is an important healing response. He needs to know that though the group members and leader will miss him, they want what is best for him. If he has been in the group for a long time and leaves cleanly, this support will naturally be forthcoming, but if he leaves before he has done all he could or for questionable reasons, the group members may challenge him. On the one hand, this is appropriate, for he might be running from an issue. On the other hand, he needs to be supported in his act of separation, unless it is clearly inappropriate. This is sometimes hard to judge.

Occasionally a client will terminate from a group primarily because of his need to separate rather than because he has truly finished his work. In this case, the leaving itself can be seen as healthy experimenting with new behavior, and it should be supported even if the termination is otherwise premature. When this happens, frame the situation for the group so they can see why he is leaving and support him in this act. With this kind of healthy termination, he may return to the group when he is ready for more work.

The Confidence to Terminate.   Some clients, instead of leaving too soon, may stay too long. This is not as big a problem, but such a person may need help in terminating. She may have become overly dependent on the group and is afraid she can't make it on her own. You may have to bring up the issue of termination and help her explore her reluctance to trust the growth she has achieved. Don't say anything that would give the impression that you want to get rid of her, but help her develop confidence that she can survive and flourish without the group.

☐ Processing Leaving

Once a client has decided to leave, there needs to be enough time for considerable exploring to be done by both the person leaving and the other group members. Encourage your clients to allow 2 to 4 weeks for termination if they have been in the group up to a year and more if they have been there longer. In addition, make sure that the group doesn't avoid the issue. Some groups will spend these weeks dealing with other work rather than their feelings about the person who is leaving. If necessary, keep reminding them about the impending termination so they don't postpone this work until the client's last meeting.

Dealing with Loss.   Termination is a loss for both the group and the person leaving, especially if she has been a long-time member with many close ties. This tends to bring up issues of bereavement and abandonment (Rutan & Stone, 1993, p. 242) which should be explored both interpersonally and intrapsychically. Some clients may react with extreme upset to the impending loss while others will pretend that they aren't affected at all. Clients may try to avoid feeling the loss by not saying good-bye or by pretending that the person is coming back or that they will see him outside of group. The person who is leaving may use similar defenses. Of course, it may happen that some group members will continue to see each other outside of group, but even so, it is a significant loss not to see the person every week in the group setting. Make sure that this loss is felt and processed.

> For example, Lois had suffered serious losses of family members as a child and adolescent, which she had not mourned at the time. Once her therapy group became close, whenever a member terminated, Lois would feel devastated because this stimulated the old pain of these losses. Each time this happened, I helped her to access and process her feelings of grief about one of these old situations. Then she would also deal with her feelings of loss in the present about the person who was leaving. After a few years and three or four terminations, her reactions to further leavings began to diminish. She eventually responded to terminations in a way that simply reflected the intensity of her current relationship with the person leaving. The overreaction to loss had been worked through.

Other Reactions.   Group members may have other feelings as well about the person leaving—resentment, envy, pride on his behalf. Encourage them all to be expressed and explored. The client terminating may also have other feelings to be explored, for example, guilt, sadness, or excitement. In addition, there is other work to do in the group. Every moment need not be spent on termination.

When the Leader Terminates.   It is not uncommon for the leadership of a therapy group to change, especially in institutional settings. This often brings up even stronger feeling reactions in group members, which they may be reluctant to share. It is important to encourage them to deal with these feelings while the therapist is still in the group, especially their anger at being abandoned. It also helps for them to process their feelings about the new leader who will be arriving. Any feelings toward the departing leader that aren't expressed before he leaves should be explored with the new leader afterward.

Worries About the Group.   Group members may also have feelings brought up by the termination that are not related to the specific person leaving, but rather to the group. They know a new person will be coming in soon and may be upset about the change. If two people are terminating at roughly the same time or the group is getting small, the members may be worried that the group is falling apart. All these feelings should be explored. You may be concerned that to have these feelings expressed could demoralize other group members, and this is a small danger, but the much greater one is that the feelings aren't expressed and therefore can't be dealt with. If some members are worried about the future of the group, you can encourage them to band together with the remaining members and support each other in reconstituting the group. Some clients may have a tendency to give up in the face of such difficulties, but you can work with them on this and encourage healthy coping behavior.

Finishing Interactive Work.   The termination period is often a time for very important interactive work. Sometimes a member has unresolved feelings toward the person leaving that she has previously avoided, and now is her last chance to deal with them. This can lead to profound work. Sometimes positive feelings of closeness that haven't been fully expressed come out during termination.

Group members who haven't had much of a relationship outside the group may need to deal with the question of whether they will have any contact with the person once he leaves. Help them to be honest about this and work with the feelings involved rather than glossing it over with a perfunctory statement of "Let's get together. I'll call you." This can be an avoidance of feelings of loss.

Reviewing One's Growth.   It is valuable for the person who is leaving to review the work she has done and the growth she had made during her time in group. Encourage other members to contribute their perceptions of the changes she has made, and be sure to add anything you have noticed that isn't mentioned. This can be important validation for the client who is graduating. It is also valuable for the client to discuss her personal growth work for the future—the things she still needs to work on and her future goals for herself.

The termination period can also be a time for reminiscing about significant group events and memories involving the person leaving. This both acknowledges her value to the group and also underlines the value of the group to its members, increasing cohesion.

If the person leaving was a significant member of the group, it is probably wise to leave a few weeks after she leaves for further processing and regrouping before bringing in a replacement.

☐ Group Termination

In short-term groups and occasionally in long-term groups, the entire group may terminate together, and therefore the themes of loss, abandonment, and mortality are triggered for everyone at the same time. In addition, because the termination has not been chosen by them, clients have to deal with issues of lack of control and lack of perfection. We must learn to accept those things in our lives that we truly cannot control. In addition, we human beings are not perfect and cannot be made so even by the best therapy. Time-limited therapy brings this out in a more obvious way because clients often have to terminate before they have fully worked through the issue that brought them to the group. Even if they have reached their goal for the group, the presenting problem may only be partially resolved. They need to deal with the feelings this elicits while nevertheless making plans for how to work on the issue in the future.[11]

---

[11] For further information on termination, see chapter 14 of Rutan and Stone (1993) and the special section on termination in the January 1996 issue of the *International Journal of Group Psychotherapy.*

23
CHAPTER

Group Roles and Positions

Clients tend to assume specific roles and positions in the group. This chapter explores how this affects their therapy and the group's process. A group role serves a certain function, positive or negative, for the group, while a group position reflects a client's personal issues. I examine how roles and positions develop and change and look at a number of specific ones, with an emphasis on the scapegoat.

☐ Containing Feelings for the Group

When a group member expresses a feeling response to an event or dynamic in the group, this may stimulate other members to express similar feelings. However, the opposite can also happen. When one person expresses a particularly difficult reaction, others may feel that they don't have to. Because that person is doing the job, they can avoid speaking up.

> For example, a number of group members are angry with the leader but are frightened to express this anger directly. Perhaps they fear abandonment or retaliation from an authority figure. If one person expresses his anger, the rest may feel relieved. Now it has been said; the challenge has been made. They don't have to take the risk because someone else did.

The other group members may even deny that they have the threatening feeling. If the feeling is not fully conscious, they are now relieved of the work of bringing it to awareness because it has been expressed by someone else. That person can take the flack. The others can pretend that they have no anger at the leader.

When this happens, this is called *containing* a feeling for the group. The person who speaks up is containing a feeling that other group members are feeling as well. He is a spokesman for the group, though this role may be unconscious or denied. The person who contains a feeling for the group is usually performing some function for the group. *In the above example, the person who confronted the leader may have been performing the function of taking back some of the leader's power for the group. Or he might have been challenging the leader on some issue that bothered the group.* Because one person did it, the others don't have to. The function has been performed so they can avoid the work they need to do.

It is important to realize that when a group member expresses himself he may also be carrying feelings or thoughts for other group members. Some group leaders who have a group-as-a-whole orientation assume that this is always the case, that whenever a member speaks, he is always a spokesperson for the entire group. I don't think this is true; we must examine each situation individually. Sometimes the client may be the only one in the group who feels that way. Sometimes a few other members feel similarly, sometimes most of them do, sometimes all. It is just as big a mistake to assume that the group is monolithic as to assume that it is only a collection of disconnected individuals.

☐   Group Roles

This brings us the notion of a group role. A *group role* is a function that needs to be performed for the group. It can be a function that enhances the functioning of the group and makes it more therapeutic, or it can be a function that hurts the group by enabling members to defend against their pain or avoid responsibility.

For example, the identified patient (IP) is one group role. This is a member who works extensively on her issues and problems in the group. The IP can take up an inordinate amount of group time talking about her life, exploring her issues, feeling her pain. The function this serves for the group is a defensive one. Work is going on, so the group looks like it is being therapeutic, but the other group members can avoid their work by focusing on the IP. She receives lots of time and attention and the rest of the group can avoid dealing with their own issues. Ultimately, this isn't even good for the IP. She may go out on a limb, making herself much more vulnerable than others, causing her to be pitied and seen as the sickest member of the group.

Another group role is the caretaker. This is a member who is caring and nurturing toward members who are in pain. When someone is feeling ashamed or scared or hurt or is accessing deep childhood pain, it is helpful to have one or more group members who can be counted on to be compassionate and supportive. This can be a positive group role that promotes safety and vulnerability in the group. However, the role could be non-therapeutic if the caretaker moves too quickly to offer gratification to others before they have had a chance to explore themselves.

Rigid Versus Flexible Roles.   Even a positive group role can be harmful if one person rigidly takes the role. At any given period in a group, some roles are flexible in that many different group members perform them, and others are rigid in that one person takes the role exclusively. For example, if one person always assumes the caretaker role, this is not good for the caretaker or for the rest of the group. The caretaker feels limited to that particular role. He doesn't feel permission to disagree or assert himself or be angry. He feels obliged to be supportive even if he doesn't really want to.

The other group members can avoid developing their caring and compassionate sides; they can sit back and let him do it all. One the other hand, if the caretaking role is flexible, then many different group members can take it, at the same time or at different times. This is the ideal situation because everyone is encouraged to develop a variety of flexible, healthy capacities. For example, each member learns how to be caring and also how to be confrontive, how to be connected and also autonomous.

In today's alienated society, it is common for people to spend most of their time playing rigid roles rather than being themselves and relating to others in an authentic way. We tend to see ourselves as parents, workers, professionals, consumers, students, teachers, doctors, patients, and so on, rather than as whole, alive people. Many of us feel that we must sell ourselves to be successful in our work and social lives, and so we we live through a persona, consciously or unconsciously. While roles are necessary and valuable at times, we have taken them to an unhealthy extreme. Though a role may help us perform a useful function, we often take ourselves to *be* the role, thereby cutting off much of our true humanity and spontaneity. One of the benefits of a therapy group is that it encourages members to be themselves, and part of this process involves becoming aware of the rigid roles they play in the group.

Roles Versus Patterns.   It is important to distinguish between a group role and an interpersonal pattern. A role is a property of a group, and an interpersonal pattern is a property of an individual. These may frequently work together because a client with a particular interpersonal pattern is likely to take over the corresponding group role. For example, a client who has a codependent pattern is likely to become the group caretaker. However, this can only happen if the group needs him to play this role. A rigid role becomes assigned to a particular person through a collusion between that person and the group, though this may not be conscious to either. The group must be looking for someone to take the role, and the client must have a psychological need for it. If a client has the pattern but the group is not looking for the role, then he may act out the pattern, but the members won't support this.

> For example, a codependent client may become overly involved in helping others to the exclusion of his own needs. However, other group members can be caretaking, he won't be the only one to offer it, and they will challenge him on his codependence. Thus the client is acting out an interpersonal pattern, but not taking on a group role. On the other hand, if the group is looking for someone to be the caretaker, they won't challenge him.

If you see that a client is trying to take on a group role by acting out a pattern, it is useful to challenge him, especially to point out the behavior that isn't allowed because of his role, for example, the fact that a caretaker isn't able to take care of himself.

The Leader.   The group leader can take on almost any of the group roles, with good or bad consequences depending on the situation. For example, at times it may be appropriate for the leader to take the caretaker role, especially if no one else is doing it. However, you wouldn't want to become the only caretaker in the group for long. It would be completely inappropriate for the leader to be the identified patient, for obvious reasons. The leader can also become a scapegoat (see below), obviously a dangerous development. Group leadership itself is a role, but it is a formal group role, designated in the situation, as opposed to the informal roles that any member can take. The leader role has powerful impacts which we have been discussing throughout the book.

There are also informal roles, such as facilitator, that can be played by the leader or by group members at times.

☐ The Scapegoat

Probably the most important and dangerous role is that of the scapegoat. This is a member who is reviled and ostracized by the other group members; he can end up leaving the group. The scapegoat role serves a defensive function for the group members by becoming the target of all their aggression and judgment. They can project all their shame onto him rather than owning it themselves, and they can direct all their aggression toward him rather than toward each other. A client may unconsciously volunteer for the scapegoat role by being defiant or provocative or needing to be different from others. A scapegoat may have an underlying issue that leads him to expect to be excluded in groups, and he may induce others to exclude him in order to feel that he is in control of this situation. Clients who are especially hostile and blaming toward others can also become scapegoats. A client may end up as a scapegoat because he *is* quite different from the other group members, especially if he is more disturbed in an obvious way. You should make an attempt to screen such clients out before they enter group, to protect them from this.

In society, scapegoating often underlies racial and ethnic prejudices. When people are unhappy and their lives are difficult, they often unconsciously look around for a minority group to blame for their problems. This dynamic may even be encouraged by those in power to prevent people from holding them responsible for a society's problems.

Unlike most other roles, a person can sometimes create a scapegoat role for himself even if the group doesn't need this role to be filled. With most other roles, if the group doesn't need the role, it won't happen, as discussed above with the caretaker role. However, a person who persists in alienating others may succeed in becoming a scapegoat anyway. If a client consistently causes trouble, if he refuses to work on himself and instead blames others, if he consistently acts in deviant and bizarre ways, this can cause almost any group to ostracize him even if they didn't otherwise need someone to persecute.

Working with Scapegoating.   There are a variety of ways to work with the scapegoating process. One involves working with the potential scapegoat and the other with the group. Whenever a group member acts in a way that seems to alienate the rest of the group, you can explore with him what is causing him to engage in this behavior, pointing out its impact on the group. If he persists, explore with him the possibility that he feels a need to distance himself from or provoke the group.

A second approach focuses on the group. At the moment a potential scapegoat acts out in some way, ask the group members to reflect on times when they have had similar feelings, even if they wouldn't act them out in exactly this way. *For example, if a client blames the group for his difficulties and refuses to look at himself, you could ask the group members to reflect on when they might have felt so ashamed or threatened that they were reluctant to look at their potential shortcomings.* If the members are willing, some of them will remember times when they felt similarly. By discussing these, they break down what looks like an insurmountable barrier between the group and the scapegoat. The members may also gain important insights about themselves and possibly realize why they were so quick to become angry with the scapegoat. This approach is useful even if the member is primarily responsible for eliciting the scapegoating process.

If the scapegoating process is further along and you sense that it is coming from the group as well as the member, another approach is useful. Explain the scapegoat role and ask the group members to explore what they are getting out of creating a scapegoat. What are they projecting onto him? What pain are they avoiding in themselves? What conflicts are they avoiding with each other? This will move them toward dealing with themselves rather than the scapegoat.

☐ Other Roles

The Emotional Member.   Therapy groups require emotional depth and openness. Ideally all members would be involved in this, but sometimes this role is taken by one person primarily. This is often a client who feels her emotions deeply in exploring her own issues and also empathizes with others, sometimes even feeling the emotions that they are defending against. This can be a functional role if the emotional member leads the way for others to get in touch with their own emotions. If the other group members remain defended and allow the emotional member to do their emotional work for them, then this is a non-therapeutic role for the group. In addition, the member caught in the role may not feel permission to express another part of herself, such as her intellectual or aggressive side.

The Aggressive Member.   The group needs conflict, confrontation, and differentiation. Sometimes one member plays this role primarily, initiating most of the challenges in the group. The aggressive member often initiates the conflict stage of group development. This role is functional if it sparks the other members to explore their aggression, but it is non-therapeutic if they avoid their angry feelings by letting the aggressive member do all the confronting. The member caught in the role may not feel permission to be soft and vulnerable. A variant of the aggressive role is the *truth teller*. This is the member who is willing to say what he sees in the group, even when this may be unpopular. Sometimes group members avoid voicing their feelings or perceptions about something occurring in the group because they don't want to hurt someone or cause friction. The truth teller is the member who is willing to tell it like it is. This can be valuable as long as the role doesn't remain rigid. A member caught in this role may not feel permission to be tactful or supportive.

The Social Leader.   Group cohesiveness is fostered when members express warmth and caring toward one other and become interested in each other as people. The social leader is the member who makes this happen. She often remembers what people have said about the struggles in their lives and asks them about it. She may initiate get-togethers for the members outside of group. She may try to smooth over conflict and help members to understand each other. Her main goal is often community rather than therapy. This can be functional for the group if it doesn't interfere with therapeutic exploration. A member caught in this role may not bother to explore herself or interact with others in a therapeutic way. She might also not feel permission to be aggressive.

The Member-Therapist.   Group therapy aims to help members see themselves clearly, perceive what is going on beneath the surface psychologically, and understand its meaning and childhood roots. Ideally, members will come to these insights themselves, but often they need help from the outside. This, of course, is one of the leader's jobs. However, it is appropriate for members to do this for each other as well. In fact, it can be very empowering for a member to realize that he can help someone else. If the member-therapist role is spread out over the membership, it can be functional for the group.

However, sometimes a member will take on this role to avoid looking at himself. He will focus on other people's issues and try to help facilitate their therapy rather than exploring himself. If a member does this consistently, he must be challenged to drop the role and work on himself. If he gets away with using it to hide and avoid his own work, then others may be tempted to adopt this posture too, leading the group in a non-therapeutic direction.

The Deviant.   In many groups, there is a member who tends to challenge or break the group norms. This can serve the positive function of expanding group norms that are restrictive. However, if a deviant member overdoes this role, it can lead to incessant conflict and possibly scapegoating.

Other Roles.   MacKenzie (1990, chapter 5) lists the four main social roles that have been studied by social psychologists and translates these into group therapy roles. Three of these correspond roughly to the roles I have called the social leader, scapegoat, and deviant. He calls the fourth role the "structural role"; in social psychology it is usually called the "task leader." This seems to include the formal role of group leader and also the member-therapist.

There are many other possible group roles. The *risk-taker* is the member who leads the way in experimenting with new behavior or deep access. The *norm-setter* is the member who has the most influence in determining group norms and activities. The *attractive member* is one with whom most members want to connect because of liking or respect or sexual attraction.

☐ How Roles Change

Working with Group Roles.   Whenever a member takes on a role, it is valuable to explore with him what is behind his need for the role. There are two parts to this. How does he benefit from engaging in the role behavior, and why does he want to avoid doing the opposite? For example, why does the aggressive member need to stir up conflict, and why is he afraid of his soft, vulnerable side? However, with a functional role, it is equally important to challenge the other group members to explore why they are avoiding taking on the role. For example, why are they afraid of confronting one another? In the case of a non-therapeutic role, challenge the group members about their need to assign someone this role.

The Development of Roles.   In the early stages of a group, roles tend to be more rigid. The members are new and are still acting out their usual interpersonal patterns. In addition, because the group itself is just being formed, members haven't yet had much opportunity to develop flexibility through their therapeutic work. This provides an opportunity to point out and challenge rigid roles. As the group moves through the conflict stage into the working stage, roles tend to become increasingly flexible. Members grow to the point where they can take on a variety of functional roles, and they refuse to be bound by the limitations of a particular role. Fewer members are willing to be trapped in a non-therapeutic role at all. Healthy groups develop to the point where they have less need for rigid roles or non-therapeutic ones.

☐ Group Positions

In some cases, a member will get herself into a certain position in the group because of her way of relating, despite the fact that this is not a role that the group needs. I call this a *group position*. This is usually not functional for the client or the group. To illustrate this, let's consider the scapegoat, which can be either a role or a position. If the group members need a scapegoat for their own defensive purposes, then it is a role, but if a member becomes a scapegoat entirely because of his own issues without the group's collusion, then it is a position. Whether a member is acting out a role or position becomes clear if the member stops the behavior or leaves the group. If a scapegoat leaves the group, will the group create another scapegoat to take his place? If they do, then it was a role that the group needed to have filled. If they don't, then it was probably a position created by the client's interpersonal pattern. The following are typical group positions.

The Mascot.   Sometimes a relatively low-functioning member of the group will be affectionately tolerated despite the fact that no one really wants to be close to him. This position is usually non-therapeutic for the member. Clients who are likely to end up in this position should be screened out beforehand if possible.

The Frightening Member.   Sometimes one member is so angry or judgmental that the other members become afraid of him. They avoid confronting him, and they may not even interact with him very much. In some cases, they become too frightened to allow themselves to be vulnerable in front of him. This is clearly not good for all concerned. In addition to encouraging the frightening member to explore where his hostility comes from, you may have to go even further and stop him whenever he starts to attack people. The group members need to be protected from intense, inappropriate anger. Encourage the other members to take the risk to interact with a frightening member even if he may become angry. Clients who are extremely hostile should be screened out in the pre-group interview if possible.

The Brittle Member.   One group member may become so easily upset or shamed that the others avoid saying anything to him that might trigger this reaction. They tiptoe around him. This is typical for narcissistic clients. (See chapter 24.)

The Silent Member.   Some members participate little in the group because of fears of being judged or a need to keep distance from others. This position is also discussed in the next chapter.

The Monopolizer.   The monopolizer is a member who takes up far more than his share of the group's time and attention, usually without any awareness that this is happening. This can be a role or position depending on whether it serves the need of the rest of the group to avoid doing work. This position is also discussed in the next chapter.

24 CHAPTER

Difficult Group Members

Certain types of group members, especially those who would be diagnosed with borderline or narcissistic personality disorders, can be hard to work with and disrupt the group's functioning. This topic has accumulated a massive amount of literature in recent years, but this chapter looks only at a few issues that are particularly relevant to group work. I explore how to work with narcissistically brittle clients and with clients who tend to monopolize the group's attention. I look at difficulties in providing healing responses to borderline and narcissistic clients. I also discuss the defense of splitting, and explain how to work with silent group members.

☐ The Narcissistically Brittle Client

Some narcissistic clients are so sensitive to criticism that they seem to be brittle. They unconsciously carry a great deal of shame, but they have constructed their defenses so that they conceal this from themselves and others. Criticism can puncture these defenses and bring on the shame, devastating the client. When this happens the client may react with one of a variety of brittle defenses. She may become defensive, desperately trying to prove that she really doesn't deserve that criticism, that she really isn't a "bad" person. In the process, she may deny any evidence of the accuracy of the criticism. She may refuse to deal with the criticism, ignoring the person or withdrawing emotionally. Her conscious statement often is "You don't understand me." She really wasn't understood as a child, and now a challenge brings up this old feeling. The underlying thought is "I am terrified that I am bad (worthless, guilty, etc.)."

When confronted, such fragile clients may even withdraw from the situation altogether. They have been known to leave in the middle of a group meeting to avoid having to face a relentless challenger. A client may respond to confrontation with rage, retaliating against the person who criticized her. It is also common for a brittle client to respond by trying to demean the other person. The client feels demeaned by virtually any criticism, so she is just trying to even the score.

This brittle reaction and the attendant feelings of shame prevent the client from making any constructive use of confrontations in the group. This means it is hard for her to own her part in problems that arise in group. And of course, it also makes it very difficult for the client to engage in constructive self-criticism. In fact, clients with severe narcissistic vulnerability can become so devastated by criticism that they are not good candidates for an interactive group, where confrontation is an important part of the process. They may need to be placed in a support group or individual therapy until they have developed enough inner sense of value that they can tolerate being in an interactive group. Another alternative is to place such clients in a group that is oriented toward self-psychology and is therefore designed to handle their vulnerabilities.

Avoiding Confrontation in Early Stages.

This narcissistic fragility is typically a bottleneck issue, because it prevents the client from being able to take in and use negative feedback from other group members or from the leader. It may even prevent the client from being able to remain in the group. In the early stages of group, it is advisable to avoid challenging a brittle client yourself and prevent other group members from doing so. For such a client to be confronted when she has little support in the group can be so devastating that she will leave the group. If a client is engaging in some behavior that you sense will annoy other members, such as monopolizing, it may be best if you work with her on it in order to forestall their confronting her. She could react in a brittle way to your interventions, but this isn't as likely as her reacting to confrontations from group members. If you engage her in a gentle and understanding way, this minimizes the chance that she will be deeply hurt, while if you allow her to go on, someone in the group will become angry at her. This could cause irretrievable harm if she hasn't yet had a chance to develop supportive relationships with some of the other members.

Empathic Interpretation.

Once someone has criticized a narcissistically vulnerable client and she is beginning to react, you must immediately forget about the content of the criticism, even if it would have been useful for her. As long as she is caught up in her reaction, it is impossible for her to learn from it. Instead you should focus on empathizing with her underlying shame in accordance with Kohut's approach (1971, 1977). You put yourself empathically in her shoes, understanding what she must be feeling as a result of having her compensatory shell cracked. You communicate this understanding in a compassionate way, so that the client feels cared for and gains understanding about where her brittle reaction is coming from.

What you express is not simple empathy, because that would mean resonating with the client's surface experience, what she is consciously in touch with. What is needed might be more accurately called *empathic interpretation*, because you are interpreting what she is likely to be feeling underneath. She was defending against underlying shame, perhaps by being charming or prideful, and this defense has been pierced by someone's criticizing her. This has triggered either the shame or brittle defenses against it. Your empathy includes her conscious pain and experience of being misunderstood but also points gently toward the underlying issue.

For example, Lucy was interacting with a group member who accused her of being sarcastic and cutting with him. She began to deny that she had done this when another member spoke up to say that she saw Lucy that way, too. Lucy got a frightened look in her eyes and began to talk angrily about not being understood and not feeling safe in the group. Knowing that Lucy had a brittle defense, I moved in and said, "It must be frightening to have two people accusing you of something at the same time." She agreed, and we discussed how it made her feel unsafe to show herself in the group if she were going to be attacked. I said, "I wonder if you felt frightened that you would believe their accusations and end up feeling bad about yourself." Framed in this way, she could acknowledge that this was true and that she did sometimes go into a depression for days when something like this happened. Notice that I dropped any attempt to help her see that she might have been sarcastic and cutting. She couldn't have handled this at that time.

Working with the Group.   It is also important to frame the issues clearly for the other group members, so they are more likely to understand why the brittle client is overreacting and less likely to continue confronting her. *In Lucy's case, the group members understood from my interventions and Lucy's responses how vulnerable she was and didn't push their challenge at that time.* Work with the other group members in whatever way is necessary to prevent them from continuing to criticize her. If a number of people are confronting her, evoke the group norm against multiple confrontations (chapter 8) and allow only one person to interact with her. If the confronting person is harsh, you might work with him on what issue of his has been activated.

Once a brittle client feels understood and cared about, she is usually able to regain her inner stability. Going through this process helps her to understand her fragility more clearly and to develop a better therapeutic alliance with the leader. The group also comes to understand her better, and if they communicate this to her, she may come to trust them, too. Over time, she may develop more inner and outer support so that her brittle reactions diminish in intensity, allowing her to make better use of the group.

☐ The Monopolizer

A major issue for certain narcissistic clients is taking the attention of the group. They tend to need a lot of the group's attention and be insensitive to other people's needs, with the result that they take up far more than their share of the group's time. They often have no idea that this is happening because of their tendency to see others as extensions of themselves. They may have received a considerable amount of attention from their parents, but not quality attention that was really nourishing. They often got attention for performing or pleasing the parents, and it took the form of praise rather than true contact. Therefore they now equate love with attention and praise, and they have little idea that anything more meaningful is possible.

Clients often have considerable difficulty dealing with the issue of needing attention. To be accused of taking up too much group time is perceived as particularly shameful by most clients. In addition, many monopolizers also have a brittle pattern, so if the group challenges a client who is monopolizing, he may be so hurt that he won't be able to make constructive use of the feedback. He may collapse or withdraw in shame, or he may defend himself in various ways, but it will be hard for him to look at his behavior responsibly. In addition, since this issue affects the whole group, you can't allow a client to monopolize even if this risks his being shamed.

Protecting the Client from Shame.   In the early stages of a group or with a particularly brittle client, it may be best if you subtly turn the group's attention away from a monopolizer after a while without making the issue explicit. This prevents him from monopolizing without subjecting him to a potentially harmful confrontation that might lead him to terminate prematurely. When he has been in the group long enough to have developed some supportive connections with other group members and a good therapeutic alliance with you, or when he has developed more inner strength, then you can bring up the issue directly. It is best to arrange it so that the client gets the feedback in a way that is least shameful. Try to avoid having more than one person confront him at the same time. In some cases, you may want to bring it up with him in a consultation to minimize the shame of public exposure. If it is brought up in group, by you or a group member, point out that this is just another issue like any other, and that he doesn't need to feel ashamed of his difficulty in this area.

Experimenting and Healing.   Make sure that the client doesn't just try to suppress his need for attention. This may be of temporary benefit to the group, but it will only last for a few weeks, and the client won't learn anything about himself in the process. The client should explore his need for attention, with an emphasis on what he really needs. Usually, if he examines his actual experience, he will discover that the attention he is getting is not really satisfying, because he is performing or is too self-absorbed to make genuine contact with people. The client really needs a more personal kind of connection with people, where he is open and vulnerable, and people understand and care about him. You can help him to realize this and then to experiment with healthier ways of relating to others that will foster this kind of connection. As he gradually learns this, he will develop relationships with the group members that are more intimate and satisfying. As a result, he will need less attention and will be more in tune with other people's needs. This is the most powerful kind of healing for such clients. As this inner healing happens over time, the client will develop a feeling of personal value independent of the amount of attention he is getting. This will help him to be more sensitive to other people and their needs.

☐ Healing Responses

Cautions in Healing Responses with Borderlines

In individual therapy with borderline clients, it can be dangerous to be too forthcoming in meeting their needs, even after they have accessed the underlying pain. This can encourage them to regress and open up levels of archaic need that are greater than could possibly be met in an ordinary treatment situation, even with multiple sessions per week. (In a full-time residential treatment setting this might be feasible, but this is so rare and expensive as to be out of the question for almost all clients.) When this occurs, some borderline clients can regress to states of rage and disintegration that entail dangerous acting out, harmful addictive behavior, quitting treatment, or suicide attempts (Adler, 1985). The group setting provides some protection from this danger because the transference and dependence are spread out over the group. However, the precaution still applies.

Related to this is the possibility that some borderline clients may regress in their functioning in an unconscious attempt to compel others to take care of them. The client has an unconscious desire to have someone take over his life like a parent and handle everything, and he may attempt to achieve this through a deterioration in functioning. If it seems that this is happening, the client must be challenged in a gentle way so that this self-destructive behavior doesn't escalate. In either case, be aware that it can be dangerous to nurture borderline clients to the extent that they might wish.

Challenging Defenses Versus Healing Responses

Another difficult question arises when a client expresses need in an indirect way, such as being seductive or acting helpless, or asks for something that is a compensation for what she really needs (e.g., asking for attention when she needs contact). Ideally you would like to work with the client's defenses until the need is expressed directly and access has been achieved, but with narcissistic clients this may not be possible. The client may need to receive some healing to be capable of more undefended access. If you try to work with the defense, this may be too wounding for the client.

Therefore sometimes it is necessary to provide some healing responses even before the client achieves any access. *For example, if Martha is acting helpless as an indirect way of expressing need (as opposed to asking for help she really needs), do you challenge her helplessness (or encourage the group members to do so) or do you and the group provide some caring with the hope that this will be a healing response to her deeper unspoken need for love?* Of course, in a group setting, the leader can't completely control the responses of the group members, but it is still important to know the direction that is best at a given time— toward meeting the need or working with the defense.

This situation is made more complicated by the following question. When a client expresses a need for nurturing, is it a legitimate expression of an unfulfilled developmental need, or is it a response to the parents rewarding dependence and/or punishing autonomy? If it is a legitimate need, it should be met (eventually, after access). If it is dependence that was shaped, the need for nurturing should be challenged (or at least not gratified), and the person should be helped to develop autonomy, which is what she really needs.

If the need is expressed in an authentic (undefended, direct) way, then it is likely to be legitimate. If not, it is harder to tell, because a legitimate need can often be expressed in a defended or manipulative way. In addition, it could be both. The client might have been both deprived and rewarded for dependence as a child, and so be lacking in both connectedness and autonomy.

Empathic Understanding

As a good initial compromise, you can validate the need through empathic understanding, as discussed in the previous section. *For example, you could empathize with Martha's deep unmet need for nurturing and caretaking without implying that there is anything wrong with her playing helpless.* If you lead with this kind of response, the group members are more likely to use it also. Empathically understanding does partially meet the need, but it is not the same as fully gratifying the need, *which in Martha's case might take the form of offering advice and encouragement as a response to her helplessness.* Empathic understanding, and other forms of caring, runs the least risk of reinforcing problematic behavior. The most dangerous kinds of gratification are giving advice and direction and physical touch, because these can play into regression and helplessness. Other kinds of responses, such as expressing approval and liking, have a moderate degree of danger. In most cases, a need should only be met fully when you are sure it is a legitimate need, expressed in an authentic, direct way; when the person will not be too threatened by having it met; and when she has already achieved a fair degree of access, so that inner healing can occur. Otherwise there is a danger that the gratification will reward helplessness or lead to destructive regression.

Degree of danger	Form of meeting needs
Most	Physical touch, giving advice and direction
Moderate	Liking, approval, appreciation
Least	Caring, empathy, understanding, acceptance, compassion

If empathic understanding eventually leads to growth or more authentic expression of the need, then the need is probably legitimate and you're on the right track. If this approach produces no change or leads to greater need or greater defense, then the need may be shaped and the client may really require help in developing autonomy and assertiveness.

Empathy and Challenge

Another way to deal with this situation is to support the legitimacy of a need, while challenging the expression of it. Explain that you are challenging the expression of the need in order to help the person get her real need met. By challenging the defended, indirect, or manipulative expression of the need, you can help the person develop healthier ways of expressing her need, and then allow the group to meet it.

> For example, you could suggest that Martha has a need that deserves to be met, but she is going about it in a way (acting helpless) that may not work too well because it irritates people. Offer to help her identify her real need and learn how to get that met. She might really need to be seen or nurtured, for example.

As a general rule, emphasize empathic understanding of the need in the early stages of group when the person might be narcissistically injured by too much challenge. This is also a way of developing trust. Emphasize challenge in the later stages of therapy when the therapeutic alliance and group cohesion are solid and some inner healing has occurred, as a way of helping the person learn to nurture herself and develop maturity. It is also wise to encourage empathic understanding with more narcissistic (brittle) clients and challenge with those having borderline traits, especially those who tend to play victim. This is Masterson's (1981) approach.

It is also important to take the group into account. You may need to emphasize challenge with certain borderline or narcissistic members to protect the group from their destructive behavior. As mentioned previously, a monopolizer can ruin a group if not challenged. Sometimes the welfare of the group must take precedence over that of one member. If the group is capable, let them do the challenging so you can stay in an empathically supportive role. If the client is too brittle to deal with an emotionally loaded challenge from the group, you may have to do the challenging, at least when the person is new in group.

☐ Borderline Splitting

Splitting (Kernberg, 1975) is a defense in which borderline clients see other people and themselves in black–white, good–bad terms. It is common for a borderline client to see one person as the embodiment of goodness and another person as evil and not to be trusted at all. These extremes can also happen with one person, where at one time the client sees him as all good and at another time as all bad, and the client doesn't have any recognition that there is a contradiction in holding these extreme views of the same person. *For example, Ray had a reasonably warm relationship with Laurie until one session when she became angry at him. He suddenly decided that she was a horrible monster, and he had to protect himself from her at all costs. His previous connection with her was completely forgotten.* A borderline client also may see herself in two extremely opposite ways without being able to resolve or integrate them.

Group therapy is particularly helpful in working with splitting because of the feedback from group members. If a client is seeing another group member or the leader as all good or bad, the other members can challenge that perception, providing their own views of that person, both good and bad. This challenges the extremity of the split perception and shows the variety of ways that a person can be perceived, thus helping the borderline client to see the complexity of real people. As a leader, you can contribute to this by emphasizing that a person has different sides. *For example, you might say to Ray, "The group seems to be saying that Laurie is a caring person who sometimes gets quite angry."* The group's feedback can also be helpful when the client sees herself in such an extreme way.

This is not all that is needed to work through a splitting defense. The splitting often involves early childhood issues, so a great deal of access and healing will be required over an extended period of time. Nevertheless, the group feedback can make a significant contribution to this.

☐   The Silent Group Member

Some clients have a difficult time speaking in group at all. They are so self-effacing that they don't feel entitled to any of the group's time. They frequently feel that what they have to say isn't valuable or that others have more pressing needs. They are usually afraid of being judged and rejected if they do speak, and being the center of attention of the group can be terrifying. Notice that this is an example of a bottleneck issue because it blocks the client from working on any other issues until it is resolved.

In the early stages of group, it may be necessary for the leader to call on a silent client to help him participate. The group members may also ask to hear from him. Sometimes this is enough, and gradually the client feels more comfortable speaking in group. If, after a time, a client doesn't increase his degree of participation, then you must work directly with him on his fears. A good way to do this is to help him explore what it is like to have the group's attention. What is he afraid of? What does he imagine the group members are thinking of him? What feelings does this bring up for him? This work can then move into accessing the origins of his insecurity. *For example, the client may have been consistently ignored as a child or even punished for asking for attention or making noise.* After experiencing the pain of such childhood experiences, the client may be open to receiving healing responses from the group. Frequently the other group members will tell him how much they value what he has to say, and how much they appreciate his sharing himself with them.

The tricky thing is how to begin this work if the client is silent most of the time. The leader may need to take the initiative. You can discuss this whole problem with the client in a consultation when he is less anxious, explain the work he can do in group, and, if necessary, elicit his permission to initiate this work for him. If the client is too frightened to agree to this, then the exploration may have to be done in consultations at first until he has gained enough insight and developed enough trust to risk doing it in the group. You can also encourage the client to process his fears silently on his own during the group.

Occasionally a client who is afraid of initiating work or speaking in the group will find that his fears quickly vanish once he gets started. In this case, you can't initiate the work by calling on him, because once this has happened there is no work left to do since the work is specifically related to initiative. Here you have no choice except to work with the client on this in consultations or have him do some exploration silently during group.

A silent client may have to work on this issue a number of times before he reaches the point where he can participate sufficiently to make good use of the group.

☐   Countertransference

One of the biggest problems for group leaders dealing with borderline and narcissistic members is the fact that these clients can stir up strong countertransference reactions. The intense anger and splitting defenses that borderlines often exhibit can cause a leader to become frightened of the client's anger or to become angry in return. Narcissistic grandiosity and demeaning comments from group members can also elicit powerful feelings of envy or rage in the leader (as well as members). It is also common to have countertransference reactions to monopolizers, to narcissistically fragile clients, or to group members who show extreme neediness. There is also the danger that the group leader will become protectively angry at a member who is attacking other members.

These countertransference reactions can, of course, happen in response to any group member, but borderline and narcissistic clients tend to provoke more intense feelings. It is therefore important to watch for such reactions in yourself and to avoid acting on them as much as possible. Chapter 19 contains further discussion of counter-transference issues and how to handle them.

25

CHAPTER

The Group as a Whole

This chapter covers a variety of group-as-a-whole issues that have not been previously discussed. First I examine the question of choosing the appropriate intervention level at any given time. Then I discuss various ways that members may experience the group—as a container, a mother or other person to relate to, a family, a community. Next I look at how groups develop common themes and emotional dynamics and how to explore these. Finally, I look at functional subgrouping and group decision-making.

☐ Choosing the Intervention Level

I believe that the importance of whole-group issues derives from the fact that the group provides the context or container for the therapeutic work. When therapeutic group norms are in place and the group is developing properly through its stages, when there is a healthy group climate and clients are not stuck in unproductive roles, then the therapeutic change process can unfold optimally. Therefore, as a leader, it is important to pay attention to group-as-a-whole issues at two times: (a) in the early stages of a group, to make sure the group develops properly, and (b) when something seems to be wrong at the group level. If you sense that something in the group is interfering with the therapeutic process, then you must examine the group level of dynamics and make interventions at that level to clear up the problem. Otherwise, you can focus your attention primarily on the individual and interpersonal levels.

These levels are not without overlap, however. It is fairly common for a group member to have important reactions to the group as a whole as well as to other members or the leader; this was discussed in chapter 17. In fact, the group as a whole can be an important activator of transference. *For example, a client who was excluded from her family of origin felt excluded by her therapy group. This was a transference reaction to the group as a whole, not to any one person.* The group can also provide crucial healing responses for a client. *For example, many clients have never before felt accepted as themselves and loved by a*

260

group of people. This is profoundly healing. When exploring issues such as these, you are simultaneously working at the intrapsychic and group-as-a-whole levels.

Some group leaders tend to favor group-as-a-whole interpretations and interventions, reasoning that this is the best way to use the power of the group. However, it seems that when there is too much reliance on this level, the group members often feel ignored by the leader as individuals, and this can lead to dissatisfaction and a poor therapeutic alliance. An overreliance on group-as-a-whole interpretations can also cause members to focus too much attention on leader-oriented transference as opposed to their work with each other (Kibel & Stein, 1981). To prevent these problems, some leaders (Horowitz, 1993) give group interpretations only after first paying attention to the individual members involved at a given time. I prefer to use group-level interventions only when they are needed because of a difficulty at the group level. Otherwise I focus directly on the intrapsychic and interpersonal levels which have the greatest potential for therapeutic change. This is similar to Yalom's (1995) attitude.

☐ How Members Experience the Group

There are four common ways in which members experience a therapy group—as a container for their therapeutic work, as an object to relate to, as a family, and as a community.

The Group as Container

A therapy group is a special, delineated space (Ettin, 1996), separate from the rest of clients' lives and with different norms and goals from most social and family interactions. Part of the power of a group derives from this function it serves as a "sacred space," where special healing events and relationships can take place. When a group is functioning well, its members experience it as a place where they can be themselves in an authentic way that may not be possible anywhere else in their lives. They experience it as a place where they can show parts of themselves that seem unacceptable elsewhere—their pain, their shame, and their perceived weaknesses. A good group encourages members to be completely honest, to say things and express feelings that are otherwise forbidden, to take risks that would be too dangerous elsewhere. A group becomes a place of closeness and caring, a place where a person knows he is loved and appreciated. And most important, a therapy group is experienced as a place for change, where clients can understand their dynamics, heal their pain, and learn healthy ways of relating.

All this takes much time and work to develop and maintain. It requires healthy group norms, clear boundaries, a positive group climate, and the ability to understand and resolve snags and impasses in the group's developmental process. Each individual influences the group's development, and the resulting group configuration, in turn, influences each member.

At those times when all this is not in place, the group may be experienced as a negative container—a place of danger, chaos, or even unbearable conflict and pain. It can evolve into a place of judgment or rejection, in which one must keep oneself hidden. In fact, even when a group is functioning well, a member may experience it negatively at times because of his or her issues. However, when most members experience it negatively, then there is something problematic in the whole group process which must be remedied.

Relating to the Group

The Group as Mother.   A therapy group is often experienced by its members as an object or person to relate to, whether or not this is conscious. Each group member has a relationship with the group as a whole as well as with each member and the leader. This relationship can be positive or negative or have elements of both. It is especially common for group members to relate to the group as a mother (Durkin, 1964; Scheidlinger, 1974). This is not surprising given our previous discussion of the group as a container, for that is part of the mother's role with young children. She provides a safe space for them to grow and develop just as the group provides a space for its member to grow. Thus in relating to the group as a mother, members can experience it as a warm, loving presence or as a dangerous, engulfing threat. When a member experiences the group as a good mother, this can activate hopeful transference, fostering regression to early, primitive feelings and needs and promoting access. The client, often unconsciously, feels that at last he is home, in a place where he can finally let himself feel all the needs that he thought could never be met. He feels that perhaps now, in this group, he will finally be loved or seen or respected. And indeed, often this does happen, with important healing consequences.

On the other hand, when a member experiences the group as an engulfing mother, he may feel frightened of being overwhelmed or trapped in the group. He may fear that he will lose himself and be taken over. This may cause him to become distant, to start fights, or even to run from the group. Alternatively, a member might experience the group as a depriving, rejecting mother, causing him to become clinging, pleasing, or distancing, depending on his defensive style.

Other Ways of Relating to the Group.   A client can also relate to the group in other ways—as a positive father who is powerful and protective, fostering a sense of safety, or as a cruel, judgmental father, which may evoke anger or placating behavior. A group can be experienced at times like a lover; for example, a client's difficulty in committing to the group can mirror his difficulties in committing to love relationships.

In all these cases, the group as a whole functions as a part of the therapeutic change process just as an individual might. The group can activate a client's core issue, producing transference, and leading to awareness and access. It can provide an opportunity for a client to experiment with new healthy ways of relating to the group, and it can provide healing responses for the client.

> For example, Penny had been a member of a very cohesive and well-functioning group for 3½ years. She had received a great deal from the group and had come to trust the members deeply, investing a lot of her emotional energy and needs in the group. During a weekend retreat she did a very important piece of work related to her father. As a child, Penny had been neglected by her depressed mother who was hardly present at all in the family. Her father was more successful in the world and provided Penny with her only hope for parenting, despite the fact that she didn't get much from him either. In her desperate need

for parental love, Penny did everything she could to please him and constructed an idealized image of him as being supportive of her despite the fact that he really wasn't. In the process, she buried all of her anger at him for neglecting her.

At the weekend, the group members supported and encouraged Penny to access and express her anger at her father through role-playing, thereby undermining her false idealized image of him. To do this, she formed an idealized view of the group to substitute for her idealized relationship with her father. Without this crutch, it wouldn't have been possible for her to let go of the idealized image of her father. However, we didn't realize at first that she had done this. Later that weekend, when Ralph confronted Penny on another issue and expressed some anger at her, this felt like a devastating betrayal to her. The regressed part of her had imagined that the group had promised to always support her. She became furious with Ralph for not living up to this, and when the group didn't side with her against him, she became angry at the group, too.

However, even though the incident with Ralph was painful and difficult, it had a positive side. She felt free to express her anger at Ralph and the group in a powerful way that she never could with her father. Therefore even though her anger was based on a transference distortion, her expression of it constituted healthy experimenting. Later that week in a consultation, I helped Penny to understand these dynamics. After a few weeks of work on the issue, she was able to take responsibility for what had happened without apologizing for her anger and reconnect with Ralph and the group. In the end she had grown enormously in her capacity for autonomy while retaining her bond with the group. This example illustrates the power of a person's relationship with the group as a whole.

The Group as Community

We human beings originally evolved to be who we are while living in extended families, bands, and tribes. Community is part of our blood and one of our most important needs. Today's world has witnessed a marked breakdown of community because of high mobility, social alienation, and the impact of the market economy (Earley, 1990, chapter 12). Many group members have a great need for community in their lives, even if this is not conscious. This is one of the reasons that groups can be such a powerful experience. It is very different to be part of a close group of people than to have a number of friends who don't know each other well.

Paying attention to and reflecting on the experience of the group as a whole tends to promote cohesiveness and the feeling of community. Because group therapy is necessarily only temporary, I hope that as a result of their group experiences, clients will be encouraged to create community in their lives.

The Group as Family

A therapy group is frequently experienced by its members as a family. This can bring up a wide variety of family-of-origin issues—exclusion, attention, power, sibling rivalry, jealousy, and competition. The leader is usually related to as a parent; if there are two leaders, they are seen as father and mother, especially if they are a man and woman. Other group members may also be seen as parents, and anyone may be perceived as a brother, sister, uncle, aunt, grandparent, or other family member. If a client was ignored and excluded in his family of origin, he will probably expect the same from the group, and he may respond to this by making himself invisible or by fighting for attention.

Clients can relate to a new group member as a younger sibling being born into the family, and a terminating member as an older sibling leaving home. Difficulties between co-leaders (even if not spoken) can be experienced as conflict between parents, as can arguments between members. Group members may feel sibling rivalry for the approval of the leader or a popular member. There may be an adolescent rebellion against the leader. The group as a whole may be experienced as similar to a client's family of origin—a cold, distant place; a chaotic scene; a dangerous situation for betrayal; a sticky, engulfing trap; and so on.

All of these possible family transferences should be made explicit by the leader and explored by the group members. As always, begin by asking members to explore what their transference is, and only if necessary should you offer your interpretation. As these family issues are worked through and the members grow, the group can become cohesive and loving like a healthy family, where each person feels deeply connected to the group and also free to be uniquely herself. This is a transformative experience.

Triadic Transference

Clients have transference not only to the group as a whole but also to pairs of other members, recalling oedipal conflicts or other family dynamics. The following are examples of this.

Melissa got upset with a man when he said something about her to the female group leader. This reminded her of how her brother would lie about Melissa's behavior to get her in trouble with her mother.

Whenever Marlene received warmth and appreciation from the female group leader, she became frightened of Charlotte's reaction. As a child, whenever Marlene had gotten positive attention from her grandmother, her mother became jealous and took this out on her by attacking her later. In the group, Charlotte represented Marlene's mother and the leader represented her grandmother.

Anne felt rejected by her father as a child. He was interested only in his relationship with Anne's mother and not much in Anne. As an adult, Anne re-experienced this with men she was attracted to. She felt that she could never compete successfully with another woman. In the group, if an interesting man started relating positively to another woman, Anne would immediately withdraw from him. She assumed that because he was making a connection with the other woman, he couldn't possibly have any interest in her. This transferential reaction threatened to become a self-fulfilling prophecy because her withdrawal would make it harder for the man to be interested in her or connect with her.

The Leader as Healing Parent

Providing Healing Parental Functions.   When the group is experienced as a family, the leader is usually seen as the parent. Because most group members have had relatively difficult childhoods, they need the leader to relate to the group as a good parent, providing healing responses. A good parent provides guidance, structure, nurturing, acceptance, love, and protection for his or her children, and therefore the leader needs to carry out these functions at times. The leader does this especially as the group is first developing, and then, with his encouragement, the group members can take over and give to each other, as they are ready.

However, certain clients will especially need one particular function from the leader. One person may have a strong need to be protected by the leader because this was absent in childhood. Another will especially need acceptance, and so on. When a client seems to need or demand one of these functions from you, don't just assume that she is avoiding responsibility for herself. It may derive from a legitimate need for a healing response from you.

In addition to the needs of individual clients, the group as a whole needs these functions from the leader as part of the healing process. The functions of guidance, structure, and protection are important to note because some leaders purposely don't provide these as a matter of principle. Leaders of psychodynamic groups often take the stance that the group should be free-form, and their only job is to provide interpretations to help the members gain insight. As a result, they do not provide these important leader/parent functions, to the detriment of the group and the healing of its members.

Since I previously discussed the need for a leader to provide guidance in the early stages of a group, this section examines structure and protection.

Providing Structure.   Some leaders may allow a group meeting to become chaotic, or they may not provide much protection if a group gets into destructive conflict. I believe that this does not take into account the need for a healing parental response from the leader. If a group meeting becomes chaotic because many members are speaking at once or interrupting each other, this may recreate a client's chaotic family life with parents who provided little structure. The leader should provide some structure by preventing members from interrupting each other and making sure that each client (or pair of clients) has the room to complete a piece of work before someone takes the group in a new direction. This not only helps the group's process but also provides a healing relationship for clients who came from chaotic homes.

Providing Protection.   If the leader allows a group to become hostile and unsafe, for some clients this may re-create the experience of a hostile, violent family of origin. The leader should protect the group from this by ending destructive arguments between members and encouraging them to explore the issues behind their anger. You may even have to go as far as raising your voice or forcibly stopping quarreling that is getting out of hand. When the leader offers this kind of protection, it not only benefits the therapy process, but also provides important healing for members who grew up in angry or violent homes.

Of course it is valuable to encourage the group members to take care of these problems themselves if possible. It would be a sign of growth if the group as a whole could prevent chaos or protect itself from too much anger, but this can come only from a relatively mature group. Even then, it is often difficult for group members to provide protection without becoming involved in the conflict, while the leader has the right distance and authority to do this. In addition, because of parental transference, members have a need for structure and protection that comes from the leader. Even if you do want to help the group take over these functions, this can be done without sitting back and allowing destructive events to occur. You can provide the structure or protection and then ask the group members to explore why they couldn't do it themselves.

Summary of Transferences.   In summary, there are four common objects of transference or activators of issues for a client in a therapy group: (a) the leader, (b) another group member, (c) the group as a whole, and (d) a pair of other group members. Each of these can activate transference, provide healing responses, and offer the client an opportunity to experiment with new behavior.

☐   Common Feelings and Themes in a Group

Group members affect each other quite strongly, not just as they interact, but also through empathy and identification with each other. In addition, group members often have comparable reactions to group events. Therefore it is not uncommon for many group members to feel similarly at a certain time or to be interested in exploring a common theme.

Group Exploration of a Common Theme

For example, if one member begins to talk about his grief over losing a parent, this may trigger similar feelings in other members. If they also talk about their losses, this intensifies the group interest in bereavement. This can lead to group exploration of a common theme, in which many of the members participate in exploring what the theme means to them. This can happen with virtually any theme, for example, shyness, abusive parents, standing up to authority figures, or fear of intimacy. When a group is sharing a common theme, make sure that the members really explore the issue rather than talking superficially, gossiping, or complaining about it. As each person explores the issue and its meaning for her, this also provides stimulation for other members in their explorations. While one person is working, the others may consider such questions as: Do I have this interpersonal pattern, too? Was my childhood similar to hers? Is that what this issue means to me? Do I use a similar defense? Could I solve this problem in the same way that she did? Thus group members can help one another to go deeper in their explorations not only with empathy and caring, but also through identification.

> For example, Laura talked about how her father praised her for performing but never seemed to be interested in who she really was. This prompted Thomas to realize that he received approval from his parents for taking care of his younger siblings but his own needs were ignored. He talked about how angry he felt about that. Manfred said that he was appreciated for his intelligence, but his parents didn't see other parts of him. This made it hard for

him to value his emotional or intuitive sides. Listening to the two men, Laura recognized that her parents ignored her intellectual side, and this might be the reason she felt so insecure in that area. She also realized she felt angry about this.

If any members seem reluctant to join in, encourage them to share their experiences or explore with them why they are having trouble participating. Be alert to the possibility that the group theme may ostensibly refer to outside issues but may actually be an unconscious, veiled reference to events in the group. *For example, the members may discuss their angry reactions to forbidding authority figures in their lives because they are feeling frightened to confront the group leader.* If it looks like this might be going on, encourage them to bring the issue directly into the group.

Group exploration reduces the likelihood of one member feeling agonizing shame about an issue. Because any shame is shared, it is diminished considerably. Involving the whole group also minimizes the chance that one person can alienate herself from the group by talking incessantly. Group exploration also creates a sense of warmth and cohesiveness, so it is particularly useful in the early stages of group development.

Common Feelings and Dynamics in the Group

Group Climate.   Because of the empathic emotional connection between group members and their unconscious influence on each other, it is not unusual for many group members to be feeling similarly at any given time. They may be feeling cautious or bold, frightened or safe, distant or close, focused or distracted. This produces a group climate that affects everything that occurs in the group. The *group climate* is the emotional feel of the group at any given moment. This is similar to the concept of group culture discussed previously except that the group climate is a more transitory phenomenon. It helps to pay attention to the group climate, comment on it from time to time, and encourage the group members to do the same. If the group climate is detracting from the group's ability to work therapeutically, this must be explored so it can be changed.

The group climate is often related to a certain group event that has affected most of the members emotionally. Perhaps a couple of important people have terminated recently, or too many new members have left prematurely, or there has been a change of leadership, and the members feel that the group is unstable. Perhaps there has been too much hostility in the group, or members have been attacked when vulnerable, and people aren't feeling safe. Perhaps the group has become very close recently, and members are more deeply invested in the group as a place where they can receive healing. Other significant group events might be the leader's vacation, a weekend retreat, moving to a new stage of group development, or a serious crisis in one member's life. These events can affect the group as a whole without members necessarily being aware of what has happened. If you point out the possible relationship between the group climate and a group event, this gives members a chance to explore how the event affected them. This provides an opportunity for good individual work and it encourages the group to work on and change a negative group climate.

Even less significant group events can affect most members of the group in a similar way. For example, a deeply satisfying piece of individual work may leave most members feeling open and connected. An unresolved conflict may leave people feeling edgy. A challenge to the leader may result in members feeling rebellious or frightened.

Differences in Members' Responses.   However, even though they affect each other, not all group members react in the same way to group events; be careful not to lump them together. It is not uncommon for five or six people to express similar feelings about some event while two or three members feel differently. Often the two or three members are afraid to speak about their feelings because each of them feels that he or she is the only one who feels that way, and they are afraid to go against the group. This may cause it to look as if the entire group feels the same way when this is far from true. At times it is valuable to check with a silent member to see if she is feeling something different from the majority, and to encourage her to express herself even if she is the only one who feels that way. The person often discovers that a couple of other members also feel as she does. And even if she is the only one, she still has the right to express her feelings. This is a valuable lesson—that it is OK to be different.

Group Resistance.   Not only may group members have similar feelings at a given time, they may also have similar dynamics, especially with regard to desires and resistance. Some of the creative early work on group therapy focused on this aspect of group process (Bion, 1959; Ezriel, 1952; Whitaker & Lieberman, 1964). If most of the group is resisting in the same way, this is often called *group resistance*. The following are examples:

> The group members might be resisting talking about their reactions to a group event that is affecting them all strongly, such as the impending termination of an important member.
>
> They might have just started to feel close to each other and are resisting bringing up any conflicts for fear of destroying their new found intimacy.
>
> A new group might be colluding to keep discussions on the surface in order to avoid dealing with pain or difficulties.
>
> Group members might be afraid to confront the leader with their dissatisfactions, and as a result the work becomes cautious and boring.

If you suspect that group resistance is operating, point out what is not happening in the group and ask the group members to explore what they think is causing this problem. Contribute your interpretation during this process if it seems necessary.

☐ Functional Subgrouping

In her systems-centered approach to groups, Agazarian (1992) maps out a a method of working with group process that is excellent for preventing problems with group roles and positions and for encouraging discussion of common themes and feelings. The following is a brief description of this technique, which is called *functional subgrouping.*

Forming Subgroups.   Each group member is encouraged to express his feeling reactions in the moment and to explore what they mean for him. Other members who have similar feelings are encouraged to talk about these feelings directly to the first person. They form a subgroup of people who have roughly similar reactions. The members of this subgroup explore their feelings with each other, using the stimulation of each other's work to take their own explorations deeper. Then members who feel differently are encouraged to speak, and they form another subgroup, sharing and exploring their feelings with each other. The two subgroups don't argue with each other or try to convince each other that they are right. Instead each person explores the meaning of her feelings within her own subgroup. Rather than the differences causing dissension in the group, they serve to help each person learn more about his own process.

The two subgroups tend to take complementary positions about a psychological issue. The following are examples of pairs of subgroups: Those members who want to become close and those who want to remain separate; those members who are oriented toward emotions and those who want to understand things intellectually; and those members who feel defiant toward the leader and those who want to go along with the leader.

Opening Up Subgroups.   As the members of two subgroups continue to explore their feelings, the groupings begin to break down in positive ways. As the members of one subgroup explore their own personal reactions, they begin to see that they don't all feel exactly the same way about the issue. Their individual differences come out, breaking down any artificial feelings of sameness. Furthermore, after a while a person in one subgroup will realize that her reactions are similar in a certain way to someone in the other subgroup. In this way, connections are seen between the opposing subgroups, breaking down any false perception of irreconcilable differences. In the process, each person gains insight into his patterns, moves beyond stereotypes of himself and others, and more fully embraces his authentic experience.

> For example, a client challenges the leader about not revealing enough of herself to the group. Some other members feel similarly and they form a subgroup to explore how they feel about the leader not disclosing more and what this means to them. Some of them feel unsafe because they don't know if they can trust the leader. Others feel one-down because the leader hasn't revealed her shortcomings the way they have. Another subgroup forms of members who are happy with the amount of self-disclosure from the leader. Some of them think the leader has revealed a fair amount about herself. Others don't want much self-disclosure from the leader, for a number of reasons. You can see that quite a bit of variety has already emerged within each subgroup. As the exploration continues, it becomes apparent that some members of each subgroup feel shame because they feel inferior to the leader. This brings out connections across subgroups. One option for continuing work at this point would be for these members to form a new subgroup to explore their shame.

Advantages.   This method prevents one person from being in the position of containing a feeling for other group members who remain silent. The other members are always asked to contribute any similar feelings they may have. It is almost impossible for a member to feel alone or isolated with an issue she is exploring because she always has a subgroup, and this reduces unnecessary anxiety in the group. It is difficult for one person to become the identified patient because a single person doesn't work by himself. Similarly it is rare for someone to become a scapegoat when a group uses functional subgrouping. No matter how extreme a position a member takes, other members are encouraged to find a part of themselves with similar feelings. This way no one is left to take the rap alone.

Functional subgrouping can be a good way of dealing with prejudice. If one member feels prejudiced toward another, the other group members can identify with both sides—what it is like to also to feel prejudiced and also to have prejudice directed at them. This prevents either person from being alone in their position.

This method tends to prevent polarization of a group and divisive subgrouping. It can be also used with other kinds of groups, such as work groups and community groups, including those that are larger in size than a therapy group.

☐   Group Decisions

Occasionally a therapy group will have to make a decision, not just explore feelings and relationships. For example, a member may suggest that group meetings start with a brief check-in from each person. Decisions may have to be made about scheduling a group weekend or about how soon to admit a new member. Situations requiring an explicit group decision don't happen often, but when they do, they provide an opportunity for group members to learn more about how they deal with power issues. Some decisions don't have to be made explicitly. For example, if a member wants to change the group norms in a certain area, this can be discussed and explored among the members, and the norm will automatically change in the direction suggested by the group's consensus.

Consensus.   Make sure that members realize that in addition to making the decision, they are also engaging in group therapy so they should be paying attention to and exploring their actions and feelings just as they normally do. Decisions that must be made explicitly should be arrived at by consensus, not by majority vote. This encourages members to deal carefully with each others' desires and reactions. A consensus is not the same as a unanimous vote even though consensus means that everyone in the group must agree to the decision. When a consensus has been reached, this doesn't mean that everyone prefers the decision, but those who don't are willing to let it stand. Any member who strongly disagrees can block a consensus and force the group to continue discussing it. Consensus is a more cooperative and caring method than majority vote.

Power Dynamics.   The decision process brings up issues related to how people assert what they want. Some members will try to force their will on the group or manipulate others into backing them. Others will hang back and go along with the majority. Some will state their preference clearly but not take the time to explain why they feel that way. Some will be very concerned about other people's desires, and others will only care about getting their own way. Exploring these issues can provide important insights into members' power dynamics that ordinary group process may miss.

Society.   In addition, this process also gives some insight into our decision-making problems as a society. Though we pride ourselves on being a democracy, our system of political decision-making is far from being as democratic as it could be. Too often decisions are made from an adversarial stance rather than in the cooperative spirit of finding the best solution for everyone. Too often those with money or influence exert power over others to serve their own interests rather than caring about the good of the whole. Group therapy can be a place to learn a different way of making decisions.

V

SPECIAL ISSUES

The last part of the book deals with a variety of special issues related to group therapy. Chapter 26 addresses gender, race, culture, and prejudice—how they can impede or enhance the functioning of a therapy group and how to use group therapy to overcome difficulties in these areas. Chapter 27 covers a variety of other topics—consultations, concurrent group and individual therapy, weekend retreats, coleading, training, and ethics. Chapter 28 examines some group modalities other than unstructured interaction (which has been the focus of the book) and then discusses therapy groups that are designed for specific populations or issues. Chapter 29 relates group therapy to larger societal issues.

Gender and Diversity

This chapter covers gender issues in group therapy, including gender conditioning, women's oppression, men's difficulties with therapy groups, gender and leadership, and same-sex groups. It also deals with cultural differences in groups, the psychological effects of oppression, and strategies for working with prejudice in groups.

☐ Gender

Gender Conditioning

A client's problems don't derive exclusively from dysfunction in the family of origin, and often family problems reflect societal or cultural conflicts. The family may just be the vehicle through which a cultural problem is transmitted to an individual. In our culture, gender is a prime example of this since both boys and girls are socialized according to gender lines in ways that can cause psychological problems.

Male and Female Conditioning. Women are taught to value emotions and to feel inadequate in intellectual discussions. Men are socialized in the opposite way, to value their competence and their intellect and to avoid their feelings. Women are trained to value connection and relationship; many end up believing that their only worth is to be found through relating to and caring for others. Men are taught to value independence and autonomy and to feel shame about any sign of dependence on others. Women are conditioned to feel that they can't take care of themselves, especially with regard to money, career, and "the ways of the world." Many expect men to take care of these spheres of life.

Women are often taught to be compliant and pleasing to others, especially men. They are given the message that too much self-assertion or success may lead to rejection by men. Therefore women often inhibit their anger and aggression. Men are trained to value their aggression and power and to defend against their softness, vulnerability, and heart feelings. Men are socialized to value themselves for their success in the world as measured by money, power, competence, and status; they are told that it is their job to take care of women financially. Women learn to value themselves for physical beauty and nurturing ability; their job is taking care of children and the home.

Even though some aspects of these gender roles are based on real biological differences between men and women, the differences are exaggerated by socialization. Fortunately because of the women's and men's movements, this conditioning is being challenged, and boys and girls brought up today are less likely to be handicapped in these ways. Nevertheless, most of our clients are still struggling with what it means to be a man or woman.

Working with Gender Conditioning.   Though gender issues affect everyone, they are especially problematic for certain clients. When a client is dealing with one of these issues, it is helpful to make the connection between the person's difficulties and his or her gender conditioning. This helps to avoid shame and facilitates women connecting with other women (and men with other men) with respect to their common issues. In a therapy group, the support of empathy and identification from others who understand one's gender struggles can be very valuable. This is especially important in those areas where each gender is prone to shame—men about vulnerability and dependence, women about attractiveness.

In order to grow, clients often need to experiment with healthy behavior that has been devalued for their gender. Women need to experiment with anger, assertiveness, intellectuality, competence, and self-reliance. Men need to experiment with feeling their emotions, vulnerability, and needs, and with expressing caring and developing intimacy. Group therapy can help both men and women escape from their gender conditioning and emerge as whole human beings with a full range of healthy capacities and sensitivities.

Gender Role Freedom.   As gender issues are explored in a group, some members may make statements about how men and women really are. Some of these can be useful in pointing out gender conditioning or even possibly innate differences between the sexes. However, even if well-intentioned, these comments can sometimes pigeonhole people. For example, even if men tend to be more practical and women more emotional, this doesn't apply to all men or all women. Some men are quite emotional and some women very practical. Make sure that each group member is allowed to define for himself or herself what it means to be a man or women, and to object if others define it for them.

Women's Oppression

In addition to gender conditioning, which applies to both sexes, women have the additional problem of living in a society that is still largely patriarchal, where men hold the balance of power and privilege. This is also in the process of changing, but women's oppression is still very real. This affects not only women's opportunities for financial stability, but also issues of personal power and self-esteem.

Masculine Ideals.   In many ways, the ideals of our society still conform to men's needs and conditioning. This causes many girls and women to have difficulty with self-esteem because they fail to live up to these standards. Self-esteem problems have other causes, and men can also have self-esteem issues because of not living up to societal standards, but the problem is greater for women. They often feel inferior because they aren't more intelligent or stronger or achieving at a high enough level. Educating women in therapy groups about these issues can help them to see through these unreasonable standards and boost self-esteem.

Sexism.   In addition, some men and some women have been conditioned to believe that women are inferior to men, and this can have a devastating effect on a woman's inner sense of value. This form of sexism is becoming less prevalent, but it still holds considerable sway, especially in older clients.

   An example of this is that until recently most psychotherapy theory has valued the male perspective over the female. The oldest theories actually stated that women were inferior, and later ones have valued autonomy and achievement over women's strengths, such as caring and relationship. In the last 25 years, feminist theory has made inroads by articulating revised theories that better understand and value women's realities (Chodorow, 1989; Gilligan, 1982; Herman, 1992).

Power.   Power is also an important issue for women (Lazerson & Zilbach, 1993; Schoenholtz-Read, 1996). They have been trained to cede power to men, and men have been taught to take it. This is also reinforced by the power structures of society. In addition, men are bigger and stronger physically and therefore have advantages in situations where might can determine power. Many women have been abused, raped, or assaulted by men, and this leaves them with scars and issues around the basic need for safety. All these factors conspire to make it difficult for women in a therapy group to exert power and deal with anger. Though this doesn't apply to all women, it affects enough for it to be an important consideration for a group leader. Women should be helped to explore their emotional reactions to anger and power exerted by other group members, especially men. Women should also be supported and encouraged to take power as part of their growth.

Men's Difficulties in Therapy Groups

Therapy Ideals.   Men also have unique problems in therapy groups that are related to their gender conditioning (Krugman & Osherson, 1993). Societal standards may be biased toward men, but therapy group norms are biased toward women. The norms of group therapy put a premium on things that women tend to do well—caring, vulnerability, relationship, emotion. Of the things that men are especially good at, only assertiveness is a highly valued group norm. This means that women tend to have an easier time in therapy groups than men. Many men find the atmosphere and goals of a group difficult and threatening. For a man to acknowledge needing help or to reveal pain and vulnerability can bring on a great deal of shame.

Reverse Sexism.   As feminism has alerted women to their conditioning and op-pression and helped them to value themselves and gender, some women have come to believe that women are actually superior to men. They have perhaps experienced vio-lence, domination, or insensitivity from men and they feel much more comfortable with women, who are oriented toward relationships and emotions. Especially in a therapy group, it is easy for women to believe that men are inferior because many men have difficulty with the therapy process. It is important to remember that men's natural strengths are just as valuable as women's, though in therapy it may not appear this way. For example, when in trouble, women tend to want to talk about their feelings and men tend to give practical solutions. Both approaches are valuable and healthy, though in group therapy, we usually emphasize feelings. However, for every man who has trouble feeling, there are as many women who have trouble acting in the world.

Gender, Transference, and Leadership

Transference issues are usually played out according to gender, with father transfer-ence projected onto men and mother transference onto women. This is one of the rea-sons why it is valuable to have a fairly even mix of men and women in a group, so that one man, for example, doesn't receive all the father transference. This is not always the case, however; be alert to the possibility that transference sometimes crosses gender lines.

The gender of the group leader affects the group, not only because of gender-related transference but also because of gender role expectations. A male leader may be expected to be more authoritative, intellectual, incisive, and protective, and a female leader may be expected to be more nurturing, empathic, and supportive (Doherty & Enders, 1993). In fact, a good leader must be all these things, and therefore you may upset the expectations of some of your group members by exhibiting qualities they expect from the opposite sex. Help them to voice the feelings that come up about this and explore the meaning it has for them. Some men (and some women) may have difficulty developing a therapeutic alliance with a female leader because they are un-willing to give her enough authority.

Be aware of your own gender conditioning and how this may limit your ability to perform all the tasks that are necessary as a leader. You may need to develop those sides of your leadership ability that have been blocked because they don't match tradi-tional views of your gender. If you are part of a male–female co-leading team, it is more likely that the two of you can provide everything your group needs. However, if you take leadership roles according to your gender, this will support the limiting gender conditioning of our culture. Ideally a leader should provide a model of healthy func-tioning that includes both "masculine" and "feminine" modes, where you can be prob-ing and caring, powerful and loving, protective and nurturing.

Cross-Gender Interactions

Sometimes the "war of the sexes" gets acted out in a therapy group. A man may make a traditionally sexist remark and then be challenged by one or more of the women. A woman may express her anger or mistrust toward men, and some of the men may take exception to this. This is normal therapeutic grist for the mill, caused by gender differences, sexism, reverse sexism, and personal histories of harm from the opposite gender. Some cross-gender misunderstandings also occur because our society is in the midst of a transition from old gender roles to new conceptions of the relationship between the sexes. Though this transition is positive, people who are on different stages of this road can become quite angry with each other.

Though conflicts between men and women need to be understood in their larger social context, don't allow the interactions to stay too long on the level of judgments and social polemics, and try to prevent a splintering of the group along gender lines. Even though these gender conflicts derive partly from societal issues, in a therapy group they can be worked through only on the personal level. Most issues of this nature are both personal and social in origin. Make sure that the men and women involved have space to work through their personal feelings toward each other and, in the process, to explore the origins of the issue in each person's history. You may need to encourage one man and one woman to interact with each other, keeping other people out of the dialogue for a time, so they can fully engage each other. As each person works through his or her personal issues and comes to understand the other, they will learn to care about and appreciate each other. This contributes not only to their personal growth, but also to a better appreciation of the other gender. When the work is finished, you might want to refer back to the social context of their issues.

Men's and Women's Groups

Despite the advantages of groups with a fairly even balance of men and women, there are also important advantages of same-sex groups. For men or women who have serious trust issues with the opposite gender, perhaps because of early abuse, it is often best to have one's first group experience be in a same-sex group. This provides the safety this person needs to take risks and make him or herself vulnerable without fear from the other sex. It is also a safe situation to share one's fears of and anger toward the opposite sex. This can be especially important for women who have suffered abuse or violence from men (Lazerson & Zilbach, 1993). It is also easier for women to deal with their feelings about being oppressed in a group of "sisters," as was demonstrated by the power of consciousness raising groups in the 1960s and 1970s.

A women's or men's group can also be an excellent place to explore and break through gender conditioning. It is easier to share the difficulties of such conditioning with people who understand it firsthand, and it often feels safer to experiment with new behavior in such a secure setting. It can be easier for women to experiment with aggression when they don't have to worry about aggressive responses from men. Similarly, it can be easier for men to experiment with vulnerability and grief if there are no women present who (they fear) might shame them for not being manly enough. Of course, the other men in the group could shame them, too, but they are taking the same risks.

However, there is a danger with this approach. Without proper leadership, same-sex groups can avoid taking on the issues that are difficult for its members. Women's groups can easily lapse into being caring, nice, and merging together, while avoiding confrontation and autonomy issues. Similarly, it is easy for a men's group to spend too much time in intellectual discussion and conflict, while avoiding dealing with feelings, vulnerability, and closeness.

☐ Diversity and Prejudice

Cultural Differences.   Our cultural heritage also affects our psychological makeup. Therefore, when a client comes from a culture different than yours, it is easy to misunderstand her reactions and psychodynamics. For this reason, the client's nationality, religion, race, ethnic group, subculture, or social class can present problems in therapy. If you work with many clients from a given culture, it would be wise to study the psychology of that group to be able to work with them effectively. If you treat clients from different cultures only occasionally, you may not have time to become familiar with each new culture, but it is still important to recognize that you are probably misunderstanding vital issues. At times you might ask your client to explain to you and the group how his culture is different from mainstream American culture.

Oppression.   When a group of people is oppressed by the larger society, they are often denied equal opportunity and devalued in the eyes of the average person. This can also happen because of their culture or because of noncultural issues, such as sexual orientation or a physical handicap. In any case, oppression produces a sense of alienation, rejection, and rage toward both others and the self. Clients often internalize the oppression and struggle with feelings of inferiority and self-judgment. Don't underestimate the incredible power of societal oppression to leave deep wounds on a person's psyche. These will emerge intensely in a group setting because of its social nature. The client will need to spend time exploring and working through both his internalized oppression and his anger about external oppression.

While it is hard to miss the effects of prejudice about race or sexual orientation, it is important not to ignore the effect of class on self-esteem. Our culture looks down on people in lower socioeconomic groups, and this can have a profound effect on a person's sense of value. Even a middle-class client who grew up poor or working class may have a deeply buried sense of inferiority linked to this background.

Working with Mixed Cultural Groups.   It can be very beneficial to deal with cultural issues in group therapy, but it isn't easy. Salvendy (1993, p. 76) suggested that "the larger the degree of social and racial polarization in a particular community, the more difficult it becomes to work with mixed groups. The author's experience in working with minority members indicates that dealing with the issue of sociocultural backgrounds early in therapy is a prerequisite to the successful functioning of the group."

Some clients from oppressed groups will lead with rage about their oppression, even to the point of alienating other group members. If they, in turn, react with anger or prejudice, this can result in destructive subgrouping. Other minority clients may completely hide their feelings, even from themselves, especially if they are the only member of their cultural group in the therapy group. They may need much understanding and encouragement to come out with their feelings. Their biggest fear is that their experiences of dismissal and scorn in society will be repeated in the group.

Some clients are members of an oppressed group, but this is not obvious, such as with some gay people. They should be allowed to take their time about bringing up the issue, until they feel some sense of connection with the group. When a client does reveal his feelings about oppression and prejudice, he should be helped to explore in depth what this means to him. Then he will want to hear what the other group members feel toward him about what he has revealed.

Interactions About Prejudice.   Having one or more minority members in a therapy group is a difficult but potentially rewarding situation. Occasionally a group member may express blatant prejudice, and he obviously needs to explore where this comes from. In many cases, however, the group members believe they have no prejudice at all or feel a need to hide any prejudice they do feel. It is a good idea, however, to bypass political correctness and have group members own whatever degree of prejudice they have. The minority client will probably pick it up anyway, and he should certainly be encouraged to speak if he doesn't trust someone who disclaims prejudice. In fact, most of us have some degree of prejudice, great or small, toward oppressed groups, even if we don't believe intellectually that this is good. We have all been raised in a society full of prejudice and this leaves its effects on our psyches no matter how enlightened we may be. It is much better if this is acknowledged, so that people can be honest with themselves and each other.

In fact, if group members can acknowledge their prejudice without feeling too much shame about it, this can allow them to do some important work. The prejudiced person can explore where it came from in his history and work on learning more about the minority person (or persons) in the group. The person who is the object of prejudice can explore her feelings about this and work on how she deals with her shame and anger, and both people can work on their relationship with each other. Earnestly working on the relationship between two such people can be a powerful force of healing for both. Group therapy is a promising modality for working on such difficult societal issues.

Make sure that a minority person is not allowed to tyrannize the group through his victimhood. Some groups, out of their guilt, may refrain from confronting an oppressed person on the way he expresses himself, allowing him to indulge in his rage or suffering. Though members of oppressed groups have experienced real harm at the hands of society, they nevertheless have as much psychological work to do as anyone with respect to this issue, perhaps more. Make sure that you don't shortchange them by focusing only on group members who are prejudiced.

Prejudice and the Leader.   Needless to say, be aware of any prejudice that you may have toward group members different from yourself. Don't assume that because you believe in equality you have no bias. Our social conditioning can have deep and subtle effects on our feelings toward others. If you are a member of a minority group, your group members may have prejudiced reactions to you. Try to help them bring these out and explore them without feeling guilty or shamed. Otherwise your therapeutic alliance with them may be compromised.

Other Issues

Chapter 27 covers a variety of other group issues. I discuss the value of having individual consultations with members who are not in individual therapy with the leader. I look at how to handle concurrent individual and group therapy, and I examine the value of holding weekend retreats with an ongoing therapy group. I also explore the advantages and disadvantages of co-leading therapy groups, and how to work together as co-leaders. Finally, I briefly discuss group psychotherapy training and ethics in group therapy.

☐ Consultations

Over the years I have found it useful to meet individually from time to time with group members to help them with their group work. For those who are also in individual therapy with me, I occasionally devote part of an individual session to this purpose. I meet with others for a consultation approximately once a month. I call it a consultation to make it clear that it is an adjunct to group therapy and not an individual therapy session. I generally meet with clients for a half hour to reduce the cost to them, though an hour is sometimes preferable. In the early stages, consultations can be seen as a way of continuing the pre-group interviews once the person has joined the group. I find it helpful to schedule the first consultation fairly soon after the person starts group. Consultations are then scheduled on a regular basis, but I let clients know that they can ask for a consultation earlier if they feel a need for one. I also will suggest a consultation if I think it is called for.

Consultations serve a multitude of functions. I will discuss each one in turn. The following applies to both consultations and the equivalent work done in individual therapy.

Additional Group Preparation

In the early stages of a client's group work, consultations serve to prepare the client for the group just as the pre-group interviews did. However, you have the advantage of not having to do all the preparation before the client begins the group. It can be very helpful to perform additional preparation after the client has attended one or two group meetings and has an initial sense of what the group is like. The client will often have more specific concerns that can now be addressed in a more incisive way.

Learning to Initiate Interactive Work

At first new members often don't understand how to initiate interactive work. Though it has been described to them and they have observed other group members interacting, it is so threatening for many people to initiate interactive work that they avoid comprehending what it means. In a consultation, away from the anxiety and pressure of the group setting, clients can reveal their feelings about the group and other group members and learn how to bring them up in group. I frequently ask how the client feels toward the group as a whole, what it is like for her being in the group, and how the group is working for her. These feelings are then discussed so they can be brought up in group. The discussion is never done in place of the client's speaking about these things in group.

In early consultations, I frequently ask the client to consider each group member in turn and share with me her feeling reactions toward that person. *For example, a client might say, "I like Joan, but I'm afraid she's not interested in me. She hasn't seemed to notice me." Then I might say, "You could tell that to Joan."* Sometimes clients are shocked about my suggesting that they be so direct, but this brings home in a clear way how to initiate interactive work, and people are often able to do it. It also gives the client an opportunity to express reservations and fears about direct interactions. You can then address her reservations and work with her on her fears.

> For example, a client may say that she doesn't want to say certain things because she doesn't have the right to judge others. I can then explain that she is supposed to express her feeling reactions to others and this is not the same as judging them.

Whenever you set up work in a consultation for a client to do in group, it is important that the client be in charge of when (or whether) to do the work. Remember, you are a consultant, not a director. People often have fears about initiating work, and you don't want them to unconsciously resist you rather than dealing with their fears. If a client consistently does not initiate the work she needs to, you must challenge her. However, do your best to convey that you are concerned about her not getting what she needs from group, not that you are displeased that she didn't follow your suggestions.

Dealing with Feelings from Group

There are various reasons why a group member may need to use a consultation to discuss feelings that came up in group. The general principle is that consultations should be used to discuss feelings that aren't being talked about in the group for the purpose of bringing them out in group. Consultations can sometimes be used to go further than this and explore the feelings, but there should be a clear reason for doing this individually rather than in the group. If the client is too frightened to broach a feeling in group, then the consultation can be a good place to work on her fear of revealing it, which may be separate from the feeling itself. *For example, a client might feel sexually attracted to a group member but might be too afraid or ashamed to talk about it in group. You could then work with the person on her fears about revealing her sexual feelings.* Make sure that the client is not exploring the feeling in the consultation as a way of avoiding doing it in group.

A client may have difficulty talking about a feeling in group for several reasons. She may not feel safe enough to broach a shameful or frightening subject; she may be afraid of hurting someone; there may not have been enough time; she may be afraid of speaking at all; or she may be afraid of feeling vulnerable.

Sometimes a person will talk about a feeling in group but need to process it further in a consultation. This is acceptable as long as she isn't trying to avoid doing it in the group. Sometimes the client is quite upset and needs to do some exploration before the next group meeting in order to resolve her high anxiety or be in a better place to deal with a difficult conflict. She might be so deeply hurt that she needs individual help to be able to return to the group at all. She may need help to return in a constructive way rather than in complete withdrawal or intense rage. In these cases, it can be helpful to allow her to do the exploration outside of group. *For example, sometimes when two group members get into a blame cycle that deteriorates into hurtful name calling, it can be helpful for one or both of them to explore the underlying feelings in the safer circumstances of a consultation. Then, at the next meeting, they can be ready to interact in a more constructive way.* Whenever someone does a significant amount of exploration of a group matter in a consultation, make sure the group is told that this has occurred.

Giving Embarrassing Feedback

Sometimes you need to give a group member feedback about some problematic behavior, perhaps because the other group members aren't doing this or because you think it will be less painful coming from the leader. If the feedback proves very embarrassing for the client, it may be best to give it in a consultation, where she won't have the additional shame of receiving it publicly.

> For example, suppose a client is monopolizing the group's time and the group is allowing this. For someone who is very vulnerable to shame, this feedback could be difficult to hear, especially in the public setting of the group. It might just produce pain and resistance. However, if it is done in the privacy of a consultation, the person might be able to use it constructively.

Rapport

Consultations are also good places to develop better rapport, especially with those clients with whom you have a weak therapeutic alliance. This, of course, should be worked on in group, but sometimes the intimacy of a consultation provides a more congenial atmosphere for this. Consultations are not a substitute for working through the underlying issues behind the lack of rapport, but sometimes a minimal alliance is required for the client to be able to do this work.

Information

In a consultation, you can also afford to spend time obtaining detailed information about a client's current life and history. If done in group, this task might be boring for other group members and bog down the flow of the group's process.

Strategizing About Work

Consultations are an especially good place to help a client strategize about the best way to use the group to work on a particular problem. Sometimes it is preferable to do this exploration in group so that the other group members can add to the discussion. However, it doesn't always happen in the group. There may be too much else going on to allow for this more individual, self-reflective kind of processing. Sometimes a client needs to take more time for this kind of exploration than would make sense in the group. The following are some examples of strategizing.

One client realized that she was afraid of other people's anger, and this made it difficult for her to handle conflict in her life. She wanted to work on this, but no one in the group was getting angry at her. In the consultation, it became clear that she was unconsciously trying to please and placate the group members to prevent them from becoming angry with her. The strategy we developed was for her to let go of this defense and speak her mind even when it might annoy others. Then she would have a chance to work on her fear of anger. Of course, this strategy itself brought up her fear of anger.

Another client told me that he became frightened and tongue-tied when he was called on to talk in front of a group. He had joined the group to work on this, but his fear of talking in groups hadn't materialized in the therapy group. Though he had become comfortable talking in the therapy group, his outside fears hadn't changed. In a consultation, I suggested that he tell the group about his fears, and then notice what it felt like at that moment to be the center of attention of the group. When he tried this at the next group meeting, his stage fright came up immediately, and he was able to work on it directly in the moment.

Re-Evaluation

Sometimes clients no longer know what they should be working on in group, and no work is coming up spontaneously in the normal flow of the group. This can mean either that the person is finished with her work in group and ready to terminate, or that she needs to think more deeply about her goals. In any case, this is a good time for a re-evaluation. The person should ponder her larger goals for herself in therapy and in life. In what ways does she now want to change, especially in the interpersonal area? Once she answers this question, she can explore whether the group might still be useful in this process. This often results in a clearer understanding of goals and renewed interest in participating in the group. Or if the person is indeed ready to terminate, this will become clear. Though a client can do this work in the group, consultations are sometimes a good place for it.

Translating Group Gains into Life

Sometimes a person will make significant changes in the way he relates to people in group, but this doesn't naturally translate into improved behavior in his outside life. Then additional work is needed to understand how he may be blocking this from happening. This could be done in the group, but sometimes a consultation is a more appropriate setting for this.

Concerns About Dissipating Group Energy

Many group therapists worry that a client may dissipate her energy for a group issue by exploring it outside group. For this reason, some are wary of consultations. Although it is certainly true that you don't want clients doing work outside of group that should be done inside, I haven't found this to be a significant problem. In consultations, I encourage clients to mention any group issues that might be on their mind. In most cases, we explore these issues only enough to prepare the client to talk about them in the group. However, in some cases, as discussed above, I do explore an issue more deeply with a client, and this usually enhances her ability to use the group rather than detracting from it. In an interactive group, the most important issues are interpersonal ones with other group members (or with the group as a whole), and these can't be fully addressed except by talking with that person (or the group). Therefore, even if I help a client access, in a consultation, the deeper intrapsychic origins of a reaction to a group member, she still needs to deal with that person at the next session. Although it may be preferable to do access work in group rather than in a consultation, nothing crucial is lost, especially if the client tells the group about her individual exploration.

☐ Concurrent Group and Individual Therapy

The Value of Concurrent Therapy

It can be very effective for a client to be in group and individual therapy at the same time. In fact, for most clients who can afford the time and money, I recommend concurrent therapy. Each modality provides a different therapeutic environment with its own special advantages. The advantages of group therapy are discussed throughout this book. Individual therapy provides a more intimate setting for the transference relationship and more time for the client to discuss outside issues.

Additional Information About the Client.   When a therapist has a client in both group and individual therapy, this is called *combined therapy* (see Lipsius, 1991; Porter, 1993). When this happens, the therapist is often surprised to see completely different sides of the person in the two settings. This may give you important insights about the person that would otherwise be unavailable. In individual therapy, you only have the client's report on how she relates to people and your observations of how she relates to you. When you also see an individual client into a group, you may get surprising information about how she actually relates to others. The person may be unexpectedly narcissistic or hostile, for example, outside the protected individual setting. On the other hand, you may be surprised at the client's wealth of interpersonal resources that you never see in the individual setting. In any case, these additional perspectives on clients can be enormously helpful in understanding them.

Adding Individual Therapy to Group.   Some group members need to be in individual therapy in order to benefit from the group. Some are so stirred up by the power of group work that they need to take a significant amount of time in individual sessions to process material that emerges in group. Others have difficulty talking in group and need the individual setting to explore this block, so they can begin to use the group more productively. For some clients, in fact, concurrent therapy is the only way they can tolerate being in a group, and the individual exploration and support makes it possible for them to benefit from a group that would otherwise be overwhelming or impossible for them. When doing this kind of out-of-group processing, it is helpful when the client can bring into the group what happens, either by reporting on it or using it to initiate interactive work.

A group member may also profitably add individual therapy on a temporary or permanent basis under the following circumstances (Rutan & Stone, 1993, pp. 227–228): (a) The client uncovers material during group, such as sexual abuse, that requires individual exploration. (b) The client has an external crisis and temporarily needs extra support. (c) The group work itself creates a crisis for the client, who needs individual help to deal with it.

When a group member decides to begin individual therapy with the group leader, you often find out much more about the details of the person's inner life and history. These things may not have come out in group because the person didn't feel safe enough to access them or because there simply wasn't enough time. This additional information is often helpful in working with the person in group. In addition, the work on access that typically occurs in individual therapy sometimes provides clients with additional therapeutic skills and insights that become useful in the group context. In the middle of a dialogue, when access is needed, the client who is experienced with individual therapy (currently or in the past) often can quickly achieve the depth required. There are also times when deep feelings emerge in group that can't be fully processed because of time constraints or the needs of other group members. If the client is concurrently in individual therapy, she can take up the work later that week.

Problems with Concurrent Therapy

According to Salvendy (1993), Rutan and Alonso presented the following possible reasons for not using concurrent therapy:

Concurrent treatment is contraindicated when another treatment modality would be an expression of resistance, when the patient cannot tolerate competition for the primary object, and when the differences between the two treatment modalities threaten to overwhelm the patient's defenses. (p. 83)

Conjoint Therapy

Often a client will be in individual therapy with one therapist and group with another, called *conjoint therapy*. This arrangement can be quite successful, especially if there is good communication between the two therapists. Whenever someone joins a group of yours who is in individual therapy with someone else, make sure to contact the individual therapist (after getting the client's permission) so the two of you can work together in treating the person.

Conjoint therapy can be problematic if the two therapists use methods that conflict with each other, either in their general approach to therapy or in their understanding of how to work with their joint client. This can confuse the client or create a situation where the therapists are working against each other. However, this is rare; in most cases, different approaches to therapy can complement each other, especially if the two therapists are collaborating with each other.

Another danger of conjoint therapy is that the client will split the therapists, perceiving one as all good and the other as all bad. Borderline clients are notorious for doing this. They will tell the "bad" therapist what he is doing wrong and how much he is hurting them, and how wonderful the other therapist is. If you aren't on the lookout for this, it can pit the group and individual therapists against each other, where one therapist begins to believe that the other is incompetent and the other feels angry and defensive, thus derailing the person's therapy. The best remedy for this is clear communication between the therapists and an understanding of the dynamics of splitting (Porter, 1993, p. 322).

☐ Weekend Retreats

I hold weekend retreats for my long-term ongoing groups once or twice a year and have found them extremely valuable. The entire group goes away for a weekend to a rural setting where we sleep in the same house, cook meals together, and hold five or six group meetings during the weekend. These retreats have a profoundly positive effect on a group throughout the year even though they happen only at roughly 6-month intervals.

Depth and Intensity of Work.   It is common for therapists to offer weekend workshops, but usually these are open to all clients in their practices or to the general public. This means that most of the participants are strangers to each other at the beginning of the workshop. These workshops can be intense and quite valuable, and to have a retreat for an ongoing group has a number of additional advantages. Because the group is already cohesive and the group members already trust each other and the leader, they can move into their work more quickly and with greater safety. Compared with a weekly 2-hour meeting, a retreat allows work to build in depth and intensity throughout the weekend. Clients don't have to pull themselves out of an introspective and emotional place after 2 hours to go back out and function in the ordinary world. Therefore weekend retreats often produce a depth of access and degree of healing that goes beyond what usually happens in weekly meetings, and a degree of connection that is impossible in workshops with strangers.

Group Bonding.   In addition, group members have a much greater opportunity to get to know each other in extra-group settings—carpooling to the retreat, planning and preparing meals together, taking walks in the country, chatting between group meetings, and engaging in other social activities during the weekend. This brings up much additional material to be dealt with in group. In fact, some clients have an easier time relating in the semi-structured group setting, and more trouble in social settings. Therefore a weekend retreat may trigger additional anxieties that are valuable to work on in group. For example, people may feel insecure about their conversational skills, anxious about being left out of social groupings, or afraid of being trapped with the group for the weekend.

During the weekend, the group feels even more like a family than usual. This also brings up powerful feelings—positive and negative—that lead to deeper work. The intensity of the work and the extra personal contact produces a much higher level of group bonding and cohesiveness during the weekend.

Human beings evolved to live in extended families and tribes, and yet the fragmentation of our modern society tends to preclude the kind of close group connection that we need for our soul's nourishment. The live-in nature of the retreats touches deeply into clients' psyches by capturing some of this communal experience. Weekend retreats are often the high point of a group's time together, with members feeling deep levels of caring and love for each other and closeness with the group. This then carries over into the regular group meetings, propelling the group forward in its work together.

Suggestions

Retreats usually need to be scheduled 3 or 4 months in advance so that everyone is free on the same weekend. I usually wait until a group has been meeting for 3 to 6 months and has developed a certain level of cohesiveness before scheduling a weekend. People should be encouraged to explore their fears about a weekend retreat when it is first being scheduled and also during the meetings preceding the weekend.

Handling Vulnerable Clients.   Because the work can be intense during a weekend, pay close attention to any clients who may be catapulted into deeper material than they can handle. Make sure that extra support is provided for them, either by you or other group members. If a client seems overwhelmed, make sure that he refrains from further work until he regains his inner stability. Clients may need to defend against deeper feelings that are triggered by the intensity of a weekend. Respect their caution.

It can be difficult for some clients to make the transition from the intensity and openness of a weekend retreat to ordinary life afterward. Some may feel depressed at the loss of the closeness; encourage these clients to call you or other group members for support if necessary. Others may have difficulty readjusting to life with a spouse or other family members who aren't as open and accessible as people on the weekend. It is wise to end the weekend with a discussion of how to handle the transition to one's regular life.

It usually isn't a good idea to bring in a new group member soon before a weekend because she won't be integrated into the group. If she gets into emotional trouble during the weekend, she won't have the support she needs.

Post-Weekend Processing. It is usually valuable to spend the entire group meeting after a weekend processing what transpired during the weekend and afterwards. Often a great deal of opening and healing has happened. Some people simply need to share with the group the growth they have made. Others may have opened up deeper issues that need to be explored further. Some may have encountered difficulties after the weekend that need to be processed. The group also needs to reflect on and consolidate the increase in closeness that has occurred. For this reason, it isn't advisable to introduce a new person into a group for a while after a retreat.

☐ Co-Leading

In this section, I discuss group leadership by two therapists. Co-leading has many advantages as well as some dangers.[12] However, despite the many points in its favor, economic considerations will probably curtail its use in the years to come. It introduces an extra expense for group therapy at a time when cost effectiveness is more important than ever (Rutan & Stone, 1993, p. 162).

I personally think that co-leading is an excellent way to learn how to lead groups and to develop one's skills as a group therapist. I co-led exclusively for the first 10 years of my experience as a group leader, and it was valuable for me during that phase. Since then I have rarely done it because I now rarely feel the need for a co-leader.

Advantages of Co-Leading

Advantages for the Leaders. One of the obvious advantages of co-leading is that there are two therapists present to notice hidden dynamics, group resistances, interpersonal patterns, and non-verbal clues. There are two people who can tap into their creativity in dealing with the multitude of group interactions. If you are having an "off-day," your partner will likely catch things you miss. If you have difficulty conveying a meaning to a client, your co-leader can help. If a client is resisting you on a given day, he might be more receptive to your partner.

Co-leading provides an opportunity for the two therapists to take different roles in the group (Levine, 1979, p. 304). One can be more supportive and the other more challenging; one more empathic and one more insightful. It allows one leader to focus

---

[12] For a fuller discussion of coleading, read *The Art of Cotherapy* (Roller & Nelson, 1991).

for a moment intensively on one client or pair of clients while the other scans the group as a whole to see how this work is affecting the other members.

Co-leaders can also learn from each other (Roller & Nelson, 1993, p. 305). When you are having a countertransference problem, your partner can notice it and help you explore it. It is very helpful for co-leaders to spend time after each group meeting discussing what has transpired, sharing their ideas and intuitions about the meeting, supporting and critiquing each other's work, coming to a joint understanding of each client's patterns and underlying issues, and planning strategy for the next meeting. Co-leading keeps you from being isolated, which is a big problem in private practice. Co-leaders should schedule enough time to discuss each group meeting fully, and institutions that use co-leaders should set aside time for them to do this.

When a group member has negative feelings toward one leader, it is especially helpful to have a co-leader to facilitate, so you don't have to wear two hats at once (Yalom, 1995, p. 415). This is discussed further below.

Advantages for the Members.   Co-leading has direct advantages for the group members as well (Roller & Nelson, 1993, p. 307). With a male–female co-leading term, the members have a chance to work on both mother and father transference with the leaders. Such a group closely resembles a family, with all the possibilities this brings for both accessing old pain and creating a healing situation. The co-leaders can model a healthy relationship with each other, thus helping clients to see what is possible and providing healing for clients who grew up in families with troubled marriages. A male–female pair of co-leaders also guarantees that each client will have a leader of the same gender to identify with.

Clients who have serious difficulties with one gender have the opportunity to be supported by the leader of the "safe gender" while dealing with their issues with the other leader (Roller & Nelson, 1993, p. 307). *For example, a woman who is terrified of men might not be able to be in a group led by a single male leader, but with a male–female team, she can rely on the support of the woman leader while dealing with her negative transference with the man.*

Disadvantages of Co-Leading

Relationship Problems.   The primary disadvantage of co-leading is that the relationship between the leaders has a major impact on the viability of the group (Yalom, 1995, pp. 416–417). Difficulties in their relationship can be so destructive that the group would be better off with only a single leader. If there is competitiveness between the leaders, lack of respect, buried resentments, feelings of hurt, or other problems, these must be actively worked on for the sake of the group. These difficulties cannot be swept under the rug or the group will suffer. Group members will sense problems between the leaders, consciously or unconsciously, causing them to feel unsafe and recreating dysfunctional family dynamics. The group therapy situation is an intense emotional cauldron and the leaders are not immune to the affective pulls of a group. Any problems between them are likely to be magnified in such a setting and can wreak havoc.

Most pairs of therapists must go through a phase of working through difficulties between them before solidifying their working relationship. Various authors have delineated the developmental stages of a co-therapist relationship (Roller & Nelson, 1993, pp. 305–306), and these have some similarity to those of a therapy group (see chapter 21). These stages must be negotiated by the co-leading team with as much honesty, attention, and commitment to work on themselves as is required for the group members. Of course, most if not all of this work should happen outside of the group, in meetings between the leaders or in supervision, but for co-leading to be successful, it requires considerable effort.

A co-leader team won't work well together if the leaders have significant differences in theoretical orientation to leading groups, because they might not respect each other's perspective and would often want to go in different directions. Similarly, co-leaders with personality clashes should not try to lead together. This means that co-leaders should exercise considerable care in choosing each other (Yalom, 1995, pp. 417–418), and they should not be lightly thrown together. Likewise, it is not advisable for co-leaders to become involved romantically, because if they break up, the group is left with either a dysfunctional co-leading pair or the loss of one leader.

Splitting.   Another disadvantage of co-leading is that it sets the stage for the possibility of splitting, a defense commonly used by clients with borderline issues. A client might see one leader as all good and the other as all bad, and he might pit the therapists against each other in order to drive them apart. If not seen for what it is, splitting can cause considerable difficulties between the leaders. Similar problems can come up when some (or all) of the group members seem to favor one leader over another in certain ways. If most of them see one leader as more accomplished, more insightful, or more caring, this can be very difficult for the other leader. The two leaders must have genuine respect for each other professionally to weather such a situation and use it for the group's benefit.

Differences in Leader Activity.   A co-leader can feel inadequate in certain ways even without negative feedback from the group. This commonly happens when one leader is less active than the other. It is easy for him to think he isn't contributing enough or that the group members see him as secondary. The co-leaders must explore this together. If one leader is less active because of insecurity, he must work on this, perhaps in his own therapy, and the other leader must be sure to make enough room for him. If the difference in activity comes more from a disagreement over therapeutic orientation, this must be worked out between the leaders. Perhaps the less active leader believes that the group needs less intervention, and the other leader is talking too much and robbing the group members of the opportunity to take more responsibility for themselves. A leader who favors a less active style can't assert this by simply doing it, because when he is silent, the other leader will take over. The leader favoring less activity must have the courage to challenge his partner, and the leaders must resolve this difference between them, usually outside of group. They need not completely agree, but there must be room for both leaders' ideas about how to run the group.

Technique

Working Together.   It isn't a particularly good idea for the leaders to split up their work in a contrived fashion, such as one leader facilitating an entire piece of work and then the other taking over. This should be done only when first co-leading together or to get through a particular situation when they are experiencing difficulties in their relationship. Otherwise the leaders should share the facilitating and learn to support each other's efforts.

Once one leader has started in a certain therapeutic direction with a client (or the group), the other leader should support and augment this direction unless she feels the first leader has made a mistake. If it seems that the leader in charge has made a serious blunder, she should bring it up explicitly at the time and suggest a different direction. Otherwise, it is better to allow the first leader to try his approach for a while and then if it hasn't worked, the second leader can move things in a direction she prefers. Be sure to avoid undercutting the other leader by taking the work in a different direction without discussion. This usually happens when the second leader doesn't realize that she is undercutting the first leader's approach. If this happens repeatedly, it leads to resentment from the other leader and confusion in the group.

Handling Disagreements.   It can be valuable for co-leaders to discuss differences in strategy in front of the group if they have a good enough relationship to handle any disagreements with cooperation and mutual respect. This is good modeling for the clients and keeps things explicit that otherwise might be confusing for them. More serious problems between the leaders should probably be worked through outside of the group unless they have a mature working relationship and a seasoned, high-functioning group. If difficulties between leaders become apparent to the group, it may be necessary to acknowledge this and explain that you will be working on it with each other later.

Clients' Interactions with a Leader.   When a client initiates an interaction with one of the leaders, especially a negative one, the other leader should take the facilitator role. This allows the leader who is involved in the interaction to attend to her own feeling responses and to choose how to share these for the benefit of the client. The facilitating leader can concentrate on helping the client explore his feelings, and the involved leader can concentrate on her responses to the client. Even though the involved leader may occasionally need to also provide some facilitation, this division of roles helps to prevent her from being thrown off by a client's attack. In addition, the client often feels safer and more supported by the facilitating leader and is therefore more willing to explore transference and to own his part of the problem. The facilitating leader must be careful not to defend his co-leader. If this happens, or is perceived to be happening by the client, he may feel that the leaders are ganging up on him and become mistrustful of both of them.

☐ Group Psychotherapy Training

Though much could be said on this topic, I will restrict myself to a few remarks directed to therapists who seek training in group therapy. There are three crucial aspects of your training: (a) a theoretical understanding of group therapy; (b) your own personal experience in a therapy group or training group; and (c) supervised experience leading groups.

Personal Therapy.   I think that the most important part of a therapist's training is her own therapy, for several reasons: (a) This gives you a chance to work through any personal issues that might limit your effectiveness as a therapist. (b) It provides an opportunity to experience and observe another therapist in action. (c) It gives you an understanding of what your clients are going through from the inside. For such an intimate, personal, and intuitive undertaking as psychotherapy, this is absolutely necessary. Therefore, I believe that every therapist needs extensive experience with her own therapy, including each particular modality you intend to practice. Thus, if you are going to lead groups, you need to have experience as a member of a therapy group. You can join either an ordinary therapy group or a training (or process) group with other students or therapists, where you gain personal experience as well as professional understanding.

It is customary in some training centers to make a distinction between therapy groups and training groups. The difference is that training groups don't go into as much depth and members don't share as much of their personal lives and history (Day, 1993). There seems to be an assumption that the members don't feel safe enough to go into as much depth with other professionals or students, and therefore they need a different kind of group. However, this has not been my experience. As part of my group therapy training center, I have led many training groups over the years. These long-term groups provide both group therapy for mental health professionals (and students) and training in leading groups. In these groups, the members have no difficulty engaging in fully vulnerable work with professional peers. If anything, these groups go even deeper than ordinary therapy groups because of the psychological sophistication of their members. Therefore, I see no reason why training groups can't be full therapy groups.

Supervised Experience.   There is also no substitute for leading your own group under supervision. It is valuable to do this with a co-leader, if possible, because you can learn a great deal from each other as well as from your supervisor. I recommend taping your group sessions and listening to each one afterward in detail. You will learn a tremendous amount from going over what happened in the group and noticing how your intervened, and you will have much more pointed questions to bring to your supervisor. Each therapy group is different, so get experience with a number of groups if possible.

In addition, many other training modalities have been used successfully, such as co-leading with your trainer, taking turns leading a practicum group, and paying attention to process in a supervision group.

Life-Long Learning.   Don't expect yourself to be an expert leader after 1 or 2 years of training. Group therapy is very complex, as is the human psyche, and it takes many years to become accomplished at this endeavor. Allow yourself to be a learner rather than having to impress others with your skill, not only when you are a student but also during your first 5 or more years as a professional. In fact, we all need to keep learning, no matter how experienced we are.

Even after your training is finished, make sure that you have someone you can turn to for supervision when necessary. If you are leading only one group, you may not need weekly supervision or even regular supervisory meetings, but make sure you have a good supervisor on call, even if you simply rely on an experienced colleague.

☐ Ethics

The primary ethical mandate for a group therapist, or any therapist for that matter, is that your priority should always be the growth of the clients. Sometimes you may have to choose between the needs of a client and the needs of the group, but you should never place your own needs above those of a client. No matter how much satisfaction you gain from leading a group, your primary job must be promoting the growth of your group members. This is especially important to remember because clients are often vulnerable and dependent when they enter therapy. Because of emotional problems and lack of knowledge about therapy, they may not be able to assert their own needs. They are trusting you to put their interests first, above your own.

Most ethical guidelines apply to all forms of therapy, not just group therapy, and therefore I will not cover them in this book. Two guidelines are specific to therapy groups: (a) Do your best to prevent group members from exploiting each other in their contacts outside of group. This was dealt with in chapter 20. (b) Be careful of dual relationships between a leader and group members within a training setting. The problem is that students or trainees in group therapy need to have a personal group therapy experience as part of their training. This often occurs in training or process groups set up by the school or training organization. If the students are also being graded or evaluated, this should not be done by the leader of a training group, because this is a therapeutic relationship that shouldn't be contaminated by evaluation. A client needs to be able to trust his therapist to be nonjudgmental, and this is impossible if the same person is also evaluating the client as a student.

Specialized Groups

So far I have focused on general purpose, interactive therapy groups for adults. This, of course, is just one of many possible kinds of groups; however, it is a good baseline for understanding groups. It includes the broadest range of clients and holds the greatest potential for deep character change. It is also the kind of group that has been most studied. This doesn't mean, however, that it is the best type of group for most clients. Many need to be placed in other kinds of groups for any number of reasons.

In addition to a variety of groups, there are also a variety of different types of work that can take place in a psychotherapy group. This book has focused primarily on unstructured interaction between members. This chapter will first describe other group modalities, which can be used in a variety of ways by the creative group therapist—sharing and support, individual work, psychoeducation, advice and homework assignments, social skills training, structured exercises, and role-playing. This information is then used to discuss how to design groups to deal with special problems, populations, and settings.

Any of the following modalities can be included in an interactive group or can be the basis for a specialized group. Sometimes a group consists almost exclusively of one modality, such as a support group or a psychodrama group. In other cases, a group may use three or four different modalities. For example, the interactive groups that I have described in this book consist primarily of unstructured interaction and sharing/support, with occasional individual work and role-playing. Other groups might have different mixes of modalities.

☐ Sharing and Support

This is the primary activity that occurs in what is called a "support group" (Carroll, 1993, p. 205; Lederberg, 1993; Lego, 1993, p. 471). Group members talk to the group about events in their lives that are difficult for them. This sharing usually includes expressing feelings that are evoked by these events. It may or may not also include some exploration of the personal issues and psychodynamics behind the events and feelings.

The group members respond with respectful, empathic listening and support. They often express empathy and compassion, and they may also describe how they identify with what the person is sharing. They may or may not give advice or try to help the person solve specific practical or psychological problems that are presented. This modality does not include access or other extended psychotherapeutic work. It also doesn't include interactive work between members or between one person and the group.

Sharing/support is particularly good for groups of people who have a lot in common, because when they share their life struggles, they really understand each other. This modality is frequently used with homogeneous groups, such as those for incest survivors, alcoholics, or cancer patients. It is a relatively unthreatening modality, because it involves neither deep psychological work nor interpersonal confrontation. Therefore, it can be used with cautious or unsophisticated people.

I discussed earlier the powerful benefits from sharing potentially shameful things in a group and receiving acceptance and understanding. This is especially true when a person is sharing with other people who have been through something similar, because their understanding is based on personal experience.

With a little structure, this modality can be the basis for leaderless self-help groups (Lieberman, 1993) because there isn't too much danger that such a group can get in trouble without professional leadership. This modality was pioneered by Alcoholics Anonymous and other 12-step groups. To ensure safety, there is usually an agreement that the person who is sharing will not be not interrupted until he is finished. There may also be restrictions on how members are allowed to respond to the person sharing. Sometimes no response is allowed at all, and sometimes there are rules against expressing judgments of the person who is sharing. If a skilled leader is present, such restrictions aren't necessary because the leader can prevent or handle potentially harmful interactions.

Sharing/support in homogeneous groups is especially useful for clients who feel ashamed about their psychological problems and may hide them from others, such as bulimics (Harper-Giuffre & MacKenzie, 1993). It is also valuable for clients who have been rejected or judged by society, such as gays (Hawkins, 1993). It is also helpful for clients who may feel that they are the only ones with this problem or with such a severe problem. It is a wonderful relief to share with others who feel the same way, who have gone through similar struggles and who know from the inside what the person is talking about. This builds community and trust and guards against isolation and self-denigration.

☐ Individual Work

This modality includes individual work focused on outside issues or individual work that was triggered by a group interaction but then evolves into extended depth work. Individual work that involves an interaction with the group as a whole is included under "unstructured interaction" and has been covered earlier in the book, especially under the *Intervention Choices* section in chapter 17.

Advantages of Individual Work in Group.   This kind of work is similar to that done in individual therapy so I won't say too much about it. However, it is worth noting the advantages of doing this work in a group setting. One is that individual work may be triggered by an interaction between the client and other group members or by feedback she receives from the group.

> For example, Jennie became enraged at the way Sylvia was acting. The leader encouraged Jennie to explore her childhood for the possible roots of her vehement reaction. She realized that it derived from mother transference, and this led to an extended piece of work about Jennie's relationship with her mother. Because of the potent trigger of the transference, Jennie was able to achieve deep access.

One person's individual work may be triggered by simply watching another person's individual work. In groups where individual work is the primary modality, if one client does deep, emotional work, it may strongly affect several other group members. Whoever works next will already be launched into her process, so it is usually easy to uncover new insights and access deeper levels of emotion than if the work were done in an individual session.

Another advantage is that other group members can be used as projection screens by the client who is working. When a client needs to experiment with new behavior, the leader can suggest that she try saying certain things to the other group members. This is not the same as interactive work, because the other members are generally not asked to respond. They are just there as people to project onto. This process can evolve into role-playing (see below).

Feedback.   After a client does a piece of individual work, even one that does not involve the group, it is important for her to receive feedback and support from the other members. These responses are often healing for the core issue uncovered in the work. It also helps the client to know she is not alone with her struggle and that she is understood and cared for. As I have discussed earlier, there is something about the public nature of such work that has additional healing consequences for many clients. The person experiences that she has done important processing in a healthy community rather in isolation.

Clients often learn a lot from simply watching others work. They learn about how to work on themselves, and they may identify with specific aspects of the work that is being done, giving them insight into themselves. This process can be enhanced if, while one person is working, you encourage the other group members to notice what similar feelings they may have and explore themselves silently. In a mature group of this nature, the other members can often do profitable work on themselves during each person's individual work.

☐ Psychoeducation

An important part of psychotherapy, especially with new clients, is educating them about psychology and the therapy process. This is done partly through the normal interventions used by a therapist—questions, suggestions, or interpretations. In a group, new members learn a lot by watching experienced members work. Education can also be done explicitly in a group; whenever a question arises, the leader may explain a concept to a particular client or to the group. In interactive groups, I explicitly educate clients especially during the pre-group interview and the first few months of a group.

In some groups, this educational component can be a very important part of the process. This is especially useful in short-term groups for specific populations or problems (Golden, Halliday, Khantzian, & McAuliffe, 1993, p. 272; MacKenzie, 1993, p. 427). If you are leading a group for eating disorders, for example, it would be useful to discuss the typical psychodynamics behind eating disorders and to teach members how to manage their eating process. This is much more efficient than having to educate each person separately in individual therapy.

Some groups are designed to be entirely psychoeducational, with little or no actual psychotherapy. There may be an organized curriculum to be covered on a week-by-week basis. This can be especially helpful in introducing certain populations to basic psychological knowledge about a specific problem. Because the members are not expected to reveal any personal material, these groups are even less threatening than support groups, and therefore they may be accessible to an even larger number of people, especially as their first taste of psychological counseling. Group members may discuss some of their personal struggles, but only if they chose to, and the leader usually doesn't encourage them to explore this to any depth.

Advice and Homework Assignments

Advice.   In some cases, especially with lower-functioning or younger clients, it may be helpful to give a client advice about how to handle a specific problem. *For example, a client who is in crisis and isolating herself may be told to call friends when she is upset. A woman who is having difficulty with her landlord may be encouraged to approach him in a particular way. A man working on sobriety may be told to call a group member or his sponsor when he is in danger of taking a drink.* This advice can come from the leader or other group members. In an interactive group, we minimize advice-giving, but with certain populations and group formats, it can be quite useful. This is especially true of problem-focused groups, because the advice may be relevant to many of the members and because more experienced group members may give useful help to newer ones.

Outside Contracts.   In an interactive group, when a client becomes aware of problematic behavior patterns, it can be useful to suggest ways to work on them outside of the group. In chapter 9, I discussed various forms of contracts that the leader might make with a group member for work in the group. For example, the member might agree to be aware of certain feelings when they arise or to experiment with new behavior. These contracts are also useful for work outside the group. *If a client learns that he tends to please others instead of thinking about what he wants, the leader might ask him to try to be aware of when this happens during the week.* I tend to use in-group contracts for interpersonal issues because the group is such a powerful place for this work, but some issues must be explored outside the group. For example, eating, sex, and work issues all occur only outside the therapy setting, so outside contracts are necessary.

Homework Assignments.   Cognitive-behavior therapy often features home-work assignments (Fay & Lazarus, 1993), and they are useful in other types of therapy as well. Assignments are particularly useful in problem-focused groups, where all members are dealing with a similar issue, because they can easily learn from each other's work. Homework assignments work especially well in group settings because clients feel an added pressure to do the assignment knowing they will be reporting back to the group the following week. In addition, clients are encouraged by seeing what other members have gained from doing their assignments. In a more structured group format, the same assignment may be given to the whole group, to be discussed at the next meeting. This also helps the clients to take the assignment seriously and to learn from each other. *For example, in an eating disorder group, clients might be told to keep track of everything they eat during the next week, or to notice what emotions they feel whenever they have an impulse to binge or purge.*

☐   Social Skills Training

Groups are especially useful for helping members to learn new social skills or improve existing ones. This can be done in three different ways.

1.   Groups may be designed for low-functioning clients who need help in developing minimal social skills (MacKenzie, 1993, pp. 426–427). The leader is directive and supportive and uses education and feedback. Members learn by interacting with each other in the group and through homework assignments, sometimes to be done with each other.

2.   In an interactive group, clients improve their social and communication skills through the ordinary workings of the group process, especially through feedback and experimenting. Though there is a focus on deeper interpersonal and psychodynamic issues, clients also get concrete feedback on difficulties they have with interpersonal skills and have a chance to learn new, more effective behavior.

3.   Behavior therapy groups can also be designed to help clients learn or improve social skills (Fay & Lazarus, 1993) through role-playing and homework assignments. Some groups are designed for clients to learn a specific social skill, such as assertiveness or dating skills, whereas others work with a variety of skills.

☐   Structured Exercises

There are a wide range of different psychological exercises that can be done with groups.

1.   *Guided fantasy or meditation.* The therapist leads the group through a certain imagined scene or story, leaving parts of it open to be filled in by the images of each member. This can be used for accessing core issues by having clients imagine scenes

from their families of origin. It can also help to access healthy capacities such as need, love, aggression, or wisdom by creating stories in which these emotional states are elicited, or by evoking inner images of figures who embody these capacities. Guided fantasy can be used for healing core issues by contacting inner images of healing figures (Earley, 1990). *For example, a classic guided fantasy involves taking a journey to the top of a mountain to meet an ancient wise person who answers questions about the direction of one's life.*

2. *Role-playing.* The leader sets up a scene involving a client's family of origin or other important figures in his life, and group members assume various roles. Frequently this is arranged as one person's work with the rest of the group playing the supporting cast. This can be used to access the origins of core issues in the family of origin, and it can also be used for healing by having members play ideal parental figures who provide exactly the healing response that is needed. Role-playing is also excellent for experimenting with healthy behavior, where a client plays a role related to a difficult real-life situation and then tries out specific healthy responses, as in assertiveness training. (See below for a more detailed discussion.)

3. *Questions and exploration in pairs or triads.* The group members form into groups of two or three. The leader specifies a series of questions or discussion topics that are answered in the pairs or triads. The leader often provides some structure to keep the members on track. This is often used for developing insight. With sophisticated groups, it can lead to emotional access or to awareness of one's here-and-now process (see Macy, 1998). *For example, in an eating disorder group, the members of a triad might all be asked to describe their memories of how they felt at the family dinner table.*

4. *Expressive techniques.* Group members engage in forms of self-expression to bring up feelings, clarify meaning, or experiment with fuller expression of emotions. This can be done with expressive gestures and actions, movement or dance therapy, open-ended expression of sound or forms of singing, and various kinds of touch. *For example, yelling and hitting a pillow can be used to express anger and rage. Reaching out with the arms can stimulate yearning or need.*

5. *Art.* Drawing, painting, working in clay, and other art forms can be used for access and expression. Art therapy, of course, is based on this approach.

Jean Houston (1982, 1987) has been very creative in designing structured exercises for psychological healing and personal growth. My book *Inner Journeys* (Earley, 1990) contains detailed examples of exercises inspired by her work, including most of the above types. It also gives group leaders specific guidelines for designing and using such exercises.

Structure Versus Spontaneity.   There are varying degrees of structure involved in these exercises. Some are planned and orchestrated by the leader ahead of time. They may be used in a certain sequence as a group develops, especially in a short-term problem-focused group, or the leader may choose an exercise that seems to fit a certain situation that arises naturally in the group. *For example, if you have an exercise that deals* *with evoking and healing a need for nurturing, this might be used at the point in a meeting where a number of group members are discussing their unfulfilled needs or how they defend against them.*

On the other hand, exercises of this nature can also be created spontaneously to fit whatever an individual member or the group seems to need in the moment. *For example, in the above situation an exercise about nurturing might be created on the spot.* This spontaneous creation is usually done by the leader, but the member who is working or the group as a whole may also create an exercise. When this happens, it may not even be correct to call them "structured exercises." At this point, they are better conceptualized as alternative modes of operation in a group or as a more elaborate forms of experimenting. Gestalt therapists often create experiments of this nature (Zinker, 1977, chap. 7).

Sometimes an exercise is designed not for the work of just one individual but for the whole group. For example, a role-playing situation or certain expressive techniques may be a way for a group to explore its current emotional climate. Furthermore, if there is a common theme or feeling in the group, an exercise may evolve that addresses this group experience.

☐ Role-Playing

I will present a more thorough discussion of role-playing because of my familiarity with it. Role-playing can be used in a structured exercise, such as family sculpting (Satir, 1967) or inner child work (Bradshaw, 1992). However, it can also be used whenever the need arises, as I have discussed at times in this book. In an interactive group, it is especially useful when a client is angry at a member who doesn't really deserve to receive it, and yet the client needs to experiment with expressing the anger. Then it is best to use role-playing to help the client express the anger toward the person involved in the origin of the anger, usually a parent. Role-playing can be used with emotions other than anger as well, but experimenting with transferential anger is a situation that requires it.

Empty Chair Versus Psychodrama

There are two basic ways that role-playing with a parent can be done. (1) The client imagines that the parent is sitting in an empty chair and talks to the chair, as is done in Gestalt therapy. (2) A group member role-plays the parent, as is done in psychodrama.

Advantages of Empty Chair.   The advantage of the empty chair approach is that there is no need to choose a person to take the role and no danger that the role-player's personality and responses will cloud the situation. If a dialogue develops between the client and the parent, you can have the client switch places and sit in the empty chair to role-play the parent, and then switch back, effectively taking both parts of the conversation. The client often learns important things when playing the parent as well.

Advantages of Psychodrama.   One advantage of using a person to play the parent is that some clients have a difficult time talking to an empty chair. They seem to need the presence of a real person to allow them to speak. In addition, sometimes the client needs stimulation to get in touch with his feelings, especially when they involve anger. He may need to hear the parent saying characteristic phrases that embody the way he was harmed or deprived as a child in order to evoke his feelings. In this case, the client should tell the role-player exactly what to say to make him angry. *For example, Ted was exploring his anger at the way he felt judged by his mother. He instructed the woman role-playing his mother to say, "You're not doing it right," and "Why can't you be as good as your brother?"* It can be especially powerful in accessing archaic feelings to hear such phrases said to one's face. Another reason to use group members to play roles is that other family members can be included to produce a fuller experience of the family of origin.

A big advantage of using group members to play parental or other family roles is that they are directly involved in the work. When the client who is working plays all the roles, it becomes individual work with other members just watching. A psychodrama can conceivably involve quite a few group members. This makes the group more lively and interesting for them and may stimulate their own issues as well.

Other Roles

Ideal Parent.   In addition to having members play parents, you can set up role-playing to include healing responses from ideal parents. The is commonly done in psychomotor therapy (Pesso, 1991). An ideal parent is an imaginary figure who provides exactly the healing response that the client needed as a child. *For example, after Ted expressed anger toward his mother, she withdrew from him. The leader arranged to have someone role-play an ideal mother who wasn't frightened of Ted's anger and could remain connected to him.* This should be a different person from the one playing the real mother (actually a negative aspect of the real mother). The ideal parent often says simple sentences that can have a powerful impact because the client is so open after access. *In the above example, the ideal mother said, "I love you even though you are angry at me."* You can obtain the words that need to be said verbatim from the client, if necessary. Touch can also be a powerful part of the healing response, especially if the client is emotionally regressed in playing himself as a young child.

Doubling.   *Doubling* is a technique from psychodrama that can be used to help the client who is working to get in touch with his feelings. A group member (or the leader) briefly pretends to be the client and expresses what she thinks the client is feeling. *For example, when Ted was having trouble getting in touch with his anger toward his mother, a member doubled for him and said to her (as Ted), "I hate the way you always told me I wasn't good enough for you."*

Right after a person doubles, the client reflects on whether the statement was an accurate expression of his feelings. If the double was accurate, the client expresses the feeling in his own words. *For example, Ted might say, "I hate the way you always told me I didn't measure up to you standards."* If it wasn't right, the client expresses what he really feels instead. *For example, Ted might say, "That's not quite right. What I really feel is, 'I hate the way you always told me I was worthless, especially comparing me to my brother.'"* Thus this technique is useful even when the doubling isn't accurate, because it stimulates the client to articulate what he is feeling.

Support Roles.   It can be useful to have group members play support roles, especially when the client is having difficulty expressing anger and is afraid of a hostile response from the parent. The support people usually stand next to or behind the client and also express anger toward the parent. *They may make statements to the parent that are protective of the client, such as "I won't let you harm her," or angry statements such as, "How dare you treat her that way. Stop it right now."* They also may encourage the client to exercise more strength and personal power in the role-play. Support may also be expressed physically through touch.

Choosing Roles.   It is usually a good idea for the client to choose who is to role-play a parent. The more a member resembles the parent, the more he can aid in stimulating the client's feelings. However, make sure that the person chosen really feels OK about playing that role. You don't want a member to comply with the request and then be hurt when the client starts directing intense feelings directed toward him. This can happen even in role-playing. When working with anger, it is also dangerous to use the person in the group who stimulated the client's anger, though this is often the one who most closely resembles the parent. If this person is used, the client may mix up the parent and the group member, and the role-play may become more real than is intended. It is better to use a different group member.

This discussion merely outlines some of the possibilities for using role-playing in groups. This approach has been developed extensively over 60 years in the psychodrama literature (Moreno, 1959), and recently the psychomotor approach (Pesso, 1991) has added to our knowledge of this area.

Expressive Techniques

It can be useful at times in role-playing to have the client use various expressive techniques. For example, in working on the expression of anger, it can help to have the client sit upright or stand up and clench her fists. This gets her body into the natural flow of expression and may undo some of her defenses that are operating at the muscular level. The client might also be given a pillow or other soft object to hit and be encouraged to raise her voice or yell. This is designed to help the client express the anger fully rather than constructively (see chapter 16). These techniques have two purposes: (a) They are designed to aid the client in accessing the buried anger and pain, they can sometimes have a dramatic effect on the person's ability to feel her emotions. (b) They help in accessing and developing healthy capacities, especially those related to autonomy and safety. By expressing anger in a powerful way that is experienced in the body, the client feels a greater sense of healthy aggression, personal power, and ability to protect herself.

Expressive techniques are useful for working with other emotions besides anger. These techniques, which go beyond the scope of this book, are commonly used in Gestalt therapy (Perls et al., 1951), psychomotor therapy (Pesso, 1991), and bioenergetics (Lowen, 1975).

Role-Playing in Supervision

Role-playing can be quite useful in supervision groups. One way to structure this is to have the therapist who is presenting a client role-play that client and the supervisor can work with her as therapist. This gives the supervisor a chance to demonstrate how to work with such a client, but perhaps more important, the therapist often learns a great deal about her client by role-playing him. By stepping into someone else's shoes in this experiential way, you often pick up information about the client that you knew only unconsciously.

Another way to use role-playing is for another member of the supervision group to play the client and have the therapist work with him. This may demonstrate how the therapist is stuck with that client and may also reveal useful countertransference information. The supervisor can facilitate the therapist during the role-play, helping her to access feelings and also to experiment with new ways of working with the client. There are other possibilities. The therapist can play the client and another member can work with her as therapist. This way both can learn from the situation. If the therapist is presenting a group he is having trouble with, the members of the supervision group can role-play the various members of the therapy group.

☐ Homogeneous Groups

In an interactive group, there is a significant advantage to having a heterogeneous mix of personality styles, as discussed in chapter 7. However, for other types of groups there are important reasons for having the group be more homogeneous. In this section, we discuss the properties and advantages of homogeneous groups.

Definition.   Problem-focused groups are homogeneous by definition because they are composed of clients with a similar problem. Groups may also be homogeneous by age (e.g., groups for teenagers), level of functioning (e.g., groups for the chronically mentally ill), gender, race, ethnic group, and so on. Therefore a group may be homogeneous in one way and heterogeneous in another. *For example, an eating disorders group will be homogeneous with respect to problem and probably gender, but it is likely to be heterogeneous with respect to age and other demographic variables.* The crucial issue is whether a group is homogeneous with respect to the major issues that clients will be dealing with in the group. *Thus an eating disorder group is homogeneous in this way, whereas a gay group is homogeneous with respect to sexual orientation and therefore members will share some issues in common. However, if much of the group work revolves around issues not related to sexual orientation, then it may actually be a fairly heterogeneous group.* Time-limited groups are often homogeneous, but many homogeneous groups have no time limits. In fact, there is an advantage to having longer-term homogeneous groups because it means that the group will contain members with varying degrees of experience, and long-time group members can often help those who are new.

Advantages.   A homogeneous group tends to develop trust and cohesiveness quickly because the members can easily identify with each other (Yalom, 1995, p. 262).

Many group members have felt alone with their problems and alienated from others. When a client joins a homogeneous group, he is often profoundly moved to discover a whole group of people who have similar problems and therefore really understand his feelings. It is easy for members to empathize with each other and to respond with compassion and caring. This facilitates rapid self-disclosure and bonding, often moving the group quickly into deep feelings and explorations. This can be very helpful for a time-limited group.

Because of their similarities, group members often have comparable emotional reactions, so they can support each other in expressing and processing them. *For example, rape victims all need to deal with their feelings of violation and rage. Seeing other group members express these feelings helps even a repressed client to get in touch with hers.*

Seeing that others have similar inner struggles helps to universalize one's experience, reducing feelings of isolation and shame. If the group contains experienced members, they can model how to work effectively in the group, and it is easier for clients to learn from people who are similar. In addition, if the advanced members have clearly benefited from the group, they also provide the beginning members with hope that the therapy can work for them, thus enhancing motivation.

Disadvantages.   On the problematic side, homogeneous groups tend to promote merging among the group members, in which they pretend to be more alike than they actually are (van der Kolk, 1993). Such a group can become conformist, with members afraid to take positions that are different from those of the others. Group members can also become overly dependent on one another in a way that is not healing because of a lack of differentiation and individuality. This, of course, corresponds to the entrance and inclusion stages of group development, and if the group moves on into the conflict stage, this will change. However, in groups that aren't designed to include intragroup conflict, this stage doesn't happen. Lack of differentiation can especially be a problem with populations who tend toward compliance and merging anyway, such as adult children of alcoholics, eating disorder clients, and trauma victims. With such populations it may be best to limit the time of a homogeneous group and then move clients into a longer-term heterogeneous group to promote differentiation (van der Kolk, 1993, p. 557).

Technique.   Here are some suggestions for handling the problem of lack of differentiation. If the group structure does allow for open conflict between the members, the leader must be direct and forceful about moving the group into the conflict stage when it is time. You might discuss the lack of confrontation in the group and encourage members to explore their fears of conflict. You may also need to explicitly direct members to experiment with conflict. *For example, I sometimes ask a member to pick someone in the group and express negative feelings toward that person, even if they are minor.*

If the group structure doesn't include conflict, then you will need to emphasize that it is OK for members to be different from each other. Look for clues that a member is suppressing or whitewashing a difference or disagreement with another member, and encourage her to express it. Especially encourage the member to explore her fear of being different and have others discuss their similar fears. This can be an important topic for group exploration. Because the members will all probably have fears of being different, this makes the exploration easier.

In a homogeneous group, there may be a tendency to idealize the group or the leader. "We are special and better than others." "No one understands us except you."

This can help to bolster low self-esteem; it is only a problem if it becomes extreme or if the group turns against the rest of the world. In some cases, it can develop into an "us and them" situation, where people outside the group or people who don't share the group's issue are disparaged or seen as the enemy. As the group matures and is ready, this attitude must be challenged.

☐ Designing Specialized Groups

Let's now look at some additional principles for designing a group for a specialized problem, population, or situation (Yalom, 1995, pp. 449–455).

Level of Functioning

The group will need to be structured differently depending on the age and level of functioning of the members. Groups with younger or lower functioning members will need more structure and input from the leader. All groups need a certain amount of direction from the leader at first, but as the group develops maturity and responsibility, the members should take over many of these functions. Lower functioning groups may not be able to do this because they don't progress as far in the stages of group development (Levine, 1979). Groups of early adolescents or chronic schizophrenics, for example, are not capable of the same kind of relationships with each other that relatively normal adults can achieve, no matter how long the group runs. If you realize these limitations ahead of time, you can organize the work accordingly, and you won't be frustrated when the group doesn't develop beyond a certain point.

Lower functioning members are less able to handle the psychologically demanding aspects of group work, such as emotional access and interpersonal conflict. Groups for these populations should be designed to avoid these stressful areas or to go into them gradually and with extra support.

You should know the level of functioning of each population, so a group can be designed to reflect its vulnerabilities and limitations. Groups for adolescents, children, borderlines, and mentally ill elderly, for example, all have their own limits and possibilities the leader must take into account.

It is crucial to formulate clear goals (for the group and each individual member) that can be reached within the limitations of the population and the group format.

Know Your Population

It is crucial that you know the special characteristics of the population for whom the group is intended, not only to be able to work effectively with them during group meetings, but also to design the group properly. Each population has certain unique needs, vulnerabilities, resistances, psychodynamics, personal goals, and external stressors. For example, with a socially isolated population, you might encourage the group members to have outside contact with one another and perhaps even assign homework related to this. Likewise, a population that needs extra support to deal with suicide risk might benefit from using phone calls or a buddy system. On the other hand, a population known for destructive acting out may need to have very clear rules against outside contact.

Other examples include the following: Children's groups are often designed around crafts or physical activities because of their developmental needs and lack of verbal skills. Certain populations must learn to manage a medical or emotional problem and therefore their groups may be built around psychoeducational work and homework assignments.

Phases in Treatment

Certain problems have defined phases in the treatment process, with different kinds of group work relevant for each phase. For example, it is accepted within the addictions field that clients in early recovery should not be plunged into emotional access because of the risk of relapse (Flores, 1993). However, later in the recovery process, when their sobriety is more solid, they will need to tackle those deeper emotional issues that were behind the need for the substance originally. If the treatment phases are long enough in duration, such as with recovery, this is usually handled by having a different type of group for each phase. If the phases are such that they can be included within a single group, then the group can be structured and organized around the treatment phases. For example, some therapists see the following sequence of phases in the treatment of sexual abuse in children—acknowledgment, stabilization, mastery, uncovering, integration, and transformation (Rice-Smith, 1993). It can be useful to organize a group accordingly. Even though all children in the group will not go through these phases in the same order at the same time, it provides an overall structure that matches the treatments needs of the members.

Know the Context

Be aware of the institutional context in which your group will operate (Yalom, 1995, p. 451). Be clear about what limits are placed on your group design by the clinic or hospital or other situation in which you work, but also recognize what power you may have to change those constraints that are not therapeutic. *For example, if you are expected to lead a group without doing pre-group interviews, you might be able to change this policy. In a hospital setting, if group members are routinely called out of group for other treatment, this can be very disruptive. If you can explain to administrators how this detracts from the efficacy of treatment, this policy might be modified.* Know what attitudes your clients are likely to arrive with, both toward the institution and toward you. *For example, is group therapy seen as a second rate form of treatment in your institution?* Know what other treatment your group members have had in the past and what, if any, they will be having concurrently with your group. Make sure to have as much communication as possible with the professionals providing the other treatment.

Designing the Group

Format and Boundaries.   Use all this information to decide whether the group should be homogeneous or heterogeneous based on the advantages and disadvantages we have discussed. Decide how much can be accomplished in a limited-time group and how many sessions will be needed for this. Does this population require longer term work, and what can be accomplished in this way? Decide how much structure to use and what activities to rule out as too dangerous for this population. What should the rules be with respect to outside contact, payment, attendance, promptness, termination, physical touch, etc.? Any of these boundaries may need to be handled differently with different populations.

Types of Modalities.   Decide what type of psychotherapeutic work will most benefit this particular population and how to provide it. Sharing/support is especially valuable for populations that have been stigmatized or isolated or have to deal with issues of secrecy and shame, as discussed in the last chapter. Psychoeducation work is valuable when there is a straightforward and useful body of knowledge to be imparted. Some issues virtually require deep emotional access work, and with others, useful results can be obtained through social skills training or other behavioral work.

Don't try to use too many different modalities in one group. *For example, an eating disorder group might conceivably include psychoeducation and homework assignments about food, body image exercises, depth work about the mother–daughter relationship, and interactive work on conflict and assertiveness. However, if you try to include all these in one group, there won't be enough time to do any of them very well.* It would be better to stick to a couple of modalities that can be done successfully.

Review the Literature.   Therapists have experimented with a great number of different kinds of specialized groups recently and many of them are being written up in the literature. Check to see what has worked with the problem or population you will be treating. There are a number of good journals covering group therapy, including the *International Journal of Group Psychotherapy* and *Group*, and these contain articles on different types of specialized groups. In addition, there are books containing collections of articles on group therapy, some of which describe specialized groups (Alonso & Swiller, 1993; Kaplan & Sadock, 1993; McKay & Paley, 1992).

CHAPTER

Societal Issues

In this chapter, I look at the relationship between group therapy and society. I examine models of psychotherapy and how they need to place clients within a social context. I explore the current state of the world and its impact on the practice of psychotherapy and consider the possibility that certain forms of psychotherapy can contribute to social transformation. Finally, I look in more detail at how group therapy can promote certain healthy qualities in its clients that can enable them to become transformative citizens.

☐ Models of Psychotherapy

The Medical Model.   Let's step back from the details of psychotherapy and examine what this endeavor really consists of. Originally it grew out of medicine and psychiatry and was intended for the "mentally ill" and other people with rather severe psychological symptoms. Because of these roots, psychotherapy developed according to a medical model that labeled people in therapy as "patients" and identified them as suffering from a disease. Many therapists use medical terms like "prognosis" and "psychopathology."

However, I personally don't find medicine a very useful analogy for understanding what happens in psychotherapy. Psychological problems have their own particular character and need their own model, not one borrowed from a different field.

The "Factory Models."   More recently with the advent of cognitive–behavior therapy, sophisticated psychotropic drugs, and managed care, the medical model has been combined with what we might call a "factory model," which involves an attempt to fix people as if they were malfunctioning machines and to mass produce therapeutic change. This has resulted in efforts to define discrete psychiatric problems that can be cured or ameliorated by either medication or short-term courses of therapy. This approach even spells out how to treat each supposed disease entity in detailed treatment manuals. The person is not treated but rather the "disease." This can be understood as an attempt to provide some form of treatment when there are limited financial and human resources. However, looked at from a societal perspective, it represents a reduction of complex psychological difficulties to a mechanical model that ignores their human, relational, and social implications.

The Growth Model.   Fortunately, there has been another development in the therapy field. More and more people have come to psychotherapists for help in improving their lives in a wide variety of ways. People who don't have severe enough symptoms to warrant an official diagnosis are seeking help with their marriages or problems at work, or want to overcome social alienation or find more aliveness and meaning in life. In addition, many people who initially came to therapy with specific symptoms have stayed to make deeper changes in their personalities and lives. In other words, psychotherapy has evolved into much more than just a way to treat psychopathology.

In the 1960s, humanistic psychology (Maslow, 1971) brought a growth model to the field, reflecting this new orientation. This model sees therapy clients as involved in personal growth aimed not only at resolving conflict and pain, but also at enhancing their ability to relate to others, connect with themselves, and be alive, spontaneous, creative, and spiritual. Human growth is conceptualized as a path with limitless possibilities. I find this model more compatible with the full range of the practice of psychotherapy.

The Person and Society.   However, both these models understand psychotherapy as applying largely to individuals and have little recognition of the relationship between the person and society. Though certain selected theorists (Fromm, 1955; Herman, 1992; Reich, 1970) have made this connection, it has been largely missing from the psychotherapy literature.

In fact, society has a profound impact on the psychology of its citizens. This is obvious in the case of people who are faced with poverty or prejudice and those who are addicted to drugs or are involved in crime. However, the societal impact on individuals goes far beyond this. For example, it is well-known that the types of symptoms and personality disorders that are often seen now in psychotherapy are quite different from those of Freud's day, reflecting how society has changed in the last century. The dysfunctions and distortions of a society are passed on to its members, affecting them psychologically. If, for example, a society overvalues success and undervalues caring, this will be reflected in workaholism among some people and poor self-esteem among others.

In addition, the reverse is also true. The psychology of the members of a society has a profound effect on the society itself. Their relative health and their particular dynamics, strengths, and defenses have an impact on social institutions, and can enhance or impede efforts toward constructive social change. Ideally we need a model of psychotherapy that reflects an understanding of the relationship between individual psychology and society.

Psychotherapy and Society

The Planetary Crisis

Looking at our society historically, we are currently in the midst of a major transition from one era to another (Capra, 1982; Earley, 1997; W. Harman ,1988). For the last 500 years or so, we have been in a historical era called the modern or industrial era. This has been characterized by the triumph of science and rationality and by an emphasis on material consumption and personal ambition. Like all eras, it has had its pluses and minuses. It has brought us a large educated middle class, personal freedoms, and tremendous technological advances. But it has also fostered a mechanized attitude toward life, where other people, other nations, and the natural world are treated as machines to be controlled, conquered, and exploited. We even treat our own bodies and minds as machines, leading to a loss of our aliveness, earthiness, and spirituality. The modern era has also brought us to the edge of ecological catastrophe because we treat the natural world as nothing but resources to be consumed. The increase in social mobility and the dominance of the market economy have largely destroyed our sense of community, and families are disintegrating into increasingly smaller units, creating vast social alienation.

We are currently in a transitional period where the ways of the modern era have become outmoded and our society is breaking down, causing social and environmental problems. Our very success at controlling the world has increased our population and our technological prowess to the point where they are now causing immense problems. Unfortunately, when we try to solve these problems with this same world view, we only make them worse. However, a new world view is emerging that could lead to a new healthier society. It sees nature as a vast interconnected web of life that has value and beauty in itself (Macy, 1998). It sees human beings as precious, emotional, spiritual beings who deserve an opportunity for initiative, creativity, and personal fulfillment.

The breakdown of modern society has led to a profound planetary crisis. We are threatened with ecological disasters (Meadows, Meadows, & Randers, 1992), computer system breakdowns (Laddon, Atlee, & Shook, 1998), or other crises, any of which could also lead to social disintegration, and few of our leaders have any understanding of this. Our most pressing human concern is to facilitate a transition to a healthier society to avoid societal destruction.

Influence of Society on Psychotherapy

Both our psychological problems and psychotherapy itself have been strongly influenced by the current historical situation. The beginnings of the breakdown of our modern society have greatly increased psychological difficulties. The disruptions of family and community, which are vital forces for healthy child rearing, have resulted in greater psychological problems in our children. This transition has been accompanied by a variety of social problems and anxieties that make living in today's world more difficult—drug abuse, homelessness, health problems, terrorism, and genocide. These issues contribute in a myriad of direct and indirect ways to the psychological problems our clients bring to our offices.

On the other hand, the modern era has achieved unprecedented success in solving material and technical problems. This has resulted in an increase in leisure and an expansion of our goals for ourselves and our sense of what is desirable and possible. We are no longer satisfied with simply making a living and raising a family. We now want true intimacy in our relationships. We want initiative, responsibility, and creativity on our jobs. We want satisfaction and meaning in our lives—and people come to therapy to learn how to attain these things. Therefore psychotherapy is facing more prevalent psychological difficulties on the one hand and loftier psychological goals on the other.

☐ Psychotherapy and Social Transformation

Psychotherapy is a diverse field covering a multitude of problems, goals, populations, and attitudes toward healing. Different forms of therapy attend to and represent different aspects of this spectrum. Some types of therapy solve only circumscribed individual problems and otherwise contribute to maintaining the societal status quo. Others foster the kind of therapeutic change that not only makes their client's lives more fulfilling but can contribute to the creation of a new healthy society. The world is in such a serious crisis that if things continue on their current path, we are likely to encounter ecological and social breakdown which will cause immense pain and suffering. Therefore I think that it is our duty as mental health professionals to do what we can to address this global threat to the well-being of all humanity.

Here I will discuss how psychotherapy in general and group therapy specifically can play a small part in promoting the kind of social change we need to move through this transition. As a profession, we can't address all the immense social issues society faces, and we can play only a limited role in contributing to solutions, but we must do what we can.

Is This Ethical?   First let's consider whether psychotherapy should focus on this area at all. Some people would say that isn't our job. Our clients come to us for alleviation of pain or improvement in the quality of their lives, and our job is to give them that and nothing more. Anything else would involve introducing our own agenda into the therapy situation, which is not ethical. I certainly agree that if we were faced with a choice between promoting social change and helping our clients, this would present a difficult ethical dilemma. Convincing clients of a certain political viewpoint is questionable. However, this is not what I propose. I see psychotherapy as contributing to social change in two ways: (a) helping clients develop healthy capacities that will both make their lives more fulfilling and also make them healthier citizens; and (b) educating them about the relationship between their personal problems and society. This doesn't involve distorting the therapy process or promoting partisan political views. If anything, a focus on social issues can enhance what we have to offer to our clients rather than diminishing it.

Symptomatic Relief Versus Character Change.   Psychotherapy can contribute to either maintaining the societal status quo or transforming society in a healthy direction. Forms of therapy that focus exclusively on symptomatic relief or crisis resolution rarely contribute to real character change at an individual level, let alone to social change. They look only at how to help a given individual feel better in the moment, not how to make deeper changes in his personality or world view.

> For example, if a client comes to therapy with a fear of flying, a therapist might design a behavioral treatment involving systematic desensitization. This might actually allow the client to fly, but it wouldn't address any of the deeper psychodynamic reasons for his fears, which are probably affecting other parts of his personality as well. Focusing on these issues would take longer but might produce deeper changes in the person's character, perhaps leading to greater self-esteem or personal power. Even though this more probing therapy doesn't address the issue of social change, it is a step in the right direction, because a healthier person is more likely to contribute to the creation of a healthy society.

Consciousness Raising.

Psychotherapy can contribute to social change by educating clients about the relationship between their personal problems and society, especially about how social conditions contribute to personal problems. This is an explicit goal of feminist therapy dating back to the consciousness raising groups in the seventies, where women explored the relationship between their personal pain and societal oppression of women (Doherty & Enders, 1993, p. 377). This kind of education is especially appropriate for problem-focused groups, where the members share similar problems and perhaps relationships to society.

> For example, in a group for bulimic and anorexic girls, it might be useful to educate them about society's overemphasis on sexual attractiveness for women and its high standard for slimness. They could learn that this is not the only way for women to value themselves.

Consciousness raising is not restricted to feminist issues. *A group for patients with hypertension or ulcers might educate its members about our society's overemphasis on professional success and power as the measures of a man's (or woman's) worth and how this can lead to workaholism and medical problems.*

Adjustment to Society or Health.

Some forms of therapy focus more on helping clients adjust to society rather than achieving personal health, which may require challenging social norms.

> For example, suppose Mike comes to therapy with anxiety about his performance at work. He is actually quite competent and works hard but is afraid to face his boss in meetings and presentations where he is being evaluated. The therapy might address his anxiety about performance and even deal with his deeper need to please authority, which derives from his fear of being judged by his father. However, Mike's anxiety is also related to an intense need to be successful professionally, which he pursues to the detriment of his family life and other personal satisfactions. This need is encouraged by a society that overvalues professional success for men. Will his therapy examine this? If it simply accepts this drive as normal for a man, the therapy would merely help Mike adjust to society instead of helping him find a fuller form of mental health.

If a form of therapy promotes what is most healthy for the client rather than helping him adjust to society, then its clients are more likely to challenge destructive aspects of society. In addition, some forms of therapy have built-in values that intrinsically contradict some of society's shortcomings or lead in healthier social directions.

For example, group therapy challenges the individualistic bias of modern society by the very fact that it happens in a group setting. These kinds of therapy can foster personal attributes in clients that make them more likely to contribute to creating a healthy society.

Personal Qualities and Social Institutions.   Can this really make a difference? Let's look at the relationship between the personal attributes of the members of a society and its social and political arrangements. It is well-known that one can't simply introduce democracy into any existing society and have it work. In order for democracy to function properly, the population needs to be reasonably well-educated and empowered. They need to be able to discuss societal issues with some understanding, form political parties and other democratic institutions, and take an active part in the governing of their nation. They must have values that include, for example, a belief in the right of citizens to govern themselves and a disdain for corruption. If one introduces democratic forms, such as elections, into a country with an uneducated, disempowered, corrupt citizenry, it will quickly revert to some form of authoritarian government.

The same applies to our current crisis. We must create a new healthy society whose attributes go far beyond democracy as we know it. We need democracy that is much more participatory and cooperative than we have now. We need an economic system that is democratic and ecological. We also need other institutions that are more oriented toward personhood and community rather than bureaucracy and impersonal market transactions. We need families that are more extended and intact. We need personal and societal values that place a premium on understanding and compassion for people who are different from us. We need to value learning and human development rather than economic success and consumption. In order to build such a society, we need citizens who have compatible personal qualities. Though having such citizens is not enough to create such a healthy society, without them the job would be impossible. I will call such people *transformative citizens.*

Personal Qualities of Transformative Citizens

Here I explore personal qualities related to social transformation that are promoted by some forms of psychotherapy and group therapy in particular.

Psychotherapy

First let's look at those personal qualities of a transformative citizen that can be promoted by some forms of individual psychotherapy.

The Inner Life.   One of the problems with our modern society is that it is overwhelmingly oriented toward the external material world, with little understanding of the importance of the inner life of the person and its effect on that person's quality of life. This causes us to value superficialities such as looks, power, and money and disparage or ignore love, creativity, and the quality of relationships. Psychotherapy can introduce people to the depth and richness of their inner world and awaken an appreciation for this side of life. This is accomplished by those types of therapy that focus on what is often ignored in our society—emotions, motivations, desires, dreams, fantasies, and values.

Vitality.   Psychotherapy can engender aliveness and vitality, replacing the deadness and mechanical way of living that our society fosters. This happens through the cultivation of what I call "participatory consciousness" (Earley, 1997), which means an immediacy and vitality of experience, as opposed to an overly rational, detached consciousness. Most forms of therapy help clients to be more in touch with their emotions. Certain kinds of therapy (e.g., Gestalt, Jungian, and art therapy) can help increase intuition, spontaneity, and creativity. Other forms can help clients to be more in touch with their bodies (somatic therapies) or open to their spiritual sides (transpersonal psychology).

Our society fosters a kind of deadness in people which may not even be consciously experienced, but because they miss their vitality, they attempt to compensate for it. They may use drugs, alcohol, power, money, status, appearance, or passive entertainment, all of which contribute to the alienation and destructiveness of our current culture. When psychotherapy opens a person to the richness of participatory consciousness, she is more likely to focus her life energy on those vital endeavors that are truly satisfying, such as creativity, community, and spirituality. These activities don't contribute to ecological and social problems, but instead point in the direction of societal well-being.

Self-Esteem.   Self-esteem is related to social issues in a number of ways. People who feel bad about themselves often try to compensate for this through achievement, power, or any of the other compensations discussed above, thereby contributing to competitiveness, consumerism, and other problematic aspects of our society. I believe there is a basic need to feel intrinsically worthwhile without depending on any externals, even those that genuinely justify feeling good about oneself. Therefore forms of therapy that help clients feel a genuine sense of value rather than a false sense of self-esteem are helping to create transformative citizens.

Personal Power.   One of the things that keeps our society stuck is a felt lack of personal power among its citizens. Many people feel that they have little power over their lives and less power to change society. Therapy often helps people to have more power over their lives, and in some cases, this can help them to feel that they can also change society. However, ideally we needs forms of therapy that would also help clients feel a sense of social power.

Group Therapy: Interpersonal Qualities

Group therapy, especially interactive groups, can foster a number of interpersonal qualities that are relevant to creating a healthy society.

Empathy and Compassion.   Too often we treat other people as objects to be used rather than people of intrinsic value who have their own fears, hopes and loves. Many of our institutions see people as bureaucratic cogs in a machine or consumers to be manipulated. This extends to the way we deal with other nations and the natural world. Group therapy can help clients develop their capacity for empathy and compassion for others, through hearing other people's struggles and pain and learning about each person's unique inner process. This can play a part in changing this objectification in our society.

Cooperation.   Our democratic and economic institutions are all built on competition. Our politics is adversarial in that every special interest group fights for its constituents and the majority takes all. We would be better off with a more cooperative system in which legislators worked together to find the best solutions for a problem taking all people into account. Our national economy is based on competition between firms, and the world economy is based on competition among nations and multinationals. This is not all bad, of course; some competition is necessary and valuable. However, a healthier society will need to be designed more fundamentally around cooperation and synergy. Group therapy helps clients work on their competitive urges and their desires to win arguments or be proven right. Interactive groups especially help clients learn to care about others and to resolve conflicts in a way that benefits everyone. This attitude could help to create a more cooperative society.

Autonomy.   Many of our societal difficulties are exacerbated when citizens compliantly go along with destructive cultural norms, outmoded values, manipulative advertising, and demagoguery. In therapy groups, clients are continually struggling with their ability to be autonomous rather than just giving in to the group or one powerful member or the leader. This can help to produce autonomous citizens who can think for themselves.

Problem Ownership.   Some of our societal problems derive from the fact that people try to blame others for social problems instead of looking at themselves or our institutions. Minority groups, foreigners, or other nations are used as scapegoats to avoid looking at the problems of our own nation. Group therapy teaches clients to take back their projections and to own their own part in interpersonal conflicts rather than blaming others. This attitude would be very helpful at a societal level.

Appreciation of Diversity.   Prejudice and lack of international understanding often derive from a fear of people who are different. In therapy groups, clients learn about each other in depth and gradually come to appreciate others in profound ways. Therefore the more diversity there is in a group, the more the clients have an opportunity to develop their ability to tolerate and appreciate people who are different.

Group Therapy: The Group Setting

There are a number of other personal qualities and insights that are often fostered by conducting therapy in a group setting.

Universality and Societal Problems. In a general purpose therapy group, especially one that contains clients of relatively normal functioning, it soon becomes clear that everyone suffers from various psychological problems. This helps group members to understand that they are not the only ones who are struggling. It also contradicts negative self-images and helps to awaken clients to the fact that our society has shortcomings. When everyone has problems, it becomes obvious that they aren't due entirely to individual or family issues; social issues must also be involved. Being in group therapy can engender the understanding that our culture needs to be improved.

This doesn't necessarily mean that we live in a "sick society" as some would say. I believe that our society has its own particular strengths as well as faults. However, we are far from what we could be, and we are experiencing a host of problems during the current planetary crisis.

Group Culture and Societal Culture.   Once a group has developed a therapeutic group culture, it becomes clear to group members that the group is a better place in many ways than the outside world. This can trigger an understanding of the need for social change. Why can't our society be as safe, open, caring, and honest as a therapy group? Of course, a therapy group is a specialized environment, and it wouldn't be appropriate for a society to have the same norms as a group. However, we would all be better off if our society bore a greater resemblance to a healthy therapy group.

When group members are encouraged to have outside contact with each other, this gives them the opportunity to extend the group culture into their ordinary lives in a natural way with other members. This paves the way for them to do this with others in their lives. Many group members who are entering the world of therapy and personal growth for the first time become excited about this new way of being and relating; some resolve to extend it to all aspects of their lives. They change their way of relating to old friends and develop new friends who share their commitment to personal growth. They may let go of friends who don't want to relate in this way. I find this encouraging because it means they have the courage to reshape the fundamentals of how they live. If enough people do this, it will contribute to changing society in ways that are needed.

Community.   A good therapy group is a close-knit community. The members understand and care about each other and participate in each other's lives. Even if members don't have outside contact, the group forms a kind of community. If they do have outside contact, this can deepen their involvement with each other. Most important, this sense of community provides a model for what is possible in people's lives. It gives them a taste of the experience and some tools to help make it happen. Since community is so seriously lacking in today's world, this can encourage group members to create it for themselves in their lives, especially after they leave the group.

Limitations

Group therapy cannot begin to do all that is necessary for social change. It can't even accomplish the entire job of developing the personal qualities that are needed for social change. There are some qualities of a transformative citizen that cannot easily be developed through group therapy. For example, because of our immense ecological problems, it is very helpful if citizens have an intimate felt connection with nature that will be reflected in their attitude toward ecological issues. Ordinary therapy doesn't help with this; it is the goal of the new discipline of ecopsychology (Roszak, 1992). In addition, our citizens need to have a greater awareness of societal problems, processes, and solutions, and this is unlikely and perhaps inappropriate for a therapy setting. Furthermore, social transformation requires much more than just change at the individual level; our social values, institutions, and political and economic structures must also change. Nevertheless, even though group therapy can play only a small part in social transformation, it is important that we do what we can.

GLOSSARY

The glossary contains concise definitions of all terms that are introduced or defined in a unique way in this book, and also terms that are not commonly known in the psychotherapy field.

Access: An aspect of the therapeutic change process that involves exploring the deeper parts of the psyche that are buried behind defenses, especially childhood memories. This includes uncovering core issues or healthy capacities that have been blocked.

Aggression: A person's capacity to change his environment to meet his needs, to go after what he wants and protect himself from harm.

Autonomy: A basic capacity characterized by being a powerful, self-activating individual who can be oneself without being unduly influenced by who others want her to be.

Awareness: Noticing and labeling what you are experiencing at the moment that it is happening.

Basic capacity: A healthy capacity that is the result of having a basic need met in childhood.

Basic need: A need that is central to human motivation in that adult behavior is powerfully influenced by it, and in addition, is crucial to the healthy development of children. If a basic need was not met adequately in a person's early years, she will feel a deficiency, causing pain and perhaps difficulty in functioning. There are four basic needs: connectedness, autonomy, safety, and value.

Blame cycle: Two people in dialogue argue about who is to blame for their problem.

Bottleneck issue: An issue that can impede the flow of the therapy process, so when the bottleneck is blocked, not only is work on that particular issue halted, but nothing else can move through either.

Combined therapy: When a therapist has a client in both group and individual therapy at the same time.

Compensation: Behavior or attitude that gives a temporary, partial, or distorted experience of a healthy capacity without developing it in any permanent way.

Concurrent therapy: When a client is in both individual and group therapy at the same time.

Conflict stage: The third stage of group development where conflict, power, and autonomy are the most important issues.

Conjoint therapy: When a client is in individual therapy with one therapist and group with another at the same time.

Connectedness: A basic capacity characterized by feeling close to important others, connected with people in general, and accepting and loving toward herself.

Consultation: A group member meets individually with the group leader for help with her work in the group. For clients in combined individual therapy, this happens in an individual session. For others, separate meetings are scheduled.

Contact: The quality of presence in interpersonal meeting; the directness of relating in the moment; the active engagement of the person with the environment.

Containing: When a client contains a feeling for the group, it means that he is the only member who expresses the feeling even though other group members are also feeling it.

Contract: An agreement a group member makes about work she will take responsibility for in the future in the group. This can involve awareness, access, experimenting, or feedback.

Core issue: A structure in the psyche that influences and distorts the way a person sees and relates to others and feels about himself.

Defense cycle: As two people interact, they trigger each other's defenses through their reactions to each other's defenses in a cyclical reinforcing pattern.

Deficiency in a healthy capacity: When a healthy capacity is blocked by a core issue, the person either doesn't have the capacity developed or doesn't have it available.

Deficiency issue: A core issue that represents a situation where the child was not consistently given enough of what he needed, especially nurturing, mirroring, caring, and support for healthy behavior. This has the effect of leaving the person feeling deficient or inadequate in some way.

Elicited countertransference: A leader's problematic response to certain behavior of a group member is considered "elicited" when this response is fairly natural in that the client tends to elicit this reaction from almost everyone.

Entrance stage: The first stage of group process where members are just beginning to interact and deciding whether the group is right for them.

Experimenting: An aspect of therapeutic change that involves trying out new healthy behavior.

Gratification: Meeting a client's needs without his first achieving access or when he could have met them himself.

Group-centered group: A therapy group where the members interact primarily with each other rather than the leader.

Group climate: The emotional feel of the group at any given moment, similar to the concept of group culture, but a more transitory phenomenon.

Group cohesiveness: The degree of closeness in the group. The degree to which the members value and like each other and the group.

Group exploration: A situation where many of all of the group members explore a similar issue in themselves at the same time.

Group norms: Agreements among the group members about those ways of being that are preferred or expected in the group and those that are frowned on or prohibited. These can be unconscious or unspoken. Therapeutic norms are those that promote the group's therapeutic effectiveness.

Group position: An interpersonal position in the group system that is dysfunctional for the person. It differs from a role because it doesn't fulfill a function for the group.

Group role: A function that needs to be performed for the group, which can be therapeutic or defensive. A flexible role is performed by many of the group members and a rigid role by only one.

Group rules: Explicit rules of a group that are not to be broken without good reason.

Harm issue: A core issue that originates when a child is actively harmed—by anger, judgment, physical abuse, sexual abuse, excessive control, intrusion, or other means.

Healing mismatch: When a client needs a certain type of healing response and the person she is interacting with has a different response, especially when it is a response that reinforces the client's core issue.

Healing response: An aspect of the therapeutic change process. The client receives something that redresses and heals the effects of the trauma or dysfunctional pattern from childhood that originally caused a core issue.

Healthy capacity: The ability for healthy behavior and experience in a certain area. This includes the person's capacity to act in a healthy way in the world and the inner experience or sense of self that comes from the capacity.

Homogeneous group: A group in which all the members are similar in some way, especially with respect to the reason for being in the group.

Inclusion stage: The second stage of group process where the most important issues are disclosure, acceptance, inclusion, belonging, and commitment.

Inner healing: An aspect of the therapeutic change process. The actual internal therapeutic change, where the person reorganizes her sense of herself and others.

Interactive work: Group work that deals with the feelings or relationship between two people or between one person and the group.

Intimacy stage: The fifth stage of group development where closeness is the most important issue.

Leader-centered group: A therapy group where the members interact mostly with the leader rather than each other.

Leadership stance: An emotional stance of non-involvement and caring that a group leader takes.

Outside issue: Group work that deals with an issue from outside group, a person's past, or other topics. Contrasted with interactive work.

Parallel process: When the content of a person's statements is being enacted at the moment in her process.

Personal countertransference: A reaction the group leader has to a client (or the group) that derives primarily from a core issue of the leader's.

Presence. Being vital, embodied, and in contact with oneself in the moment.

Problem-focused group: A group focused on a specific problem, symptom, or population.

Problem ownership: A client recognizes that certain behavior of his is contributing to an interpersonal problem—either a problem in group or a problem in his life. He is willing to see his part rather than only blaming others.

Prohibition: Group norm that specifies what behavior is not allowed in the group.

Protection: A healing response to a harm issue where the client is protected from an action that is similar to the way she was harmed originally. Protection can come from the client herself or from the leader or another group member.

Punishment issue: A core issue that derives from a situation where the child was regularly punished or threatened or received negative consequences when engaging in a certain healthy behavior.

Relational healing: Healing that happens as the result of developing a healthy relationship with another group member or the leader.

Resistance: Any behavior that attempts to avoid cooperating with the therapy process or the therapist.

Responsibility: A client recognizes that *she* is ultimately in charge of her progress in therapy and takes it upon herself to make her work successful (to the extent of her ability to do so).

Safety: A basic capacity characterized by feeling safe from attack, intrusion, or judgment and having the ability to protect oneself if necessary.

Scapegoat: A member who is rejected and ostracized by the other group members, sometimes because they project their own shame and aggression onto that member.

Self-direction: A client understands his issues and how he needs to work on them and uses this information to direct his work. He also keeps track of his feelings toward other group members and the growth he has made.

Self-fulfilling prophecy: Any situation where the client elicits from others the response he is expecting and fearing according to a core issue, whether or not this is his intention.

Support: The various ways a client feels her internal strength (inner support) and/or receives help and healing from others (external support).

Support group: A group in which the main activity consists of clients sharing their problems and receiving caring from each other.

Taking in: When a person receives a compliment or a healing response, "taking in" means allowing it to affect him emotionally, so that he feels better about himself and inner healing can occur.

Therapeutic alliance: The working relationship between the group leader and a group member that allows the client to use the leader's help in the therapy.

Therapeutic dissonance: When a person receives a healing response, the experience of the discrepancy between that response and the core issue. This leads to inner healing.

Transformative citizens: People with personal qualities that naturally promote the movement toward a healthy society.

Value: A basic capacity characterized by feeling worthwhile and valuable as a person.

Vulnerability: The capacity to be open to one's emotions and connections with other people, even when there is a risk of pain, shame, or hurt. A healthy capacity and also an important group norm.

Working stage: The fourth stage of group development where the preliminaries have been completed and the ordinary work of the group occurs.

APPENDIX

The following article was written for group members. It is mailed to prospective group members as a way of introducing them to group therapy and my particular style of groups.

☐ The Interactive Group Experience

Interactive Groups provide an exciting and powerful journey into psychological healing and personal growth. Though they can be either long term or short term, I will focus on long-term groups in this article. Interactive Groups focus on growth through relationship, specifically through your relationships with the other group members. This is an intense and very effective learning environment, because instead of just talking about how you relate to others, you learn from your interactions with the other group members, right in the moment. At another level, an Interactive Group is a vehicle for an aspect of spiritual development, because it is an exercise in the creation and expression of love—acceptance, compassion, appreciation, and intimacy. Interactive Groups also have social relevance, because they provide that deep sense of bonding with a group, that sense of community that is often missing in our fragmented, alienated world.

This paper describes what it is like to be in an Interactive Group, from your first few weeks in the group to the stage when you are an old-timer with close relationships. It is an abridged version of a larger 50-page article. It is intended to give prospective group members an understanding of the group experience so you can decide if you want to pursue it.

☐ Before You Enter the Group

The Initial Call.   The first step is to call the leader to get more information about what the groups are like and to find out which groups have openings. This initial call is an important statement to yourself that you are ready for more growth. However, it doesn't commit you to joining a group. In fact, each additional step—the interview, the first weeks in the group—can be done as an experiment to see if the group is right for you. You can decide to discontinue at any time.

The Interview.   If you want to carry the process further, the next step is a pre-group interview or interviews. During this time, you and the leader get to know each other, the leader tells you more about how the group functions, and you share more about who you are and what you want to get from a group. If you decide you want to join a group, there is a discussion of which group might be best for you. The leader also helps to prepare you for group by discussing any fears or reservations you may have.

☐ The Entrance Stage

I have divided this paper according to the stages of development of a group, which are also the stages each person goes through when they join an existing group. There are four stages: Entrance, Inclusion, Mutuality, and Intimacy. I will describe what a person's experience might be who joins an existing group as he or she goes through each of the stages.

Checking Out the Group

The Entrance Stage begins when you join the group and is usually brief. During this stage you will probably check out the group to see if it is right for you. You may check out the leader to see if you feel he or she is competent and caring. You may check out the Interactive mode to see if this style of group can help you make the changes you want. You will also be checking out the group members to see if you want to get close to them. During this stage you will probably be observing for the most part and only occasionally making small forays out into the group. You may be tentative until you decide that the group is right for you and you begin taking the risk to do significant interactive work.

Beginning to Participate

Your first participation might be to talk about what it feels like to be in the group. Most people feel a fair amount of anxiety at their first meeting. Some are also excited. It can be a relief to talk about whatever you are feeling.

For example, one person introduced himself as follows: "Hi, my name is Willie. I joined this group because I want to learn to be assertive without getting into so many fights with people. I also want to figure out what I'm doing wrong so that my love relationships don't work out.... Boy am I nervous right now. This is hard talking to a group of strangers, especially about stuff like this."

You also can begin by giving feedback to other people who have worked.

For example, after Jill finished interacting with another group member, you might say, "Jill, I really identified with your struggle to speak your mind instead of smoothing things over. That's a big problem of mine. I appreciate the way you hung in there with what you believe instead of giving in."

At the beginning it is important to let the other group members know who you are. When you feel safe enough, you will want to tell them about the important issues in your life and why you have come to the group. You may need to share some pain with the group. You may need to let them know about what really troubles you and what isn't working for you in your life. This isn't always easy to do with a new group of people because you need to develop trust that they will care about you and not judge you. However, the sooner you can share yourself with the group, the sooner you will get something out of it.

Almost everyone feels nervous and uneasy at the beginning of a group. At times you may also feel excited, connected, curious, cautious, or many other things. It is very helpful to simply express these feelings to the group when they come up. Invariably there will be other people who are feeling similarly. This is a valuable way for the group to work with its process and for you to begin to learn how to be aware of your experience in the moment, which is an important skill for getting the most out of an Interactive Group.

The Interactive Format

We make a clear distinction between "interactive work" and "outside issues." Interactive work doesn't just mean people in group talking to each other. It means people talking to each other about their feelings toward each other or about their relationships. It can also mean one person talking to the group about his or her feelings in the group. "Outside issues" refers to sharing what is happening in your life or what your psychological issues are or any other general discussion. The focus of the group is on interactive work. Outside issues need to be brought up occasionally, but they are secondary to the interactive work. However, during the Entrance and Inclusion Stages, outside issues play a more important part in the group because people are still getting to know each other and developing trust.

The assumption is that you will learn about how you function in your life by participating in the group. The group becomes a microcosm of your life, and since you are the same person, almost all the issues you have in your life will come out in group sooner or later. You can learn about them in a much more direct and accurate way through your own awareness in group and through feedback from others. You can also experiment with new behavior right in the moment during group. This is a much more effective growth situation than just talking about your problems.

This focus on interactive work means that there isn't a lot of free floating discussion unless it is about what is happening in the group. Sometimes there are even silences in the group. During these, members think about what work they have to do, or perhaps get up their courage to begin some difficult work. The group usually doesn't focus on one person exclusively for a long period of time, unless that person is dealing with their feelings about group. Even then, the work will probably expand to include other group members. The leader doesn't structure the group much by setting up topics or doing exercises. The group members initiate the work they need to do. Once a piece of work is initiated, however, the leader is often active in facilitating the work.

In the beginning stages of a group, outside work is more important, because you are just getting to know each other, but as the group progresses we move more and more toward interactive work.

Your First Interaction

At some point the leader will encourage you to begin doing some interactive work. You will be encouraged to pick someone in the group whom you have initial impressions of and reactions toward. Actually you probably have them toward everyone. After a fairly short period of being around anyone, we all have initial reactions to a person, so it's just a matter of picking someone in the group to start with, probably someone that you feel safe talking to. The reactions can be positive or negative, big or little. Many people start out with positive reactions because they find these less threatening. This also helps to build initial trust and safety.

For example, you might say, "Mary, I really like the way you come across. You seem really honest, and not afraid to say exactly what you are feeling. And you say it in a way that doesn't offend people." Then the leader might ask you to tell her how that makes you feel toward her. "I feel warmly toward you and I feel like I can trust you." Mary would then respond with her reaction to what you said. For example, "Thank you. That makes me feel good. I've been working on that for a long time. It's nice to be recognized. I like you, too."

Your first interaction might begin with someone in the group telling you their initial impressions of you. For example, someone might say, "It seems like you're a nice person, but I'm not sure you would ever say anything negative even if you were feeling it. So far it seems like you're mainly trying to please people." It would then be your turn to respond. You might feel embarrassed or hurt or angry in response to what she said. If so, it would be important to say that. Or you might just respond to the content of her perception of you, by saying whether you think you have been trying to please people in group. The dialogue between you would continue until it came to a conclusion that was satisfactory for both of you. In the Entrance Stage, these interactions are usually brief.

Receiving Positive Feedback

One of your first interactions might involve receiving positive feedback. For example, Betty says, "I really like what I've seen of you so far. You seem warm and caring and really perceptive, especially for someone so new to the group. I feel like you've been really understanding and supportive with me, you know, especially last week." You might take in her feedback, allowing it to make you feel good about yourself, and respond to Betty in a warm way. Or you might get embarrassed or deflect the compliment. In that case, the leader would encourage you to examine why it was hard for you to take it in. For example, you might not feel worthy, or you might feel afraid of the contact with Betty. You would then experiment with taking in Betty's feelings, and then you would respond with your feelings toward her. A short dialogue might ensue.

Moving On

After a while, you may decide that the group seems right for you. You decide that you like the interactive format. The group feels relatively safe and you decide that you want to be there. You are ready to begin taking some greater interactive risks. When you do this, you have moved ahead to the Inclusion Stage.

☐ The Inclusion Stage

This stage deals with acceptance and power and commitment. It deals with the question of whether you are included in the group or not. You also learn how the group operates—the group norms and the group culture. You learn about how people function psychologically and you learn awareness and communication skills.

Initiating Interactive Work

There are two ways to initiate interactive work in group. One is to allow yourself to respond in the moment when you have a reaction to something that happens in group. When something happens that generates feelings in you, I encourage you to speak up, to let your feelings be known, so that you can benefit from processing them at the moment they happen. These will often be feelings toward another person in group, so an interaction often follows.

The second way to initiate interactive work is to plan it before group. You can think through your feelings toward each person in group and notice where there are feelings toward someone that you haven't expressed or feedback that you haven't asked for. These don't have to be strong feelings. They can be positive or negative feelings. You can bring up these feelings without waiting for something to trigger them in group. At the beginning of group, or when there is a pause, simply say that you have some work to do, and begin by telling the person your feelings. An interaction will follow.

Awareness

Awareness is the ability to notice and label what you are feeling and experiencing at the moment it is happening. In most instances, this is no easy accomplishment! Of course if you are experiencing a very strong emotion, you will be aware of it. However, most of the feelings that are important are much more subtle and hard to grasp. It is especially hard to be aware of your feelings when you are in the middle of an intense interaction with someone, yet this is the time when it is most needed. Awareness is a skill to be developed over time. Some people have it highly developed when they first join group, but most have to learn it gradually. There are many levels of awareness; the first feeling you notice in a situation is only the beginning. As you become more adept at aware-ness, you will begin to be aware of subtler and deeper aspects of your experience.

> For example, suppose Sandy tells Mike that she thinks he talks from his head too much and is out of touch with his feelings. At first he thinks about whether this is true or not. He is focusing on the *content* of what she said, not his awareness of *feelings*. The leader suggests that he talk about his feeling response to Sandy. Then Mike becomes aware of feeling re-sentful or angry about what she said. At the leader's suggestion he looks further and be-comes aware that he also feels hurt by Sandy. As he explores deeper he discovers that he feels hurt because he likes Sandy and he wants her to like him, so he is especially vulner-able to hearing something negative from her. Even deeper, he might realize that he was criticized a lot during his childhood, so hearing any criticism now makes him feel bad about himself. Notice how many levels of awareness are possible.

A Full Interaction

> If Mike tells Sandy that he is angry at her, he might get an angry response back and then the two of them would work on resolving the conflict. If he tells Sandy he is hurt because he wants her to like him, she might explain that she *does* like him, and that she was just telling him about one thing that gave her trouble. Mike would then have to decide if he believes her—if he thinks she really meant it when she said she liked him, or if he thinks she was just smoothing things over. If he tells Sandy he feels bad about himself because of old mes-sages, she might be sympathetic and caring. No matter which feeling Mike expresses, he and Sandy will then engage in a dialogue to see if they can work things out between them.

> In addition to working out his feelings with Sandy, Mike might also decide that he is inter-ested in the issue of his being too intellectual. He asks Sandy to give him examples so he can understand what she means. He asks the other group members if they also think he is too much in his head and if they can give examples. If Mike decides that it's true and he would like to change, he might ask Sandy or the group to let him know the next time it happens. Then he could practice expressing himself in a more feeling way.

Self-Revealing and Acceptance

Notice that part of Mike's interaction with Sandy dealt with learning about himself and part of it dealt with acceptance. Now that Sandy has told him something she doesn't like, does it mean that she doesn't accept him? Acceptance is the number one issue in the Inclusion Stage. You want to reveal yourself, but only if you are going to be ac-cepted by the group. You want to tell the group about yourself, especially about your problems and your pain. You also want to be able to *be* yourself. You want to show your anger or your insecurity, your tears or your fears, your strength or your neediness, but it is critical that you be accepted as you are.

An important part of most people's work in group is to share things about yourself that are important to you and that you have strong feelings about. Perhaps you need to talk about how you were abused as a child. Perhaps you are gay, or you are going through a painful divorce, or having anxiety attacks. Even though this is not officially "interactive work," it is very important work, especially in the beginning stages of group.

As you feel ready, you will probably take the risk to reveal more and more of yourself, especially parts of yourself that you feel ashamed of. These are the hardest things to reveal, because you expect to be judged and rejected. But they are also the most urgent because you really need to be accepted *with* these shameful parts. You will discover that when you reveal these parts of yourself in an open way, not only are you accepted by the group, but people actually appreciate you more, because of your courage and vulnerability.

This is one of the magic things that happens in an Interactive Group. There is actually something beautiful about a person when they are being very open and vulnerable, whether this is because they are showing some deep pain or insecurity or because they are being open and loving toward someone they feel close to. Everyone has a great need to show these vulnerable parts of themselves and be accepted, and in fact the group atmosphere makes if easy for this to happen. People want to be able to love each other if only they are in the right environment to bring this out. Most people in group find it natural to be loving and compassionate toward someone who reveals pain or weakness. The pain is experienced as something precious and beautiful, and most people in the group welcome this kind of sharing, especially from new group members. It makes them feel closer to the one sharing the pain. It's one of those poignant, special moments in group that everyone cherishes.

Negative Feelings and Conflict

One of the big challenges for many people at this stage in the group is the expression of negative feelings. It is valuable in an Interactive Group to express all of your feelings, not just good feelings that won't get you in trouble. It is important to say when something bothers you. It is valuable to be able to express annoyance, disagreement, hurt, or discomfort. It's also important to express stronger feelings such as fear, anger, and jealousy, but these can be put off until the Mutuality Stage when you feel safer in group.

Some people find it hard to believe that expressing negative feelings of any kind will be helpful to anyone. *"It will just hurt him unnecessarily, and it's not a big deal anyway." "It's probably just my own material anyway. I should just work it out myself." "It's not something she can change. Why make her feel bad?"* This is usually because you are afraid of hurting her and feeling guilty about it, or because you are afraid of her being angry or rejecting toward you.

In fact there are several reasons for expressing negative feelings. It gives you a chance to practice asserting yourself. Many people are afraid to bring up difficult things, and this is an ideal way to learn how to do it. It also gives you a chance to learn how to work through any hard feelings that come up. In addition, it gives the other person some useful feedback about how they affect others. When you react to someone, it's usually not all their fault, and it's usually not all your fault. In fact it's not necessarily anyone's fault, but it's usually a combination of something real about the other person and some issue of yours. So both of you have something to learn from the interaction.

For example, Carole says, "Jan, when you had that interaction with Max last week, I didn't like the way you treated him. I felt you were being defensive and controlling. You didn't really give him a chance to explain himself before you attacked him." The leader asks Carole if she was feeling protective of Max. "Maybe a little, but I was more just scared for myself. I wouldn't want Jan to do that to me." Jan responds, "I don't see what was wrong with what I did. I was just standing up for myself." The leader explores with Jan how she is reacting to Carole, and she discovers that she is feeling defensive. She even realizes that she is responding to Carole the same way she did to Max. This helps Jan to recognize a pattern of hers that involves defensiveness, and she decides she'd like to change it.

In the midst of this, the leader asks how Carole is reacting emotionally to Jan. She discovers that she is feeling frightened of Jan's anger. They check this out with Jan and find out that she *is* feeling a little angry at Carole, but she also appreciates Carole's taking the chance to confront her because it gave her an opportunity to learn something about herself. This gives Carole a chance to begin dealing with her fear of other people's anger. Here she finds that she can tolerate Jan being a little angry at her.

Asking for Feedback

Like many people, you may join an Interactive Group partly to learn more about how other people react to you and to learn what you may be doing to keep your relationships from working out the way you would like. You will get plenty of information of this kind through the ordinary working of the group, as people express their feelings toward you. However, if you want to make sure you get it, and make sure it's relevant to your concerns, you can ask for it explicitly. You can also ask for general feedback or for feedback about something specific that you are concerned about.

For example, Lilly said to the group, "I'm concerned that I may be pushing away people whom I'd like to be close to without even realizing I'm doing it. I end up alone so much when I really do want people around, and I never knew why. Recently someone suggested that I was unconsciously pushing people away. I'd like to know if any of you think I've been doing that." In response a male member of the group said that she discounted the good things he said to her. A woman said that Lilly acted sour and complaining even when they had nice contact. The group helped Lilly to sort out what she was doing and how she might want to change.

Consultations

Each group member consults with the leader individually on a regular basis to help you get the most out of the group. The consultations have a number of purposes: (a) They help you learn how to initiate interactive work in the group. (b) They help you get in touch with subtle but important reactions you have in group but don't bring up. (c) They provide a chance to talk about feelings from group which you don't feel safe to explore in group. This gets you ready to deal with them in group. (d) Sometimes you have a specific issue you want to work on, but you don't know how to do this in an interactive way. In a consultation you and the leader can strategize about the best way to make this work happen in group.

Commitment

It is a big emotional step to commit yourself to an Interactive Group. You're not just committing yourself to come each week and work on yourself in this environment. You're also committing yourself to be involved emotionally with the people in the group—to care about them and to let them care about you and be important to you. In fact, if you have no emotional room in your life to get close to people, an Interactive Group will not work for you. You may get something out of it for 6 months or so, but then you must be willing to get involved emotionally or not much more will happen.

The commitment issue usually comes up during the Inclusion Stage. People ask themselves questions such as: Do I really want to get involved with these people? Are they good enough for me? Am I good enough for them? Will they accept me? If I commit, will I have to give myself up? Can I be myself and still be close to these people?

These are the kind of questions that also come up for people in love relationships. People who have commitment problems in love relationships often have commitment problems with group at this stage. So this can be an excellent opportunity to work through your commitment problems in your life by working on them as they come up with respect to the group.

Moving On

At some point you feel ready to really commit yourself to the group. You have probably revealed most of who you are—especially parts of yourself that you may be ashamed of—and discovered that you are really accepted by the group as you are. You probably have confronted people and have been confronted by people, and you've worked through these confrontations to strengthen your relationships with these people. You have probably asserted some power in the group to make it operate in ways which you need.

All this combines to allow you to feel safe to be yourself in the group and to feel that the group is really yours. You are entering the Mutuality Stage.

☐ Mutuality Stage

In this stage, the preliminaries are over and you move fully into the major work of the group. Not that you haven't been doing significant work already, but now you probably feel safe enough to let out all the stops. So your work deepens.

Growing Edge

You can think about your work in group in terms of the question: What is my growing edge (or edges)? In other words, what are the areas where I need to grow and where I am now ready to take the step? We all function within a certain circumscribed area of behavior and feeling that is safe and comfortable for us. Your growing edge is that part of the boundary that you are ready to push back, the place where you are ready to take a risk to try new ways of being.

> For example, if you usually fight to defend yourself in ways that keep people from being close to you, your growing edge might be to allow yourself to be vulnerable. If you usually are self-effacing, your growing edge might be to speak up with your opinions and feelings. If you usually take care of people instead of expressing your needs, your growing edge might be to ask for support. If you usually control yourself and your environment so that you avoid feeling uncertain, your growing edge might be to initiate work without a plan about where it is going and allow yourself to be spontaneous in the moment.

There are hundreds of possible growing edges. At any one time you might be working on just one, or perhaps two or three.

How Growth Transfers to Outside Life

Communication Skills. In the group you learn various communication and awareness skills. You learn how to confront people directly without judgment. You learn how to be open and vulnerable. You learn how to be aware of and express your emotional reactions. These skills can be valuable in any of your outside relationships—friends, family, spouse, work relationships, acquaintances, and strangers.

Awareness and Choice. Many of our interpersonal issues go beyond just communication skills. They require that we change some of our deeper interpersonal patterns—our growing edges. In group you learn to become aware of these patterns, not only in the abstract, but also in the moment.

> For instance, suppose you have a pattern of saying "yes" to everyone who asks for help, no matter what the cost to yourself. You will not only learn that this is a pattern of yours; you will also learn to become aware of it at the moment it happens. You will learn to notice when you are about to give in to a request when if wouldn't be good for you.

> Once you have learned to do this in group, you can start noticing it outside as well. Then you can choose to act differently. Even though you may still have the urge to say "yes," you can say instead, "Let me think about that. I'll get back to you." Then if it is something that really isn't good for you, you can tell the person "no." You can use awareness and choice to change your behavior.

Deeper Change. The major learning in an Interactive Group goes even deeper than this. Through becoming aware and trying new behavior in group and getting positive responses, you grow. As this happens repeatedly, you change at a deep level. Your natural responses begin to be healthy.

> For example, suppose you are afraid of being close to people because you fear you will lose yourself in trying to please them. In group, you will have many opportunities to practice being assertive rather than pleasing. You will also have many opportunities to practice opening yourself to being close to people, and then working on not losing yourself. Even-

tually, you will know at a deep level that you can hold your own. You will know that you can be close without giving yourself up. Closeness won't feel so frightening. You will find yourself just naturally opening to closeness rather than closing down or running away.

Relationships Outside Group

Unlike some therapy groups, there are no rules against having contact with other group members outside of group. In fact, I think that it enhances the value of the group if people develop relationships with each other outside of the group. In the later stages of the group, it adds depth and intensity to people's relationships, which provokes work, which goes deeper into the psyche and is therefore more potent for healing and change. It also brings the group experience closer to "real life" and helps people to transfer learnings from group to their regular lives. Usually during the Mutuality Stage, some people begin to reach out to each other to make contact outside group—calling to ask for or offer help and support, getting together for lunch, and so on.

Weekend Retreats

Each group periodically goes away together for a weekend retreat. These weekends are very powerful, in the depth of the work people are able to do, in the openness and vulnerability people achieve, and especially in the bonding that happens among the group members.

The extra contact between group members is very important to encouraging bonding at a deep level. Driving out in car pools, cooking and eating meals together, sleeping in the same house, playing together, hanging out, taking walks—all these add to the sense of being a caring family. This sense of healthy family, of being with a group of people who really know you and care for you, is incredibly valuable for the level of work that people can do in group and the depth of healing that happens.

The intensity of the weekend experience also contributes to bonding, but more important, it leads to more potent work which goes deeper into the psyche and therefore is more healing. The commitment of going away for the weekend and devoting all that time to personal growth adds to the intensity. By working frequently during the weekend, you have time to open up gradually throughout the weekend and to open at deeper and deeper levels as you go. You don't have to leave group after 2 hours and go back to your ordinary life, which may require you to close down again. People are stimulated to get in touch with deeper material by watching others work, and often on a weekend, one person triggers another who triggers still another, as the depth and intensity build throughout the time together. The weekends seem like an amazing, magical time because so many wonderful things happen. People often come away with a sense of having had an almost spiritual experience.

After the weekend, the bonding which happened now feeds back into the ongoing group. People trust each other to continue working at deeper levels. The intensity, of course, can't continue, but the group connection does, and it changes the whole complexion of the group. Because of the potency of the weekends, I see them as an integral part of the whole group experience, almost as important as the weekly meetings.

Moving On

As your relationships with the other members deepen, some of them may become genuinely important to you as friends in your life, not just as companions in therapy. This means that you are moving on to the Intimacy Stage.

☐ The Intimacy Stage

The Intimacy Stage continues the work of the Mutuality Stage but at a deeper level. Time-limited groups usually don't reach this stage. Some of your relationships have deepened to an intimate level, and therefore, the issues and growing edges that come up for you reflect that depth and intensity.

Deeper Work

As your relationships in group become more important to you, many issues that were resolved before come up again because of the deeper intimacy. This is also true in outside life. You will often find that when you first enter a love relationship (or when you end the honeymoon phase) old feelings and issues crop up which you thought were resolved. This doesn't really mean that the growth you made wasn't real. You had resolved your issues at that level, but now the increased intimacy has brought you to a new depth, and the old issues must be worked through at this level.

Group as Healthy Family

By the time a group enters the Intimacy Stage, there are not only close relationships between certain pairs of people in the group, there is also a profound sense of group connection. This is partially based on all the strong relationships between pairs of group members, but it goes beyond that. By this time, you've been through a lot together. You've challenged each other and fought each other. You've helped each other and cared for each other. You've revealed some of your darkest secrets and been accepted and appreciated. You've shown your pain and also your strength and joy. The group has become a unit, a community, a healthy family, in which each person is valued and loved and in which each person can be autonomous and powerful. This bonding is already strong in the Mutuality Stage, and it becomes even clearer and stronger in the Intimacy Stage.

This gives the group enormous power for healing. The reason for this becomes apparent when you look at the origins of our psychological problems. Most of them come from the way we were treated as children, primarily by our parents, but also by other important people in our lives. We are very dependent and vulnerable as children, so the relationships we have with our caretakers shape our psyches to such a large extent, in both positive and negative ways. This is why individual therapy so often focuses on childhood issues, and why "inner child" work is so popular these days.

If the origins of many of our problems are in our early relationships, then our healing will also be through relationships. In individual therapy this often happens through the relationship with your therapist. In an Interactive Group it happens through your relationships with all the group members. The group becomes like the healthy family you always wanted and needed. When you open yourself up to pain (which often comes from childhood) and are then offered a healing response from someone in the group (or from the whole group), you are able to take it in fully and let it truly change you. You can do this because you trust your group. You have a sense of coming home.

This also happens, of course, in individual therapy, but it's sometimes easy to feel that your therapist is the only person who understands and accepts you. In a group you know it's the whole "family," and this gives it a greater sense of reality, a stronger feeling that you actually deserve it. You also participate in other people's healing and growth, and this promotes a recognition of your own value and worth. You have the experience of feeling yourself as part of a larger whole that is loving and growthful.

☐ Conclusion

I have been leading Interactive Groups since 1978, and I love the process. I love the excitement and the intensity. I love the genuineness of people's responses and the depths to which people go. Most of all, I love the deep caring and love that people share. I hope that this article gives you some idea of the richness and possibility of these groups.

REFERENCES

Adler, G. (1985). *Borderline psychopathology and its treatment.* Northvale, NJ: Jason Aronson.

Agazarian, Y. M. (1992). Contemporary theories of group psychotherapy: A systems approach to the group-as-a-whole. *International Journal of Group Psychotherapy, 42,* 177–203.

Alexander, F., & French, T. (1946). *Psychoanalytic therapy: Principles and applications.* New York: Ronald Press.

Almaas, A. H. (1988). *The pearl beyond price.* Berkeley, CA: Diamond Books.

Alonso, A. & Swiller, H. I. (Eds.). (1993). *Group therapy in clinical practice.* Washington, DC: American Psychiatric Press.

Bacal, H. A. (1990). Object relations in the group from the perspective of self psychology. In B. E. Roth, W. N. Stone, & H. D. Kibel (Eds.), *The difficult patient in group* (pp. 157–174). AGPA Monograph Series, Vol. 6. Madison, CT: International Universities Press.

Beck, A. P. (1974). Phases in the development of structure in therapy and encounter groups. In D. A. Wexler & L. N. Rice (Eds.), *Innovations in client-centered therapy* (pp. 421–464). New York: Wiley.

Beissler, A. R. (1970). The paradoxical theory of change. In J. Fagan & I. L. Shepherd (Eds.), *Gestalt therapy now* (pp. 77–80). New York: Harper & Row.

Bennis, W. G., & Shepard, H. A. (1956). A theory of group development. *Human Relations, 9,* 415–438.

Berne, E. (1964). *Games people play.* New York: Grove Press.

Bion, W. (1959). *Experiences in groups.* New York: Basic Books.

Bradshaw, J. (1992). *Homecoming: Reclaiming and championing your inner child.* New York: Bantam.

Capra, F. (1982). *The turning point.* New York: Simon & Schuster.

Carroll, K. W. (1993). Family support groups for medically ill patients and their families. In A. Alonso & H. I. Swiller (Eds.), *Group therapy in clinical practice* (pp. 201–215). Washington, DC: American Psychiatric Press.

Chodorow, N. J. (1989). *Feminism and psychoanalytic theory.* New Haven, CT: Yale University Press.

Dahl, H. (1991). The key to understanding change: Emotions as appetitive wishes and beliefs about their fulfillment. In J. D. Safran & L. S. Greenberg (Eds.), *Emotion, psychotherapy, and change* (pp. 130–165). New York: Guilford Press.

Day, M. (1993). Training and supervision in group psychotherapy. In H. I. Kaplan & B. J. Sadock (Eds.), *Comprehensive group psychotherapy* (pp. 656–667). Philadelphia: Williams & Wilkins.

Dies, R. R. (1986). Practical, theoretical, and empirical foundations for group psychotherapy. In A. H. Frances & R. E. Hales (Eds.), *The American Psychiatric Association Annual Review, Vol. 5* (pp. 659–677). Washington, DC: American Psychiatric Press.

Dies, R. R. (1992). Models of group psychotherapy: Sifting through confusion. *International Journal of Group Psychotherapy, 42,* 1–17.

Doherty, P., & Enders, P. L. (1993). Women in group psychotherapy. In A. Alonso & H. I. Swiller (Eds.), *Group therapy in clinical practice* (pp. 371–392). Washington, DC: American Psychiatric Press.

Durkin, H. (1964). *The group in depth.* New York: International Universities Press.

Earley, J. (1990). *Inner journeys: A guide to personal and social transformation.* York Beach, ME: Samuel Weiser.

Earley, J. (1996). Healing through relationship in an interactive Gestalt group. In B. Feder & R. Ronall (Eds.), *A living legacy of Fritz and Laura Perls: Contemporary case studies* (pp. 219–232). Montclair, NJ: Feder & Ronall.

Earley, J. (1997). *Transforming human culture: Social evolution and the planetary crisis.* Albany, NY: SUNY Press.

Ettin, M. F. (1996). Do you know where your group is? Development of a group-as-a-whole compass. *Group, 20,* 57–89.

Ezriel, H. (1952). Notes on psychoanalytic therapy: II. Interpretation and research. *Psychiatry, 15,* 119.

Fay, A., & Lazarus, A. A. (1993). Cognitive-behavior group therapy. In A. Alonso & H. I. Swiller (Eds.), *Group therapy in clinical practice* (pp. 449–469). Washington, DC: American Psychiatric Press.

Festinger, L. A. (1957). *A theory of cognitive dissonance.* Evanston, IL: Row, Peterson.

Flores, P. J. (1993). Group psychotherapy with alcoholics, substance abusers, and adult children of alcoholics. In H. I. Kaplan & B. J. Sadock (Eds.), *Comprehensive group psychotherapy* (pp. 429–442). Philadelphia: Williams & Wilkins.

Fromm, E. (1955). *The sane society.* Greenwich, CT: Fawcett.

Gilligan, C. (1982). *In a different voice.* Cambridge, MA: Harvard University Press.

Golden, S., Halliday, K., Khantzian, E. J., & McAuliffe, W. E. (1993). Dynamic group therapy for substance abuse patients: A reconceptualization. In A. Alonso & H. I. Swiller (Eds.), *Group therapy in clinical practice* (pp. 271–288). Washington, DC: American Psychiatric Press.

Greenson, R. (1967). *The technique and practice of psychoanalysis, Vol. 1.* New York: International Universities Press.

Grof, S. (1985). *Beyond the brain.* Albany, NY: SUNY Press.

Harman, R. L. (1984). Recent developments in Gestalt group therapy. *International Journal of Group Psychotherapy, 34,* 473–483.

Harman, W. (1988). *Global mind change.* Indianapolis, IN: Knowledge Systems.

Harper-Giuffre, H., & MacKenzie, R. (1993). Group psychotherapy with eating disorders. In H. I. Kaplan & B. J. Sadock (Eds.), *Comprehensive group psychotherapy* (pp. 443–458). Philadelphia: Williams & Wilkins.

Hawkins, D. (1993). Group psychotherapy with gay men and lesbians. In H. I. Kaplan & B. J. Sadock (Eds.), *Comprehensive group psychotherapy* (pp. 506–514). Philadelphia: Williams & Wilkins.

Herman, J. L. (1992). *Trauma and recovery.* New York: Basic Books.

Horowitz, H. (1993). Group-centered models of group psychotherapy. In H. I. Kaplan & B. J. Sadock (Eds.), *Comprehensive group psychotherapy* (pp. 156–164). Philadelphia: Williams & Wilkins.

Houston, J. (1982). *The possible human.* Los Angeles: Tarcher.

Houston, J. (1987). *The search for the beloved.* Los Angeles: Tarcher.

Kaplan, H. I., & Sadock, B. J. (Eds.). (1993). *Comprehensive group psychotherapy.* Philadelphia: Williams & Wilkins.

Kaul, T. H., & Bednar, R. L. (1986). Experiential group research: Results, questions, and suggestions. In S. L. Garfield & A. E. Bergin (Eds.), *Handbook of psychotherapy and behavior change* (pp. 671–714). New York: Wiley.

Kernberg, O. (1975). *Borderline conditions and pathological narcissism.* New York: Jason Aronson.

Kibel, H. D., & Stein, A. (1981). The group as a whole approach: An appraisal. *International Journal of Group Psychotherapy, 31,* 409.

Klein, R. H. (1993). Short-term group psychotherapy. In H. I. Kaplan & B. J. Sadock (Eds.), *Comprehensive group psychotherapy* (pp. 256–269). Philadelphia: Williams & Wilkins.

Kohut, H. (1971). *The analysis of the self.* Madison, CT: International Universities Press.

Kohut, H. (1977). *The restoration of the self.* Madison, CT: International Universities Press.

Krugman, S., & Osherson, S. (1993). Men in group therapy. In A. Alonso & H. I. Swiller (Eds.), *Group therapy in clinical practice* (pp. 393–420). Washington, DC: American Psychiatric Press.

Laddon, J., Atlee, T., & Shook, L. (1998). *Awakening: The upside of Y2K.* Spokane, WA: The Printed Word.

Lazerson, J. S., & Zilbach, J. J. (1993). Gender issues in group psychotherapy. In H. I. Kaplan & B. J. Sadock (Eds.), *Comprehensive group psychotherapy* (pp. 682–692). Philadelphia: Williams & Wilkins.

Lederberg, M. S. (1993). Staff support groups for high-stress facilities. In A. Alonso & H. I. Swiller (Eds.), *Group therapy in clinical practice* (pp. 171–184). Washington, DC: American Psychiatric Press.

Lego, S. (1993). Group psychotherapy with HIV-infected persons and their caregivers. In H. I. Kaplan & B. J. Sadock (Eds.), *Comprehensive group psychotherapy* (pp. 470-476). Philadelphia: Williams & Wilkins.

Levine, B. (1979). *Group psychotherapy: Practice and development.* Prospect Heights, IL: Waveland Press.

Lieberman, M. A. (1993). Self-help groups. In H. I. Kaplan & B. J. Sadock (Eds.), *Comprehensive group psychotherapy* (pp. 292–303). Philadelphia: Williams & Wilkins.

Lipsius, S. H. (1991). Combined individual and group psychotherapy: Guidelines at the interface. *International Journal of Group Psychotherapy, 41,* 313–327.

Lowen, A. (1975). *Bioenergetics.* New York: Penguin.

MacKenzie, K. R. (1990). *Introduction to time-limited group psychotherapy.* Washington, DC: American Psychiatric Press.

MacKenzie, K. R. (1993). Time-limited group theory and technique. In A. Alonso & H. I. Swiller (Eds.), *Group therapy in clinical practice* (pp. 423–448). Washington, DC: American Psychiatric Press.

Macy, J. R. (1983). *Despair and personal power in the nuclear age.* Philadelphia: New Society.

Macy, J. R. (1990). The ecological self: Postmodern ground for right action. In D. R. Griffin (Ed.), *Postmodern spirituality, political economy and art.* Albany, NY: SUNY Press.

Macy, J. R., & Brown, M. Y. (1998). *Coming back to life.* Stony Creek, CT: New Society.

Maslow, A. H. (1971). *The farther reaches of human nature.* New York: Viking Press.

Masterson, J. F. (1981). *The narcissistic and borderline disorders.* New York: Brunner/Mazel.

May, R., Angel, E., & Ellenberger, H. F. (1958). *Existence.* Northvale, NJ: Jason Aronson.

McKay, M., & Paley, K. (Eds.). (1992). *Focal group psychotherapy.* Oakland, CA: New Harbinger.

Meadows, D. H., Meadows, D. L., & Randers, J. (1992). *Beyond the limits.* Port Mills, VT: Chelsea Green.

Moreno, J. L. (1959). *Psychodrama: foundations of psychotherapy, Vol. 2.* Beacon, NY: Beacon House.

Orlinsky, D. E., & Howard, K. I. (1986). Process and outcome in psychotherapy. In S. L. Garfield & A. E. Bergin (Eds.), *Handbook of psychotherapy and behavior change* (pp. 311–384). New York: Wiley.

Ormont, L. (1990). *The group therapy experience.* New York: St. Martin's.

Perls, F., Hefferline, R. F., & Goodman, P. (1951). *Gestalt therapy.* New York: Bantam.

Pesso, A. (1969). *Movement in psychotherapy.* New York: New York University Press.

Porter, K. (1993). Combined individual and group psychotherapy. In H. I. Kaplan & B. J. Sadock (Eds.), *Comprehensive group psychotherapy* (pp. 314–323). Philadelphia: Williams & Wilkins.

Reich, W. (1970). *The mass psychology of fascism.* New York: Pocket Books.

Rice-Smith, E. (1993). Group psychotherapy with sexually abused children. In H. I. Kaplan & B. J. Sadock (Eds.), *Comprehensive group psychotherapy* (pp. 531–549). Philadelphia: Williams & Wilkins.

Rogers, C. R. (1951). *Client-centered therapy.* Boston: Houghton-Mifflin.

Roller, B., & Nelson, V. (1991). *The art of cotherapy.* New York: Guilford Press.

Roller, B., & Nelson, V. (1993). Cotherapy. In H. I. Kaplan & B. J. Sadock (Eds.), *Comprehensive group psychotherapy* (pp. 304–312). Philadelphia: Williams & Wilkins.

Roszak, T. (1992). *The voice of the earth.* New York: Simon & Schuster.

Rutan, J. S., & Alonso, A. (1982). Group therapy, individual therapy, or both? *International Journal of Group Psychotherapy, 32,* 267.

Rutan, J. S., & Stone, W. N. (1993). *Psychodynamic group psychotherapy.* New York: Guilford Press.

Safran, J. D., & Greenberg, L. S. (Eds.). (1991). *Emotion, psychotherapy, and change.* New York: Guilford Press.

Safran, J. D., & Segal, Z. V. (1990). *Interpersonal process in cognitive therapy.* New York: Basic Books.

Salvendy, J. T. (1993). Selection and preparation of patients and organization of the group. In H. I. Kaplan & B. J. Sadock (Eds.), *Comprehensive group psychotherapy* (pp. 72–83). Philadelphia: Williams & Wilkins.

Satir, V. (1967). *Conjoint family therapy.* Palo Alto, CA: Science and Behavior Books.

Scheidlinger, S. (1974). On the concept of the "mother-group." *International Journal of Group Psychotherapy, 24,* 417.

Schoenholtz-Read, J. (1996). The supervisor as gender analyst: Feminist perspectives on group supervision and training. *International Journal of Group Psychotherapy, 46,* 479–500.

Silbershatz, G., & Sampson, H. (1991). Affects in psychopathology and psychotherapy. In J. Safran & L. S. Greenberg (Eds.), *Emotion, psychotherapy, and change* (pp. 113–129). New York: Guilford Press.

Spotnitz, H. (1996). *Psychotherapy of preoedipal conditions: Schizophrenia and severe character disorders.* New York: Jason Aronson.

Stolorow, R. D., Brandchaft, B., & Atwood, G. E. (1987). *Psychoanalytic treatment: An intersubjective approach.* Hillsdale, NJ: Analytic Press.

Stone, W. N. (1992). The place of self-psychology in group psychotherapy: A status report. *International Journal of Group Psychotherapy, 42,* 335–350.

Toseland, R. W., & Siporin, M. (1986). When to recommend group treatment: A review of the clinical and the research literature. *International Journal of Group Psychotherapy, 36,* 171–201.

Tschuschke, V., & Czogalik, D. (1990). *Psychotherapie: Welche effekte veraendern?* [Which factors cause change?] Berlin: Springer.

Tuckman, B. W. (1965). Developmental sequence in small groups. *Psychological Bulletin, 63,* 384–399.

Tuttman, S. (1993). Countertransference and transference in groups. In H. I. Kaplan & B. J. Sadock (Eds.), *Comprehensive group psychotherapy* (pp. 98–104). Philadelphia: Williams & Wilkins.

van der Kolk, B. A. (1993). Group psychotherapy with posttraumatic stress disorder. In H. I. Kaplan & B. J. Sadock (Eds.), *Comprehensive group psychotherapy* (pp. 550–559). Philadelphia: Williams & Wilkins.

Weiss, J. (1993). *How psychotherapy works.* New York: Guilford Press.

Whitaker, D. S., & Lieberman, M. A. (1964). *Psychotherapy through the group process.* New York: Atherton.

Yalom, I. (1980). *Existential psychotherapy.* New York: Basic Books.

Yalom, I. (1995). *The theory and practice of group psychotherapy* (4th ed.). New York: Basic Books.

Zinker, J. (1977). *Creative process in gestalt therapy.* New York: Brunner/Mazel.

AUTHOR INDEX

SUBJECT INDEX

DATE DUE